ARCH OF FIRE

BARBARA LALLA

Kingston Publishers Limited

Published by Kingston Publishers Limited
7-9 Norman Road, Kingston, CSO, Jamaica

ISBN 976-625-089-8

Cover design by Patrick Champagnie
Typeset by Janet Campbell and Hemmings'way Ltd
Printed by United Co-operative Printers Limited, Kingston, Jamaica

To Will, Ralph and Allan

The rainbow, sign of God's desire,
is earnest of the final fire.

Edward Baugh, "Colour Scheme"

CONTENTS

PREFACE

The characters that appear in the following pages are, with few exceptions, fictional. A few historical personnages are referred to in passing (such as George William Gordon, Alexander Bustamante and Norman Manley) and even fewer appear briefly as characters (such as Alexander Bedward and Abū Bakr al Ṣiddīq). These are identified by their correct names. However, the central characters are imaginary and bear no actual correspondence to persons alive or dead.

Acknowledgements

I thank Edward Baugh for permission to quote from the poem, "Colour Scheme." I thank my father for urging me to read almost as soon as I could hold a book, and my mother for urging me to write almost as soon as I could hold a pen. I thank my beloved elderly friends for oral testimony, elicited for the most part by my sister, Elsie Aarons, without whom I could not have written the greater part of this book that is (in essential ways) as much hers as mine. I thank John Aarons and Camille Walling for assistance in discovering past and present Jamaica, and Jean D'Costa, Liz Hearne and Kim Robinson Walcott for their support and comments on the manuscript. As many of the circumstances related have been created partly on the basis of reading in the National Library of Jamaica, The University of the West Indies Library and The British Library, I thank these institutions also. Historical events are listed in the table at the back of the book. Otherwise, the situations described have no reality outside of my overactive imagination.

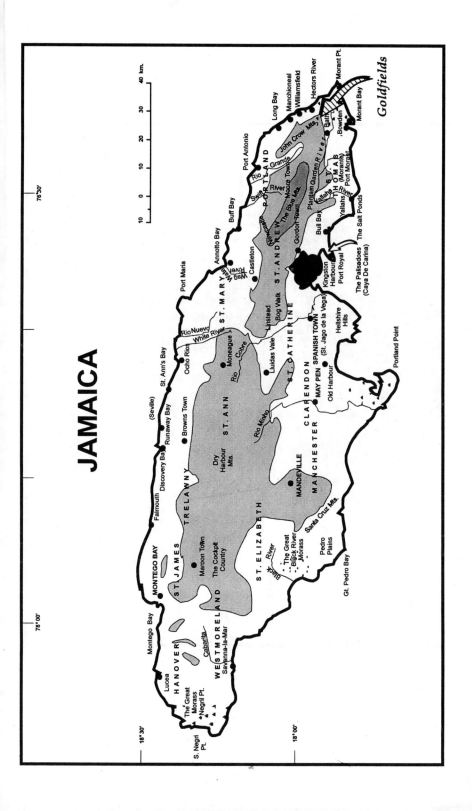

JAMAICA

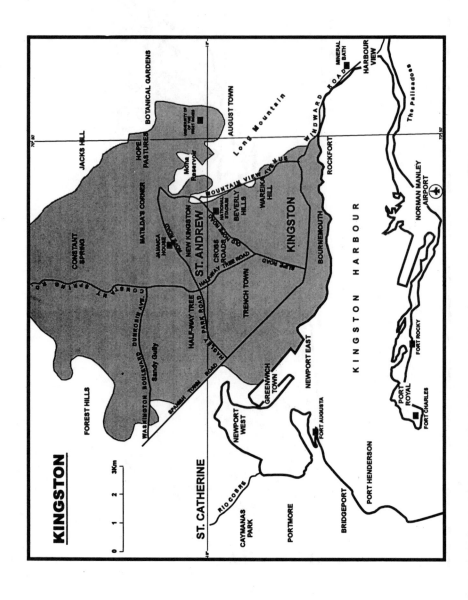

KINGSTON

ARCH OF FIRE

THE FAMILY

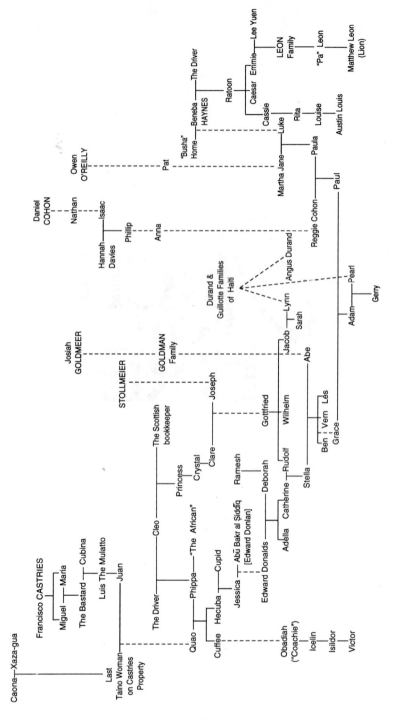

I
Falls

1

Crossings

BENEATH THE stony contemplation of the great house, the valley scooped away to a distant edge of deep green coconut fronds parted by pulses of sunlight reflected from the sea. The sky was pitiless at noon, branding the low-lying fields and roads, but at dusk it relented, salving with dew so that nothing really died forever. Even when the hurricane rode in and the wind rose cracking its whip upon the land, twisting, breaking and uprooting, still, when the screaming died away, the soft shoots sprouted again their chorus of resistance.

Through the years Goldfields had not only spread back up the mountain but sprawled down into the valley, sun-tempered, blood-soaked. Even as the sugar plantation had risen, flourished, crumbled, swirling together lives and events, the mists had rolled down from the mountain, fogging the past. Phantoms that had hissed out through crevices of the accursed grey stone and dispersed into the bamboo groaned there at night, replaced by creeping emptiness that was gradually dispossessing even current owners, now little more than living dead. But life surged on in the neighbouring families who spread with intertwining roots, jostling for space and struggling to rise from the soil, lightward.

Ramesh came late to the neighbourhood around Goldfields as the old estate declined after Emancipation. For his cottage, plot, some pence and a ration of food, Ramesh whirled his cutlass by day. By night, he immersed himself in white rum or huddled before his door, hazing with ganja smoke a past of dysentery and despair.

Months wore away the urge to escape to that end of the island where the East Indian population concentrated. He bawled a ribald comment and women stopped scraping their ginger to giggle at the out o' order coolieman. But a grizzled neighbour muttered sourly from beneath a crushing load of coals on his head, "Going get chop one day."

Out in the field again, the one-foot man who was caller chanted out the cutting song, and soon Ramesh chorused with the rest of the work gang — the rising tone of the calling, the deep response of the bobbin falling with the gleam and slash of the cutlasses. Then came evening cool and twilight smoke and, before sleep, throbbed the note of a tree frog. The croak, taken up by other snorers, pulsed from among the bromeliads where they bred and swelled in unison, sweeping wave on wave into the distant hills and dying into violet night.

Christmas came and passed in incomprehensible festivities — sacred and solemn in the church, but in the streets wild, bawdy, reeling in brilliant patches of cloth, painted horseheads and horned masks of the Jonkunnu parade. Yet he would quickly have fitted his niche in the island — only the first shipments from India brought few women. Then the news came that the Colonial Office required forty East Indian women to be loaded for every hundred men, and Ramesh drank himself into stupefaction and remained blissfully incapable of work for two days.

Yet it turned out badly — never an East Indian woman of his own. Accusations hissed and brawled and eventually one murderously determined husband waited in the canepiece, stroking his cutlass. For months, even while Ramesh nursed the festering chop on his thigh, he watched warily for the offended husband who was still bent on rectifying his earlier failure in aim. After the wound mended and the enemy contented himself with brandishing his blade and howling obscenities in an unintelligible dialect, Ramesh confined himself to local women.

When his five years of indentureship ended, he had settled

4

with one. India receded to stark, fragmented memories of disease, starvation and rejection. The neighbours laughed and congratulated him on his Madam, who was swelling with life. The voyage back churned through his mind, its monotonous heaving to the other side of the world and poverty reaching its bony fingers beyond his generation and on and on in a suppression entrenched by caste. Then the old music that haunted other newcomers for him wailed only of parting, and faded. His re-collections of sacred ceremonies hollowed to emptiness, and eventually the last blush of nostalgia for childhood memories of his mother performing rites of uncertain meaning lost shape like a lotus whose petals crumpled and swirled away on brown flood water. Then Ramesh requested cash bounty instead of his return passage to India and he postponed the homeward voyage indefinitely.

So Deborah, his daughter, was not full Indian but half negro, and a Baptist. The years that sped through seasons of planting and crop-over brought increasing hardship, but as his daughter's childhood passed he invested all he had in cementing a match that would help her to "live good".

· When the time came for Deborah's marriage, Goldfields was bankrupt. Employment was scarce in 1865, and Ramesh's cash sum had shrivelled. Word came that old Mas' Cohon of Goldfields, who had been drinking himself into the grave for years anyway, had seen spirits and staggered away from them through an upstairs window. There he sprawled on the stone walkway below with his neck broken, wide-eyed at the stars. The plantation passed through a quick succession of uncaring hands and sank rapidly into ruin.

Still, at Ramesh's cottage, there was revelry among the poorest of the dwellings around the plantation. Despite the drought and inflated prices (dem say war do it, inna America — saltfish price go up, go up), still there was food. Little was stolen. The Governor insisted on flogging for theft. Men whispered, with nostrils flaring dangerously, that the whip was back. (Blood, they said, is blood it would take....) Well. There was food, and a tea meeting had raised enough to equip the bride.

The bride's cake was draped in white lace and its candle set to burn the night through. Mas' Jackman's big son had brought the cake carefully on his head, making sure never to look back lest his neck remain askew forever. Ramesh had hidden away a little bhang for those few special guests who would linger afterwards. The tiny savings that Deborah's mother had hoarded over the years had long bled away into the tax for the Anglican Church. Among the well-to-do and educated, only Gordon, the Baptist magistrate, had denounced clergymen like Herschell who drained the poor, and Gordon had been censured for his pains. The groom, Edward Donalds, knew better than to be a Baptist in days like these. He was an Anglican, clear-skinned, educated by missionaries, able to keep his own books — a catch for Deborah.

In the long run, Ramesh reasoned, don't everyt'ing was for the pickney? He grow up the one girl straight and stric' and now she would live good. It was Ramesh, with two East Indian friends and their women, who prepared the curry goat feed. A rough table supported quarts of rum, flanked by vast pots of cock soup, rice, ram-goat curry and dip-and-flash. Into the drumming the men stamped and heaved, steeped in rum and rhythm, and the wedding night thudded about them, but on the edges of the circle the women rustled in secret laughter.

"All now so dem bathing her," one whispered from a brilliant, golden grin. "Give her de rum and ganja self."

Yes, Deborah married. Not in middle age after years of cohabitation and childbearing but at sixteen, and the men bid money to peep under her veil. She was a lady; her heart swelled with it and her feet tapped impatiently as the band struck up.

But a clatter of hooves forestalled the quadrille. A voice

6

rasped in warning. Jordan Tracy burst in, streaming fear and haste.

"Is what?"

"Wha' appen?"

One of the children at the door sang out helpfully, " 'Im nearly kill de mule come ya!"

Tracy fought for breath and pronounced, "Dem march 'pon de courthouse. Backra dead."

"Too lie!"

"...Me see de Custos body. An' Herschell."

"De clergyman kill?"

"Dem march, I tell you. Three, four hundred wi' gun, cutlass, stick...."

"Bogle lead dem?"

"Mus'."

"...An' courthouse burn."

So it should, but their deep rumble of approval died away in an exchange of glances. Not grief but shock, realisation.

"Hell fe we."

"Go on, Mas' Jordie. Run." The mule shuddered as Jordan heaved himself up again on the old bag across its back, gabbling little fragments he had picked up about the riot.

"Oh Gawd! Run, man!" they urged.

"Ride inna de bush. Don' stop!"

"But after you no do nothing!" His wife ran beside the mule bawling. They pulled her away. Fool.

"Him there inna town. People nuh did see him?"

So there must be no gathering now, for any reason. Deborah tore away the veil and plunged the money between skimpy breasts. Ramesh bundled what food he could into a sack and swung it up onto Edward's head. It was still early when the couple pressed uphill on a track in the bush.

That wedding night and for two succeeding days they crouched under the dripping cedars and plastering wet coffee

7

leaves at the back of Goldfields, straining for the tramp of soldiers. An old woman scuttled along in the other direction.

"Maroons," she croaked urgently. "Man in de pass dere tell me
seh Maroon helping de soldier-dem."

Edward and Deborah Donalds buried the remaining food lest
the smell betray them, and they doubled back. The cluster of huts
that had belonged to slaves in the old days flared and crackled
and the blaze threatened to overtake the surrounding bamboo.
They circled widely and it was evening before they came back on
a clearing they had crossed before. Now eight bodies, one a
child's, swung from the branches on the far side. Edward and
Deborah dived off the path where the bush seemed thickest.
Patoo, the white owl, shrieked above them and Deborah shuddered violently, but somehow they evaded the soldiers who
scoured the countryside, hanging, burning, shooting. The real terror was the Maroons, the hunters from the hills who were part of
the bush themselves and now helped the soldiers to track down
suspects. So the couple burrowed down into the sodden undergrowth and lay still hour after hour.

When at last they returned to Deborah's house, it was gone.
Smouldering wood and ash marked the site. A few men had
paused to clear away signs of festivity, and the officer who had
burst in forced them to dig a trench. When the soldiers opened
fire, Ramesh had not died promptly and the officer buried a pick-
axe in his head. What was left of his face stared bloodily from the
open trench when Deborah came home.

There were earthquakes after Gordon's hanging, but the
earth quieted. Then there was Bogle's hanging, just as Edward
had foreseen, and hundreds more were executed, hundreds
flogged. A thousand homes, torched in the reprisals, lit the
nights of mourning. Deborah should have worn her return-
thanks hat two Sundays after the wedding and dressed like a
bride again, but somehow 'turn-thanks never came, what with
Gordon dangling in the arch of the courthouse and Ramesh in

his wedding suit broken in the trench.

Well, she was Mrs Donalds. The neighbours muttered respectfully that "de more you chop breadfruit root de more 'im spring," for Edward built, extended his land, supported his church, resolutely forgot the things that ought not to have happened. A child, Adella, was born, followed by Catherine. Deborah spread from slender, almost brittle girlhood, swelling at the bust, broadening at the hips.

Yet even as Edward settled his family, the community heaved, split and transformed around him, slipping through his fingers. Now some neighbours attempted precariously to live in the country and the city at the same time. Obadiah Castries left his common-law wife and their smallholding and set out for Kingston to be coachman for a Jew named Jacob Stollmeier. On a tiny plot of land at the edge of Goldfields, Castries's mother sang on in strident tones the same old songs and unlikely tales the children loved. They were tales her grandfather had told of how his grandmother, Phippa, had run away with a Maroon and, when he died, returned to the estate with her children. There were tales of Goldfields and Massa and the haunting of Nanny Town.

Unlike the Donalds girls, the Castries children grew wild and unschooled along the village streets, plunging and squealing in Driver's River that tumbled away from the base of Reach Falls and splashing in and out of the sea and up the streams. They clambered after mangoes and star-apples, ducked among the roots of banyan trees, or searched out janga, the river shrimp, to take home for soup. Icelin, the youngest, toddled close to the fireplace. She reached into a nearby yabba to pass vegetables to her grandmother and watched dreamily as Old Ma quavered songs about forgotten, perhaps imaginary times and swirled together innumerable sauces, vegetables and shellfish into the pepperpot. Old Ma Castries was probably the last of the family to make pepperpot the old way, with cassareep, which she claimed preserved it indefinitely, and she boasted that her stew was a continuation of her mother's and grandmother's.

None of the Castries had ever played with the Donalds children growing up less than a mile away and descended from the same runaway slave. Indeed, Mas' Donalds's gruff interruptions cut short elderly aunts from filling his girls' heads with nonsensical old tales and sayings and from tracing ancient histories.

As his own children grew, Edward Donalds called in the sawyers and hammered together a haven of sober middle-class security. He added a kitchen that Deborah filled at once with the smell of cassava pone and conch soup and curry goat and cowfoot with broad beans and duckanoo and susumber with saltfish. Their elder daughters, Adella and Catherine, wandered about the modest property ignorant of hardship. There was little else to do. No daughter of Edward could be allowed to kick up her heels at a bruckins party, or reel in the street at Jonkunnu. Nor were they to involve themselves in low cults like Kumina, which reeked of the old days of slavery and was African and backward, though Edward himself might send his contribution of a bottle of white rum to bless the drums. As they lay in bed straining for the sounds of a neighbour's wake, the girls wondered about the power of the drumming to confine the dead, for they had heard of dancers possessed by the ancestors whom the drums roused. But Edward was determined to raise his children above the past.

Sometimes they explored what was left of the old Cohon estate, Goldfields, which abutted on Donalds's land. The plantation had finally fallen into the hands of old Mas' Cohon's distant cousin, Gottfried Stollmeier. He halted the decay of the great house and reclaimed woodland and pasture from the bush. The works lay in sad disrepair by the early eighties, but a new Stollmeier extended the domestic supply of coffee and renovated the great house. However, this Stollmeier was a Kingston man.

Rudolf Stollmeier was not tall, but had what people called presence. He sat straight on his horse, and his coat, not tight but cut to form, highlighted the hard lines of chest and thigh. He gazed appraisingly at women as he rode by.

Then his eyes held Catherine Donalds's and she stared back. Hers were black — not like her mother's big eastern eyes which were black but cool; Catherine's were fiery, turbulent black with a hint of iron. Adella thought his mouth-corner twitched with amusement and speculation, and the horse stopped, quivering. Close. Polished boots brushed Catherine's dress.

"Like a ride?"

"No, sir. Thank you."

She was nervous, but Teacher had caned children who sounded 't' for 'th', and her father insisted she speak like a lady.

The glossy legs of the horse rippled and its rider leaned to peer at her. Briefly she raised her eyes but his face lay shadowed by the hat brim.

"Come on up," Stollmeier's voice urged, soft but laughing.

Alarmingly harmless it seemed to climb up, to feel a few paces of the lovely, restless animal. Then Adella pressed a hand on her back, propelling her along.

"Cathy, come." And a moment later Adella breathed in her ear, "Is what happen to you? You mad?"

So he rode on.

But it was hard to put out of her mind — the notion of jogging behind the graceful arch of the grey mane with the sleek young man rocking behind her. Then he began to appear in unpredictable places. Of course she knew — nothing more dangerous to a brown girl than a white man. She was frightened and flattered. Easily she refused expensive presents. But then. A rose, an orchid.... After all, he wanted only to talk to her.

They walked briefly beside the horse, crossing the borders of her father's land into his without noticing. An elderly servant from Goldfields regarded her sadly and shook his head.

11

"Lizard never know whe' him dey till him find 'imself in puss mouth," he reflected.

Catherine was careful for a long time. But when he whispered promises to her, brushing her cheek with his mouth, his skin flushed with a heat that spread into her own blood, burning away Adella's warnings, the sermons of the clergyman, her father's threats, her mother's tears. The rich white princes of her story books belied them all, and the tales she had heard whispered about Rudy had to be lies. His own brother had married some fast creole girl from Louisiana, people said. And after all, Catherine thought, I'm not fast, I'm respectable.

Handsome, rich, so, so gentle. He would take her to Kingston and be good to her. Everything, everything else fled from her mind as he unfastened her hair and the orchid fell beneath the heel of his shiny boot and his lips whispering of carriages and jewellery would not lie with breath so warm, and fingers so reassuring would cherish her forever. Out of the middle of the ruined millhouse on Goldfields a spreading poinciana blazed with scarlet flowers, and the grass beneath it was tall and soft for Catherine and Rudy.

Kingston. Catherine supposed it would be the same for her as for Jacob Stollmeier's wife who was near white but not white. Rudy's brother had brought her from Louisiana and married her.

At last Kingston was the place to go. The mountains around Goldfields crouched forward to watch their people leave. The Lebanese pedlar plodded barefoot behind his wheelbarrow in which were rolled the fabrics that would make his fortune in Kingston.

He nodded engagingly to potential customers, and they grinned at him tolerantly. For now the rawness of most of the strangers gathered over the centuries was gone and essences had blended beyond recognition. Hardly anyone knew who was who any more, and the past suppressed its shadows so deep that they raged only in the darkest corners of the mind.

"Is Paradise you think Kingston is!" Edward Donalds boomed. "Everybody goin' there, eh? I tell you the only people going is them dat don' have nothing here. Is not people like us with likkle substance goin' Kingston."

"An' is a wicked place. Wicked," her mother whimpered. "Lord, blessed Jesus, Cathy. You cyan't see the man foolin' you up? Is a big white man. What him want wid you? Kingston is a Wicked Place."

Catherine was different; she was certain of it. She packed what little she had and the gifts Rudy had brought for her and she told her sister roundly to stay out of her business. Nevertheless, Adella packed up her own best things for Catherine when she saw that there was neither reason nor sense in the younger girl and gave her what little money she had.

"So at least when him drop you, you wouldn' starve," Adella snapped.

Catherine whirled out and was off in Stollmeier's carriage with her straight brown nose as high as if it were white indeed. Rudy laughed it all away, for she would need none of them now, and they would come around in the end anyway.

So they would, she thought. When she returned in her own carriage, with gifts for all of them (for she did not mean to hold a grudge), when she was Mrs Stollmeier. She would be there often enough, with Goldfields to renovate....

Adella too set off for Kingston with her few remaining possessions. She had not only talked to the Castries woman down the road but traversed a social boundary by sitting down and drinking a cup of bissy with her, and she had learnt there was work in Kingston for those who were not too proud to take it. Obadiah Castries was doing well as Jacob Stollmeier's coachman. One of the Jackman boys had come back to the country but the other had stayed in town and married a deacon's daughter.

"Hear seh Cassie Haynes's daughter, Rita, lef' the pickney with its grandmother and she and all gone Kingston. Don't know what Rita doing there. Cassie did keep her well strict les' she get big too quick, but the gyal take her rudeness inna bush and wo'tless man breed her. How she live a Kingston now me no know. Cassie not a woman fe question. But Cassie self mus' be tell Rita what fe do, for Cassie and spirit-dem talk. And don't Cassie four-eye too? Is true, Miss Adella, 'M. Everybady a go a Kingston."

It was the following year, in 1884, when Adella was just seventeen, that she found a position as a nursemaid and waited quietly for Catherine to need her. When the time came, Adella sent her money, week after week, until the baby was born, landless, nameless and fatherless as any.

Then Edward Donalds came to the mean little room Catherine had rented in Kingston. He had found a couple, childless and discreet, anxious to adopt. There was a chance for Catherine after all. He leaned forward and peered at her when she shook her head dumbly.

"Eh?" he gasped incredulously. "Then what? You don't know what a jail you put youself in, don' want married and live good? Den you mean... you not even sorry?"

Mechanically she smoothed a crease in her skirt. "Sorry? Sorry... you disappointed." He choked and she hurried on. "I shoulda never believe...." She fell silent with her finger tracing embroidery on the tiniest of linen sleeves then stroking down to the baby's hand which opened and closed on her finger. "And she don't deserve... this way. But to say give her 'way, or... or sorry I have her — no. I never going sorry for that. Look." Her voice dropped to a whisper, "Pa, look how she know me."

Edward almost looked at the baby, but somehow he slid his eyes away urgently and stepped back to the door.

"Then you good as dead."

He crunched heavily out from the doorstep without a glance,

for he knew his daughter, pride, stubbornness and all. Catherine sank her nose onto the child's stomach and rubbed it with a groan that crumpled through tears into a chuckle.

"Soft, soft. Well. I never goin' be a lady now." Then she laughed again, this time with a hint of steel. "But you. You going be twice the lady I shoulda be. Wait. Is a Stollmeier you are. I going register you so make him squirm. Me, hide? Sorry no use now, lady. Is Stollmeier you name."

The child wrinkled her nose and returned a wide, bare-gummed smile of incredible sweetness. If all Rudy's promises had come true Catherine could not have cared more for the baby and she chatted on and on to her about the future, pointing out everything from the mountains to the sea; but she never passed on tales of the country district where she had grown up, or taught her the sayings of their elders.

After all, she decided, what does it matter what old-time people say? If there were no past we would live easier together. Hn! Every man and woman in Kingston knows that black and white make brown. Why complicate matters by prying into history? The people in the middle like herself had no history — no claim, some said. Notoriously they were last to come, first to go. In fact, they never came; they happened.

So Catherine seized on the future because it was all there was, planning, building, scheming, saving. Sacrificing everything — her parents, her sister, herself most of all — for the child. It meant unlearning sayings, erasing myths, ignoring old pains. She had to leave the dead buried, the living unembarrassed, the unborn unencumbered. And if black or white rejected her, what of it? They were nothing to her in the end for it was her place, she said, more than anyone's. It was she and her kind who were "born ya". Who her old ones were mattered not at all, for they were dead. And if they came by diverse paths each from his little hell, what of it? Some things were best forgotten or left unlearned.

2

The Icon

LOWER KING STREET may not have been stylish, but in the last decade of the century it was still residential. As Catherine would remark, the neighbours were 'nice people'.

The house was one of the newer brick structures that had sprung up after the fire of '82, but it was built on the old lines. New brick walls were joined to a surviving section from some older building, to huge cut stones that formed a massive back wall of uncertain history. Ancient Carpenter Richmond would purse up his lips in the midst of whistling old choruses and rap a wooden facing with his crusty knuckle. Then he nodded in satisfaction and muttered that it was built by men who knew their trade and made a house to last.

Wicker chairs and ferns transformed the verandah into an extension of the garden. The whole house was practically a cluster of closed verandahs, for even the bedrooms opened out onto pale blue plumbago or deep green, serrated philodendron leaves. Jalousie blinds shielded the house from the weather, but normally these were flung wide open so that the sunlight slanted in upon bright cotton bedspreads and the strong salt breeze they called 'the doctor' blew uninhibited through and through.

Slender red brick pillars rose from a wealth of maidenhair and fishtail fronds to support the roof, understating the boundary between house and frontage, and implying spaciousness and dignity. Cramped or not, Catherine's front garden was fragrant with roses of all types, occasional huge, creamy blooms, delicate in the tropics but stately; and, in and out between these, incorrigible ramblers ducked in tiny splashes of crimson.

Outside, the tramcar sped past the house at ten miles an hour. As the commercial area spread, more and more pedestrian traffic filtered along their road — not always desirable, as Stella's mother remarked, her lips meaningfully compressed. Some bustled along to the cigar factory, others to the market at the foot of the street. Donkeys plodded between crisp clerks in detachable starched collars and older business men still in frock coats and boiled shirts. Harassed policemen gestured uselessly at vendors who negotiated in the middle of the street. Among them sailed ladies, rigidly elegant beneath fine-spined parasols which floated up between the heavy baskets of the higglers.

One morning a messenger sucking noisily on a mango collided with a member of the regiment and spread the slippery fruit down the scarlet, yellow and blue Zouave uniform onto gleaming white spats.

"You dutty black nega," bawled the victim.

"Who you calling black? Nosehole big like yabba!"

The injured messenger kicked sorrowfully at his half-eaten mango in the dust and emitted a stream of obscenity at Catherine's very gate.

It was true then that the neighbourhood was going down. Certainly the noise had grown. Now scraping hoes and shovels from women working on the street mingled with the trundle of mule-cars, the clop-clop of donkeys patient beneath their panniers, and the rushing tram and harsh jangling of its bell. Shrill arguments raged between vendors and their clients, and from morning till night street cries echoed: "Ripe pear for breakfast, ripe pear gwine past," "Basket around, me lady, basket, ba-asket around," and "Fi-ish, fi-ish, fi-ishi!" With all this traffic milling past the house the front wall grew more important — not only for the pleasing spectacle of powdery yellow allamanda blooms trailing on grey brick but for the measure of privacy that it lent.

Stella's mother, Catherine Donalds, was what was called a

handsome woman, solid but trim and erect. Her skin was cool olive beneath severely suppressed curls, and her chin tilted at the world as if everything, to be seen properly in focus, must be regarded along the downward angle of her nose. Of reckless gaiety or sheer abandonment to impulse there was no sign. She observed everyday proprieties meticulously, almost obsessively. Yet there was Stella, and Catherine unmarried.

Few people were bold enough to intrude on Catherine Donalds, even by speculation. How much even Stella guessed no one could tell, but they were close, tangled together in longings, in prayers and in laughter — so close that perhaps there were things that need not be asked or told. Or perhaps that was how they explained to themselves an area of silence deep and unsearchable.

Catherine herself had smoothed and hardened under years of saving face and putting up a proud front. It had not always been so. Once there had been whispers, eyebrows raised when she brought her daughter to church, and disparagingly sympathetic smiles. The likes of that little Leon girl had cut her eye off her in the street — Anita Leon same one, who would have been lucky to receive a polite smile when Catherine first rode into town in Rudy Stollmeier's carriage. (And the slant-eye Leon girl was well pregnant now for that barefoot Lebanese pedlar — not that he was barefoot any longer.) To Catherine's family, except for the sister who had followed her to Kingston, she was dead — only the wreath of purple asters missing, she had once remarked, to Stella's horror. As for the Rudolf himself.... So much for that. She had been alone with her infant and her pride. But for a few shillings regularly from the older sister who had estranged herself from her parents for Catherine's sake, God knows, Catherine sometimes thought with a shudder along her spine, God knows....

"Is a choice," Adella had snapped, tired at last of Catherine's pride. "Is either I work and mind you so you bring up the child decent or you end up 'pon street. Unless you have a next man line up already?"

Catherine had boxed her and their only contact since had been through the money which arrived, for Stella. Meanwhile Catherine's shoulders squared and stiffened her into an imposing figure, unapproachable in her tailored black bodice and leg-o'-mutton sleeves and inflexible in her two-and-ninepence Leoty corset. Now she turned out elegant embroidery and no longer depended on Adella. Both regretted losing contact but were too stubborn to admit it.

Catherine's was fine needlework which stores like Nathan's Metropolitan House were glad to take, and she and Stella carried themselves like ladies. She exacted the respect due to a widow without posing as one, for she maintained her maiden name, but she saw that Stella bore her father's name openly. Estella Gertrude Stollmeier. How it galled him. It was the essence of what Catherine's few friends called her self-respect and what those who admired her less termed feistiness. She had sunk her past deep beyond the most inquisitive minds of her neighbours and reared the child so respectably that Stella was a living reproach to her father's neglect.

Rudy himself was stubborn and self-committed. He would have his way whatever it cost him and, usually, it cost him little. This was partly because of who he was (a Stollmeier, after all) and partly because of what he was — startlingly attractive, physically and socially. It was hard to say whether his nineteenth-century waistcoat clung any more slickly to him than the genteel eighteenth-century European background his family imagined themselves to have.

He was a man of property and exuded class.

Everyone knew of attractive middle-class girls with sons resembling him, but none was a Stollmeier. What of it? When his liveried coachman flicked the horses to a gallop on Half Way Tree Road, the crowd opened and closed again under a pall of dust behind the slick Prince of Wales buggy, and that was as it should be. Times, he snapped at his brother, could change all they liked. He remembered from childhood the vast old cotton tree that had accommodated generations of market women resting on its roots to break their journey from country plots to the city market, but now the Half Way Tree was dead. Deeper rooted and more permanent than the landscape itself were other traditions. Civilisation itself balanced on a social order enshrined in upper class values.

Rudy Stollmeier's new house on Half Way Tree Road was a clean-cut white building with a roof that sloped away on all four sides. Not only the usual jalousied verandahs but a number of high, wrought-iron balconies looked out onto well-kept grounds bordered by palms. His other house, on Goldfields in St Thomas, was older, darker, forbidding, with hooded windows contemplating the wide sweep of pasture and coffee, and brooding over the valley. His personality expressed itself in the suburban house with its elegant swirls of iron, the tracery of the fanlight over its panelled doors, the complex twining of fretwork. Just as much a part of him was the old stone stronghold in the country, whose ancient twisted brackets supported the shingled hoods of its windows, and whose defensive loopholes looked out over the present and the past towards the sea. A man like Stollmeier might form liaisons with any attractive, respectable girl, but the selection of a mistress for his property and his name was another matter.

Still, Catherine's and Stella's claim, though unobtrusive, was matter-of-fact. Even his brother's family acknowledged Stella, and she moved with startling confidence in Jacob's house. Her upbringing by Catherine had instilled the manner, bearing and outlook of a lady, but her association with Rudy's niece added that air of upper-class confidence and heightened her taste.

Throughout her life Stella would recall her first impression of the old Jacob Stollmeier house on East Street. Lynn Stollmeier, her father's sister-in-law, had glimpsed Catherine in a store and stopped her impulsively. Stella was to spend Saturday with Lynn's own daughter, Sarah. From the night before, Stella was tense with anxiety and expectation.

Before first light her eyes popped wide awake and strained into the darkness, her ears waiting for the birds, the dogs, the first rumble of traffic. For a long time there was nothing but the slow drip of the garden pipe beneath the window, the green fire of a peenie wallie in its progress down the wall and occasional zig-zag about the room. Then at last the semi-black room had thinned to grey-green, with sharp wedges of light between the slats making visible lines like the slim arch of the steam bent chair at her table. Thlop, thlop, on the road. The crunch of wheels and the fresh, good-natured greetings of early pedestrians.

By the time she was up and had made her bed, the gate creaked and slammed. Then Doris's voice rang, "Yes, 'M. Yes, 'M. Me, Doris, 'M!"

Stella dived hastily across to the dresser and pushed her doll into a drawer, for she was eleven now — only she had cared for the doll so seriously, shopping on Orange Street with a quattie for half a yard of cloth, collecting gracefully curled feathers when a fowl was killed, drying lime peel to make hats. Of course she never played with it now but, at nights, when Mama moaned and tossed in her sleep and the traffic on the road died away leaving a hot thick stillness broken only by the screech owl, it was good to feel under the pillow and run her fingers over the familiar surfaces.

Outside came the regular tramping and clatter of day-clean and the clanging of the tramcar bell. A street vendor bawled, "Booby egg! Booby egg! Bwoil an' raw, booby he-egg!"

Stella stiffened and cocked an attentive ear, but they were the first for the season and would be expensive; she would not ask for them. Yet minutes later there was Doris calling, "Miss Catrin, 'M. Me get the hegg-dem. If I mus' put dem on to bwoil, 'M?"

By the time Stella reached the kitchen the little speckled shells were bumping gently in the pot.

Doris swelled indignantly in the kitchen, denouncing the booby-egg vendor to the world at large. Catherine was nowhere in sight, but the woman flounced and postured anyway, shoulders back, belly thrust forward, arms akimbo.

"If you hear all what an' what de hegg-woman come wid 'bout de price, 'M. Tell me seh how when de man-dem a come from de islands de boat overtu'n before de Palisadoes and how im husband drown and how de money have fe feed nine pickney. Laad, 'M."

Stella regarded her uncertainly.

"Well, don't it might be true?"

"'M? You gwine follow old nega, 'M? Too tief!"

Doris switched her skirts impatiently and flounced over to the high kitchen stool, where she perched with her wide enamel plate and steaming, sweet tea.

Catherine was in and out, shaking up linen so that little golden flecks of dust rose and spun in the slanted beams, and she struggled with the impossible questions Stella asked about the house on East Street.

"I tell you, darling, I never been there myself. Help me with the ackees and we get through faster."

Willingly enough the child picked up the basket of orange-red fruit and tumbled her hands through them.

"These are no good, eh?"

She dived at a few tightly closed ones that might be poisonous and pushed them aside. Her mother was out of earshot but Doris paused and grinned at her. "Whenebba me Mumma send me pick hackee, 'M, she always tell me de riddle say: 'Me fada send me fe pick out a wife, tell me only pick dem dat smile, fe dem dat no smile will kill me'."

On delivering this cheerful news she chuckled shrilly and pulled out from another bag a couple of lemon-coloured, coarse-skinned seville oranges. Catherine appeared, clucking her tongue impatiently.

"Oh, Doris, pull out the little battered-up ones, nuh? Don't I tell you we going to stew some halves? What we will stew if you take the good ones clean floor?"

The woman grinned again in unperturbed good humour, rolled the two oranges back in and pulled out two more as unselectively as before. In a minute Doris passed again with her pail and the smooth, brown brushes of coconut husk for polishing the floor.

Catherine shook her head. Well Doris was not a bad woman but it was not like the old days. When Doris finished she would walk right back across the room on her bare feet and smear up the sheen, not like the cleaning women of Catherine's childhood, who would shuffle across on cloths gripped between their toes. Hn. A decent woman, Doris, but none of the pride of them old-time people. Strange times now, eh? Strange, with a touch of madness. Watch this man Bedward (in the news now) insulting decent people, and thousands flocking to August Town for healing. Hn! When you confuse up people like that, how they going keep they mind 'pon work?

By the time Stella had torn the pale flesh of the ackees from their pods, and bundled away the plump black seeds and pinky-orange strings in an old *Gleaner* newspaper, Catherine was fastening on her hat. On the way out they called to Doris who was on her knees with her skirt bundled up around her, rubbing the floor with swift, strong, circular movements. In a cardboard box at a corner of the porch her baby dozed contentedly, his fat, creased little legs sprawled apart in an attitude of abandonment and his lips parted in a milky half-smile. On the table nearby waited his worm medicine (see-me-contract, boiled with orange peel) and this must be his last dose for that night would be full moon. Beside the cup was a small chunk of shad roe for his gums.

The morning was hot and dry but relieved by a steady wind.

Grass quits popped up and down around the dripping pipe, bobbing their heads cheekily, and a humming bird whirred from
flower to flower, iridescent among an emerald blur of wings. The
bees droned monotonously around heavy clusters of pink and
white flowers that weighed down their stems into the pathway.

Catherine and Stella caught the mule car near to the gate. At
East Street, Mama asked the driver of the bus to rein a few yards
from the gate, and she accompanied Stella to the gateway, no further. The child found herself crossing the wide courtyard and
suddenly she was small and lost in this strange broad space
where the wind whipped circles of dust thinly here and there.
She wondered whether Sarah's father would be at home, felt her
throat contract, and glanced fearfully over her shoulder. There
was Mama, framed by the tall pillars, solid and square and erect
as they were, coldly motionless and remote. A pale stone gentleman towering above Stella struck an impressive pose and glared
down critically, but even from a distance the child felt her mother's strength surge through her and her back straightened and
gained poise. Often she let go of Mama by becoming her. Stella
breathed freely and shifted her mind from her mother and the
bus that would bear her away and thought only of playing all day
in the big house. To the right the garden sprawled away but she
did not take it in beyond sensing a blur of smooth green with
smudges of roses.

All that seemed solid was the house itself, timeless and indestructible with the square hewn stones of its front steps and the
carved pillars that swirled up to dissolve into the roof through
ornate fretwork. She kept to the centre lest she forget and dull
the brass stanchions within reach of her sweaty palms. She
opened and closed her fingers, reminding herself. Mrs Stollmeier
had invited her here. Mrs Stollmeier was her aunt.

Beneath, she caught a glimpse of vaulted cellars at the massive base of the house. Then she was at the top of the broad staircase. Through the window shutters she glimpsed a dart of colour

and a voice sang out, "I think she's here, Nana. Coming! Coming!"

Then there was the girl her mother had pointed out to her as her cousin, tumbling out of the heavily carved mahogany door as unselfconsciously as you please in one of those new, scandalously short, rainy daisy skirts, and she grabbed Stella's hand and tugged her in.

As they brushed in through the doorway the heavy wood shifted painfully on shiny brass hinges. Stella hesitated, for the gallery to the left seemed so inviting with its sheen of floor slipping endlessly away and the gleaming wall slatted with sunlight that streamed in through the louvres. But they turned instead through a room forbidding with the dark gloss of mahogany woodwork and the spread claws of the tiger skin sprawled at the centre. She glimpsed her own scared face in the French mirrors between the pictures and struggled to compose herself.

In and down on them looked the dignity of the old house out of gilded frames leaning forward from the walls. The portraits were of military-looking gentlemen mostly, but there was quite a young lady too, wearing a tiara and white feathers above a pointed face with tendril-like curls at forehead and cheeks. Children too. A little girl with plump arms folded and an irritatingly self-satisfied expression under a close, frilly cap. There was even a baby, trailing gold-embroidered muslin.

Low and heavy above them hung the gold-leafed chandelier by a frail chain, and the wall beyond was dominated by an old English blunderbuss. A dark, carved door stood closed with a seeming finality Stella would never have thought to question, but Sarah grasped the brass handle irreverently and shoved. The room they entered was heavy and full. The silence loomed palpable and somehow awe-inspiring to Stella. Then she realised it was the organ, but she had thought only churches had organs. A tall, angular black girl was rubbing brassware at a table near to it and grinned readily as they entered the room. Her face was sharp-featured but pleasant.

"Where Maman, Icelin?"

"Me nah know, 'M."

Stella grew aware of an older, heavily set woman, in white from her shoes to the Dutch cap.

"So you are Stella," she murmured, gazing at her with unexpected, quiet excitement. She watched Stella so intently the child would have been frightened, but there was a softness about the face and some familiarity.

"Have we... I know you?" Stella asked.

"No, man," Sarah interrupted. "This is Nana."

"Your Mama upstairs, Miss Sarah." Nana turned them gently in the direction of the stairs. "Go quiet, my lamb."

Stella felt Nana's eyes on her till they rounded the curve of the stairway. The wall along the narrower ends of the steps was lined with pencil and wash drawings and mezzotints. Sarah caught her arm, laughing.

"We must see Maman first. Then I'll take you round."

Then Stella was mortally embarrassed, feeling they must think her a bungo.

"I'm glad you could come," Sarah burst out hastily. "My other cousins are so dull."

Stella stared at her in relief.

"How they can... how can they be dull?" she gasped incredulously.

"Dolls," Sarah moaned. "They always want to play with dolls. Of course," she seemed anxious to disclaim too close a relationship with them, "they're just second and third cousins. Not like you."

Stella stood at the top of the steps beside her, digesting this. "You don't like dolls?"

"Well. I used to, you know. When I was a child."

"Yes. I used to, too." Stella regarded Sarah admiringly. "Pity your cousins are so childish."

"Their mamas," Sarah's voice dropped confidentially, "they feel I'm... a bit wild."

"No!" Stella gasped, genuinely shocked. "Why?"

Sarah frowned, considering, then shrugged.

"I'm different." Then she threw back her head and laughed. "That must be why."

What a laugh she had, honest and open. She wasn't very proper at all. Stella loved her instantly and permanently.

Sarah pushed the door beside them at the top of the staircase. "Maman must be here."

It was a small writing room with hand-painted chairs at a fragile desk cluttered with note paper and envelopes. On one side it opened into a room with a vast bed, heavily carved and overhung by an embroidered canopy from some previous age. Near to the door was a new American sewing machine and over to the far side stood the commode press. The other side overlooked the rose garden beyond a curling glazed balustrade. From the writing table, a lady tiny and elegant as a china figurine looked up and smiled hesitantly.

Stella curtsied involuntarily to her aunt, wondering how anyone could write under the scrutiny of the smooth, hairless faces framed above her. (They did seem to be men despite the absurd little rolls of hair over their ears.) In fact, Sarah's mama did seem a bit uncomfortable — kind, but somehow uncertain about what to say.

With a start, Stella realised that her aunt was coloured. Sarah was not white, but fair enough, and somehow Stella had not imagined Aunt Lynn as obviously coloured. But of course it was common knowledge. Stella remembered the older girls in school whispering about Lynn Guillotte. One had been sent home for saying something about how she had come by her wealth before Jacob brought her from New Orleans. There were even people who insisted that he had never married her, but Mama said people were just wicked. They themselves had said he was besotted with Lynn.

The old midwife had told Mama something about obeah.

Lynn Guillotte must have used a potion, the woman said. How else would a Stollmeier have lavished everything on a creole woman? The midwife was old enough for Mama to restrain herself from putting her down quite as sharply as she wanted. But afterwards she told Stella that Lynn was certainly married. Stella's father, Rudolf, was estranged from Jacob over it. Their youngest brother, Wilhelm, who had resettled his branch of the family in Germany no longer wrote to Jacob. But people could talk all they liked. And no one but Jacob mattered to Lynn. Catherine had recognised, with amusement, that Lynn was an unorthodox woman in many ways. Obviously, she was quite contemptuous of the Jamaican proprieties. Otherwise, as even Stella realised wryly, they would hardly be meeting now.

Stella answered politely as Aunt Lynn inquired for Catherine in her strange, musical voice. The child managed a remark about the roses and instantly her aunt's eyes gleamed with interest.

"You like roses, *ma petite*? Aah. I 'ave been in the garden today already, but next time you come I take you with me and show you one very special rose. I 'ad it brought from London three years ago. Next time you must come early to go with me, *oui*?" She flashed her fragile smile, kind, lonely, curious at the same time.

The truth was that Lynn Guillotte had had a white grandfather and a grandmother who was a brown woman pretty and talented enough to have been accepted as housekeeper and mistress in Guillotte's household. She retained her place in his affection all his life — even after their daughter made a disastrous marriage with a brown gambler and died in childbirth. Lynn had passed her childhood on an estate fronting the Mississippi, nurtured in a mansion at the end of an avenue of ancient oak trees, finished in Paris, cultured beyond the understanding of Jacob Stollmeier's friends and relatives. But she was not white. Voodoo, it was whispered. Was voodoo, or she coulda never get a Stollmeier. Everyone knew the French Catholics were superstitious — not like Kingston people.

Rudy's brother, Jacob, had created for Lynn a world separate from Kingston though their home was almost at the heart of the city. It was a rare and fragile world of china and rose petals, but it was all for her, his *petite fleur,* and she could afford to laugh at Rudy's scorn of her parentage and in return disparage his morals. Above all, Lynn could afford to live in Kingston without quite seeing it and to be as kind to Catherine's daughter as she liked.

So it always was — the dutiful call on Aunt Lynn, with an offering of something special like a wedge of fruit cake or a jar of candied seville orange for this extraordinary aunt. Yet Stella knew the house well before she met Jacob himself. Then the uncle she had been dreading turned out to be a colourless, harassed man defined mainly by his courtly devotion to Aunt Lynn. He ceased to frighten the child once he materialised.

She explored the grounds avidly, for Sarah was allowed in the words of her father's cousins to run shamelessly wild, but they avoided the stables. Sarah rode well, but when she mounted Stella on the new polo horse, it had thrown her and was therefore, according to Sarah, "a confounded, venomous beast." Still, the Shetland pony that Jacob had had brought to Jamaica eight years before was gentle and affectionate.

Outside, vendors trudged in through the back gate from the lane. In the morning, fishermen displayed snapper and king fish, ran their fingers encouragingly among glistening heaps of shrimp or, high over the heads of the children, they swung live lobsters which twiddled their eyes and slapped their tails angrily on their undersides. In the evening, wrinkled red hibiscus and belladonna lilies spotted the garden, and the air hung heady with jasmine. A faint scrambling overhead announced the bats stirring between the ceiling and the roof; then they would stream out from a small hole barely visible under the eaves. Night deepened to the fluting of tree frogs from the rosy wild pines, toads snoring from loose bricks around the sundial and, last, a sharp, startling scream from a white owl sailing overhead.

Quickly Stella made acquaintances and selected favourites, apart from Nana. Cookie was broad-faced, and shiny beneath her plaid cap from close association with the fireside. Only to Stella she revealed the secret of her crystallised breadfruit blossom. Cookie's tight skin crinkled infectiously at mouth and eye corners over the texture of lemon wine or of coconut drops meltingly smooth. Old Ella, the pastrymaker, fancied herself above a mere cook, and Ella was less fun than the indiscreet Cookie, but gratifying in her respectful bob of the head when addressing Miss Stella. Ella and Cookie crammed the cupboards of the Stollmeier kitchen with jars of mango chutney, cherry peppers in wine sauce, chippolata and mountain cabbage, stewed guavas and coco-plums.

Because of them, the comfortable kitchen was more appealing than the dining room; besides, the fireside was better built than Catherine's, so the smoke went out directly. Or perhaps it was that the ebony chimney sweep came more regularly, sending Stella and Sarah scampering under the arch of the back step behind a pair of old Spanish jars. Then too, the butler, a remote, intangible figure, hovered ominously over the dining table — like a John Crow, as Sarah muttered wickedly. Still, he was not as frightening as the sweep.

One person in the establishment pointedly kept her distance and treated Stella as an intruder. Jennings, the lace-edged housekeeper, viewed Stella as the other Mr Stollmeier's brat and had no intention of waiting on her like one of the family. Sarah neutralised the rebuff by scoffing that Jennings rattled her keys contemptuously whenever she passed Stella in the corridor, and by giving Stella a matching bunch to rattle back.

Others moved dimly in the domestic background. Among them was a laundress. When Stella first saw her she was hanging out Sarah's underwear. She was magnificently built, with long powerful legs, broad shoulders and full, firm breasts. Her face was notably strong at the jaw, eyes shadowy with memory, lips forgotten by laughter — a tragic, reproachful face. But Stella saw only the swell of the wide skirt Louise had pulled up over her bulging abdomen. Suddenly, as if she sensed Stella's critical eye, the girl shot a smouldering glance over her shoulder.

"Who that?" Stella whispered to Cookie.

"Poor Louise," Cookie sighed. "Well, she soon go."

Stella waited till the yard man had passed. He plodded slowly across the brick-paved yard, burdened with earth for the toilets.

"Why?" she insisted softly.

"Well she cyan't keep on a work ya the way she stay now. Well, sir. Last time a bush man help her out of her trouble. She was well sick. Is me same one boil the penny royal fe her."

"Why she was so sick?"

"You ebba hear 'bout a bush call Ram Goat Dashalary? Well is that he give her fe do 'way with the pickney. Massa! Nearly dead."

Nana was hurrying across to them and Cookie waddled on into the house.

"My lamb," the nurse remonstrated, putting her hand on Stella's back and steering her away to the house. "You come here as Miss Sarah's cousin, man. You can't stand in backyard chattering with the servant so."

Stella hesitated, glancing back over her shoulder.

"That girl," she said, "that Louise. Why she hate me?"

"You? Oh, no. Poor Louise Haynes. She don't even know you."

"What she doing here?"

"Coachie beg Miss Lynn give her a chance. He must be know her family."

With a last firm touch of her fingers Nana pressed Stella into the house.

After Sarah and Nana, Stella liked Coachie best. Hardly anyone knew his real name, Obadiah Castries. It was he who drove Stella home, accompanied by Sarah and Nana. On a still Saturday evening it was cool under the roof of the old catherine that the Stollmeiers still kept as their family carriage. Aunt Lynn preferred the tandem for her personal use, but Stella loved the catherine for no reason but that it had Mama's name.

A pleasant drive it was, past the park at dusk. The trees quivered with sleepy birds and the flame of the poincianas blended into sunset and disappeared. If they were early, Coachie would pause for the girls to run and see the fountain shoot its fine spume up into the twilight.

"Water no short now," Coachie would be sure to remark as they clambered back into the carriage.

The city drew on the Wag Water River. Thank God, Nana always agreed, now there was water pressure enough for any emergency. After the fire of '82 they had learnt their lesson.

Out past the Metcalfe statue they rolled into that interval of evening when the sky filled with shapeless fluttery things — bats usually, but occasionally soft, dark moths brushed past, dusting them lightly. Then the gas lamps would flare as they rounded the corner. All the way, Coachie talked. How he talked. He pointed out people and objects along the way that the girls had seen a hundred times. He recounted tales they knew by heart, jokes funny again because they were so familiar. In the end they would chorus the punch line together. Then Coachie's already creased face would crumple into a million tiny wrinkles and he would call Miss Nana to witness how de young lady-dem like to mek pappy-show of old people. Other times, Coachie just sat bouncing along contentedly on the baggy seat of his trousers, muttering to the horses.

Certainly Coachie and the horses talked together and knew each other's minds. The reins he held lightly as a sort of formality or symbol of office, but really he told the horses what he wanted them to do. Once, when Stella asked if he never used a whip, he was startled into a minute's silence. When he spoke it was a low, reproving rumble.

"Well, see 'ere, Miss Stell. Whip is a ting people did use long time before dem get civilise." He paused, then resumed. "Sixteen bredda and sister me have, an' me is de baby."

Stella sucked in the corner of her mouth and avoided Sarah's eye to keep from laughing at the idea of Coachie as a baby. He spoke labouringly, anxious not to offend.

"My fada belong to old Mas' Gottfried, 'M. Das Mr Jacob fada. Different, different man to Mr Jacob. When de family buy Goldfield in de country, my fada come to dem as a bwai with de house and a few other use-to-be slave. My fada back 'ave what look like little gutter 'crass it. Plenty ole time people 'ave scar-scar 'pon dem back, but my fada — de flesh eat 'way, 'M. Mind you, Miss Stell, nega people, backra people can wicked same way 'cause me grannie did kill one of fe-her own pickney, carry go tie her down 'pon ant's nest 'causin she tief likkle sugar. Wicked same way, all dem old-time people, black and white. But people civilise now, 'M. Nobody dig up me back wid whip, Miss Stell, and me nah go beat no dumb beast. People civilise now, 'M."

Any inclination to laugh had completely left Stella. For a moment she saw him. He was distinct from the whole Stollmeier establishment, a man with parents, with stories of family and home, perhaps with children of his own.

"Coachie," she ventured, "you have children?"

He glanced back in surprise.

"Twelve, Miss Stell. Is twelve me have, 'M. Well true is nine since the boy-dem gaan Panama an' nobady nah hear fram dem. Icelin is me younges'."

"Icelin?"

"Icelin, 'M. Tell im madda seh im not goin wo'k no land and im follow me come a Kingston. Icelin what always help Miss Nana, 'M."

Yes, of course, now she thought of Icelin, that tall spare girl, older than Sarah, who ran errands for Aunt Lynn and helped with housework. No one ever thought of servants having surnames, anyway. There had been no way of knowing Icelin was Coachie's daughter. Icelin Castries, she must be.

"Icelin. She's your youngest, Coachie?"

"A good pickney, 'M," he beamed. "Never a day sick, nor rude neider. Madda keep im well stric', no mek im run 'bout like plenty gyal-pickney dat age. Im madda is one good woman though, 'M. Dis Christmas, please God, go make twelve years now we engage."

Nana interrupted his rambling to point out something quite dull. Nana was so obvious really. Sarah nudged her cousin, stifling a giggle.

"Coachie," she assumed her most grown-up voice, "tell us all about Icelin's mother."

"Now, Miss Sarah," Coachie's face shrivelled into a sly smile, "is haig you want to haig Miss Nana. You too mischief, 'M."

His eyes darted gleefully at the woman behind him, who could not check a wry twitching of her lips.

"Old wo'thless," she muttered. Then louder, "Keep you eye on the road, man. You not 'fraid you miss the gate? Please to sit back, Miss Sarah. Hold you things, Stell. Don't forget the stew cashew."

The horses stamped, shuffling their hindquarters impatiently and twitching their ears against the sandflies. Stella squinted and held her breath as she darted through a cloud of the insects, her mouth twisted in revulsion.

"What is it?" Catherine gasped.

"Flies!"

Catherine stared tensely then relaxed, but she fretted every time Stella left for East Street lest someone snub her. Still, she let her go again.

Let the child go. If anything happened to Catherine herself, Sarah and Nana would be there. And then, Jacob Stollmeier was different from... from his brother. Certainly he had married Lynn

Guillotte, and diamonds and fast horses she may have had in New Orleans but she was coloured just the same.

While Stella was gone, Catherine walked the house till she sank stiffly into the dark straight chair whose back she rarely touched with hers. In the mirror over the cabinet she caught sight of the little lines beginning between her brows. "And my mouth corners too," she mused, brushing at them ruefully. They would gather and deepen so quickly, for Stella would be a woman soon and only yesterday she had been a frail little thing with a thin wheeze of a cry. Catherine had held her with painful concentration, as if the next breath might blow the wisp of life away. Yet soon she would reach the age that Catherine had been....

Catherine glanced fearfully back into the mirror at the other face reflected from the portrait behind her chair. Rudy had ordered it. By the time she had sat for it he was wearying of her presumptuous expectations. The photographer had caught the pain in the pinched mouth and wide, hurt eyes. Still, the photographer had been kind to her. Her mouth had been fuller and her nose — she assessed it candidly — no, it was definitely not so straight. Pity she hadn't realised it. She had believed Rudy though even Jenny Parsons had been fairer than herself and the dePaz girl was near white. Mitchell, the photographer, had walked to her house with the picture from Duperly's because it was paid for and uncollected. He was so embarrassed — not a bad man, Mitchell.

But there was Stella. Catherine stood up abruptly, smoothed her skirt and tucked the scented cambric handkerchief into her bosom. The child would be home soon and today was not one of Doris's days. Perhaps a little pumpkin soup.... Rudy used to like pumpkin soup, it came back to her suddenly. Hn! Pity it hadn't choked him. She slammed the chair in so that the delicately tapered legs quivered, and she bustled out into the backyard for Spanish thyme.

Catherine was the centre of Stella's world and Stella the reason for Catherine's. As Catherine stitched, the child loosened or rewound the long skeins of glossy thread, tracing patterns onto the fine linen and making odd comments that melted away her mother's front of cool austerity.

"Where you think those big stones in the wall come from, Mama? Must be pieces of some mountain. How they bring them all this way? Old time people must have been strong, eh?"

Their lives were meshed together. They blended ginger beer and combed each other's hair for church, fretted over homework and wandered inquisitively through the cloth stores, consulting the Syrian owners about matching shades and textures. They would hurry past the cigar makers and straw hat plaiters but stop at the corner of King and Tower Streets to explore Curphey's, which Stella loved for the range and incompatibility of its supplies. Pickles lurked between fern albums, tooth elixirs, phosphoric rat poison, biscuits, turtle eggs and wines. They selected cherry toothpaste, Amalga soap and candy, and they wrinkled their noses as they passed the turtle liver oil. Even better than exploring Curphey's was roaming the Metropolitan House, a department store with chic clerks in skirts that floated six inches above the floor. When she left school, Stella decided, she would work in the Metropolitan.

Of everything they did together, Stella felt even in her early teens that total bliss was accompanying Mama to market. They set out early, before the crowd, the dust and the heat. On the sidewalks, scattered vendors would just be setting up baskets of tobacco or poultry. They were old women mostly, with cadaverous faces and blank eyes, sunk in dark hollows, and Mama said their things were dirty. At the entrance to the market a small crowd would already be drifting, dissolving, forming again. Wild, bare-legged boys darted between the baskets, pinching fruit from the open trays, spitting guinep seeds about with competitive vigour and startling the donkeys into sidelong plunges among the shoppers.

In front, a few tourists mused over doilies of lace bark ornamented with ferns and pressed flowers, while a handful of local women selected lady baskets or clay pots. By the door, vendors plagued a newly-arrived, pink and white Englishman to buy an ebony walking-stick. A massive woman leaned out to him with pursed lips, addressing him as 'lover'. When he flushed painfully she shrieked with laughter, her stomach bobbing in the loose dress and shaking against pendulous breasts which pushed out the folds almost at the waist of the print frock. Then he laughed too, a loud, free sound that made Stella smile, but Catherine's grip on her arm tightened and she pulled the child along.

"Coarse!" she muttered disdainfully. "Making himself cheap with dirty, bungo people."

Catherine and Stella bought the regular things first, a heap of tomatoes and peppers at threepence a heap, three chochos for a penny, onions and yellow yam. In the meat section Catherine came across a man selling janga, little river shrimp, and sent the child scurrying back with fivepence for vegetables to make pepperpot.

"Eightpence a pound for chicken, my lady."

They exchanged significant glances.

"You see why I bought those layers, Stell. Just as well we buy fresh pork for the money." Catherine cast the chicken vendor a withering look and moved on. "Saltfish?"

"We didn't use much since last time. We could do with little salt kine though."

"Sixpence, sevenpence. Much of a muchness. Take a chups of pork."

Catherine stopped by a woman who pushed the brim of her flat straw hat back on her head to reveal the rust-coloured cotta beneath. "Miss Catrin, 'M!" She laughed and slapped her palms down on the white apron over her thighs. "Well, Miss Catrin. If you know how long. I been sick, 'M. Is dat make me gone back Morant. Well sick. Baby dead in me, 'M. Yes, well now, tank

God."

She dived her hand into her tray and produced a rosy pome-
granate for Stella. "Pretty like youself, eeh, darlin'?"

They paused and bought plantains and a good, powdery-dry
looking wedge of pumpkin then wandered on again, glad to be
out of the smelly area of the meat vendors.

"We should keep little arrowroot around, you know,"
Catherine reflected and Stella picked it up reluctantly.

Outside, a rowdy group milled around the fountain although
the courtyard lay under a pall of dust. The old tobacco seller
cackled and flourished his knife before slicing off a length of
jackass rope. Catherine and Stella hung back to linger among the
fruit sellers, hugging each other's arms, whispering about the
prices.

"Locust, Mama. Look!" Stella laughed and pointed at a fruit
they never bought.

"Oh, no. Not that horrible thing. Lord, the smell."

"That's why they call it 'stinking toe'."

"Shh!"

"No one hearing me."

"What a smell, though. Is no wonder really."

And they squeezed each other and giggled softly like sisters,
for Catherine was still a young woman and Stella, at fourteen,
almost a lady.

Stella occupied two worlds alternately, each almost but not
quite complete. Catherine never failed to remind her that she was
a Stollmeier, with a right to more than her mother alone could
provide. To the outrage of Jacob's cousins, Lynn Stollmeier
bought bicycles for Sarah and Stella and identical white serge cos-
tumes. Yet Stella never changed in the upstairs rooms when Sarah
was away.

This was not Lynn's doing but Nana's.

"But why Nana so?" Stella fumed to her mother.

"She just protecting you."

"From *what?*"

"Never open youself to no snub, child. Better they think you ungrateful. But never open youself to a snub from them or they servants."

"Like Nana."

"Eh?" Catherine stopped and looked at her startled.

"Well, is Nana who don't want me upstairs, and don't she just one of the servants?"

Catherine spoke quietly and rapidly. "Never say that."

Cautiously Stella extricated herself from a topic turned perilous. She could not grasp the understanding between her Mama and Nana, who visited often now and even spent a night when Mrs Stollmeier could spare her. Stella herself had grown as close to Nana as Sarah was, and it was as well too, for in the November of her fifteenth year, Stella contracted typhoid.

They sent word to East Street at once. Nana could not return to the Stollmeiers from her visit with Catherine and Stella until the danger of contagion had past.

It was strange. Now, more than ever, Stella seemed a child. The most trivial illness had always brought to Catherine the grey shadow of speculation, the spectre that hovers at the back of the mother's mind whispering... Suppose. The thing never put into words because the mother is too busy, too practical, too religious, but it was there, at the back. What if... It had been so through every little gasp of asthma. And this was typhoid.

Catherine passed an icy hand over her eyes and tried to go about what had to be done, but she was almost out of control. Her legs folded uselessly and Nana caught her.

"I not leaving you," she snapped.

Catherine stared at her dazedly.

"Pull youself together," Nana shook her, "or I going have fe hit you. You can't stand up?"

Nana tugged at her and talked roughly, cajolingly, threateningly in turn till Catherine revived slightly.

"I never see you so before."

Catherine shook her head dumbly.

"Typhoid." Her mouth could hardly frame it.

But consciously, stubbornly, she crushed the doubts, wiped blank the corners of her mind and moved about her work with the strength and automatic efficiency of cold steel.

Stella herself was vaguely conscious. Pain and terror solidified in her abdomen till it swelled hard, patched with wide flat spots that stretched nearer, up to her chest. The days parched restless by and jumbled into headache, nosebleed and a strange pressure under the navel. The fever roasted and shrivelled her.

At the end of the second week she lay as if dead, yet somehow aware of her abdomen bloated above her like a thing separate from herself. The room was a soft slushing of voices. Mama, Nana, Dr Eliot. Their voices melted and the room became a fluid that washed against the foot of a hill that sloped ahead endlessly, its top lost in swirling clouds, painfully bright. Mama would have climbed it, and though Stella felt her breath shortening and her joints aching she climbed and climbed with the valley cutting away deeper than she could see. She tried to force herself not to look but an iron gate beside her swung open and something stepped through to her. Then it was a strange, uneven box, resting unsteadily, and she let go with one hand to reach over and level it. For a second she glimpsed the inside — a tunnel, and she could not see the end. Then at her touch it jolted, nearly dislodging her from her grasp on the slope, but she dug her fingers into the grass as the thing jerked loose and slid back, back down.

She could hear it clanking hollowly through the stones and glimpsed its polished surface disappearing into blue-green depths. Then there was a splash and the gate clanged shut. Voices swelled around the slope, washing over her.

Nana was crying.

"Cathy, darling. Cathy, Cathy."

"Watch her though," Dr. Eliot was saying. "If she starts haemorrhaging... hmm."

There was a tepid trickle around her skimpy breasts as they bathed her with the cassia bush thing. Just a little way away she could hear her own voice, "It fell through itself."

Wonderful that she could talk, whatever nonsense. They sopped her with cassia bath, beaming encouragement. They boiled the cassia too, and raised her head to make her sip the tea. Dr Eliot's instructions droned on. Milk. Disposal of stools. Acid to soak the linen. Days later she noticed the sheets, stained with the stuff they had sponged her with. Nana caught her glance and shrugged gently. They would just burn the linen anyway.

Nana and Mama moved easily about the house, knowing each other's minds. Nana would hold out her hand and Mama place a spoon in it wordlessly. The fever had passed and Stella lay sleepily confident that she would be sponged and fed, cooled all over with rum and given ginger tea. Afterwards they dressed her in the nightgown with the torchon edging.

"From Sarah," Mama smiled, "and the roses from Aunt Lynn."

Nana held out a fine Venetian vase with three perfect blooms from the garden at East Street.

"But those are her London roses," Stella gasped, almost tearfully.

"I going make little Tallawah Tonic, build you up," Nana promised softly, running her fingers over the bones and hollows of Stella's face.

They opened the door wide so she could see them in the kitchen. Nana scrubbed the bryal roots and put them to boil with sarsaparilla, chew-stick, nerve withes, 'strong back', and a young coconut. When it had boiled down and cooled, Nana and Catherine argued anxiously about the amount of dark sugar, rum and brandy. For some reason it was Catherine who had to grate the nutmeg. For a day or two the tightly corked bottle stood on the sunny windowsill of Stella's room.

When she was better, Aunt Lynn insisted that she have supper with Sarah and spend the night. It was a special dinner, for Sarah insisted on turkey and Cookie stroked the seasoning into it lovingly and roasted it with plantains and yellow yams. At night Stella sat with Sarah on the carpet in the music room while Lynn played the piano, and in the morning they romped in the terrace bath. Then, as they sauntered out from between the stands for china basins and goblets, into the back garden, Sarah's father rode off to polo.

"Go in, out the sun," he inclined his head to Stella as he passed.

His voice, never harsh, was kindlier now that the rift between his brother and himself had widened. Rudy's officious advice on business investments had driven the brothers further apart.

The girls wandered downstairs, shyly overjoyed to be together again. Stella peeped in through the open doors to the billiard room and library. The library seemed strangely masculine to her with its rows of richly bound volumes, leather-covered fauteuils and inlaid furniture. The bookcases, tables, armchairs and a massive desk glinted with decorative insets of cast ormolu. On a shelf in the far corner stood a peculiar, ornate figure which Sarah identified as an icon. She whispered that her father could not bear it.

"He calls it a graven image," she chuckled.

"Then why does he keep it?"

"Maman. Her grandfather brought it for her grandmother from one of his travels east — same time he brought the cloisonné plates. It's all right for her. She's Catholic."

"And your Papa?"

"Oh." Sarah looked at her for a moment in wonder. "Well, they were Jews, you know."

"And now?"

"Aah. Now? Well I don't think they are anything in particular...."

"What about you, then? Where do you go to church?"

"I don't go much. Sometimes with Maman."

"Come with me too," Stella begged, squeezing her hand. Then she hesitated. "At least.... Of course Mama and I are Anglicans, and Catholics don't recognise... and of course Jews...." Then she stopped, confused, and glanced away, her face suddenly gone blank. "Besides, Mama and I don't sit in the front, you know."

Sarah gurgled.

"Let's march up and see what they say. What they do? They make you move?"

"Well, we never do it. We won't have anyone ask us!" Stella gaped at her.

"They better ask me," Sarah's eyes sparked.

"Hmm. Well is not you they going ask." But Stella regarded her in wide-eyed admiration just the same.

Nana dropped in at Catherine's that evening to bring word of a laundress in need of work.

"I well need someone now Doris gone again," Catherine sighed. "One child after another. They can't learn, these people." She met Nana's eye and stopped abruptly. "But how I can pay her if she accustom East Street?"

"No, man. Louise Haynes just want a work. She get into trouble and have to leave the job. The child come, but it not... right. I never see it, but I hear seh. Anyway the girl need work."

"Send her."

"But after you don't even speak to her."

"You know her. Send her."

When the laundress came Stella recognised her from East Street, though she had not recalled the name. Louise Haynes was not like Doris. They never seemed to know much about her, as Catherine remarked. Nana shrugged.

"No one ever know Louise," Nana sighed. "Louise come in from the country young and pick up with a no-good man. When she get in trouble he kick her in the belly, they say. Perhaps is why the child so. Nobody know, for Louise don' talk."

Catherine tried her. Louise was silent and powerfully built. She was strong enough to do the job and quiet enough not to offend. It didn't matter how little they knew about her for she was hardly inside the house. They spoke pleasantly to her when they saw her, but few things blur away in the common domestic haze around a backyard like a woman over a washtub. Louise's closed, shadowed face was virtually invisible and when she failed to turn out to work it was hard to really picture her.

In fact, her irregularity provoked Catherine, especially as Louise offered no explanation.

Once she said, "De pickney did sick."

Nothing more. No apology. When Catherine eventually dismissed her she left only a grey, unfocused image on the memory.

By that time Stella was fifteen and there was more to occupy them than a laundress. For in that last, expectant, half-gay, half-fearful year of the century, Jacob Stollmeier received a letter from his bank. It was the last in a series of crushing financial blows. When he jumped down from the carriage he shook hands with his coachman, Obadiah Castries — a thing he had never done before — and he locked himself into the library with his father's gun. It was a beautiful old piece with a carved handle, a collector's item. He sat turning it over vaguely for a while.

Once, as a child, he had plunged naked into a jewel green pool beneath a waterfall near his father's old plantation. Goldfields. He had never been free before or since. And there was no starting over unless he came naked again into the world.

When they heard the explosion and broke open the door his blood was trickling down the backs of the leather-bound volumes on the shelf behind him, obscuring the gold lettering and soaking into the pages. It ran across the desk, settled a dark circle around the crystal paperweight and dribbled over the edge onto the pastel pink and grey of the Parisian needlepoint. At his shattered body, slumped upon the desk, stared the icon from the back of the room, as if only it saw Jacob's death for what it was. News on the lips of strangers, questioning, probing. An event of lost roots in a minute land of bottomlessly time-tangled history. A tale in search of a beginning. Over and over. The icon stared at him with wide lidless eyes and painted, pitiless smile. And there was all the wisdom of the old world in that smile that twisted up out of forgotten centuries. Savages, it said, playing at being civilised.

3
Wilderness

THE ISLAND hung at the edge of the world. Eternity tossed and swirled formlessly around it.

In the distance, the great fish was not visible from the canoe, and the wooden bark floated smoothly, noiselessly, uninteresting as flotsam. The man had scrubbed his catch clean and left little odour of blood to excite a killer, yet faintly the current conveyed a swell of irregular motion and a suggestion of raw flesh. It was enough to draw on the shadow that had trailed the canoe for hours, and glimpses of the fin had driven the fisherman miles beyond his regular landing places. The fisherman weighed the distance and subdued a twinge of unease, knowing that excitement or haste meant certain death. Here was a bay at last where he could beach the canoe but the turn must be made without calling the fish. And land he must, because, ultimately, the shark would attack. As if his camouflaged tension scented the water with urgency, the fin sliced closer.

The man gathered the spirits around him and willed himself to be calm. It was not his time. He pulled in the paddle and froze, his eyes scouring the surface, for the fin was gone. A current jolted his log so that he glimpsed over the edge of the canoe a broad, blue-grey back. The boat tipped again as the shark swung back, keeling, and cold, flat eyes stared through him into his inmost terror and the lipless mouth grinned brutally. The Taino froze and his boat bobbed meaninglessly above the monster. Dulled by the lifeless motion of the canoe the shark sank from sight.

Now it was crucial to decide whether to float longer or to turn inland. The Taino rubbed an idol on the bottom of the boat but it was silent. Then a pelican smacked down far out from land and the fin shot up and out cleaving the water. Instantly, softly, the man turned in.

The waves slapped and gurgled under the wood and he struggled, spray-drenched, against a counter-current from some nearby river. Against the glare of sunlight on water the fin rose black and knifed inward. But the man had known the sea all his life, and even as the water boiled around and the shark's grey death sped to him the swell heaved the boat forward to the sand and beached it. Instantly the sea behind him rolled unbroken by any sign of life.

Sea foam is fragile but indestructible. It clung to Xaza-gua as he stepped from the turquoise shallows of the bay and planted his flat brown feet into gleaming sand. Cautiously the Taino eyed the river mouth. It was a dark green place, where the past flowed effortlessly into the future.

The dugout canoe was secure with its cotton nets, bark fishing lines and tools cut from the rocks of the Blue Mountains. The sea swirled between his splayed toes as he stood letting the salt wind crisp his hair and cure his skin under relentless sun fire to a yet deeper copper. But for a brief flap of cotton at the loins, he was bare, for he had earlier unwound the narrow cotton strips that normally held feathers in place at his wrists and ankles. Now his only adornment was a shell pendant, pearl pink and polished to transparency. He was well-formed, rather longer in the body than in the legs. His face was broad, but his head was decidedly elongated and his cheekbones high. His forehead was smooth, not merely unlined but flat. He had been well tended in infancy, the bones carefully compressed as the Corn Lord willed.

For a while his eyes were expressionless, for the fish were in and nothing was required of him. He had hoped to return with a turtle or a manatee but it was as well that he had had no more to madden the shark, so he had placed his lines fortunately and was content. The cassava bread must already be baking on earthen slabs in the village, and his fish, smoky and well spiced with hot peppers, would be welcome. Afterwards the adults would be dulled with tobacco, and though the night fell and the dead roamed he would sleep. His eyes wandered, their natural slant emphasised by an involuntary squint against the glare. There was nothing of pride in them for it was no more his land than anyone else's. The Tainos had drifted in and lingered.

Around the tip of the island where the waves burnt in the morning, he had paddled in the shoal water unhurriedly until the fish drove him further along the coast. Fleetingly a great loneliness overshadowed him for now the mountains towered between him and Aaomaquique, the village of octagonal, palm-thatched houses that studded land grooved by streams of cold, sweet water capering down to the sea. Spreading marl over the refuse of shells and broken stoneware behind the houses had temporarily suppressed the smell and postponed the tribe's inevitable trek further along the coast. Xaza-gua knew of a place to go when the time came, a slope of soft, gold-green. The mountains crouched about it protectively, but the slope itself looked out to sea like the face of God, aglow with sunlight. Perhaps in time they would be driven from this island as their ancestors had been from others, paddling in huge canoes hollowed from the ceiba by fire, fleeing before the savages; perhaps not. But like all the Tainos Xaza-gua knew the island was not his. Not anyone's.

His eyes narrowed, searching the vague lines beyond the glittering expanse of sand and flickering hesitantly towards the mists that the zemes curled around the mountain peaks beyond. Dishonesty was a vile thing among the Tainos, theft a crime punishable by impaling. It never occurred to him to lay hold on the place, even in his mind. He knew it was the jewel of the Sustainer. Yucahu Bagua Maorocoti was the spirit of cassava, sun and sea, born of woman, never fathered, immortal as the mountains, invisible as the wind. The place was no man's land but His, the Hunchback, father of mountains.

The island hung in an eternity of incredible blue so vast as to trouble his soul and send it groping for gods to receive and shelter it when it soared from him. It was a blue that arched interminably deep and still above him until it burnt away into white heat. And then behind him and, ultimately, all around tossed a restless blue — blue-green, blue-grey, white-tipped gold-flecked blue, sinking and sucking down into darker troughs, rising light, curling pale, spraying into white, riding the wind. It confined, supported, crushed or fed them as the spirit moved it for — placid, furious, playful — it was alive.

The shore was a brief riot of glinting sand, dense forest and incalculable peaks; rich brown, gold, red earth; greens that were wet, prickly, glossy, succulent, poisonous, delicate, tangled; mountains sloped and sheer, forested, rocky, pitted with caves, reaching dizzily up and looking out forever, shading into blue themselves as they misted out of sight. Down and out from these mountains, innumerable streams dropped, tumbled, twisted their way to the sea. They too were alive, sparkling over the rocks or shrunk sullen underground for a while, sudden and treacherous among the hills, deceptively slow in the low places, oozing in fine trickles out of fern-covered banks and soaking back among the roots. The bush concealed small game. Guavas, soursop and pawpaw dropped and rotted on the ground. All around, the streams, the rivers, the sea teemed with fish for the men to draw out wriggling silver on harpoons of bone and shell.

It was a tolerant land generally, cruel occasionally, and unpredictable if they disturbed the zemes who infused all things and were all things, who supplied and withheld health, restrained or unleashed the elements — were the elements. So he walked gently on the ground, accepted the sting of the spray, respected the forest, and glanced at and away from the mountains in awe, offending no one.

Yet he wondered what lay on the other side of those moun-tains. Vaguely he had heard of Maima from arrivals in Aaomaquique. One of these newcomers was Caona. In the wilderness of bush, sand and sea, her name flared in his mind and engulfed him in speculation. He dreamed of her dancing out the memory of the race as old Arocoel quavered tales of the grey past and the cacique passed his fingers over the tambourine that he alone dared touch. He dreamed too of her romping in the batos. The sinuous ripple of her skin as she twisted dexterous-ly beneath the elastic ball shimmered through his mind. He dreamed of the dreams that came during the celebration after the game, when the tobacco fumes filled him with oracles and the gods sent promises of her. Then he would breathe more deeply from the hot cup of leaves, the fumes would sear through the forked tube to his nostrils and the sacred sleep of the gods would slide over him.

Reluctantly he forced his attention back to the river and, idly, he tested the current. Speed, temperature, particles. Physical sense and intuition merged and mingled and his mind began to pour backwards, back through his own recollections, brief teach-ings of his elders, fragments of songs and mnemonic mutterings of old men. Moons, rains, generations. He was still as the water poured through his fingers and the memories of the race through his mind. So he began, tentatively at first and then with certain-ty, to know the river. He knew it powerlessly, as he was powerless over his own bloodstream, but intuitively and forever.

He scooped up a handful of pebbles from the mountain tor-rent then hesitated, but he was abstinent, so he bent and dared let the pebbles run through his fingers. Then he began to walk thoughtfully inland, following the river.

Upstream, where it ran faster, he found a bend with the water sweeping clean along smooth rock, and he cleared away a miniature bay. The river swirled in, dashing aside dark particles of sand and fine rock and tumbling them so that the mud dissolved and washed on with the river and the grains sank down to the rocky bottom. He crouched low to peer at them. Nothing. He wondered if this place was known to the tribe or had been known. He focused on a low rock in the river. Perhaps when the rock was higher and less smooth one of the old ones had been here, or earlier, when the river bore it down from the mountain, when the edge was sharp from cleavage, or when there was no rock, only a projection of the mountain far above him, waiting on the tireless water. He could see no one. Awareness fell on him fleetingly of generations in the island, lifetime following lifetime relentlessly; but he had no sense of any Taino on this water beside himself, now.

He returned to the beach, launched the dugout again and, keeping well inshore, paddled for Aaomaquique.

The rains came and passed before he found the place again, climbed steadily upriver and sat on a low rock. Clean-cut stone gleamed pale under the shallows, laid like shelves in the river. Between them sank holes and crevices of deepest green, not the murkiness of still water but the bottomless, transparent green of sheer depth. Above him the river plummeted white over a rock-wall, levelled green then dived again from one foaming terrace to the next. Cautiously he slid into one of the deeper pools, twisted, surfaced and ducked again more confidently.

It was a strange place but lovely, cool with ferns, bamboo and intricately twisted vines. Languorously he turned onto his back and drew it all into a flood of sensation about to become memory.

When he dived again a hole yawned at the base of the rock, a passageway into the stony heart of the mountain. He backed away from it lest he in some way desecrate his past. From caves had come both gods and men, and there was rushing water between their time and his.

51

Xaza-gua returned to Aaomaquique, and before he climbed the river again he had lost count of the sunsets, moons and rains that had passed since the waves had carried his canoe up the sandy shore. Now he swam into the cave, followed a passage up above the surface of the water and found where it opened out through the rock face. There he stood behind the sheet of water that sprayed a veil over the smoother boulders and thundered down deep channels in the wall to the emerald hole at its base.

Afterwards, he sat tumbling the sharp, clean stones over and over in his hand before dropping them into the bottomless pool. Why, he pondered, in such a place was there not to be found a trace of the little grains sacred to the fire god, so that he could fashion them to a sun-pendant for his new wife, Caona.

But then, it did not matter. The zemes said all would be gone in a while. The whole tribe would be destroyed by the gods — new gods wearing thunder in their belts. The Wise Ones thought perhaps, if there were an offering, something sacred, perhaps the little grains themselves that sparkled cold in the hand but lit a flame in the soul, perhaps the light of them would please these gods and they would move on and let the Tainos be. But then, Xaza-gua was not sure. Such a thing was not in memory and who could tell it? Who could tell where the bright stones would lead? In the end, brilliant, warming, blinding or consuming, all light is fire.

Blameless, Xaza-gua let the pebbles that had no gold slide, one by one, over the edge into infinity.

Over a century later there was no gold in Xaza-gua's valley for the Castries family either. It was a sterile place for them, isolated in a green wilderness. There seemed no escape but death.

One of the things that had swayed Francisco Castries into coming was that the island was a stone's throw from Cuba. Then he saw the stupidity of measurement. Years, miles, lifetimes — in sixteenth century Jamaica they meant nothing. In between his side of the country and the other, nearest to Cuba, the island itself threw a wall of mountains running east to west. Once he had crossed these on foot to reach the southern side, Cuba might as well have been on the other side of the earth.

The horses had skidded and stumbled behind him through a timeless stretch of green and only the thought of being left to wander alone among the dark pockets of the hills had kept him moving. His feet flamed, then lost sensation, and oblivion fringed his mind waiting to overtake the single purpose of keeping up with the others. The trail rose and fell through a green gloom of bush, then over rough grass and sharp tumbled rock until it led them down to the scalding heat of the south plains.

Francisco Castries was not an enterprising man in the first place, or he would hardly have remained. An initial brief wild dream of a vast hato like those in Pereda and Guatibacoa, of shipping pimento, sugar and mahogany to the mainland, faded swiftly as reality closed round him — the heat, the drought of the plains, the worthlessness of the Indians. The land that was finally his lay inaccessible to him under the sun. He never saw it all, let alone cultivated it. Certainly it held no beauty for him. He stripped a wide flat portion of the valley and made it even more useless to him than it had been before. In the end, Castries never settled anything, not even a match for his Maria, and Maria was the only dreamer left.

Tales of Sevilla la Nueva shot tingles along Maria's spine. A traveller named da Silva had passed at the craal months before, bringing news of the fabulous city that Juan de Esquivel had planned. It was a vast place, da Silva had said, miles of houses, miles of pavement. He gestured broadly with a dusty, sunbaked arm. Why even the church and the castle were almost a mile apart.

"The castle," Maria Castries breathed, staring at the wanderer with luminous black eyes.

"But yes," da Silva assured her, warming to his tale, *"and a church such as you would love to worship in, little saint."*

He bowed to her in deference to her father, Francisco, but with a somewhat unholy gleam in his eyes for the road to this solitary place was blisteringly dry and hot and her skin was smooth cream and damp with excitement.

"Not finished, the church. But it will be beautiful. Two rows of carved pillars run up to the altar, with festoons and cherubs, and the door arches so high."

Maria raised her head following his gestures and exposing her throat. She could see it all — the Saviour's head over the archway, crowned with thorns and flanked with angels, the saint impaled on his right and, on his left....

"Beautiful," she gasped, as he described the image of the Madonna.

"Indeed," da Silva stared at her. Actually Maria was thin and rather pale from lack of exertion, but it had been a long road and a lonely one. *"Very beautiful,"* he moaned, shifting impatiently. *"Fine houses for miles around and sugar works nearby with a great water mill such as you have never seen. They look down from the hills to the bay."*

Her attention wavered for the sea was common and uninteresting.

"But not a sea such as this," he hastened, dismissing the foam-flecked water somewhere beyond the bush. *"Smooth. Smooth as glass."* She stared at him again, for she had seen glass only once in her life. *"Two horns of land sweep out on either side of the bay, and inside the ships lie still. It is peaceful, like blue stained-glass in a cathedral."*

"Nothing ever happens here."

Her voice was barely audible but she leaned forward, a taut line of impatience, like a child wanting a story. Most of all, she wanted to be in the story. Her eyes were wide and hungry for life.

Da Silva glanced at her father desperately. Francisco was pre-

occupied with other things. Maria's mother was long dead and Francisco was unaccustomed to feeding and rooming a visitor. He had little time for Maria, and was a careless parent in any case.

It was easy.

Months after da Silva had gone, though, long after the days of fearful waiting to know whether she was pregnant had passed, the images of Sevilla la Nueva haunted Maria. The craal became a torment of lurking greenery, ceaseless dusty savannah and dragging hours. The Indians sulked and died. She yearned for the luxury of houses and furniture, for elegant dress and conversation, for the Castilian pride of the governor's friends. A mine, she thought feverishly, toying with the idea of Indian gold. That was what her father needed; or perhaps a canefield, broad as the eye could see, lush green in the morning sun.

Besides, the traveller had burst on her like a flash flood on the thirsty savannah. She dreamed of a husband in a real house with dry planks, with walls of split cabbage trunks and clean tiles. She dreamed of her father returning to Spain or migrating to Santo Domingo to see her married; even of a dashing pirate who would spirit her away.... The last was no more far-fetched a dream than any other. None of it came to pass.

The Castries had not noticed the slope overlooking the valley. They lived in a low house, whose posts were hammered deep into the ground for fear of earthquakes, and whose sides were of reeds plastered with clay. There was a porch and a parlour for sitting (hours and hours of sitting) and a room at each end. Behind were the closets and the cooking space. Above, the palmetto thatch was as cool a roof as could be managed, but Maria yearned for smooth, gleaming tiles.

When her brother returned it was better, and worse. Miguel hated it now as she did, the craal, its claustrophobic valley, the nearby hato and their unendingly long, hot days. They recalled their cousins, dispersed, married — intermarried really, for there were only a few hundred whites like themselves, scattered in small settlements. The memory of the traveller, da Silva, burnt in a secret place at the back of her mind, and after a while it seemed to Maria that if no fire came into her life she would die.

Less than a year later Maria Castries gave birth to a healthy squalling manchild and, by the grace of God, no one discovered that its father was Miguel, her brother. Francisco had whipped her and screamed for the father's name, then suddenly he had flung her against the wall and backed away. Perhaps he had guessed and feared confirmation. When the child actually appeared and was white, he asked no further questions, harshly as he treated her. And now she was truly doomed, for nothing interesting could possibly ever happen to her again. She was old and bitter at twenty. Her dreams were troubled recollections of da Silva's hands upon her, of Miguel's urgency and revulsion, of the confession she had prepared but been unable to say. She had nothing to look forward to but eternity, and Hell yawned before her.

Things changed little in the years that followed. Miguel Castries quickly put aside the sister who had shamed the family, and he found a cousin to get him real sons. Maria mumbled madly to herself and tore at her breast with her wooden crucifix. Eventually she died without effect except that with a woman less in the place an African girl was brought in to help with the cooking. Years later, this Cubina eased Maria's son through the thick, slow evenings of the hato.

Luis Castries, the mulatto son of Maria's bastard, was neither Spanish nor African. He was a tall, tough man whose servitude hung loose and irrelevant on him. Free of both dreams and property, it was Luis who learned to understand the valley from the soil up and to know the mountains and the forests. The dimensions of his life were wide and shifting. His days followed the sun. Time began when he set out and distance was a function of weather and terrain. The valley was his place.

The official masters of the Castries land remained strangers to it. Generations later, one or two may have heard of some ancient scandal about the mulattos on the ranch, but the men of the family continued to interbreed with them. There was an easy, open relationship between the white and the brown descendants of Maria and of Miguel, but in some ways it was the mulattos who were more truly masters of the land, for the owner still understood nothing of it or of its Indians.

It infuriated him how obtuse these Tainos were and how idle. They would escape work by any means, and when the dogs chased them down and they were brought forcibly back they shrugged it away by suicide during the night. What with this attitude, throughout the island thousands had died. Now there were only five Indians left on the property which sprawled largely uncultivated despite the arrival of the Africans.

Of course Castries could always leave, perhaps not the island but Morante itself. And yet... the nearby hato sprawled down to the cape, with its wild horses and horned cattle his for the taking. His own valley was half-heartedly planted with ginger but flourished with giant trees like ceiba and cedar which were used for ship-building. Everything grew here — mahogany and lignum vitae reaching back to a time beyond recall, cassia weeping its yellow blooms on the porch over the long summer evenings. Even the strange new avocado had caught and borne fruit. If Castries left now, where was there to go?

Miguel's white descendant dreamed of Villa de la Vega. Seville was desolate now, black and overgrown, and a tree grew out of the ruined tower. French pirates had razed it, leaving it fit to shelter only fishermen and a hardy group of corsairs from Tortuga. Nowadays it was of Villa de la Vega one dreamed. But of course there was no question of it. Castries had no livelihood there. The hidalgos could doze in their mansions and live off the produce of their hatos, but Castries was not a hidalgo. Life had thrown him away.

In the valley that was now Castries land, a Taino hoed the soil and planted ginger. A year later, when the ground was covered with the plant, he watched dully for the leaves to wither and the stalks to dry, and he hoed them away. Then it was time to clean and wash the root, to boil and dry it. At times the master simply let it run uncultivated as he dreamed of the great town of the plain — Santiago de la Vega, as a few people called it now. His mind flickered through old legends and he felt so certain that the Indians could have found gold had they really cared to. But the Indians had cared eventually for nothing but to die and have done.

So it was that from birth the Taino had worked out his fate on the Castries land. He had told his wife to still the infants from birth as the other women did. The choices had haunted her to madness: the future she must bear them into, the horror of killing them, the spectre of her own survival if the rest should die before her. Her own brothers had died long ago in the mines. She bore her babies.

The Taino had watched the diseases of the Europeans waste his children till they lay upon the ground with their arms like threads. His wife gibbered over them for a while then wandered away and drank cassava juice. She writhed all day in the dust of the hato and died, eventually, under the afternoon sun. So he buried her with the children.

Then briefly, briefly, the living death of the hato bloomed for him. It was a woman of glowing flesh like polished copper and a cloud of tumbling black hair, startling in her surroundings as an orchid in the dust of the plains. She was all that was left of Xaza-gua and Caona — the only other Taino on the property. He treasured her for a few days that lifted him out of the despair into which he had been born. He discovered the softness of grass under an ancient tree, noticed the depth of blue between the branches above them and wondered if some vast spirit reigned beyond it. It occurred to him that there might come another time, a place of coolness, flowing water and children paddling in shallows. And he was so confused by hope and bewildered by sensations to which he had been numb his whole life through, so caught up in being human at last that he never saw the horse-man.

It was best for the woman, of course, to be taken before he could wear her down with childbearing or the Spanish destroy her with labour. The blade was quick for him and merciful, severing him from life only when he had dared to dream a way out and before the dream could crumble. It was without regret that the Taino was hacked down by a dark hunter from the hill country, who carried the woman off into the wilderness. So the spirit of the Tainos melted into the forest and became myth.

The wielder of the cutlass was one of the wild brown descendants of Maria and Miguel Castries. The mulatto had learnt the secrets of the densely forested interior as he chased the wild cattle which the Spaniards required for hides to export to Cuba and the mainland. And even as the woman screamed and struggled against the muscular arms that locked her safely in front of him on the horse, even as the massive animal thundered towards the trees bearing her away from the sight and memory of her race, even as the smell of blood rushed away on the wind, she knew she was saved by the murderer from the slow death overtaking the tribe. So when the panic calmed and the trees opened out along a rocky path she had the heart to wonder at the roar of the river tumbling over sheer rocks and to feel the attraction of emerald water.

Later, when the mulatto slept, she could have run from him but there was nothing to go back to and it was not as if she had never been raped before or would never be again. Unwillingly it came to her that he had tried not to hurt her. She inched her way trembling into the ancient pool and submerged shivering gratefully as the clean, cool water rippled over her bruised back. Her hair spread, floated foam-flecked and jewelled by shining droplets then drenched, and sank whirling behind her as she dipped and turned over and under and she wondered languidly at the familiarity of this place she had never seen.

Then she shivered again at the savagery of the cutlass but remembered with new surprise the gentleness afterwards of the same wild, free hands. It might be possible to kill him now, as he slept, but there seemed little point. And if she went back she would be obliterated by the blaze of the sun on the hato, the arbitrary violence of some cold and alien predator who enslaved them, or simply, eventually, by the dust of nonentity.

After all, they would all be gone in a while as the Wise Ones had foretold. Burnt away. Of course the water that slept or raged with the passion of the gods and the mountains that pondered silently upon the years — fire could not move them. The mountains and the fire were one. They belonged to the Hunchback, master of time.

4

The Stollmeiers

EVERYONE STELLA had ever met seemed to be at Jacob Stollmeier's funeral. In the midst Lynn stood alone, adrift in flowers. Nana had sent her with Icelin Castries to the garden — for flowers, she said, but really it was to get the library cleaned.

"Go to the library, girl," Lynn murmured vaguely as she wandered past the laundress and turned on the path to the rose beds. "*Vite, vite.* Take your tub."

Louise had sopped up what she could, but after a while when she wrung the cloth it oozed crimson over her hands and slippery between her fingers.

Outside, Lynn stripped the garden and Icelin pattered to and fro across the shining floors with buckets of flowers till the living room was heady with lilies, penthus, gerberas and splashes of roses. But in the library Louise Haynes sponged and squeezed while her head swam with the smell of death and she relived the sprinkling of blood from the calabash over her grandmother's grave and the Stollmeiers were nothing to her. Only old Cassie Haynes, her grandmother, mattered, and Cassie's tales of her own grandmother. The past lived on in the shadow present.

For Lynn Stollmeier though, the future was dead and the past fluttered in crushed rose petals through her fingers to lie in crimson blotches about her feet.

At the funeral, Sarah was in control of herself, but taut with contained rage. Stella had not expected her to be broken and the Stollmeiers were above maudlin displays of emotion, but Sarah was furious. She would never forgive her father. Besides Nana, only Sarah grasped at once the enormity of what he had done.

Lynn had become a stranger in her own living room, drab in a fashionable high-collared black dress that suddenly lost its elegance on her. Through the haze of condolences her lips formed confused greetings indiscriminately in French, in English, in French Creole. All the flowers she had gathered for Jacob murmured and whispered around her, some wilting now in the dry Kingston heat and shrinking from a hundred feet threading their way smartly among them. Calf. Kid. Square toes and low heels. Glacé shoes on the ladies. People who had never cared for Jacob nor accepted Lynn, his *petite fleur*. Without Jacob there was no one. She had forgotten even Sarah.

From the back of the room Nana directed all. She had finished the cleaning of the library, and ordered it locked when she realised that Lynn would wander in and sit for hours. Gently she had dispatched Lynn to see about clothes for the funeral, and eventually she had arranged that too. Apart from the family all the servants were properly dressed, thanks to Nana. Lynn was only a coloured woman after all and Jennings, the housekeeper, showed no inclination to bestir herself once the master was gone, so Nana had fired her. When Jennings refused to go, Nana had Coachie put the woman's things quietly but firmly in the lane.

So the preparations went smoothly for the servants knew who was in charge.

Now in the living room that seethed with socialising, condolences and speculation, Lynn wandered among her drooping gerberas, but the lilies turned away coldly and the penthus shrugged its florets at her feet and only the roses wept for her in petals of blood. Deep green of the asparagus creeper shadowed the afternoon and the moisture of ferns saturated the whispers of the mourners rising like steam around and overpowering her with the hot sweet scent of huddled, anguished blooms. So, numbed by their composite odour to every sensation but pain, she picked her way among the tears of her garden, responding to the veiled smiles and gloved handclasps in odd, unsuitable little comments that she never heard herself say.

Nana's mind swept through the house, properties, papers, investments — all the things none of them understood. Sarah came looking for her through the vast living room with its gilt-framed past, yawning tiger skin and smothering flowers, and Nana knew that Sarah was thrown naked into the world.

"Meet them, baby," Nana instructed calmly. "Stay near yu Mama call the names mek her hear. Send Stell."

Stella hurried to her. "You want me?"

"Yes, my lamb. You mus' go home."

Stella stared at her in amazement.

"Don't any minute now so you father going come? If he show you bad face, Miss Sarah goin' rude to him and she can' afford quarrel with Mas' Rudy now. Papers going have to see 'bout...."

Stella gathered up her things hastily but outside, at the familiar stone gate, a buggy drew up beside her and she turned unsuspectingly. It was Rudolf Stollmeier, one hand resting on his cane and the other clutching a purse. His fingers worked nervously over the brown Russian leather.

He spoke to her for the first time in her life, a halting murmur about Jacob having been good to her — like an accusation. When he drew out two American double eagles she recoiled. Flurried, he pressed the gold towards her.

"I should think you could find use for it," he stammered, "Jacob gone...."

Stella collected herself to a straight, cold line. "I have my mother. I have always had my mother."

Her back receded with a little switch of black hem and unflinching shoulders in white pequine before she swung sharply around the corner. He fumbled, steeling himself not to glance over his shoulder at the bustling courtyard. Eventually he felt into his fob, drew out the watch and sprung the heavy gold lid, glancing at the face unseeingly. Replacing it, he slid the coins away surreptitiously.

Inside he spoke meaninglessly to Lynn and promised Sarah to see her later in the week. All the way home to Half Way Tree he swore inwardly at the coachman for driving slowly, hitting ruts, swerving to avoid others. Jacob dead. Their last quarrel had been over business and investments. His mind spun back over other arguments. Jacob's marriage. Catherine Donalds's child. Still Jacob... his brother. Faceless with the gun locked in grey-white fingers Rudolf had had to prize apart. He forced his mind to the future.

Any property left... a mess. Lynn the upstart, blank and helpless. Sarah, an ungovernable adolescent. Nursemaid running the house. His own bastard rejecting his money in the street. Have always had my mother.

He must get out. Away from the tragedy, scandal, irritation. From Kingston.

His mind toyed with Goldfields but dismissed it.

He had no real friends to call on and he sifted his acquaintances distastefully. Farley might be a man to contact. The Englishman would only be in the island a few days longer and Stollmeier believed in maintaining contacts in the motherland. Besides it was someone extraneous he needed.

Golf? He needed something faster, more urgent. Even cricket was not enough. Nightfall found him over dinner with Farley.

"Yes, I don't think we can make a sounder choice than hunting," Stòllmeier said, flicking open the embroidered serviette. "I'd have suggested the ring-tail myself. We could have packed up and gone into the mountains, but it's close time. Or we might have fished up in the rapids, but again — protected just now."

"What game do you have here though, Stollmeier? Only small wildlife, I thought?"

"Well, of course no one bothers with the little things, agouti and so on. Many getting quite scarce now anyway. There were a few rabbits about once, not indigenous of course. People ate them, I suppose. They eat them in other places. Well, people eat anything, even monkeys. Oh yes," he insisted at the startled expression on Farley's face, "yes, people say they have seen monkeys here."

"Oh, but surely not even... I mean, no one eats monkey." The Englishman stared at him aghast.

"Well, I don't know anyone personally who does, but... good God man," Stollmeier was on the defensive instantly, "people do eat frogs, eh?"

"They do indeed," Farley spread his hands placatingly.

"You won't find monkeys about now anyway, though there are still supposed to be deer. I've taken the dogs after deer, to Mount Gotham, but with no success. Wild hogs are game now. Dangerous though. Wreck provision grounds, you know. But they're real game, huge beasts with great tusks." (Yes. It was a monster he needed, to devour feeling and memory.)

The other regarded him curiously and grinned. "I suppose you're not planning on us stalking a few of the natives or anything similarly exotic?"

Stollmeier guffawed and tossed the exquisite napkin to the side of his plate. "We are going to the Rio Cobre to shoot alligators."

Farley was quite still, obviously captivated. "Alligators. How big? Compared to, say, the African crocodile?"

"Oh, not as large. Ours are crocodiles too, though. We just call them alligators. And they're big enough, and savage enough to pass the time."

"Don't doubt you," Farley chuckled, reverently swirling a chunk of heavy white meat through its sauce. The cold tang of shellfish and crisp, bitterish flavour of the cress was a relief after tennis. (Should be banned in the tropics.) He tried not to attack the lobster with undignified gusto. Not that Stollmeier cared if the Englishman betrayed himself; the whole point was to patronise him carelessly — pleased, if anything, that he was a trifle vulgar and that he was furtively overawed by a level of civilisation he had never expected here. The truth was Farley's income did not accommodate lobster at home.

"We must start early." Stollmeier peered at him anxiously. "Quick breakfast, then to the swamp. By dawn."

Before light next morning, Stollmeier paced the living room. Where the devil was Farley? And how long could he keep up anyway? Accustomed to hunting in the type of terrain where he could pitch camp, that was it. Let him try that where they were going, and spend years of his life draining away in fever. Bloody Englishmen always thought they knew the colonies.

Stollmeier drew the watch from his breast pocket. Time on a chain, but ticking, ticking.

Farley burst in energetically and swung his gear down near the door.

"Oh, was that what kept you?" Stollmeier gestured contemptuously, but he was jovial again. "The boy would have seen to your things. Come. Let's eat."

They settled at the end of the long dark glow of mahogany and Stollmeier rubbed his hands in nervous good humour.

"Yes. Well, you'll try our local fruit, eh?" He turned the handle of the wide server towards Farley. Slices of pineapple and mango edged crescents of pawpaw topped with thin wedges of lime. In the middle, heavy silver fork handles jutted upwards from the centre of three or four oranges peeled of skin and pith to bare the fruit pulp.

"Tea first though, thank you. Yes, India would be perfect," Farley nodded reassuringly aside to the query of a black butler. "Those are our people too, you know."

Stollmeier ignored that with effort. "Tomorrow you shall taste our mountain mullet," he said. "I've arranged with a fellow."

"Mm." Farley gestured dismissingly with his fork. "Wouldn't be easy to improve on this." He leaned across his fried egg confidentially. "So true, isn't it? Fun trying new things, but when you come

down to it there's nothing like the real breakfast of home." He
prodded the tines at the smooth gold dome. "Perfect."

Stollmeier was provoked. Unreasonably, he knew. The man
was only complimenting the hospitality that rendered Stollmeier
palpably civilised. But at least Rudolf would have liked a little
more enthusiasm about the mullet. He pushed his plate away
now, anxious to be gone.

When they reached the bay, the whaler was waiting and the
boatman lounging nearby under a sparse almond tree, his feet
cocked up on a ravaged stump. Without delay they boarded; it
was already growing light. Behind, a good wind persisted
through the crossing. Farley looked about eagerly, but Stollmeier
was quiet, staring morosely at the water slapping the side of the
boat. Small boat, he thought, and a big sea. He hugged the gun
silently.

He had never really known his brother. He had berated Jacob
about the state of his affairs, thinking he did not care. Rudy started violently as something large smacked the water behind him.
Out of the water a pelican thrust its head to the wind and sailed
away, gulping urgently. Drab and ungainly, Stollmeier shrugged.
And yet, as it glided easily over the surface, rose, circled effortlessly on outstretched wings then plummeted again head first in
an explosion of sea spray, and yet....

He lifted his face to the early morning sky whose few clouds
kept tightly to themselves, and he squinted up to something
cruising at immense height. A frigate bird etched the sky with distinctive wide, thin wings and long, forked tail, lines sketched so
fine on his vision as to be perhaps filled in by his imagination.
Something moved by his foot and scurried into a crevice at the
bottom of the boat, distracting him from the deceptions of distance. The near, busy little thing darted again — a lizard. He sat
motionless as it grew trusting, crawled up onto the barrel of the

rifle to sun itself and spread its translucent orange throat fan.

Beyond the grey stone of Fort Augusta, the Rio Cobre opened out into the huge bay that was Kingston Harbour. Behind, at the base of Long Mountain, the green and white city was flecked with morning gold, and before the city a thin sandstrip with palm trees and a few houses marked the way to Port Royal. Inland they could make out the path of the river by the coconut trees emerging from thick clumps of foliage, and beyond hummocked the Hellshire Hills, mottled with grey limestone and split by candelabrum-shaped pillars of cactus. Above, the John Crows wheeled deliberatingly over the stench of the swamp.

"We should be dressed like the natives," Farley sang out as he plunged into warm water, and he jerked his head at the guide's brief merino.

But Stollmeier chuckled with contemptuous goodwill. "You're an Englishman, Farley, in a place where countless of your countrymen, company after company, have been wiped out by malaria."

Sand levelled under their boots, darkened to dull mud and stretched into the bush. Broken antlers of mangrove roots jutted out, pale and coated at the bottom, tipped dark with rot. From deep within the bush rasped the harsh, guttural scream of a bittern, and inland a long white streak flagged, wheeled and disappeared. Freshness of the salt breeze thickened and stilled to air heavy with waterlogged vegetation and woodrot. A cloud of white and gold butterflies smoked up, dipped again then swirled dizzily apart. Grass, bushes, trees groped out of dark, still water, black-wet lush presences with turgid origins, filmed at their bases with evil-smelling muck.

In this way, piped in by the buzz and whine of myriad insects, they found the river bank and worked inland, fondling the comforting solidity of their Winchesters. Large trees rose around them and one, huge, naked of leaves but intact in its massive trunk, reared stiff branches with twigs bone pale and thin to claw the sky. High above water level Stollmeier discovered a hole with clear grooves running from the rim. It was a nest with claw marks still clear.

"Mus' be frighten im did frighten 'way," the guide suggested.

Stollmeier breathed faster hugging his rifle, and they began to wade the streams that twisted, joined, separated again to empty the river into the sea. They surprised a grebe, silky black and grey, searching the sedgy ground, and with a flash of pale grey the long beak stabbed up, and the bird's eyes glinted brilliantly from startling black and white circles. Stollmeier flinched as its momentary glance penetrated his soul, then it was gone. Around them vaulted the complex arches of the mangrove, and dense, leathery foliage shrouded the water and sheltered insects, crabs and their attendant wading birds. Mud welled around the men's ankles, sucking at their boots, and they stumbled among half-submerged roots, but always with their rifles poised, ready for the kill.

It was the guide who sighted the first, basking dead still at the edge of a stream. Farley fired at what seemed a bar of mud and vegetation, and the soft ground surged convulsively as the beast dived beyond reach.

The next was Stollmeier's. He raised the rifle and shattered the stillness of the swamp, certain of his prey. It dived, surfaced and dived again. They waited for it, their eyes unwavering on the water, but eventually they left it for dead. Yet as they retraced their steps the water churned and it could only be the same beast, wounded but alive.

They fired together, and a huge head broke the surface then fell back, snapping desperately. Then it twisted swiftly, knifing to the shore so that they sprang back. But immediately a swirling of the murky water near the edge where it was difficult to see showed that it had turned again and was plunging around in circles, its powerful tail ploughing the water. Stollmeier inched forward.

"I'll have it," he muttered, panting, but calm with the coldness of the predator. Soundlessly he edged into the water, knife in hand. It might be too close for the rifle.

Farley was aghast. "Stollmeier. My God! We can't go in there with that thing!"

"Im right, massa. Wait likkle, sah. Wait! Im go tear you."

Furious as he was, Stollmeier was not such a fool as to disregard the guide. The last man he had come with had been badly mauled. Gruesome business. He put up his knife and withdrew. Then the green-black, mud-encrusted snout broke water almost before his face. He leapt aside, tugging over his shoulder at the Winchester and stumbled backwards to fire. The water exploded in a writhing, cavorting mass and the massive tail lashed out and slapped down into pink froth. Then it rippled and was still. They drew out the body and measured it — twelve feet of cold-blooded flesh, primitive and inscrutable.

As the guide worked expertly at the skin with his knife, their thin shirts tingled on burnt raw flesh. The exposed skin on their hands and arms puffed into pearly blisters. The water in their bottles was tepid and useless to the vast thirst of the white man in the tropics. But Stollmeier felt temporarily salved. He was ready to go back even without a memento, for he needed nothing but the hunt and the kill itself, but he couldn't have justified the waste to Farley. Even when Stollmeier thought he saw one cutting through the shallow lagoons of the delta he let it go. Another time, he thought, he would return for it.

He chatted warmly with Farley. Tramping through the rough grass of a dry place on the bank they found another nest. He crouched down to study fifteen to twenty capsule-shaped eggs and passed his hands over the hard sheen of their shells. A white, pitted band ran unevenly around the middle. Beautiful, like enamel. He raised one to Farley who bent forward with a grimace of revulsion and smashed his gunbutt into the rest over and over. Then he glanced at the dripping wood in disgust.

"Damn!" he grunted, and wiped it off on the grass.

Stollmeier gently replaced the one left intact and dropped behind, loathing him. Who was Farley anyway? Thought he owned the place. Couldn't leave anything for later or for anyone else, could he? Blasted savage. Stollmeier trudged back to the beach in a fury, answering his companion automatically, briefly. When the water swirled around his calves his resentment dulled, though in a way he was sorry to relinquish his anger and the justification it entailed.

Evening on the verandah overlooking Half Way Tree Road hung in tobacco smoke. Their skins crisped against clothes and furniture yet they chatted on contentedly with the small company Stollmeier had thought it decent to invite.

"Can't do anything big for you, I'm afraid," he had spread his hands deprecatingly at Farley. "Recent bereavement, you know. Just one or two close friends."

These included his Gemma, of course, and her genial husband, Wilbur. Only three other couples. One woman he did not know at all. Greenidge had brought her along. She looked cheap enough, Stollmeier thought, in that bishop-sleeved affair he associated with lower-class women.

This was as good as it could get, he felt, sipping sangaree and old rum in the twilight, listening to the women... blimming, as they liked to call it in London now. Gemma was so good at it, talking pleasant nonsense that made everyone else sound clever. Now and then they stopped to comment on the characters who wandered past on the street beyond. Gradually as dusk fell these became faceless, then formless. Stollmeier's eyes wandered to the soft stillness of the summer twilight. A mist of yellow blooms covered the cassia trees near the house, blurring the soft, pinnate leaves, and their gold lay strewn on the ground beneath in a last swooning glow as sunset faded. A croaking lizard crawled along the rafters emitting his brief, grating chirrup. The air whirred with crickets and here and there a tree frog plucked a soft treble note out of the gathering dark.

A tortoiseshell and gold tray supported chilled grapefruit halves, sweetened and laced with rum. Then it was time to gather at the table. A dark, uniformed figure melted back into the shadows. When the soup was cleared away, the conversation of Stollmeier and Gemma grew sophisticatedly indiscreet, but her husband's attention seemed wholly upon the table. Barbecued hog, pigeon pies, crab patties — but also, as the conversation piece of the evening, a roast of varied fowls one inside the other.

"Why Stollmeier, wherever did you get such a notion?"

"Well, last year of course, in London. But if I had really wanted to be obvious I'd have served ptarmigan pie."

This prompted an explosion of laughter at the King's vagaries, and Farley joined in self-consciously. Then he murmured, "Really, Stollmeier. All this, just for a few of us here, you know."

Farley smothered his astonishment at the table which his host shrugged away, but the dinner was just another overstatement for denying pain.

"Well, what do you say, Stollmeier," Greenidge was pressing him. "Will you buy an automobile?"

"Unavoidable, I suppose."

"What about the carriage, then?"

"Oh, the carriage is indispensable, good heavens, for conducting serious business. But an automobile — for fun, eh? Oh yes, my Gemma, we must certainly have an automobile."

"Nice for motoring to St Thomas," she smiled slyly at him.

"You have another place then, Stollmeier, in the country somewhere?" Farley queried.

"Oh yes, in St Thomas. Goldfields."

"What do you do with it?"

"Woodland and guinea grass mostly, a few cows, some sheep."

"Large?"

"Well, about thirteen acres of forest, rather nice gardens."

"Superb gardens," Gemma interrupted decisively, stretching her neck proudly and fingering the satin rosettes at her breast. "The most romantic old aqueduct with trailing flowers on it and a waterwheel at the back."

"What, all apart from the pastures?" Farley reached discreetly into a silver bonbonnière.

"And the coffee," she smirked. "A few hundred acres, reaping buildings. Barbecues."

"What you'll be having shortly." Stollmeier leaned back, looking blank.

"How much do you reap per season? I mean," Farley hastened apologetically, "I suppose you market?"

"Oh, a hundredweight or two." Stollmeier rolled his eyes up as if he were considering it for the first time. "Three maybe."

Farley glanced around uncertainly as the others chuckled. They were all familiar by now with Stollmeier's reticence about discussing his affairs too exactly.

"Meaningless though, you know," Stollmeier stared at his wine as into a crystal ball suddenly darkened. "We're to be swept aside."

Gemma stirred uncomfortably and broke in with an artificial laugh, "Why, Rudy, whatever are you talking about on such a nice evening — in the midst of all this food?"

He paid no attention to her, but Farley and Greenidge regarded him blankly.

"Look at the Legislative Council," he snapped. "Non-planters elected more and more."

"Anyway, anyway," Farley interrupted heartily, "Chamberlain will take care of you."

They stared at him. Even Gemma's husband looked up from his cup, and Farley felt horribly stupid.

"What was that about Chamberlain?" Gemma prompted him kindly.

73

"Oh, his commitment, you know, to the islands."

"To civilise us, you mean?" Stollmeier smiled blandly across the table.

Hastily Gemma switched to the war.

"How are our people doing?" She enquired solicitously.

"What horrible brutes the Ashantis are," tinkled Bishop-Sleeves.

"Well, we've made some mistakes on our side," Farley reflected.

Greenidge shook his head in commiseration. "Oh, we're in poor shape, sir, poor shape. And when I think of what we were...."

Farley relaxed. They were all on the same side after all. All Englishmen, in their own way.

When the ladies retired, the conversation drifted on in tobacco smoke and the smell of port, but Farley let his attention stray from his host and around the room, over the polished panelling of the walls, the eighteenth-century aquatints and old duelling pistols, down to the wide cedar floorboards. Under the Dutch chandelier, the laden table was equipped with Cyprian mats and Sèvres china, ornamented with silver candlesticks and ceramic flower holders for the azaleas and surrounded by twelve Queen Anne chairs.

Stollmeier broke in on his thoughts as if he knew them and shattered the natural reserve of the Englishman by commenting, "Investments, Farley. I'm just one of three sons, you know."

"I know your brother just... er... you lost him."

"Not a businessman, though," Gemma's husband interrupted regretfully, his first utterance for the evening drawing instant attention. He glanced sidelong at Stollmeier. "Nothing you could have done to advise him? He's done so much in the past to shoulder the burden of your own responsibilities.... Well, well. I'm sure you did what you could."

Stollmeier whitened to surprised loathing. He glanced around at the other faces whose eyes slid away from his. Gemma had always told him that Wilbur was neither as stupid nor as genial as he looked.

"I told him to get out of sugar...." he stammered.

The room grew uncomfortable and tense as everyone except Wilbur strained for something to say, something that would sound natural. Gemma's husband resumed his air of stolid contentment and said nothing more for the evening.

"Let's join the ladies." Greenidge rose abruptly and led the way through the carved mahogany arches. They passed into the living room where the women chatted in embroidered chairs sunk deep into blue carpets before the wide log fireplace that was a mystery to Farley. On either side of the mantel were panels with Wedgwood roundels set into the timber. Above the mantelpiece rose an antique mirror.

Gemma handed Rudolf his cup. In answer to her unspoken question, Stollmeier paused before the heavy Venetian glass and gazed joylessly into it, smelling the rich mountain coffee of Goldfields, seeing his reflection sip black fluid from a gold-chased cup and tasting nothing whatever.

"Joseph eventually agreed about the mirror. He sent it to me the day before... the accident."

He looked around wonderingly at the company. Everything circled back. The blood, the funeral, the household. Stella. The excitement, the food, the... things — they distracted only briefly.

For the months that followed, Rudolf and Sarah were at war. It was undeclared and civil, at least on his side; but it was war.

The year after Jacob's death passed in gruelling adjustments. One by one the trimmings of Sarah's life shredded away. No income remained to support the life to which she had been born. The scent of malingering flowers still filled Lynn's brain and she hung suspended in bygone days. Rudolf redeemed the more embarrassing debts and infuriated Sarah by deserving her

75

gratitude.

After a period of juggling bank and insurance loans, Sarah eventually convinced her mother to cut staff and close some of the rooms. The notion of selling the house plunged Lynn into a cold sweat.

Strangely, it was Rudolf who helped to manipulate her when Sarah's patience wore thinnest. He took over older servants such as Coachie and Ella and agreed to pension them off in a few years. Nana, of course insisted on staying with Sarah and Lynn, unpaid. Icelin simply refused to go, either back to the country or to "de Mas' Rudolf him," and they were afraid to turn her out lest she end up on the street. They reduced Louise's duties to fit into a single morning, once a week. Occasionally there was a gardener, shared with some other neighbour.

Still the house hung upon Sarah and sucked at her youth, for her mother managed nothing. Lynn fluttered vague directions and fingered her pearls nervously, and Nana and Icelin showed her gentle deference but managed the house and what they could of the garden. Sarah struggled fearfully with the papers at night and eventually took a job at the Machado tobacco factory. Relief came when Rudolf offered to buy Hedgemont.

Unpleasant as it was to think of him at the country house near Hope, Sarah was relieved. The money from Hedgemont would buy her time to persuade her mother to sell the house on East Street. She watched her uncle speculatively, wondering whether he was taking the place to spite or to assist them.

"*Non, non.* Jacob would never 'ave sold it," Lynn fretted. "Never."

Rudolf turned the talk to Sarah.

"You'll be eighteen in some weeks, I hear," he remarked good-naturedly. "I was thinking. We should have something. Some sort of celebration, I don't know."

She sat in a trance listening to him discuss it with her mother. Lynn stirred, coloured, concentrated. Nothing had moved her like this since Jacob's death. Rudy's voice droned on. What a party he would give. Dinner, dancing. So many invitations. So many pounds. Whoever they pleased could come, within reason. Sarah was intractable about Stella. Lynn pointed out that Stella would never attend at her father's house even if she were asked. East Street no longer had the servants necessary for such a function. Eventually, before Sarah's stony face, Lynn broke down in tears.

Sarah tried to get a grip on herself. No money to fix the roof and her mother throwing a party.

"I don't want this," she hissed, closing her eyes and seeing bills on her father's desk, blood bespattered. "Don't you understand, I can't... dance money away again."

The silence stopped her. She opened her eyes and saw the bewilderment and anguish of her mother's face. Stollmeier swore under his breath.

"Do what you like and be damned," he snapped, grabbing up the papers for Hedgemont. "If you want, I'll let you have servants and money. But it won't be at Half Way Tree."

Sarah turned on him. "We don't need a party."

He grasped her arm and propelled her out of the room.

"You don't," he said scathingly. "You don't need anyone, do you? Not even a husband? Well your mother needs... something to keep her out of the madhouse." He released her and grinned suddenly, wryly. "You're carrying too much for a girl your age. It's turning you sour. Dance a little."

She stared at him and an answering gleam of merriment in her eyes reminded him of the Lynn her father had brought home from New Orleans.

"I won't come, of course," he said, "but then, you won't miss me."

"No," she agreed, lit again by that hint of a smile. "But I won't forget you either."

They turned back to Lynn together.

"Why not have it at Hedgemont?" Rudolf suggested.

77

For that brief time, Lynn revived. She spent hours of planning at her writing table. Invitations. Sketches for decorations, dresses.

"Bien. Bien. Why we did not we think of this before?" She gestured at the girls with a handful of papers. "We really 'ave not used 'Edgemont enough. At least now, even if it is going...." A new thought diverted her. "So. We set flambeaux up the walks, at each palm, *oui?* And outline the terraces. And at the entrance, flowers — flowers along the colonnades."

Sarah interrupted, softly for Sarah. "Careful, Maman. The cost."

"Nonsense! Ring for Louise. She can go up there and see about the floor."

"When she comes next I'll send her."

"Pas possible. Ring for her, Stella. Now."

"The bell, Aunt Lynn."

"Eh?"

"The bell hasn't worked for months, Maman."

"What? Why Jennings 'as not...?" Lynn caught sight of Sarah's face and recovered herself. "That's right. Jennings gone."

"Long ago. Years."

"Well. But it must be fixed somehow."

"Maman, there is no money for bells."

Lynn pouted and the confused, stricken look hovered over her again. Sarah touched her hair lightly.

"Hedgemont, Maman. Flambeaux and flowers."

So it was at Hedgemont. The gravel walks were illuminated by torches, Their light picked out the pillar-like trunks of the palms and, in between, glowed greenly against feathery bamboo that overhung the way. It was all ablaze with light. On each side were tiny pinpoints from the terraces and bold flares between the paws of stone lions like those at East Street. A glimmer down in the distance marked the way to the grotto, though no one was likely to stray so far from the house itself. In front, the fountain trapped the blaze of the torches to throw up spumes of gold, fading into the evening sky then drizzling down brighter and brighter into the brilliant froth and ripple of the pool.

From the fountain, the way to the house up the steps was paved with Spanish stones which a previous owner had dug from some ruined church long before anyone cared to remember. Now the torchlight set the ghosts dancing across their worn surfaces. Out of the sash windows at the front and from the pillars near the entrance the air was warm and exciting with candlelight, music and rich food.

Sarah was a myth of pale pink chiffon, white lace and pink roses. "Maman," she whispered in explanation to Stella. She linked arms with her and kept up a muttered conversation, nodding politely at the same time as her guests flowed in. "Major and Mrs Warne. (Maman insisted on pink, even the flowers.) Thank you, I loved your gift. (Feel like little Bo Peep in this thing.) Reverend Jackman, my cousin, Stella. Aah, Mrs Delgado... delighted. (Uncle Rudy's sulking in the study, won't stay for dinner — which is a spectacle and one *he* dreamt up. Maman made him come, for appearance sake. Even....) Oh, everyone's inside, do go ahead and make yourself comfortable. (She even told him not to bring that 'Gemma woman' into *her* house.) The roses, Jennie? You like them? And they'd be perfect with your gown, do have them... no really. (Lord, I can't get rid of the beastly flowers on anyone, Stell.)"

Inside, the mood was mellow with madeira from Jacob's fine old cellars. And the table. Stella paused bemused.

Expanse of mahogany, white linen, Georgian silver. Fish, hot and cold, pickled and plain. Masses of fried conch, arranged around a shoulder of wild boar stuffed with forced meat. Pepperpot with black crab. Turtle, naturally, a great favourite of Jacob's — but also goose. Cold slices of ham, tongue and game fowl. In between were regular dishes like rice and peas, baked and whipped yam. But the centrepiece presented a dish that only a few guests from long established families might have heard tell of from their grandparents. A roasted peacock spread its iridescent tail feathers in a spectacular display over the English china.

"That's what I meant, Stell," Sarah whispered. "It's not a dinner, it's a monument."

"Well. Enjoy it though. It's for you."

"Is it? Well, I'll dance. But who ever heard of eating peacock?"

Afterwards, sweets. Acid fruit and ginger jellies, and of course the brandy, swirling gold at the bottom of deep, swelling crystal.

Unwillingly Stella realised she was looking for her father. She glimpsed him as she passed the library. He was slumped deep in the Chippendale sofa, his head bent to a newspaper, unable to look at the feast he had recreated from tales of past splendour. He would eat little, she knew. She had heard he ate frugally, and suffered from indigestion. A strange surge of more than curiosity stirred her. All her life she would wonder why he had done this.

The music changed. Sarah was on the floor with Jonas da Silva. Stella stopped in the doorway, hypnotised as Sarah turned and turned again with the music and into the music till she had no substance as a separate entity from it but melted and merged into melody. It seemed to Stella that in Sarah the music took meaning and shape, swelling and drawing down to soft curves and hollows and that it rippled through her hair and sang in the hopeful fullness of her body.

The young man she danced with was elegant in a lean, slick way and glided easily along with her through the steps, but he was separate from the music. Jonas was graceful and competent but contained, aware of his image on the floor. Sarah was thoughtless sound and motion echoing through Stella in deep chords, but they remained Sarah's chords, mellow and mature, for in this first year of the new century she was a woman. It was strange and magical to Stella who did not feel like one as yet but caught only the delicate strain of it through her cousin.

Jonas, smooth and exciting, fascinated with Sarah and her setting, brought a new, rushing sensation to Stella at a distance. And in Sarah's eyes the little sparks of fire were muted to a warm glow, dreamy with speculation about the years to come, and her lips parted in waiting for the song life promised to put into them.

5
The Cross

JONAS DA SILVA cut a fine figure, tall, slender-built — too slender, Catherine said.

"Oh, Aunt Cath," Sarah wailed. "How can you? He's just... elegant. Have you seen him in the grey flannel with that soft blue shirt? You don't think so, Stell?"

Catherine's face relaxed, softened at the jaw. How well she remembered. Then her eyes narrowed.

"He's... a solid man?"

Rudy in grey and blue and that... place, its filthy brass ashtrays, battered porcupine fish on the wall, common bamboo furniture. There would be ladies there like herself, he had said. Well, the women were coloured too. But silver bracelets jangled their forced gaiety, and the paste stones flashed, and painted blushes showed false under the guttering lamplight. The air hung heavy with tobacco and cheap scent, the women's faked British accents cloying the brief, desultory conversation. One played the mandolin and sang tonelessly.

"Auntie? Where are you?"

"Sweet Jesu. Nowhere."

Catherine rose abruptly and smoothed her skirt. "Evensong, girls?"

Evensong was quiet and intimate. Family name tags on the pews were ignored. Women kissed on parting, and girls strolled home arm in arm.

At Evensong it was a joy to have given oneself into the hand of God. The Reverend Augustus Jackman let the strain of a long day and a large, exacting congregation, roll away. He stretched his arms over the close group of faces, embracing the cool dusk of the church. Go forth into the world in peace.

Light faded behind the stained glass at the back and a few faces fell in shadow. One he searched for — only for a special benediction, he told himself hastily. Then, overtaken by honesty, he reflected, If we say that we have no sin, we deceive ourselves and the truth is not in us. His eyes roamed the congregation. Among the innumerable black and white muslin gowns glowed a few soft blurs of colour. Pink and white, mauve and white. Blue. Let us depart in peace.

Jackman was dark and what Jamaicans called cool-skinned, with closely cropped curly hair. From the full vestments tucked into the barrel-shaped sides of the pulpit resounded his deep, rather ponderous voice. He was young, but solid.

That week he called again on Catherine and Stella and left, as usual, riddled with doubt. Stella was intimidatingly polite, listening to his plans but never entering into them. Yet she distracted him.

She was a prim, poised figure with an unsettling tilt of the head and no humility. Her image intersected all others and filled him with forbidden sensations in the middle of divine worship. First he had lost his place somewhere between the Exhortation and the Comfortable Words. Then he had forgotten to pray for that Rescue Home for women that the Archbishop was opening. His control slipped, plunging him into confusion. Last Sunday he had found himself contemplating her figure while consecrating the elements.

Suddenly he realised that they were sitting in silence. Her mother moved restlessly in the next room. He drew a damp finger around the inside of his collar, crossed and uncrossed his legs. Stella's deft hands lay strong and still on her lap. She showed no inclination to fidget.

He sprang to his feet clumsily and began without knowing

what he was going to say.

"Will you... will you...." His voice trailed away. Dark and steady her eyes were, looking straight into his soul and smiling, a little mocking, a little compassionate. "Will you be at the tea on Saturday?"

He released her hand and looked down at it, ashamed to see white imprints for a moment where he had gripped her and damp glistening on her skin from his palms. He sank miserably back into his chair before she could answer and launched into a description of how the Salvation Army was preparing Marble Hall for the Rescue Home.

Then he stopped and looked hopelessly at his shoes. He was not normally a clumsy man and was at a loss to cope with this compulsive, disastrous fumbling. Gently she led him to another topic, but he forced the visit to a close. He felt a fool. He could not bear to be in her presence; he could not bear to have her out of his sight. The gate swung angrily behind him.

"Well," Stella smiled wryly at her mother, "what a threat I seem to be."

At the tea on Saturday he was needed everywhere at once. By the time he had sped over to the vestry to change his collar and slipped out again in the hope of walking her home, a man hovered uncertainly at the main entrance.

Jackman swore inwardly but paused, held by the other's wide, searching eyes in a rather boyish face.

"Just passing and... looked in. Thank you."

The stranger turned away, but Jackman stopped him, reluctantly, in an agony to get back to the hall before Stella left.

"Come tomorrow, won't you? To our morning service." He hesitated, then added bravely, "I'm quite free now, if you'd like to talk."

"I'm a Jew."

"Yes. I thought perhaps you were. Tomorrow?"

The other man pressed his hat firmly in place and shook his

head. He began to walk rapidly away, seeming even younger from behind. Jackman stared after him in relief, yet called involuntarily,

"Wait!" and the Jew hesitated without looking back. "Tomorrow at nine."

Dapper little man, Jackman smiled, turning quickly to the hall and searching for a glimpse of Stella's distinctive black and white hat. But she was gone.

The next morning was a hot, glazed Sunday. Mango leaves hung sharp and still and blossoms clung motionless. The girls carried new fans to church, hand-carved and threaded with fine coloured silk. Very pleased with themselves they were, Sarah in soft blue with white tulle bow and ostrich feather nodding cheekily at each step, Stella unapproachable in grey, boleroed and belted in rose with a matching toque.

The clouds had thinned to distribute sunlight in an even glare, and dust rose in tiny puffs underheel. Along the pews with the name tags older heads turned disapprovingly as the girls slipped into a centre row, faces peeping alluringly carefree from behind the fans and the little silk tassels fluttering gaily.

Brief, disparagingly compassionate smiles flickered near the front. The Upper East Street ladies compressed their lips. Immodest, their eyebrows signalled, if not bold. One glanced at the minister, who had slipped in to consult with the organist, and then back at Stella with a delicate shrug that disclaimed responsibility for a lost generation.

"A bit too much," Miss Holmes murmured regretfully, smoothing her black and white gown.

Another elderly spinster sighed, flicking back an exposed grey strand beneath her blue toque with the pink malmaisons. "Girls from such quiet homes."

"Monied people the Stollmeiers were till recently and, all their misfortunes aside, respectable."

"Well, there are Stollmeiers and Stollmeiers, you know." Mrs

Clarkson tapped her wedding ring significantly. "Background will tell."

Upstairs, the young Jewish businessman smirked at the stir in the front pews. Clannish in their own way, these Christians. The black families in the rear pews were inscrutable.

The beadle turned from the procession and the Jewish visitor winced as morning light glanced off the polished brass of the cross, piercing his soul. He shrank under a raw sense of nakedness, reaching involuntarily for the silk hat on the bench beside him.

Reverend Jackman raised his hands tiredly to invoke the Almighty unto whom all hearts be open, all desires known and from whom no secrets are hid. In the flutter, the turning, the whispering, he must choose. "That we may perfectly love thee," he intoned. Perfectly. Nothing to spare.

He glanced upstairs and started. He had forgotten the Jew. Now he strove to concentrate on prayer for his conversion. That fan again. Even upstairs the Jew glanced away from the altar. Yet so composed her face was above the rose and grey dress, lost in the epistle. Perhaps she was above distraction, but the rest were not. Neither was the minister.

He announced a lively hymn to regain the congregation's attention, but as the unusually heavy rhythm of its music swelled up a disturbance at the back startled him and a black woman shoved her way, clapping and sobbing, from her pew. She wheeled around in the aisle and staggered up to the altar where she cast herself on the ground groaning and shrieking in the voices of the spirit.

For an instant Jackman froze, appalled at his predicament, then hurried forward to raise and hand her over to the beadle who conducted her away smoothly. Ladies in the front row stared incredulously and he knew, he knew they were registering that it was when a coloured man took over a church that this type of dirty nega display could break out in the presence of decent people. Stella's fan stirred briefly again, and the ladies shook their heads confirming to each other that she was part and parcel of the entire moral collapse.

At the end of the service the members filed out and shook hands with the minister under the pointed arch of the doorway. One interruption in the service was too far below decent attention for anyone to refer to it, but the ladies knew of their minister's visits to Catherine's porch and a word to the wise, as Mrs Clarkson intoned, should be enough.

"Inspiring service, Reverend Jackman. Do pardon our young friends' little indiscretion. I've spoken to them myself. In a motherly way." She leaned forward confidentially. "You just have to be brought up in correct circumstances to appreciate the dignity of the Church, don't you think?"

Amazing, he thought uncharitably of Mrs Clarkson. She took such care to look like a girl. Pink and white Liberty silk and her hat wreathed with roses. If she had ever been young, she had forgotten how it felt. Miss Holmes, of course, did not appear to greet him, having sailed out through another door, never to return.

Sarah was shaking his hand. "Reverend Jackman, some of the ladies — well it seems we disturbed the service. We... we're sorry."

But she wanted only to mend things; her eyes flashed rebellion. Stella said nothing. He must make every move, every choice. Her fingers touched his from a great distance.

"I hope the ladies said nothing... nothing hurtful," he stammered in a low voice. "What happened to our unfortunate sister from the back pew had nothing to do with... I wouldn't for the world...."

Her fingers slipped away and at once the Jewish visitor grasped his hand with easy familiarity.

"Well, but you are not for the world, Mr Jackman, are you?" It was a strong sincere grip, though his eyes wandered to Stella. "I'll come again, if I may."

"You'll be most welcome. What about our evening service?"

The man bowed to him and turned away, bowed again to Stella and raised the tall silk hat.

"Permit me, Miss Stollmeier. You seem to have forgotten your fan in the pew. Too elegant to be lost. Yes, I enquired your name so as to return it. Abe Goldman, Ma'am. The evening service, then?" He raised that confounded hat again and was gone.

That Evensong there seemed to be only three of them in the church. Oh, it was well attended as usual, but the three struggled with each other in the stillness of twilight.

The sacrifices of God are a broken spirit: a broken and a contrite heart, O God, thou wilt not despise. Red gules from the Saviour's robe in the stained-glass image above swam across the prayer book on the lectern, across his mind, and Jackman's voice seemed to echo between the dim stone walls.

Rend your heart and not your garments.

Such a fuss, Stella thought, over a little fan. Involuntarily she glanced at the Jew, encountered his gaze and looked hastily away.

There began a sort of delicate dance between the three. Jackman subtly, patiently, irresistibly strained for Abe's soul, but with Stella he stumbled and eventually halted altogether. Abe waited and learned her. He introduced himself to Catherine with such propriety that she lamented him afterwards as "such a nice-spoken young man, for a heathen." He saw that Stella was proud and distant through an excess of caution. The intensity of the clergyman fired him but then afterwards came the cool gospel of calm among the ferns on Stella's porch, and he relaxed watching, waiting, never touching.

Jackman baptised Abe and Catherine came to view him as 'promising'. Stella began to trust him. Wrong, she brooded, to trust any man completely and she guarded her feelings, but his restraint disarmed her. Jackman agonised over her, wanting but not quite approving of her, so his hesitation was rebuke. But Abe's reserve was adulation. Strategically, relentlessly, he drew her to him by never quite grasping her.

She was timid, and unprepared for physical intimacy, but not unfeeling. Provided he was never crude, provided he never pounced on her or startled her she would relax with him. Abe contained himself, quivering with impatience and with the fear that even in marriage she might never quite lower her defences. Still, he wanted her on any terms.

The months of courtship were not irrelevant. They were a time for gaining confidence, laying plans that made such vast and vague undertakings as marriage and changing faith seem workable. But in a sense it had been fixed within an evensong of doubting, longing, rebellious sensations, human lives gambled on a moment of passion, as human lives almost invariably are.

Stella had felt the need gathering in the man who sat demurely on Catherine's porch, courting the mother's good opinion, enlisting Nana. Even Sarah could not hold out against his persistent charm, not in spite of but *because* they saw through him. It touched them, even as they chuckled about it, that he should accept Stella's reticence, seek and unerringly recognise every support she had, and deliberately range himself with them.

"But it is not so simple," Stella insisted.

"Of course not," he agreed suavely. "But why have my plans complicated by the disapproval of others who share my good taste?"

"And what are these plans?"

"To worship from afar for as long as necessary, but for no longer."

"Let's go in and sit with the others."

"Tell me how I have offended you."

"You haven't," she protested quickly, and added before she could help herself, "you couldn't."

He tried to reach her hand but she moved it from the handle of the chair to her lap.

"So it isn't that you cannot... like me?"

She shook her head, and her voice was almost inaudible. "The situation is just impossible."

But she refused to say why. It was Sarah who explained later, gently, "You are a Jew."

"With respect, Miss Sarah, so are you."

"That is quite another matter, and you know it."

Abe reminded Stella that he was taking instruction from Reverend Jackman and was to be confirmed. Their children would be Christians, he wanted to say — but that would be too personal.

"Our lives would be everything that you could wish."

She looked away in confusion, but collected herself and shook her head. "Your family. From what you've said, they are devout in their faith — and I respect them for it." Near white too, she reflected hopelessly. "Your whole background is different. It would cause such... dissatisfaction."

"They will come round. And if they don't it can't be helped." Quickly said, but shadowed by anguish. "At least, I cannot help it."

Still she was troubled and distant.

"It wasn't just a sprinkle of water, Miss Stell. My beliefs have changed. And my feelings are... well they cannot alter. Whatever you decide, whatever you do, I'll never be the same again." But he was an irrepressible tease. "You've changed me from one thing to another *without* a kiss. What will become of me if I ever get one?" The laughter in his voice was real, but charged with desperation.

"But suppose," she whispered to Sarah, "suppose he changes his mind. Perhaps your uncle really meant... at first. Suppose at the last minute... or worse, afterwards, when he realises what he has given up...."

"No." Sarah could read Stella's fear. She saw Rudolf with his back to Stella, and the library door that locked Lynn out forever. "No. He is different to them. Stronger. And he doesn't just want you. He *must* have you."

It was true. There was something, like a current sweeping them together. And that raised another issue. She was absolutely ignorant.

She was persuaded by Abe's delicate combination of persistence and restraint, stirred by his presence, impatient in his absence, but two days before the wedding she sat on the porch, frozen in terror. She had no idea how to conduct herself... well, after the wedding. She was excited and curious, but totally uninformed. And she had no means of finding out. Because there was no one to talk to and it could not be talked about. A figure shaded the tiles before her and she started. It was Abe.

"You are very quiet," he observed after a while.

"Am I?"

"Sometimes, I think you're frightened and feel to run away."

"Sometimes I don't feel to run away. Then I'm more frightened."

Without warning, that tug, like an unseen force drawing them. He crushed his face in her hair.

"People will see us," she urged, scandalised.

"No. The ferns."

"But still."

"Why does it matter so much?"

"I must behave properly in public."

"And when you are not in public?" It was soft, teasing, but she could hear the hunger and she shut her eyes, breathing quickly. He released her but clasped her hand, gently weaving his fingers through hers. "Miss Stell, your behaviour is always appropriate." He raised the hand and kissed the ring finger deliberately. "And always will be. Automatically."

"Automatically?"

"Automatically."

It was an unspeakable relief.

At the wedding, in a trailing two-tiered gown and broad hat, sprays of white flowers on the shallow scoop of its brim, Stella was poised and erect way beneath the celluloid supports and bones of the snug white bodice. Respectable. Catherine's spirit soared. Secure. Sarah glanced back and caught Nana's eye, glistening in thanksgiving.

Icelin was grinning, but shone with perspiration. Sarah had posted her at the church door before the wedding, with precise instructions.

"And when you see Mas' Goldman walk into the church and sit down to wait," she whispered, "you must run back to King Street and tell Miss Stell I say, 'He is there.' And hear what I tell you, Icelin. Miss Stell goin' be dressed and ready. *Run* there and *run* back."

It was a simple gown, of classic lines and occasional delicate lacework. Stella's hands were steady with their sheaf of soft, half-opened rose buds. Above them, her face was petal-smooth, controlled, but aglow with suppressed emotion.

Exquisite. Abe's head swam with exultation and anxiety as he slipped the ring solemnly onto her slim, unshaking finger. Like the filigree brooch he had given her. But so, so proper. In public, anyway. For a moment she thought... then, no, even Abe would not have winked at a time like that.

On the verandah at King Street, the maidenhair ferns fluttered on shiny black stems which rose hard and wire-thin in a spiny cluster at the base of the pillars. Nana and Catherine were in the whirl of activity inside. Lynn Stollmeier hung, vaguely, near to the door. Sarah hovered between Jonas and the wedding party. The rest of the small gathering drifted in and out through the polished doors, brushing the plants unconsciously.

Reverend Jackman alone concentrated on them, forcing himself to notice the uneven line of fine brown seeds which crusted the edges thinly. He studied the wide arch of the fishtails, wondering at their forking stems and peering at tender shoots, coiled at their ends in pale, tight promises of life. He brushed the knuckle of one finger over the transparent green of baby's breath foaming over red clay. He waited to bless the cake, as the ferns cast their delicate lace shadows before his feet.

Stella passed and smiled at him readily and directly, and he felt a hot surge of anger because she had never done so before. Her glance showed that now he was a priest solely, and not a man with a man's feelings. His soul hardened with resentment.

Lynn Stollmeier wandered by and her eyes wavered gropingly over his face before she smiled absently and lowered herself onto a wicker chair, confused at finding herself in Catherine's house. She looked around blinking rapidly, questioningly into the sunlight. Jackman felt sudden kinship to her, dazed and out of place. He still could not believe he had married them himself. The ferns and their shadows and the little patches of sunlight in between scattered across his mind like confetti, but the empty spaces among them ached.

"You're a plant enthusiast too? Like Stella?"

ᐧIt was Goldman, distastefully friendly and cheerful, hand outstretched to thank him. Strange fellow, Jackman thought, full of unpredictable depths and shallows.

Abe was a sound businessman, yet not always discerning in his judgment of character. He made and spent money easily. He was careless, though never untidy; negligent, never callous; deeply concerned about religious truths, incurably materialistic. Jackman had come to know Abe in the past months leading to his baptism. He was warm, but a little blind. Involuntarily the minister drew back.

"I must thank you," Abe insisted. "After all, you have changed my life in every way for the better." He paused and looked down at his highly polished shoes, a little self-conscious. "I... I have something I'd like to give you."

Jackman looked down at the pool of light in the centre of Goldman's hand. It was a cross of flat, polished gold, knife-edged at the sides, with the chain matted under it. The minister flinched despite himself.

"I can't."

Abe laughed, a distressed, coughing sound. "Oh but you must. I could think of nothing good enough but this. I wanted you to know how.... Well you have given me everything. Even Stella."

Jackman froze to the floor but something dark and bitter rose in him. Up from his gut he could feel it searing through his chest, flaming along his skin.

"Christ," he gasped. He went taut with the strain of trying to contain the heat that spread across his face. Even Abe could not misunderstand. They stood there for a minute feeling horribly exposed, horribly responsible. Now they were desperate to escape each other but unable to move.

"I never knew," Abe breathed.

A soft pressure on his arm and Stella was beside him, slipping the soft, bell-like folds of her sleeve through the crook of his elbow.

"What is it?" She tilted her head over his shoulder and drew a deep breath. "Oh, beautiful."

But she knew Augustus Jackman could not wear it.

"One day, when you are Bishop," she teased. Still, it was not such a big cross as that.

"I'll wear it under the vestments till then," Jackman managed a smile. Next to his skin, he thought. Like a hairshirt.

The minister's fingers closed over the cross, raised and slipped the chain over his head. "A memento from your husband, Stella."

How like Abe, she reflected.

Sunlight struck the smooth surface of the gold to a glow upon the minister's chest as he turned back to Abe, and Jackman was the bush that burned but was not consumed. He smiled and grasped Abe's hand self-consciously. It was cold and damp. "Well," murmured the minister genially, "what was it the Lord said to Abraham? Get thee out of thy country and from thy kindred, and from thy father's house, unto the land that I will shew thee. Which reminds me — I have one more duty to perform for you."

He left later than he had hoped. Edging past the buggy Abe had hired from Eden's, he glanced up at the sun. He walked quickly but when he arrived at Aaron Goldman's door the Sabbath had started. The thin, quavering voice of the old Jew was raised in prayer.

Jackman waited, fidgeting. There were more than the regular Sabbath prayers. Abe's father called on the God of the wanderer, and struggled with him, debating, reminding, praising, beseeching, but at last his voice rose in affirmation, "Hear, O Israel, the Lord our God, the Lord is One."

It was finished.

The minister knocked reluctantly and stepped back, off the porch.

Aaron Goldman unlocked the door himself and greeted Jackman politely, stepping down into the courtyard a little uncertainly while the others gathered in the doorway.

Clustered in the dark entrance, the three pale faces were poignantly alike and unmistakably resembled Abe — half-brothers, from his mother's previous marriage, Abe had said. He was his father's only child.

And I have torn him away, Jackman thought. But he said, "It's about Abraham."

Mrs Goldman pushed one of the younger boys away impatiently so as to stand on the doorstep. She was short, very white, and too thin for her build. Her cheekbones were low and this, with a pinched mouth and heavy lids flattened her face. There was a sweetness in it; she might even have been pretty once. But pain had etched a hundred tiny lines about the mouth and eyes.

Anxiety had shrivelled her, Jackman thought. And now he had come. Conciliatory phrases he had planned dried in his mouth leaving only the bald fact of Abe's conversion and marriage.

A few things etched into Jackman's memory. Crinkled hair thinning on an old man's head which sank, crushed by his message. The Jew's pale fingers groped for the neck of his clothes, ripping them wide across a thin, defenceless looking chest. His hands groped in the dirt around his feet and scooped it up, crushing it onto his head. Slowly, slowly the mother's ruined face turned up then sank into her hands. And all his life, even when Aaron Goldman had long been in his grave, Jackman carried in his head the high thin wail of lamentation:

"Abraham is dead!"

So this was the day that separated the past from the future for Jackman. His whole system of belief was uprooted and replaced with new vision. Love, he had thought, was gentle and binding. But now he knew.

He had hesitated over the personal consequences of marriage, but now he saw the violence of love. The very union transformed other relationships. Other lives it tore apart.

Now that Stella and Abe were settled in a modest house near the bottom of East Street, Catherine was alone, but at the upper end of East Street Sarah too began a new life. In a sense, she too was now alone. Her mother sat for much of the day, lost in the past. Sarah should have sat with her more. There was nothing Lynn would have liked better than to wander with her through that incredible, exhilarating afternoon when Jacob had asked her to come with him to Jamaica. In thought, Lynn strayed among the corridors and rooms which were bolted now and heavy with dust upon the throw covers of what little furniture remained. But Sarah refused to look back. Not for a moment, not for anyone. She tried to speak of the present and the future, but it was useless. Lynn did not even recognise Jonas, however frequently she met him.

Over and over Sarah explained to her mother why they must sell the furniture. The disposal of each piece brought new hysteria. Only once, just after Stella's wedding, Lynn volunteered to part with something. "The desk, Sarah. I'd like to give them the desk."

Sarah peered at her curiously. "Your writing table, Maman?"

"*Non, non.* The desk. In the library."

Sarah turned sharply, came and sat close to her taking both her tiny hands in one firm grasp and looking steadily into her face. What was there to say to her. Her husband's blood had sprayed over the ormolu inset in the far corner. If she had forgotten, God was merciful.

"Maman, Stella doesn't need a desk."

"Nonsense. Every house needs a desk. A man does. She's furnishing a house."

"Abe sells furniture. He's had everything made."

"But do they have a desk?

"Oh, Redeemer."

"Well?"

But that weekend Stella and Abe visited them together. Lynn rarely went out now and Stella could not forget that Lynn had first asked her to East Street in different days. As they entered the room, Stella's mind went back to the birthday party. Lynn's eyes were bright and her hands lively with quick, birdlike little movements. A man needed a desk, she said, and she was sure Abe hadn't made one for himself. He chuckled and shook his head.

"No, Mrs Stollmeier. That will have to wait a while."

"But it won't," she insisted. "We're not using it and I have one that must stay in the family."

"Well, it's hard to refuse anything offered quite that way," he conceded easily.

Sarah came in with tea.

"Stop. Sarah, what is this desk your Mama means us to have?"

The other girl started, rattling the china and setting down the tray unsteadily.

"Oh, it's all arranged, Sarah, all arranged," Lynn crowed.

"Stella, no!" Sarah burst out. "You're not really taking that thing?"

Stella regarded her blankly, then her eyes widened.

"Right. That's what she's giving you."

Abe and Lynn chatted on. He would send the men for it, he said, once she was certain.

Abe would laugh at them for being superstitious, Stella knew. And then, she could not think what to say to Lynn. While she was deliberating, the desk settled down in the corner of the Goldmans' living-room and became a part of their life.

Sarah saw it in place by the following week. Reverend Jackman accepted his teacup from Catherine and rested it on the nearest corner of the desk.

"You foolish girl," Sarah scolded her. "You couldn't stop them? Why didn't you take the beastly icon too and be done?"

Stella chuckled, and Reverend Jackman grinned at Abe despite himself, "Ah, but, Miss Sarah, a graven image?"

Sarah stared at him in irritation and affection, then laughed boisterously. Yet she had lost it all, the traditions of generations, property, parents, and now Stella. All she had left was old Nana, and the maid, Icelin Castries, who refused to return to the country for any reason. It was different for Jackman, she thought wryly. He did not have her past, and anyway he had what little he had started with.

6
The Island

AS EARLY as 1654 there had been a Jackman, private soldier, who
had started with little enough. Indeed he had hardly a clue of
what the voyage from Portsmouth was about. The truth, which
was not his business, was that there were not enough men. The
rest would be collected in Barbados, St Christopher — wherever
some earlier expedition had abandoned them — if they were still
alive. Once the blighted expedition had reached Barbados at all.
Indeed, it was more than usually uncertain whether this voyage
could get there. Mutiny was more likely with the cutthroats they
had drummed up. Cheating Tyburn, people called it.

Rumours spread down even to Jackman's level of merciful
ignorance. One rumour, about the store ships, was well-founded,
as it turned out in Barbados. No sign of the stores there.
Nothing. No pikes, firearms, carbines or ball. Not even food.
They stripped Barbados before they left. Anyway, Jackman noted
triumphantly as he boarded again, he had survived the malaria.

Santo Domingo had been a nightmare. But what sort of luck
was to be expected after stoning a statue of the Virgin with
oranges? There was a hanging too — no one knew why. They
heard Venables had ordered it. But what had the old Irishman
done? All a mystery. Jackman had kicked the box out from under
the old man when the order came, for one carried out orders.
But anger exploded in him sometimes, like the time when he had
found himself fighting at the tip of a long rod of men, thrust out
into open space, and an officer screaming, "Cowards! Cowards!"
at his own men even as the Spanish were skewering them to the

ground around him. Santo Domingo.

Well beyond Jackman's surmise, the minds directing the oper-. ation were in ferment too for there would be hell to pay when they all got back to England. Cromwell. Whatever would they take for Cromwell?

Down in the ranks, all Jackman knew was that what remained of the Commissioner after the fever was lowered into the sea, and the men were stunned by the salute of forty-two guns only a matter of hours before the mountains of Jamaica rose dark against a flaming evening sky.

On deck next morning Jackman stood as straight as he could. His belly griped and he shifted uneasily hoping it was only hunger. Six weeks of short rations had shrunk him and he was constantly hungry and flatulent. He prayed that it was not the flux. Fear? Perhaps. He had seen the Spaniards fight. Then the signal came, and the urgency of unloading safely blotted out sensation.

When the news came that the fort was empty and the Spaniards had fled before them, he laughed, "Afeared over nothing."

Jackman found that first night in Jamaica like any in Santo Domingo. Crabs rattled threateningly among low thorn bushes irregularly lit by fireflies, and mosquitoes whined and needled them. The hunger gripe was familiar now, almost reassuring (though he grew giddy at times, especially in the heat, and he must zave a mite of food to avoid being too leery at noon, he noted).

Next morning the company marched beneath Spanish breast-works between the hills. The road wound empty ahead and the town waited eerily. Without resistance it was theirs.

The Cayo de Carina seemed solid enough to the men who walked on it. Really it was the end of a broken peninsula, and the rest of the spit was little more than a linear scattering of out-

crops. Superficially these might join each other by sandy residue washed down from the mountains but all around, the land fell away abruptly. Underneath, out of sight, a shifting base of sand, silt and gravel reached fluidly down for a hundred feet or more. From the surface they looked out over a remarkable harbour where they could accomplish much, given time. They had no way of knowing that anything accomplished over decades or even centuries could disappear in a matter of minutes.

Jackman stared sullenly at the sea and the mountains after only a couple of months working on the Cay, or Cagway, as they had come to call it. The boat was late. He ran his thumb over his forehead to flick the sweat away, leaving a trail of grime beneath his hairline. He would willingly have exchanged for the damp December greyness of Portsmouth all this mythical gold of the tropics.

It had been a soaking, trickling day, that last day in Portsmouth. All of it — the waterfront, the sky, his wife's face now. (He'd not zeed the missis these many months past.) Incredible, year-long months they had been and her face was fading in his mind but for the trickling of tears. When the gun discharged the recall signal she had jerked as if it fired into some vital place, and her face melted. Long agone.

Jackman leaned upon a rock and stared murderously out to sea. Now the food was finished. He was slipping into an apathy from which only hunger and hatred could raise him. And the food was done.

Except for the cattle. That was another thing. He was no farmer. He was no carpenter and he was no bloody farmer. He hadn't come to build anything or to mind animals. When he wanted meat he would hunt and kill; and what he could not use could wait for the vultures. But now the men were not to hunt. Nobody fed them, but they were not to hunt. (Wanted to learn zoldiers to be carpenters, they did.)

A younger soldier wandered over and squatted beside him.

"The men are talking of meat. They'll go when we get back, you know."

"None left on the plain," Jackman snarled. "Cattle driven off."

The lad nodded cautiously. "They'll go to the woods."

Jackman tensed, eyeing him narrowly. "Ross 'n Charleton went Vriday," he pointed out.

The other nodded, chastened, and admitted, "Brought Ross in this morning."

"Dead, was he?"

No answer was necessary. It was the Spanish who kept Jackman loyal to the army. If he ran, the Spanish would get him along the way. He got up without a word to the boy and plodded back towards the site. If he did not work they would shoot him. Besides, work gave the day a certain shape.

The days were identical then indistinct, eventually hazing into each other feverishly as they fortified the harbour.

Under the July sun they tore stone from the giant limbs of the mountains and took over the nearby lime-kiln abandoned by the Spaniards. He pounded out the seconds, minutes, hours of his life, under the white heat of the island. He grew accustomed to the sharp edge of famine, but he slowed. Raising the pick became strenuous and required a supreme effort of will. The lad who had hunted cattle in the woods survived the guerrillas to succumb to malaria, and Jackman buried him. Then the fever raged through Jackman and left him wasted but alive.

August was arid, dust-laden. In September, the air thickened and choked out even the determination to survive. In October he paused with the pick in mid-stroke and let it fall. He dragged himself away under the shade of a thorn bush and lay wondering idly when they would shoot him. But they were all in it together and would all sooner die than work. No one bothered to shoot him. (Probably have to ax them to shoot me, he grunted.) So occasionally, from lack of anything else to do, he went back and broke a few stones.

Yet, somehow, in November they could see progress. Guns were mounted. They measured the progress in guns. Nine, ten... twenty. Over the next two months as his companions died around him, Jackman began to pick out new faces, seamen pressed into service.

"Might as well 'ave been in the bluddy navy," grumbled another who had boarded with him.

The fever rarely bothered Jackman again. When they talked of a round stone tower he found strength for anger, and by April, when it was already five feet high, he was court-martialled for a drunken outburst of obscenity. Yes, there was liquor now, and the traders bought and sold it along with their provisions. Business boomed. Success spread, even beyond the damn Jews.

Yet, somehow, his life never steadied on those shifting sands of the Point that projected from the island's edge, and one day, three years after his arrival, after returning to the main shore, he took his life in his hands and walked inland.

There were valleys that the island kept secret, unsuspected by those who saw only the wind-scrubbed shores and thorny land-ing places. Those who worked out on the Point were unaware of them; and even Spaniards like the Castries, who had possessed land in the interior for generations, had fled without ever really seeing it. After all, the whole island itself was barely more than a rumour.

The mountains looked out through their mists for a child who would be their own, but they settled their roots firmly into the green tangle of generations and waited, for as yet the faces of the people were unformed. Strangers drifted in raw from their own pasts, unconnected to each other, irrelevant to any conceivable common future. Some were hopeless of the future; some strove to hew it out for themselves. Meanwhile, by a sort of tacit agree-ment, all were committed to the obliteration of the past.

The strangers were nobodies, all of them. No common story. Detached shadows that came and went across a rumour. Among the shadows tossing under a giant silk cotton tree was the English soldier, Jackman.

The Point that they called the Cagway was distant now and, with it, his superior officers and the damned navy. If he got far away enough, in towards the mountains, they need never find him. With the Spanish driven back, there was land for the taking; and Portsmouth was a fading dream in any case. And if the stubborn residue of Spanish or their negroes in the hills fell on him in the isolation of the bush and left his mutilated remains for the hopeful vultures wheeling overhead, he no longer cared.

In the mythical interior sat Juan Castries almost invisible against the brown tree trunks. His father before him had been a hunter, scarcely limited by servitude, and his mother one of the last of the Taino women. His father had killed to steal her from the Spanish settlement in the valley but no one there had noticed. More and more the brown Castries had mastered valley and forest, but none of them had roamed far along the coast. The Point was a place the lad had never seen nor did he even quite believe in it, though he knew that changes were afoot near the shores of the island. So Juan squatted on his heels near the edge of the forest and pondered the flight of his Spanish master from what had been Castries land for generations.

Juan speculated too on the likelihood of his own survival under the newcomers. In the first place he had heard they spoke an outlandish tongue no one could understand and he recalled two English deserters he had heard as a child during a raid in Morant. It was unsettling, such discord. Whites should speak alike.

Juan squatted motionless, his face impassive despite the turmoil within. He cursed the Spanish for abandoning him, and the British for threatening the even, carefree life of the hato. His eyes, already slanted in a flat, chocolate face, narrowed as he stared at the unkempt edges of the Castries land. He recalled, he recalled. His mother had told him stories.

There was a place. There was his mother running with him, her long hair flying. There was water running. Rushing, falling. A cool, deep place in his mind, in the forest. His mother had loved water. Her father had told her... something... the old ones had said, and their fathers, and their fathers. In the beginning, was a cave....

Into the cool, green darkness of his mind sliced the bright open hato before him like a shaft of pain to come. On a path in the distance, something stirred, neared and took shape. It was one of them, the new whites, in the garb he had seen before. A British soldier. It would be easy to chop and dismember him, but pointless. The bush would swallow the stranger effortlessly.

Juan Castries shifted uneasily, foreseeing some enslavement less leisurely than before. The Spanish blacks might be more confined, cut off from the hatos and the forests. Now, their growing awareness of the intruders was driving them together, impelling them towards the deeper forests. Slowly he rose to his feet, backed into the bush and melted into the silence of the Blue Mountains.

Hours later, Castries was not the first to arrive in the clearing, nor the last. They fell into step together, black men and dark brown. In and up they retreated. The rocks grew steep and the trees clustered darkly protective. The wilderness embraced them. They picked fruit and brought down a few birds. By the side of a slow river they laid lines and drew in five or six small fish.

Jutting from a rock stood a huge dead tree with a nest of wild bees. The men circled, gesticulating until at last Juan sprang forward, clambered over the rock and up the trunk and leaped down with the honeycombs dripping from his hand. He had only a few stings, and his heroism was the greater for them. The men licked the honey away and sprawled dazed with sugar in the thick, sticky afternoon.

They awoke out of a drunken sleep, suddenly aware of a new presence and glared curiously at a tall, heavy-set man, older than they, on the far side of the clearing. Beside him was a woman hugging a small child against her legs, and two older children crouched at her side. He gripped a cutlass in his right hand and, in his left, withes by which he led a couple of meagre hunting-dogs.

Women, children, shelters. A village. In the mountains they welded into a community cut off from the rest of the country, an island within an island. Over the years, the life of the bush became their own and they hunted and were hunted.

They had been stalking the hog three days. Nostrils quivering, eyes feverish, the dogs darted along the trail, lost it, wheeled, ears alert, snuffled frantically this way and that, picked it up and sprang forward again, ears flat. But it was almost dark. The men hacked their machetes at the smaller branches and made the night's shelter squarely on the trail of the hog. It must double back when it reached the end of its normal route and they slept restlessly. The bush was dry and the waterholes empty. Wild pines which trapped water clung to the rocks further up in the mountains. Soon the hog must burst back, heading uphill, and the dogs would head him off. But the dogs came back, and the men tied them and slept again.

At dawn they loosed the dogs once more and waited. The barking was intermittent, questioning, then, hours later, it grew louder, deeper. But then after a furious snapping and frantic, throaty barking the snarling grew shriller, thinned to tortured squeals and stopped. The men glanced at each other, irritated, yet resigned and with something of respect on their faces. The dogs were dead.

They consulted briefly in the common language of the slaves who swelled their numbers by escaping from the thin scattering of English plantations. Then they heard it. Twigs snapped and crunched; stones skidded under heavy hooves. Juan squeezed the hilt of his knife and a longer shaft in his other hand, and his soul screamed a jumbled prayer to Ananse, the great weaver, and to Mary. Then there was no time.

It hurtled out of the undergrowth, a massive beast with curved tusks brilliant with blood, and plunged into the midst of them. They sprang onto rocks and low branches, tensed to clamber down, but by the edge of the clearing it swung and charged around. Then it broke circle, ripped in again to the boulders in the centre and wedged into a cleft.

Juan gripped his knife and raised the shaft with a longer, brutal blade and slid from his rock. Distrustfully, the others watched the aging hunter sidle across the clearing. Yet, one by one, they eased down and edged in. When he reached the boulders where the hog sheltered, it charged, but he was safely on the rocks by then and the others scattered in time. The small eyes glinted as it trotted round and made its stand again. Above it, Juan closed one eye, held his breath and plunged the shaft in. The hog leapt then stumbled, and they all jumped down and raced towards it. It staggered to its feet and charged wildly, wavering but crazed with pain. Juan was nearest and the tusk ripped him in the thigh, missing the groin by inches. When he screamed they knew they had been right about him, but they turned, closed in, and plunged forward and aside as the beast struggled till they had finished it.

They locked their arms under Juan's to draw him gently near the carcass, and the healer cleaned and bound the wound. They embraced over the hog, unrolled the spices and began to prepare the meat. Soon the pyre of dry wood blazed high and hot in the clearing, but it took their conjoined efforts to sweat, singe, clean and split open the hog. Juan lay near the *old hunter who seasoned the pale slabs of meat.*

"More pepper," Juan snapped.

The other made a contemptuous click of his teeth and muttered, "Bwai, go 'way from me!"

He stroked the pimento into the white flesh. But Juan jerked his head stubbornly. "More pepper," he insisted.

Again the others shrugged at his arrogance, but one bawled out tolerantly, "Put de pepper pon de haag, man."

Then it was skin downwards on the sticks and they added pimento leaves to the fire.

Hour after hour it cooked and the voices round the fire rose and fell. They talked, slept, woke and talked again. Of the hog, of other hogs, of hunting in the old days, of the cattle that had overrun the hato like a plague so that men stripped the hides and left the carcasses to rot in the sun. There seemed to be fewer cattle now. They talked of the old masters' flight, and of new plantations to creep down to at nights, and they boasted of children they had fathered there.

The smell of roasting pork rolled away from the pyre and curled about them, and they paused and inhaled sleepily. For a long time they huddled together singing, spinning old tales far into the night, half-dazed though they were by the constant crackle and sizzle of dripping fat, the savoury smell of the lean, and the spices stinging their eyes. They chuckled at the thought that they themselves were the subject of tales now in the settlements and plantations.

Some of these properties were growing wide and threatening and it was sensible to avoid them except in carefully planned raids, but there were others. One was a small plot with a runaway soldier-man. The two Spanish women on it had not seen their own men for years and their lives improved when Jackman moved in, built walls and penned cattle. Soon, under their guidance, he had thrown up a wooden frame, fixing rocks in the frame with masonry. The women urged him to mix more mortar and spread it smoothly to finish the walls by which he extended the house, but Jackman grumbled that he had not deserted the army to take orders from women.

There was a small trade between the farm and the wild blacks of the mountains and there was an African woman within the Spanish enclosure who welcomed Juan Castries when he scaled one of the walls by night. The Englishman had joyfully thrown away the last rags of his uniform and the two Spanish women bore a child for him alternately each year. Most solitary Englishmen wandering alone in the forest died suddenly and violently, but it amused the blacks to let Jackman live. After all, he was no longer a real soldier, the Maroons decided. Probably, he never had been.

7
Shadows

So MUCH for the Reverend Augustus Jackman, Sarah shrugged. He had had his chance to win Stella. Still she felt a sympathy for him. Why, with Stella married, Sarah herself grew lonely.

There was Jonas, of course, and although the wedding had been postponed twice there was a date again. Sarah visited the Goldmans with details of wedding plans but Stella was slipping further and further away, especially with the baby on the way.

It seemed that as Stella's burden increased her frame grew frailer. Then, weeks before the expected time, Sarah and Abe found themselves staring down at the limp, wasted little infant and looked away, at each other, at Catherine.

"You're not accustomed to seeing newborn babies," Catherine whispered. "They pick up after a while... and this one is so early." She tried to smile and glanced back into the basket. Then her face settled into stern determination. "We will just do everything...."

Stella threw up a wall around herself and the child. Sarah came immediately after work to sit in the nursery, leaving Nana with Lynn. Icelin Castries moved permanently to the Goldmans and took over the heavier work. She moved tirelessly about the house, swinging her body easily in its dark, blousy cotton dress. She turned her hand to anything, and even when the gutter outside choked and stank she laid aside her frilly cap, took cover under a battered jippi-jappa hat, reefed her skirt up under her waist so as to clear her ankles and went to work on the debris with a coconut broom. In the days, when Sarah was at work,

Catherine was always with Stella. But Stella would not relinquish the child for an instant.

Stella's daughter was born in August and, by September, buried. In the cemetery Reverend Jackman officiated in his familiar deep, measured tones, but inwardly he bled to see her, fragile to the point of transparency but dry-eyed, and her back, if anything, straighter than before.

It was a small, tight group before him. Catherine and Nana. Sarah, between Jonas and Lynn. Abe, standing behind his wife with his fingers moving compulsively around the brim of his hat. Stella. The rain trickled from her hat and rolled unheeded down the marble scroll of her face.

For weeks it seemed to Abe that Stella had buried her heart with the child. Fear tightened in him to a thick knot under the ribs. Anything to do with the baby was a little cold stone of silence that might grow into a wall.

Reluctantly she agreed to accompany Sarah to Bath for a few days' rest before the wedding. Stella argued that two pounds ten a week was exorbitant, but Abe was adamant and the slender-limbed trap that he had ordered bore the women off to St Thomas. They swung out between the Pound and the Lunatic Asylum, past Chelsea Pier and towards Long Mountain.

"Look!" Sarah gasped, pointing. "Rudolf Stollmeier got a motor car."

Then, sure enough, with a flash of huge beetle eyes and elegant cream fabric roof he roared past in a cloud churned up by shiny spoked wheels. The dust parted only to allow a disappearing glimpse of the huge spare at the back.

"He would."

Sarah's chatter was tiring at first, then a relief, for she was filled with light-hearted disclosures. Yet what a solid girl she was — a woman, Stella made a mental note — impossible to picture as aging. Sarah was stunning rather than pretty, with her too prominent hooked nose and the slightly pointed ears that lent her face its artful expression — even when her mind was innocently employed, as was infrequently the case. Her eyes gleamed dark but brilliant with humour alternating with curiosity and wickedness. Even her fiancé and approaching wedding were unsafe from accurate little comments.

"I can see the label on the back of the bridal buggy now: Eventually Married. Can you imagine Jonas? Chewing the end of his moustache ... so ... and carrying himself stiffly. You know how seriously he takes himself."

Stella smiled but shifted uncomfortably. Of course she didn't really know Jonas. But then, shouldn't she by now? Her eyes narrowed as she thought of him swinging loosely alongside Sarah. If there was one thing she didn't like about him it was that... walk.

Down they lurched to the uneven bed of the Hope River and the wheels clattered bumpily across the stones. A tight coil loosened in Stella and she felt guilty, then grateful. The valleys beyond sank grey-blue with mist but between them higher ground curved sharply green in the crisp air. Water tapped on the fabric of the roof from the leaves that hung dripping over the road. Trickles had found their way down the inside of the buggy and Stella stretched out her foot and regarded her damp shoe in wonder. Her sudden movement sent a tiny polly lizard wriggling briskly into a crack between floor and seat.

"Why, Stella, didn't you realise it was raining?"

Stella stared at the other woman, awakening from past to future.

"Then, Sarah, what about your flowers, girl? The bouquet?"

The air was rich with wet soil and vegetation and the road slick and dark on either side, dotted with little cubes of donkey droppings. Stella began to wonder about the Yallahs River, but by the time they drew level with Bull Head Mountain the puddles disappeared and soon the low shrubbery bordering the road was filmed with dust. Stella sighed in relief and Sarah's eyes prickled with gratitude that the other woman cared at least to live, but she hid her tears in memories shed carelessly and irrelevantly.

"When I was little, my cousins hardly visited and when they did they played with each other, not with me. Their parents had told them my father should never have married Maman. Supporting me was his duty. But he shouldn't have given the family name to a coloured woman. It messed up his business connections too. Still he took us up, and he shouldn't have laid us down, should he, Stell?"

"No. Who you played with then? At first."

"No one, till Maman thought of... the daughter of that brother who had known better. The thing is, then all my other cousins resented my preferring you. That was revenge. Sweet, eeh?"

"You're a wretch."

"I like to think so," Sarah sighed contentedly.

The sky greyed to a slight overcast, but somehow rain seemed unbelievable with the pale powder from the road coating the prickly scrub trees. Already these cringed, suffocating, under matted yellow brown tendrils of love bush. Here and there a twisted battlement of dildo reared up; or tuna cactus spread weirdly, spawning out flat, conjoining oval faces, brutal with thorns.

Then rapidly the land changed again, mushing into swamp, edged with bulrushes. Then streaky grey boulders, scattered among temporary-looking shrubs, indicated a wide, disorganised flood plain. Uneventfully, the treacherous Yallahs fording dropped behind them.

Away stretched the canefields, dark under a dark sky but threaded with the pale gleam of irrigating streams and bordered eventually by lines of brick quarters. Then up slid the stone and brick buildings of Albion, severe looking, but relieving the atmosphere with the faint flavour of rum. Ox teams trundled past, carting barrels and accompanied by barefoot men with their pants rolled up and shirts loose, exposing ripples of brawny flesh. The soft brims of their hats flopped as they ran.

"Imagine," Sarah said dreamily, "Goldfields could have been like this."

"What is it like really?"

"I don't remember... I think... nice, but not really sugar any more, you know. Just a place for Rudy to take his...." After a while she added, "We can drive in."

"No."

"It should be yours. It isn't fair."

"I don't even want to see it."

Sarah looked through the window.

"One day," she said, "it will come to me. Since he feels he has no children. Then. If you won't take it, I'll see that your children do."

"Darling, you can't just decide that. You will have your own family. Your children. For me, Goldfields is a thing of the past. Something to forget."

But Sarah tightened the corners of her mouth stubbornly and muttered, "Goldfields is yours."

They stopped for tea in Yallahs, where even Stella could not resist the thinnest of cassava wafers, then rolled out past the white-rimmed salt ponds — stink as usual, according to Sarah — and the bushes flashed glimpses of foaming waves as they approached White Horses.

Past Morant Point, women clustered at a river's edge, spreading clothes to dry on the flat rocks. The land basked rich and green now with tall silky brown plumes of corn.

"Near here, isn't it?" Stella murmured, preoccupied with sudden curiosity about Goldfields.

"Up there. Through the trees. Look now."

Stella stared at the grey stone and watchful windows warily, and hid mentally from the image of her mother's seduction that slid out from a corner of her mind.

Sarah cut into her thoughts irreverently.

"Must be full of endless old duppy." Then her voice softened. "But there is something about it, eh?"

Stella nodded dumbly. It was beautiful and terrible.

Before the Port they swung sharply north and soon they were high enough to look across a valley to hills covered with thousands of coconut trees. Immediately beside the road the earth exploded into life, blooming, bearing, coiling, chirping around them. Laden breadfruit and banana trees; brilliant flashes of hibiscus. Cataracts of yellow-streaked philodendron trailers tumbled from trees far above their heads and dark serrated leaves sprang from crevices in the mountain face. They caught a smell of roasting breadfruit long before they glimpsed the brown ball smoking in a hollow in the roadbank. Star-apple trees emerged from thick clumps of cocoa and the poincianas swept their careless flame over the ferns that laced the rocks. Streams trickled down over the stone faces or sprayed in a continuous fine mist to the mossy places beneath. Stella inhaled thankfully.

Then the hills rose up in a solid, almost forbidding wall on the other side of the Plantain Garden River. The road across seemed to run straight into the mountain but, in fact, twisted sharply at the very base of rock and they followed the mossy side with the ravine slicing away the ground on the other hand. A mongoose sprinted across the way just before they swung hard to the right, beneath a burdened jackfruit tree, into the Bath of St Thomas the Apostle.

It was a different, foreign-looking town, solid with its tall, strong houses and the striking, carmine carpet of downy otaheite blooms under the trees bordering the road. They stopped at a lodging house by a vast rubber tree frosted with orchids. After supper they found their way to the other side of the town and explored the church with its circular windows and thick walls.

"And they say it's made from white lime and molasses," Sarah observed. "Icelin always says if you tek likkle molasses regular you wi' last fe' ever. And I do, you know. She's insisted on it."

It was probably true. Clumps of boston and maidenhair ferns sprang as healthily from the brickwork as from the mountain itself.

Beyond the church, they strolled along the gravel path into gardens dim and hushed as a cathedral, stately with towering century palms, with the vast span of the knotted barringtonia tree and the purity of frangipani blooms. Here and there the frangipani gleamed on the darkening grass like fallen stars or floated down delicately onto the rough stone rim of the well.

They paused to stare at the pale splendour of two or three spectacular bursts of white and pink against the strange, ropy trunk of the cannonball tree.

"We should go back now," Sarah urged. "Miss Duffy will be expecting us."

The next morning they breakfasted solidly as befitted the country.

"All that!" Stella protested at first. But she was uncertain, dislocated from the immediate past and isolated with Sarah in the careless intimacy they had known before her marriage.

"Lord, I shall smell of red herring forever," Sarah chuckled. "When Jonas bends to kiss the bride it will issue forth — fumes of onion and pepper and smoked fish."

"Oh Sarah, you're not really going to? Not in front of all those people?"

"Not going to what, Stell?" Sarah tantalised.

"Oh go on, you misery. You know."

"Kiss him, Stell?"

"Sarah, man, there are other people around."

"Yes. And some of them may even have been kissed at some time. Shall I ask — ah, Gladys!"

Stella froze as the woman put down her tray and ambled over. No. Not even Sarah would. Would she?

"Gladys, I wonder if I could ask you something. Have you ever been... to Cuna Cuna pass?"

"Oh yes, 'M. Up de bridle road, 'M. Any s'm'addy will show you, 'M." And Gladys flashed a grin brilliant with gold and disappeared.

The road up to the bathhouse wound between steep banks, which were trickly, ferny, coated by the continuous drip of water, tangled with vines trailing from old trees along the way. By the roadside, branches sank laden with full mangoes; ripe and rotting ones squirted under the wheels even as birds gossipped among the branches above, stabbing at the brilliant fruit. The river flowed fast and low among the rocks, shadowed on its far side by massive plumes of bamboo. Nearer, a golden burst of allamanda somersaulted wildly over a stump.

Half a mile along the deep river gorge the road stopped abruptly in a rocky glade. The bathhouse rose up hard between the river and the hill, shaded by two nutmeg trees, male and female, which communed together with a mature and settled peace that hung over the whole valley. From upstream a faint mist marked the source of the hot fountain.

Their lives had melded again.

On the morning after their return to Kingston, Sarah sauntered into the office, and the girls applauded. One hummed the wedding march, moderating her typing to the rhythm.

"Look," Mr. Best himself had brought her mail. "Letter for the bride."

Sarah glanced at the writing. Jonas. Suddenly she wished Stella was with her. She read it and turned tight-lipped into the bathroom.

Before she could pull the chain the door handle rattled and

she could just distinguish Best's voice, urgent but discreetly modulated. When she opened the door he was relieved and embarrassed.

"Something seemed... I thought you might be ill. Forgive me. I have a daughter your age."

Sarah smiled reassuringly. "I was only flushing the ring."

She was calm and completely expressionless. Clumsily he pushed past. Sure enough, at the bottom of the bowl was a tiny circle of gold, glinting with red and white fire. With a muffled exclamation he dived his hand down. Wet from elbow to cuff he snatched the letter, skimming it.

> Such a final step... not ready... your own changed situation having made our future less secure, though of course none of that has mattered to me over the years... I think next year... both our sakes... not ready....

"You see," Sarah explained coldly, "I had already ordered the lilies."

"Yes." Best stared at her with all the anger and hurt she should be showing surging into his face. "But send the stinker his ring."

She considered and nodded. At her desk she typed a brief businesslike letter. It began, "Please find enclosed...." and concluded with a request for a receipt at Jonas's earliest convenience. Then she typed another letter withdrawing her notice. She completed her day's work and caught the tram home.

Here there was only Icelin to cope with. Her mother had never fully grasped the notion of the wedding anyway and Nana had moved to the Goldmans so that Icelin could return to Sarah and help with the packing.

Icelin would help her dress for the dance. It had taken Sarah no time at all to decide that she was still going to the party arranged in honour of Jonas and herself, but it took several minutes to dispel Icelin's superstitions about the wedding dress.

Eventually Sarah snapped at her.

"You foolish woman, you. The thing is not a wedding dress if there isn't going to be a wedding. It cost a fortune I no longer have and I'm damned if I don't get my money's worth."

Icelin collapsed in tears of disappointment. Sarah was apologetic but cool.

"I'm sorry you're disappointed. But don't cry here."

Icelin hurried away for the sewing basket, threading her way between crates and suitcases.

When Sarah was ready, Icelin drew back and regarded her from a distance, like an artist spellbound by her creation. Sarah regarded her reflection in the mirror with an ironic smile.

"I stay good, Icelin?"

"Oh, Miss Sarah. Laad, 'M!"

Deliberately Sarah scrutinised the sleeves they had shortened and the neckline adjusted to the décolleté of an evening gown. Without the veil, her figure showed to better advantage. The smooth sheen of the bodice curved down over the bust to the pinched waist and followed the swell of her hips to flare out in the deep folds of an extravagantly wide skirt, bordered with lace ten inches deep. They had picked off the delicate buds that seemed too fluffy for evening wear.

Above the ceremonial white, her skin glowed smooth gold in the lamplight with little shadows where the elbows dimpled and between the swell of her breasts where the bodice plunged daringly. Her face was perhaps a trifle colourless, but cool. She glanced at her bare neck poised above well-covered shoulders and exposed by the soft upswirl of hair. It looked... vulnerable. Mechanically, without taking her eyes from her reflection, she stretched her hand into a velvet-lined case and groped for her mother's pearls. They had never sold Lynn's engagement gift from Jacob. Another deserter. Round and round she wound them to a reassuring stranglehold on her throat.

At nine-twenty the carriage turned under the entrance arch of the hotel and clattered between palms and crotons up to a building ablaze with lights. On the wide verandah, tables set for al fresco dining bloomed with a rare hibiscus which would remain open all night and with crotons, carefully placed to avoid marking the white linen. Japanese lanterns outlined the verandah, and outside, from the centre of the lawn, spouted a huge, fountain-like palm brilliant with red and white lights.

Sarah drew a deep breath before the main doorway to the ballroom where she was expected to enter on Jonas's arm. Well. She had always wanted to enter one alone, just out of curiosity. And now.

The glow from the ballroom diffused out and into her. Out of the soft yellow glow and contented buzz of voices the music swelled full and deep around her, quickening her blood and sweeping breath and pulse into waltz time. Her feet stirred under its current and she was carried forward on a surge of expectation. In the doorway she paused again, conscious of the sudden hush, a slowing of couples on the floor.

Sarah Stollmeier. Alone.

Coldly she surveyed them, a motionless figure, frosted with white lace. She seemed to see all their faces at once, incredibly clearly, some stunned, some twittering with shock, speculation, disbelief. But they didn't matter. They faded into drab shadows as she approached the floor. For a moment she was crossing the living room at East Street after her father's funeral. Faces, clothes, entire persons thinned to transparency for none of them could have done what she was doing now. They were limp and makeshift. The men especially hazed into unreality. Jonases, most of them. She struggled for a minute to understand, then the smell of lilies angered her and she shrugged them away. Spinelessness had no reality to her. Only the music was real. She was here to dance. She could waltz with any of them. She had practised waltzing with shadows.

The ripple passed and couples on the floor felt awkwardly for their places again, unsure of what was expected of them. They were to have clapped when Sarah and Jonas arrived together. Now they felt for their partners in embarrassment, avoiding each other's eyes.

Sarah felt a swell of satisfaction at having disturbed them. A new sensation rose and fell in her, something warm and heady. Her chin tilted a deliberate challenge and she let her eyes wander directly over the male faces turned inquiringly at her. Slowly, confidently she came down the three low steps onto the hard gloss of the floor.

The crowd rustled again on the other side of the stand, and a well-shaped man, notable for a sort of languid elegance, detached himself. Hugh McCallum, the test of feminine success at any ball, sauntered between the staring couples to grasp her hand in an attitude of relief.

"Sarah, my dear! Thank heaven you've come." He leaned forward confidentially. "I had given up hope of being able to dance tonight. I mean, just look at what some of them are doing."

"Come now, Hugh, you didn't think I'd miss my own engagement party?"

He deliberately avoided the issue by turning up one palm in supplication.

"I suppose you have nothing to spare me on your card?"

She handed it to him, flashing a mischievous, sidelong smile, for they both knew it was empty. His eyes lingered momentarily on the low scoop of her neckline then travelled up to her throat in its tight, cold noose of pearls.

"It all depends," Sarah sighed, feeling her power and toying with it. "How many do you want?"

"Oh but I am determined to have all — every one. Well, later I may spare one or two to some poor deserving wretch. Not a waltz though."

He qualified his generosity in a strictly admonishing tone.

"On no account a waltz. And the final waltz — well we shall take over the floor."

By now, three or four were hovering in the background, laughing and signalling to her not to let him take them all. In moments the card was full. Hugh McCallum drew her to the centre of the room and whirled her into the music.

She dipped and rose, circling, approaching, withdrawing. The lower tier of her skirt flared as she turned and turned again. The lace threw strange patterns on the floor, folding, spreading again. At the centre of the room, under the candles, the light touched the lace to white fire and her skin to gold. One after the other the shadows came, circled and turned with her. Tiredness swept her then exhaustion. The pain she had postponed engulfed her and burnt itself away. Soon she felt nothing but the glow of the great light, the music licking through her and the soft fabric caressing her legs. At last the waltz again. Other couples drew back to watch them, but by now she could barely distinguish them as dim forms on the outside of her circle of light.

The room dipped and swung around her; the light was above and then below. Dizzy and satiated she sank into it, losing herself in rhythm.

She was not sure how she got home. Icelin opened the door as the spidery wheels of the buggy grated to a halt. The woman's cheeks were sucked in anxiously so that the long slant of her jawline showed prominent under the gas lamp above the door, and her cap slipped in frilly disarray off the tight plaits at the back of her head.

She drew Sarah in, stripping away the shredded white satin slippers, and scolding that it was four o'clock. When she tried to unfasten the back of the gown, Sarah pushed her away gently and burst it open from the plunging neckline, ripping it to the hem. As she stepped out of it Icelin started forward, but Sarah kicked the torn lace aside without a glance.

"Burn it," she whispered.

Screech Owl

IN KINGSTON, at the Goldmans' house, Christmas came and passed and came again. December brought skies of stunning blue, strewn briefly with white flowers of cloud, and crisp fresh evenings on the porch. It was a good time. The breeze curved cool and smooth over Stella's cheeks, rustled the poinsettia bushes outlining the low verandah wall, and set the heavy scarlet bunches dipping and swaying. Then, yes, there again, an upheaval at her very core. Holding her breath, listening, almost, with her fingers, she tested the side of her abdomen where the bulge had gone tightest.

Now she rested more determinedly, but she felt glad and confident about the child fighting and tumbling within her. The first had made weak, listless movements which she had thought normal, knowing no better. A deep thud made her gasp with laughter and she hugged her arms against the swelling, rippling cloth. She raised her head to the cool finger of the December evening stroking her neck, and stretched her thickened feet to as comfortable a position as was proper on a porch that overlooked the street.

Stella smiled at the little yellow rose blooming near the gate. It was her first rose, grown from one of Lynn's. There was yellow allamanda too, that Catherine had potted herself, and Lynn would set other slips for her, in her own time. Dear Lynn, receding into her world of memories — only Nana truly managed her.

Icelin had moved permanently to the Goldmans. Something subtle, heady, drew Stella's attention, and there was Icelin

beside her with the newspaper and a glass of egg flip, whipped
to a stiff froth, laced with cognac and fresh with a spiral of lime
peel. Stella ran her eyes over the woman wonderingly. Icelin
Castries had grown quieter yet closer over the years. She had little to say about herself, but she watched over them fiercely.

"Aah, Icelin." Stella smiled up, loving her blindly.

"S'm'addy must make you eat, eeh, Miss Stell? No care 'bout
youself, 'M."

The woman bustled away, preoccupied.

Stella was aware, in a vague way, of a world outside where a
different wind was blowing. The time would come for change to
blow gale force through the lives of those she loved, but not yet,
not for years. Perhaps it would be after her time. Abe said something would come, but could not say what exactly. Dim shadows
of unrest haunted his imagination, but it was speculation only.
Life was predictable like the Christmas breeze, like May and
October rains. The newspaper was a pastime and a record of
remote events. Still, far outside, the climate was unsettled, and
attitudes of people Stella did not know formed, evaporated,
formed again.

Occasionally she read things in the *Gleaner* and tossed it aside
in disbelief or impatience. Bedward's teaching was an outrage.
He denounced the upper and middle classes as Pharisees and
Sadducees, and some said he had prophesied that their world
would be shaken apart and destroyed in flames. Years ago they
should have put a stop to him. They'd had him once on a charge
of sedition and lost him on a technicality. But it was not the
incitement Stella feared so much as the blasphemy, the promises
of healing from a mountain stream and the hysterical claim to
being a prophet of Jesus.

Icelin heard it differently. It was the news on the street.

The Leons' maid had attended Bedward's church, and the
withered dressmaker in the lane was one of the elders. Icelin
overheard others beneath her station. The old broom-and-bottle

man asked her in his cracked falsetto if she had not been to hear Bedward. The women working on the road whispered excitedly about him, and the fishman cocked his head in surprise that Miss Icelin had never seen August Town.

Icelin began to know more as the pieces of gossip fell together, and the knowledge troubled her. From what they said he drew you with his eyes, wove spells about you with his hands and his voice broke and remade you. They said he set you on fire with the Spirit.

So one evening found her on the way to August Town. She was surprised and frightened for it was unintentional. At no point had she actually decided to hear Bedward for herself. She rarely roamed from the Goldmans (fe her grannie did tell her seh when crab walk too much him lose him claw).

She found herself among the women in white dresses and the men in black suits pressed shiny, and she was dismayed. The ridicule of Mr Abe rang in her ears and the image of Miss Stella, scandalised and disappointed, haunted her expectations. Icelin's experience was bounded by childhood in St Thomas and by her introduction to Kingston under the gentle discipline of Miss Lynn's big house and the watchful eye of Miss Nana. Her treatment had been different from that of the majority of such 'schoolgirls' brought from the country to Kingston for domestic work. She knew Miss Stella's background through the gossip of the East Street house and idolized Miss Lynn for recognising her niece. Now Icelin was responsibile for the frail, brave and puritanical Miss Stell herself and the careless but hardworking Mas' Abe. Their opinion mattered.

Of course they need never know she had gone, and it was harmless after all. (Not fe say she believe in no Bedward. Just curious she curious.)

Near August Town the mountain rose straight ahead of them and swept down and away to the right. At first she moved with the crowd. Then she grew tense, confused. The throng jostled her, sending little washes of anxiety over her. She hung back, embarrassed, pressed around by spectators and genuine believers who crammed the roadsides on the same pilgrimage as herself.

"Move nah, woman. Wha' do you?"

She began to feel less conspicuous but lost as the mass of bodies churned around her. She could not go forward or turn back. A woman in white took her hand.

"Come, sister. Don't 'fraid, sister. Welcome to the blessed."

Frightened and relieved, she allowed the evangelist to draw her into the centre of the crowd.

Then gradually a new sensation formed and spread, rippling away her sense of separateness. She was alternately buoyed up and submerged by the tide of the crowd. Her body seemed to bob away out of her control and her will ebbed in a slow receding trickle into the greater body of the faithful.

Then they were craning, pointing, nodding to each other. He was the big man with the space around him. Everyone else was jammed together but there was a space around him even in the crowd pressing in to see and touch. The elders thronged near him in the purity of ceremonial white robes, but even from them he was set apart in his strange, clear circle. He turned his eyes over the crowd and looked at and through and beyond them. His glance searched her as he passed and she felt he had penetrated clear through her in all directions, into her past and future and along the intricacies of her dealings with the Goldmans and her few other acquaintances. He had startling eyes, wide, bright and upturned, giving his face a rapt expression, almost shaping his body. His form seemed to strain upwards.

She found she was not even listening to him. At first, when he spoke, she could hardly hear, so drained she was of energy. But there was no need to grasp specific words, only to float limp upon the swell of mass emotion while his voice washed over her. Behind her the song leaders burst into fast, pulsing rhythm and the elders, evangelists and station guards took it up, clapping and nodding their heads with a conviction that swept the crowd along in a compulsive thunder of hands and voices. And under the irresistible pressure of the rhythm she shook and moaned because she did not know the song that beat upon her from every side. But then the chorus came round again and the words were ripped out of her, and her hands flung up in the storm of clapping and her feet among hundreds stamping the ground to dust.

Then through the diminishing roar of voices there resounded one, a voice with the power to cleave the songs of the multitude, echoing into the corners of her soul.

"Rise."

Bedward's voice rolled through her like thunder, dissolving her into the assembly yet reverberating in every cavity of her body.

"Angels in the sight of the Lord," he boomed, and don't it was what dem did always want. Way, way down in the gut, the hunger. "Black angels. God will make you shining white!"

His hands stretched, compelled, embraced. All. A gasp went through the crowd for the ground stirred beneath their feet and they could feel the... heaving. He could lift them as one body, effortlessly.

"Come, rise with me and see Jesus in the flesh. I will take you, I, Alexander Bedward, His prophet — fly with me to the throne of the Lamb."

Then he put them down and the hope pealing through them died away. He stared sadly, almost with loathing, and they bowed seeing themselves for the first time. And they were vile.

"You are black with sin and shame, with filth plastered on you by the white man. Will you stay black forever? Will you grovel under oppression? Hell will be your portion!"

The deep, sonorous voice rose and thinned, whipping them till a frenzied plea wailed from the middle of the crowd, "Save us, Shepherd!"

127

It began to rush behind her, on either side, an intensity of need, their collective yearnings sweeping together, gathering to a force that redefined gravity until there was no pull but this Voice, and the broad, rapt face whose eyes searched the sky became the energy centre of a tide of swirling souls.

"Bedward!" Hoarse and urgent. Who? "Wash us, Bedward, wash us!" Her own desperation sobbed in the distance.

But they wouldn't wash her yet.

"Not yet, sister, not yet. You must learn with us. We have to set you up. Den you can baptise."

She was cold and ill with disappointment.

When she went back to the Goldmans it was different. Bedward was a dream her mind toyed with, fled from and surrendered to. At night she pulled away the bags and boxes at the back of her cupboard to see the little vial of blessed water she had hidden there. It was all she could have for now since they wouldn't wash her.

Her room at the Goldmans' was empty of clapping and singing, and Bedward was far away. Miss Stella said Bedward was the work of the devil. Good or evil, Icelin knew his was powerful work. Still, if Miss Stella said it was evil, perhaps it was. She pushed the vial of spring water onto the very bottom of the press and rested boxes against it but she looked at it sometimes to make sure that it stood upright and could not leak away.

Then Stella's time came.

They named the baby Reuben, but would call him Ben. He was more sickly then they had expected after the healthy pregnancy. Day after day they nursed and prayed. When he went into convulsions, Icelin shifted aside the khus-khus bush that kept fresh and fragrant the treasures in her cupboard, and she brought out her black dress to air. She took the vial out at the same time and turned it this way and that, then rested it slowly but resolutely back in its place. Miss Catherine and Miss Nana came and went, consulting, sponging, brewing teas, and Sarah crouched by the crib, this great impending loss driving out emptinesses of the past.

"Nothing must happen to this one," Abe muttered hoarsely to the doctor. "Nothing!"

Dr Eliot was a middle-aged man who had saved so many and lost so many that he regarded Abe with weary compassion.

"My boy, there is no must or mustn't with a sick baby. As for Stella — I've known her... oh...." He waved the years away vaguely. "You haven't begun to know her yet... what that girl can take." He mused, then added, "This one's not weak like the first though."

Yet one morning Stella crumpled, half kneeling, half lying across the cot, and cried from immeasurable depths, "Not again, oh my God, not again."

Icelin paused in the doorway, and she was resolved. She would stop at nothing to save Miss Stella's child. If need be, she would sell her soul for it. Furtively she opened the vial of Bedward's holy water into the bowl of rum and lime they used for sponging the baby, droplets of hope and healing running through her fingers. She carried it to the mother.

"Make we cool him down, 'M. Morning well hot."

"I just did it, you know. Still...."

Stella took it thankfully, sponging the child.

"Im will pick up, you know, Miss Stell. Me feel seh dis chile gwine pick up from now."

"Oh, Icelin, I pray God." Stella's face was pinched and shadowed with exhaustion.

"What 'bout de love bush tea, 'M?"

"Lord, I 'fraid it Icelin. I hear it can be dangerous, you know."

"Miss Nana prefer de ganja tea, 'M. And old time people say...."

129

"Jesu! I don't know."

"Make we wait likkle, 'M. See if im pick up now."

Reverend Jackman prayed that evening over the cot. Icelin watched him distrustfully. Minister meant well, she knew, but she feared anything he might do in conflict with the power of the water.

That night the screech owl flew high above the house, lingering, circling under the pale, white haze of moonlight with a few monotonous cries. Icelin shivered, glancing up sidelong through the kitchen window, and she muttered the curse.

"Pepper and salt fe you fada, pepper and salt fe you madda, pepper and salt fe you fada an' madda you brute-beast!"

Days passed and weeks. At first they thought it was their own eagerness, but no, it was genuine improvement. Ben gained weight, grew lively, grabbing and batting at things, kicking his feet at the world and screaming from sheer temper when he could not get his way at once.

Inevitably, as the year wore on, Ben monopolised their attention. Nana coddled him, the others said, capitulating to his every whim. But Sarah too romped and tumbled him about, adoring the fight in him, and Catherine delighted in rubbing and flexing his limbs, carrying him about in the morning sun and whispering to him, "Grow, boy, grow. Grow into a real boy, man. Show them."

Abe swung him up on his shoulders and crowed that he was bigger and taller than everyone in the house and could lick any of them in a fair fight.

So the year turned to gold for all of them. The child stood, toddled, ran with sweet tottering clumsiness barefoot under the mango tree and laughed to find the grass sticking up between his fat little toes and tickling his ankles. He stooped to touch shame-lady, the sensitive plant that Icelin called 'dead-and-wake' and he squealed in triumph when it folded abruptly. They watched him, breathless with the wonder of it.

A sort of magic diffused through everything. Abe's business expanded beyond the showroom of delicately carved yacca and mahogany furniture to fine houses in residential areas of the expanding city. Sarah escaped the mindless chatter of the general office by moving to the switchboard. Stella secured a post in Nathan's Metropolitan House where she presided over Fancy Goods. Icelin returned to August Town to prepare for her vows.

Even for Rudy Stollmeier the year dawned fresh with promise. He had heard of Ben's birth, at polo with the officers at Camp, and had hardly paused over it. Stella and her child were ٦one of his concern. Yet the thought that he was a grandfather brought, unbidden, the startling awareness of passing years and the draught of time rushing by. Soon he would be old. And alone. Then, hearing of the child's illness, he had been saddened. It was illogical, for the Goldmans were nothing to him. Months later, when he glimpsed Ben on the street, a fine, tough, wilful boy, he longed to give him something. But Rudy knew by now that Stella was unapproachable. On an impulse he noted in his will that Ben should have his Winchester, the treasured piece he took on hunting expeditions. Almost everything else he left to the family of his only remaining brother, in Germany. However, he made sure that Goldfields was for Sarah, his brother's child, though what good it would be to a sour old maid he could not tell. Then he went out and bought two new racehorses.

When the baby grew strong, it was time for Icelin to take her vows. One of the elders took her in his arms and rested his grizzled chin against her head, rocking her a little, back and forward.

"T'ank de Lord, my sister. T'ank de Lord for dis new soul coming to Jesus, ready to leave de world and despise the flesh for Jesus' Church. Praise His name."

Nothing they had told her prepared for the sensation of awesome finality that came during the service. The baptism would be less frightening, for then her sins would be washed away, but now she was only to be faced with them and the necessity of washing.

"Down in the valley," they sang — the old Sankey chorus.

She followed them to the altar and then came the terrible nakedness of standing there while the whole room rang with accusation. An elder pressed a candle into her hand and squeezed her limp fingers around it. He lit it and she knelt, whimpering for mercy. All her flesh quivered with exposure. Then at last they sang again, 'Before Jehovah's aweful throne,' and the prayers began.

Stella and Abe knew nothing of Icelin's decision. They were entangled in planning and building the future. At last it seemed sure. Stella was never so robust again as she had been just before Ben's birth, but her mind sang with speculation every day to watch him grow tough and vital. She worked through lunchtime at Nathan's, when he was sleeping, in order to leave work early.

Now that Ben was well and Stella tolerably strong, there were pleasant evenings again on the porch. By the time the Christmas rush was past, the black cake was moist and mellow. The fruit had been steeped in wine from months before. Catherine had made the rum punch and laid it away in good time. As usual Sarah had clamoured for her to put in a larger measure of rum and Nana had grumbled for more sugar, but the others had clung stubbornly to the old recipe. One of sour, two of sweet, three of strong and four of weak. Only you left the weak out, Stella nodded sagely, and filled it up with ice when the time came.

The mid-January breeze was cool and clean, bringing a flush to rich-toned skins among the group that chatted and laughed together on such evenings. Some of the married men were black, rather than brown, but the really dark-skinned women in the gathering tended to be unmarried. Still, it was a wider range of shades than most porches on East Street would have accommodated, for Stella was a stubborn woman in her own, guarded, way.

A white Irish linen cloth, brilliant with satin-stitched poinsettias was thrown over the table at the front door. Cut-glass dishes winked cordially in the candlelight and the jug of sorrel, deep red as a stained glass window, proclaimed that Christmas was not long past. There were bowls of fudge and cashew nuts and small plates of crystallised fruit, ginger, otaheite apple and breadfruit blossom. Off to one side were the savouries, Solomon Gundy and cream crackers, patties hot from the oven. At the other end lay a wide flat dish with sweet pastries arranged on a doily, and the ladies conferred over the mellow coconut of the chess cakes and the crunchiness of the plantain tarts.

Grinning and smiling above her crisp black dress, for she knew everyone and everyone's business, Icelin passed drinks and sandwiches while Stella cut generous wedges of fruit cake. Nathan Fletcher was sure to be called on to play a favourite tune on the old piano and one or two of the men would sing along — deep mellow tones that promised that the evening would never end. Sometimes the talk sank to only a vague murmur or died away almost in the deep blue stillness. Then a sudden burst of laughter would erupt.

Abe was in his element, puffing his Golofinos between pronouncements on British politics or local rumour. An undignified squawk from Sarah turned the ladies round, smiling indulgently. Even if her life was a balancing feat to maintain the burden of a vast house that was her Maman's last link with reality, the privileges of birth clung to her.

"But you hearing your husband, Stell?"

"Miss Sarah," Abe's voice rose above much laughter. "Thou shalt not go up and down as a talebearer among the people." Then he grew serious and continued, "No, there will be more of Dr Love, and many like him. The majority of the people will be heard."

"Oh, Abe, man," one of the gentlemen expostulated, "Love's a radical, man. Another Bedward."

"Oh but Bedward's a cuffee, and Love is an educated man," objected old man Preston from across the road. "Extremist, but highly intelligent."

"That only makes Love madder than the prophet, and more dangerous." Abe's opponent was Nathan Fletcher. They were close friends and argued politics far into the night.

There was a groan of derision and Sarah suggested that they sell Bedward to Lowande's Circus. Then the fruit cake came around, and for a while there was little noise but for the rustling of skirts against the wicker chairs and an occasional low rumble of laughter among the men until Abe laid aside the empty plate.

"Laugh all you like," he insisted, and with that little quirk of humour at his mouth-corner, Stella thought, even she could not tell if he were serious. "It's inevitable. Look at the colour of the population. It's forty to one, you know. Why does that one have to make the laws?"

His voice was drowned by immediate outcry.

"Revolution. That's what you're talking about, revolution."

"What about the Empire, man? Don't you expect Britain to put her people in positions...."

"Yes," Abe responded, "but there are educated people right here, brilliant people."

"Like Bedward?"

"For God's sake, man. We have the framework of their laws and constitutions, there are men here...." Abe's voice was drowned.

"Look at Haiti and see where you're taking us. In ten years we'll be like some little inland village on the Gold Coast. Two republics in the West Indies — double anarchy. America would never put up with it."

"*England* would never put up with it."

"Look, we don't need rhetoric from extremists. We need

money put back into agriculture. This big conference should do some good, eh?"

Abe nodded and threw a cigar butt into the ashtray on the mahogany stand. There was a chorus of agreement over the agricultural conference.

"And I hear the ball at Port Antonio was.... Oh, they say the Hotel Titchfield was a fairyland."

"Imagine what Mico will be like. Such a gathering."

Sarah clasped her hands and stretched her feet forward yearningly. "I wish I could have been at that ball."

Resolutely her mind blocked out other balls, with Jonas, without Jonas. The evening breeze rustled comfortably through her frilled skirts, stirring the flounces aside to show how elegant were her kid shoes and how genteelly placed close and parallel. All about them on the porch waved Stella's maidenhairs, fragile and seed-embroidered. They floated above the heavier leaves, caladiums and begonias with silver sheened blades, transparent shell-pink undersides and gold powdered stems. Above them a few moths flitted aimlessly, tiny things with fine pink spots sprayed on a flutter of white satin, waiting for the lamps.

The morning was clear and still, with a holiday atmosphere on the streets. Visitors drawn by the agricultural conference swelled the regular tourist season.

Something jarred on Stella as she walked briskly towards Nathan's. A dishevelled ruffian walked ahead of her slowly, deliberately placing his feet straight, one before the other to avoid cracks in the road surface. His eyes were fixed to the ground and his head tied with a red rag. A few paces past him she glanced back. He stared fixedly down and was silent, but his mouth seemed to be working in terror. She felt odd about him and hurried on. After a while he was lost in the crowd behind, yet something clung to her, tainting the morning.

At work she felt irritable and struggled to avoid speaking sharply to the girls, especially to Vio, who adored her. They were unsettled and ran constantly to the front to compare notes on the visitors. Two burst into nervous laughter near the entrance and Vio hurried over. A small, muttering group gathered and obstructed the doorway.

"What now?" Stella sighed.

"Is a man jumping deh, 'M," one of the cleaners offered, nodding and pointing in delight. "Is a madman."

"Run im!" another suggested.

Stella crossed the polished floor and glanced out. The man with the red tie around his head, the man she had seen on the way to work, was prancing outside with his hands and fingers spread in an attitude of horror. He bawled,

"Death! Death!" Over and over, "Death! Death!"

She stared at him in alarm. "What he's doing?"

"Him da prophesy, Miss Stell."

One of the floorwalkers shouted an instruction and a few men sprang forward and chased him away. As he sprang forward the crowd scattered, and he shrieked, "You go see. Four o'clock, look. Going destroy. Destroy by four. Death! Death!"

When they were rid of him the crowd dispersed. The girls still chuckled and nudged each other, welcoming excitement, then bustled back to their places. But Stella was tense and jumpy now, longing to be home with an eye on Ben.

The minute hand of the old clock above the door crawled so slowly. For a while she assumed it had stopped and ignored it just long enough for her to mark a slight change of position. It was saying three twenty-five when a pile of hangers clattered to the floor as the fat brindle cat that slept all day upon the counter started nervously.

"Oh, bother! Mother Puss, you bad as me."

She leaned across to see where they had landed and her thighs quivered slightly against the counter. She grabbed the glass top and went rigid.

"What's this?" Only her lips moved, noiseless.

The girls stared at each other mystified.

"Rain go come, Miss Stell," they suggested.

Vio noticed a stack of traycloths under a window and sauntered across to them.

"Get out!" Stella screamed, plunging at the door. She collided with a stray dog that raced in with its tail between its legs, swung around yelping and bolted out again.

"Get out! Come, get out!"

Stella was through the door and running for home by the time the others understood the rattle of the window panes, saw the cups explode from the tea tray and shower down again in a burst of thin blue splinters. The showroom behind her heaved and filled with dust and flaking plaster and short, breathless shouts and screams as the girls scrambled for the door. In seconds, Metropolitan House was a pile of rubble with Vio and two of the other girls crushed out of the world. But Stella was down the road and racing for the corner of her own street. Past her the bus went hurtling over the swelling road surface and the horses reared and lashed out as the loose stones skidded and tumbled under their hooves.

At the Goldman's, as the house rocked, a glass pane shattered and sliced Icelin's forehead at the hairline. Still she snatched Ben in one arm and darted for the door.

When Stella stumbled in through the gate, the gardener was clinging desperately to the trunk of a towering East Indian mango tree that still swayed after whipping to and fro like a reed during the tremor. The Bombay mango tree lay on its side, and she could see Icelin in the kitchen doorway clutching Ben with one hand and supporting herself on the upright with another. Her head was bleeding heavily. The earth jerked briefly, slamming Stella to her knees on the stone steps, but she scrambled up them, clawing at the rails. She snatched the child and would have turned back, but Icelin grabbed her skirt so that the seam opened.

"Wait, 'M! No go out. Dutty not safe in groun'shake."

Stella stared at her uncomprehendingly and struggled to free herself, but the woman's fingers manacled her in position in the doorway. "O Gawd! De ground shiftin', 'M. No go stand 'pon it. Massa Gawd!"

Icelin tugged again at the arms locked around the child and cried, "Lawd! Loose de pickney likkle, 'M. Him wi' strengle."

They crouched there with their arms around each other and around the child as the earth heaved more gently, steadied and rippled again.

Blocks away, Sarah had sat to receive a message, adjusting her headgear carelessly to hold the earphone firmly in place. A sound at the window distracted her, a flutter of wings and tapping so desperate as to crack the pane. A huge bird, white and utterly strange (a sea bird, she thought) with brilliant driven eyes and hooked beak wide open frantically battered at the glass.

Tearing her mind from the alien thing Sarah flicked on one of the myriad switches on the panel before which she sat, dwarfed, and the noise of the tremor split through the phone in a shattering roar against her eardrum. Only faintly against the thunder in her head came the sound of her own screaming. Ripping the gear away she lurched out of the chair and to the ground as the switchboard opened out in a sheet of flame. Her head thudded and she locked her arms around it, scrambling to a window. Figures scurried surprisingly far below in an excited, noiseless pantomime. She struggled with the door but it was jammed shut. Then the door handle shook furiously, pulled from outside. But it did not rattle. Even as they burst the door in soundlessly and hauled her fainting down the steps, she wondered at the silence.

All seemed quiet when Stella and Icelin agreed to cross the yard and sit in the doorway of the wooden outhouse until Abe came home, but Stella insisted that Icelin go ahead with the baby.

"Miss Stella, what, 'M? You not going inna house?"

"Icelin, if anything happen to the house an' I don' have them papers we wouldn' have a farthing. Is quiet now. I going bring them."

She dashed through the kitchen, through the dining room, into the living room towards the massive inlaid desk that had been Jacob Stollmeier's. One of the floorboards had lifted and she tripped, shoving off an odd assortment of papers. They slid behind, between the wood and the wall. She edged into the corner and reached down, seeing the packet she wanted, just out of reach. Her skirt hitched on something as she reached over, pinning her into the corner, and she was still struggling when an angry murmur rumbled under the house.

Glancing wildly over her shoulder she tugged faster and faster in her efforts to loose the gown. It refused to give. In her haste she could not make out where it was caught. She wrenched round, struggling. Damp folds of cloth lapped her legs, wedging her more securely. Fear trickled down her back, drenching the fabric. Her eyes riveted on the wall beside her. A thin line started at the bottom, opened to a wedge-shaped crack, zipped jaggedly up to the ceiling then yawned out, tearing the wall apart.

Her scream was lost in a rending, grating roar. Thought, decision, everything slid away in desperation that translated into strength. Possessed by a power she had never had she tore herself out of the dress even as the house crumbled between her and the door. The building heaved and split and she lost balance and crashed to her knees. Plaster rained onto her hair and bare skin, but she rolled, shredding her knees on splintered ornaments, to shove aside the heavy mahogany chair at the desk. Under the desk she flung herself, slamming head and shoulders on the unyielding wood. She had barely pulled in her legs and drawn her knees against her chin when the ceiling crunched in.

Things might have gone differently if old Coachie Castries who had served the Stollmeier family from Jacob's childhood had not been pensioned off. But the buggy had rolled more and more slowly and eventually Rudy, his new employer, had changed Coachie for a younger man. When the road lurched and split beneath their hooves the horses bolted and the new coachman was powerless.

Rudy attempted to scramble forward but jerked off onto the gravel. He sprang after the buggy then fell as the road heaved beneath him on the crest of a wave, sank sickeningly in a trough and crested again before he could regain his balance. When it stopped he got unsteadily to his feet, ran his fingers through his hair helplessly and looked around. He began to walk, slowly, stunned by the destruction. He found himself on King Street and crossed it to a tumbled grey wall under a heap of dusty allamanda flowers. He halted and stared at the doorway. Catherine clung to the doorpost.

He was never aware of going to her, yet he found their hands tightly locked in a moment of silence at the heart of the shattered city. There was nothing to say. They were cold, tough people whose worlds had long ago touched for a few months and never effectively separated again. Suddenly, distractedly, he felt he must salvage what he could for her and he turned into the house. She followed in the same haze of disorientation. They were inside when the second tremor struck, much lighter, but beyond the resistance of weakened brick. The walls bulged inward as the shattered framework crumpled around them.

Bricks tumbled from above the entrance and above them a sturdy beam that had run' front to back of the room chopped downwards. Catherine saw him reeling out of the way, tripping over glass and debris and going down with the thick beam slanting above him. The upper end wedged in the join of the old wall and the ceiling at the back of the room and the lower end pinned his leg to the ground. The tremor was over but still the building folded gradually inward. The massive stone wall behind Rudy's head slowly, slowly caved forward, still in one piece but leaning, toppling. Precariously it halted against the beam. For a while, quiet. A tiny shower of plaster. A brick sliding. They stared at each other, hardly breathing, their shoulders drawn together against the inevitable collapse of the whole structure.

Get out. His lips barely moved. His eyes fixed on the upper end of the beam that pinned him to the ground, and held there unwaveringly. The slightest movement would dislodge it and it groaned under the weight of the wall that was certain death above them. Leave me.

Eyes fixed on him she edged towards the door. He nodded almost imperceptibly. But, outside, feet and horses' hooves beat helter-skelter down the street, and above the commotion shrilled screams of fire. She eased herself through the partially blocked entrance, half blinded by dust and sweat. Only driven shadows, images of fear, rushed past. No one would stop.

Out of the shouting and the haze came the realisation that the haze was more than dust. The city was burning and from nearby buildings thin fingers of smoke groped into the street. A fair man in clericals and a short coloured woman jostled past in the crowd — Reverend Luke Horne and that O'Reilly woman he had married. Help me. She wondered who had screamed. The minister stopped and his wife was carried on in the current down the narrow space between the doomed buildings. Horne struggled to cross the street but stumbled against the crowd and then disappeared as a carriage lurched forward. His hand raised bloodily towards Catherine then sank into the dust.

She turned from the horror of the street to the horror of the wreckage, squeezing back through the entrance. Rudy was still breathing, but she could not move him any more than she could halt the fire. She could only end it, she thought, looking at the beam that shimmered now with edges rendered wavering by the heat. If she touched it.... But then. That wall would kill them both. It was unthinkable. Yet. Memories sang through her hopelessness, and they were not the memories of his leaving her but the bright ones of passion he had fought, fought because it was real, and once she had loved him. His eyes flickered open as she bent over him and for a few seconds before eternity she was infinitely precious to him. Get out. It's here. So he was aware of everything.

Now it was not dust alone thickening the air. Almost above them a soft, licking sound. His skin glistened in the heat and the low roar of the next door building grew to a thunder. He was too weak to move. There was no one to free him but her. A crisp flapping from behind the wooden partition, then the bright flare up the curtain. But she scarcely glanced at it. It would not matter. But Stella, she thought. Then, no. For she *had* loved him.

Catherine drew close to him under the shadow of the wall, and her knuckles showed pale for a moment in the flickering light as she reached for the fast and certain death that slanted above them. Lord have mercy on Stella. And on me. On us. Rudy stared at her, gasping at the heat, trying to see through the pain and confusion left. For a moment it seemed to him that he had not quite wasted his life, and then for a moment that he had wasted it indeed. Then Catherine braced herself against him and shoved the beam. The room roared around them as the darkness slammed down, locking out the flames.

9
Shards

ABE GOLDMAN squatted in the ruins of his house, clawing the debris with bleeding fingers. The sanity and order of his life creaked and slipped in crumbling brick, mahogany and china and his mind shuddered in the rushing emptiness. Then his ragged fingers, swelling with splinters under the nails, struck smooth wood.

The old Stollmeier desk had supported the shattered roof and, in the dark hollow below, Stella crouched with knees drawn to her chin gasping for air. Her mind blurred and faded, squeezing her back into a past where she curled and heaved in dim waiting.

Air, please.

Then there was noise, but still no air. Hands and an agony of rushing life. The needles of uncramping limbs distracted her from the work of breathing. Sunlight was piercing and callous.

Air, air.

They delivered her out of the flattened house into the un-created garden. Abe cradled her, trembling, and blew in her face, and Ben toddled unaware of chaos through the grass around the uprooted Bombay mango tree.

At first all she could see was Abe's face, speechless from the swift sequence of shock and relief; all she could feel were his hands searching her limbs in disbelief and praise. A man thumped his shoulder gladly, but another plucked at him to come on to the next house. Ben chuckled and she stretched her hand to him.

143

"And Mama?" she breathed.

But a voice fretted, "Me hear seh Miss Sarah and dem get 'way, 'M. But nobody see Miss Catrin yet."

Abe released her to hold Ben, and Stella's eyes widened as her mind splintered and reformed to contain the wilderness. Mama. Her feet struggled for the earth which seemed firm again then growled briefly, quivered and was still.

"Mama."

"Wait, 'M." Icelin restrained her, the black and brown fingers entwining clumsily. "You no have on 'nough, 'M. Wait take dis no walk 'pon street naked." Icelin ripped off her own dress and flung it over Stella's head. "Me will carry Mas' Ben up de street to Miss Sarah, and if dem have fe leave dere me wi' go Parade wait fe you."

Abe's oozing fingers groped over her face, her hair, and he rocked backwards and forwards blindly as the Shema of his childhood welled up.

"Hear, O Israel," he gasped. "Hear O... O Israel...."

His mind throbbed with their homelessness, the miracle of her tortured breathing and his own tormented fingers, darkening, swelling. How would he work? Still, still, they were alive. Others....

Neighbours tugged at him for help.

"Get away from the buildings," he groaned as they tore him away. "Stay out in the open. Get to Parade."

But Stella's eyes strained west to the city centre. Abe was swept away with the rescue team and Icelin, who now knew Stella's thoughts almost before they formed, made no attempt to stop her. Instead Icelin armed her ruthlessly with what truth she had.

"People run past say town mash up. But after Miss Catrin no come, 'M." She laced her own arms firmly around Ben, and told him, "We going to see you Goddie." But she went on, "Nobody no hear 'bout Miss Catrin, 'M."

An icy draught opened at Stella's back. She shivered it away, struggling to pull herself out of shock. Ben was safe in Icelin's arms and would be with Sarah and Nana.

She stumbled through the gate. People turned to glance at her as she pushed past in the wrong direction. Plaster matted her hair above a purpling bruise, and the borrowed dress sagged incongruously around the poise her mother had ingrained in her from infancy.

Out on the mangled street, the chill of doubt froze to fore boding. Split pillars and wooden verandahs tilted out, but brick walls had fallen into the road. Between these, across the shattered pavement, store clerks, shoppers, street-cleaners, well-to-do businessmen drifted bare-headed and dishevelled. One hugged an arm snapped to an appalling angle; another clutched together raw flesh gaping at his shoulder. Then came a woman crooning in a wild monotone and rocking empty arms.

Stella ploughed headlong into nightmare. At the bottom of East Street she stumbled over the fallen bricks and picked her way between tangled wires and electric poles. Almost at the crushed heart of the city she paused for breath. Between the smashed walls and gaping doorways the road was ripped and water mains uprooted and twisted. To the west hung a black haze.

Mama.

Stella jerked forward hurriedly, turning into Harbour Street. Around the tumbled heap of *Jamaica Times* scurried tattered figures, bawling for help to dig out the editor. A low thunder growled in the distance. Louder. With the creeping darkness crept gathering heat. Try not to notice. Running. Smoke and ash and cinders flying. Feet flying. Ahead rumbled a black cloud.

A scream. Voices, voices. A woman wailing. Children sobbing. Try not to notice. An agonised shriek, scarcely human. A... smell on the warm wind.

Past the corner of Church Street she dived through a hot, airless blast. Bright tongues flapped out of a drugstore down the road, and a flurry of movement in front bewildered her. They stumbled past, carrying.... God, no. It can't have been.

Don't stop.

An arm stuck up out of the rubble where Jonas da Silva had worked. A sheet of flame parted the dust and wood ripped and tumbled.

Dust billowed out of the Leon building ahead, choking her. A shrill needle of sound pierced out from far within the blaze and a man in tears with a small bucket of water plunged towards the holocaust. Upstairs, a woman sprang forward, her clothes afire. She screamed to Stella and threw down a bundle.... Jesus!

Winded, Stella grabbed automatically at the thing which had been flung against her chest and stared up among the grotesque writhing of red and black and orange where the woman flared, twisted, crumpled, arched and was gone.

Stella started forward again mechanically but heaving with nausea and clasping the squirming wad of bedclothes that had landed in her arms. Unconsciously she pulled aside the folds of the bundle so that the little creature inside could breathe. Crying, alive. But she could not stop. Clutching the infant she gathered speed. The corner of King Street loomed nearer, and for a while there was less flame, more smoke. Darker. Frantic figures salvaged where they could.

Faster. Run now, and don't look. Try not to see, to hear... to smell. Only run. This is it. Her chest knotted, throttling the long thin gasps that were left. Turn here.

"Miss Stella! O Gawd, Miss Stella!"

What?

Woman... used to wash for Mama. Louise something. Louise Haynes, struggling to her feet, which crumpled under her. She clutched desperately at Stella's hem, dragging her down.

"Mama!" Stella screamed at her and wrenched aside, tumbling the Haynes woman into the drain.

She rounded the corner, clutching the baby in its grimy bundle and gathering the bulky skirt out of the way with her other hand. Along the ruined street, figures moved at the periphery of vision wildly or hopelessly, shrill or silent. Bare hands scrabbled through rubble. Soldiers, policemen gesticulated and melted from view. All going the other way.

Even now....

Impossible. Catherine would have met her on the way.

It was hot now. Hotter. But she stumbled on, dodging a crevice. The tramcar blazed on its lines. No one was around but one man turning over the wreckage. She looked away, trying to recognise King Street, and above her mushroomed a dense pall of smoke blotting out the afternoon and beyond her the wooden remnants of the buildings on either side of the street roared into flame. She gasped and gasped but there was no air left and she fell back straining for breath. The bundle she clutched writhed and spluttered and she stumbled back further down the street to blow into the child's face. When she glanced up the whole world was burning and there was nothing to go on for or turn back to.

The heat hammered her back. A few men huddled around a moaning form among the ruins.

"Pull, pull!"

"It can't raise!"

"Leave the arm come hold him!"

"Pull im and leave de arm come!"

The baby whimpered faintly for the heat crushed down on them, and there was no further to go. She clutched the child to her. It was choking. She blew again into its crumpled, red face and glanced about. Jesu. Now there was no one. Galvanised, she stumbled along the deserted street southward to the sea. A few demented mules clattered northwards to a ghastly fate but apart from them the place was empty. At the market she slowed only to dip the end of her skirt into the horse trough for the baby's parched tongue but she dared not stop. Thunder swelled under her feet and the lane beside her exploded into flame. A roof flashed open, then another. A house almost shattered by the earthquake, caved inward as the wooden uprights burnt through. Devoured from inside the buildings split and shrank to weird configurations and the walls were eaten away in gaping holes yawning wider and wider to reveal the inferno within.

Out of the thunder behind her rang a shrill squealing and grating of hooves on the rubble and the sweet irrelevant smell of roasting pork. Then a herd of pigs rushed out of the lane and she froze, for they were mad from the flames. They were street swine, nourished in the gutter, thin and long-boned, long in the legs and wasted across the buttocks. The baked skin over their backs and ribs split and the flesh gleamed raw, and their heads were long, abnormally drawn out. Sighting her they wheeled, lunged back as if uncertain whether to avoid or attack her. Tiny crazed eyes glinted, brilliant with pain and terror and their lean flanks quivered at the sight of something in the path of escape, and they came wheeling and plunging toward her deadly and hollow-faced. Yet like a ghost herd they overtook her all around and rushed into the smoke of another street and she was left alone in hell.

Everything tumbled past now in strange meaningless patterns. Now she struggled only to breathe, to grip the child, to force one foot after the other. Not a soul all the way to the sea. Only the wind whirled through the rubble hotter and hotter.

Steel grey the water glittered but near the shore churned dark by the feet of men waiting by the boats. Her heart recoiled from the boats ahead, from the ruin behind, from abandoning the search. After the fire, she vowed, she would come back. Afterwards. The blunt hopelessness of it felled her utterly to the ground and she sank suddenly and heavily down to the muck of the pier. Not from fear or even exhaustion. Only there was no going back and the going forwards was unthinkable, a betrayal.

The baby lay on her like the finger of God. She could hardly lift it any further but it compelled her. Cold about her feet the water swirled, stinging the raw places clean and dragging at her skirt as the coarse side of the boat dipped up and down crazily before her. All around, tough, bruised hands reached for her, grasping her clothes, clutching around the breasts, shoving up from beneath, anywhere, just to crudely bundle her into the boat. They ripped her bodice and she crushed the child to her chest as she shrank onto the wooden plank inside.

Others huddled in the boat, and one started as Stella sank down almost beside her. But Stella's mind slid right past the Haynes woman whose mouth clamped bitterly together squeezing back hatred. Down on the floor crouched two men cradling a third and holding a blood-soaked jacket over the place where his arm had been. Stella looked away hurriedly, back to the way she had come.

The shore receded with its primeval skyline — distant mountains obscured by smoke columns and hazed with dust. The baby who had fallen on her without warning or history sighed as the boat rocked. Where the child came from, whose it was, they might never know. Even Stella's own beginnings had been swept away. Her house was levelled, the city fallen. And the dead, the lost. Mama. The waves gulped hungrily for the little boat and lapped against her thoughts, tearing away the centuries. What would it take, her mind screamed, to step out of the sea and begin again....

Night fell, cool and turquoise except over the torn skyline of Kingston where a lurid glow disfigured the dusk. Already over a million pounds of property lay in ashes, and the city burnt on. Losses mounted.

A vast mass of souls made homeless in an afternoon drifted outward from the city centre. Dazed, they fanned out to open places like the Parade and the Racecourse. They were homeless but not in search of shelter. Never again, they felt, could they sleep within walls, under a roof. Some shuffled cautiously on the treacherous road surface. Others ran. A few ran until they died.

Ninety thousand of the homeless.

Sarah was lucky. She sat on the floor of the coach house behind the ruins of the Stollmeier home and held her mother. Nana had drawn Lynn into the room, Lynn with lost eyes, mouthing questions Sarah could not hear. Nana knelt in the corner and Sarah knew she was praying for Stella and Catherine. But it was a pantomime, more poignant for its silence. Sarah stroked her mother, nodding quietly to comfort her. It was no point telling them yet that she was practically deaf. Lynn would not have understood anyway. All that was left of Lynn's mind after Jacob's death had fallen with the house.

Looking at Lynn, Sarah buttressed the inside of her mind against their shattered lives. She would let no man leave such emptiness to engulf her from within. She would let no mere building become reality for her. She took an oath in that vacuum left by the earthquake. The fear of loneliness rose and gripped her, but she crushed it, and in the dim room and oppressive stillness she crouched, waiting for her life to fill again. Somewhere, she felt with utter certainty, Stella was alive.

The evening breeze from the southwest fanned the city and the glow flared higher, devouring the evening. Far beyond Kingston, the country people could locate the ruined town at a glance.

One was a sturdy though greying woman who leaned on a shovel in her backyard and wiped sweat out of her eyes to look up at the wound in the evening sky. Two mules from the cart she had stolen in town to bring back her husband stamped and snorted. Martha Jane had firmly dismissed the men who had dug the hole, and now she was alone. Her daughter, Paula Cohon, lay inside.

Martha Jane peeled off her bodice and laid it beside a small and oddly assorted collection on the ground: wedding ring, clerical collar, an open prayer book. She worked in her chemise, neck and arms bare beneath the night sky. She breathed hard now and was drenched through, but she bent again. The shovel grated dirt and pebbles, scooping its load over the edge with a soft dull thud. She buried her husband.

Afterwards she sat frozen in shock and exhaustion on the damp soil. Then with a jolt she remembered Paula, her one child, inside, alone and frightened.

Martha Jane hurried in. Her daughter lay on the couch squeezing a cushion against her belly. Her hair was damp and matted and clung to her forehead. Her eyes were wide, deep and very black. Martha bent over her, her fingers testing the belly that the girl clutched spasmodically .

"It start. It start, eh?"

Paula shook her head. But Martha peered at her sharply.

"Must! Or how you look so? Don't it start?"

"No! Can't have it now. No."

Martha turned to get ready as best she could. She scrubbed her hands and hardened herself to survive the night. Walls bulged and opened in her mind, and in the smoky and scream-tattered memories Luke's gentle hand raised briefly, dustily, and the crowd bore her away.

Then she locked her mind, fastening it on Paula, and put away the day. But Paula, knotted with fear and grief, fought the pains and it was hours before Martha held her grandson. Then she cleaned Paula and left her to rest, pale and breathing raggedly. Martha Jane kicked aside the blood-stained linen and gathered up the infant who bawled healthily on the clean pillow. She clutched him to her and blotted out all else. The horror and grief of a lifetime had overtaken her in a single evening and she forced her way out on the other side, tough and timeless as the bones of the mountain.

"Hush. Not to cry, baby. You an I never goin' cry. None of them strong like you an me. Little Paul. You an me."

She rested her hand anxiously on Paula's forehead and rocked the child. But a face haunted her, determined in the midst of the crowd that shoved and trampled before the fire, a face compelling them from a smoke-filled doorway. A woman had beckoned and Luke stopped forever, trying to turn and falling, falling, and the woman turned back into the smoke with her face of stone.

Who knew anything of Catherine? Abe Goldman had enquired along the way and could think of nowhere else to look. Desperately he wanted to take for Stella some hope, some word. But at least he knew now that Stella had reached the Parade at last. On East Street he had met one of his workmen, who had seen her, but it had been hours of uncertainty once he heard that she had attempted to reach King Street. And he should have known she must, once Icelin could take Ben to Sarah.

He trudged north, towards the Parade again. A preacher hailed him sternly. The Bedwardites were out. They acclaimed the foresight of the prophet and sprinkled water from the Hope River liberally on as many of the injured as they could reach. Abe faltered and shrank, and for a moment he was a child again. Nothing was left, and if only someone would take care of him.

Along Charles Street his feet slowed before a pile of stone that loomed up near a dark corner. The synagogue was gone. At the outer ring of the debris he hesitated. Even now, among the ruins, he could not walk carelessly upon this ground. Every step turned him back. At first a gentle lapping on the borders of memory and then he bent forward, holding a broken column as the full force of his boyhood swept over him. *Lord I love the*

habitation of thy house and the place where thy glory dwelleth.
All was twisted and broken. The Arch of the Echal and the marble tablets with the commandments in gilt letters, gone. The brocaded silk and wool covering for the Tebah must be buried in dust and the huge hanging light in fragments. He laid his face against the cold, broken stone.

Wind stirred the dust and the flapping wooden panels sent the shadows scuttling around him mockingly. A light flashed, offering flickering glimpses of the wreckage, and footsteps crunched the rubble. Men held up the light and shadows fluttered as the lamp passed from hand to hand. Abe distinguished one of the dusty faces. The beard was matted and one lens of the gold-rimmed spectacles cracked. The skull-cap was crushed and stained. But it was his father. Abe stepped forward but no one distinguished him from the other ghosts that flitted in the guttering light.

Aaron Goldman knelt in the dust and began his prayers. *Be not ashamed, O Jerusalem! Neither be thou confounded. In thee shall the poor of my nation again find a refuge, when the city shall be built on her own mould.*

Then the Shema came down the ages. It seemed to Abe that it was addressed to him and that he was hearing it for the first time. All grey the men were, clothes, faces, even voices; and they melted back through the dust, but the Shema hung crystallised bright and shatterproof in the ruin. *Before Abraham was, I am. Hear, O Israel, the Lord thy God, the Lord is One.*

It was the final separation. They walked past him unseeingly and he let them pass without rebuke.

Outside, on the dim streets leading north to the Parade and the Racecourse, the people of Kingston still drew their scattered possessions in crocus bags, bed sheets, handcarts. A couple of mule-drawn carts were moving now, reeking of their unmentionable contents.

One was roughly covered with bits of drapery and straw

matting. Another was open and, on top, a prominent businessman sprawled in the careless indignity of death upon countless
others. Probably they were his store clerks, his janitor. Now they
were tangled together for all eternity. How fragile his achieve-
ments had been, the rich old Syrian. By daylight there would be
many such carts. There would be no time for ceremony unless
the authorities dared face a plague-ridden city. The dead must
be buried at once.

As he approached the Parade, Abe turned over in his mind the
directions for finding Stella. At the same time, his own ruin forced
itself on his awareness, suddenly becoming real to him. The
house was gone, not yet paid for, and the insurance questionable.
His showroom was destroyed. The workshop survived and there
was good lumber in store, but it would take months to build up
new stocks of furniture. And who would buy? The people of
Kingston would need capital for other things.

Then what of Stella, and Ben?

Stella. His legs had buckled under him when Icelin bawled
that she had run back into the house. Then a weak thumping as
he tore at the wreckage. From the street, two men had heard him
yelling and had run in. They cleared the surface of Jacob
Stollmeier's massive desk and reached around, tugging away
bricks and split wood. His finger tips just touched her. They had
drawn her out, faint and gasping for air but uninjured. Then,
unthinkably, she had vanished in the chaos of the city.

Yet Stella and Ben were safe. But homeless. Of course he had
much to be thankful for. So many had died. Something odd about
that sequence of thought. God forgive, it was not what he meant.
And yet.... A cart rumbled behind him and he quickened his
steps, fighting nausea.

Parade was less difficult to search than it had been when he
tried earlier. Still the homeless struggled in, little lost bands of
broken families, neighbours, groups of friends and visiting businessmen. Some drifted in with news of fire near the wharf,

sweeping towards stacks of coal, thousands of tons, they said. Stores worth substantial capital stood unprotected now. Some left to help salvage, a few to loot. However, most groups sat in silence, mesmerised by the fire that still raged hopelessly out of control as the breeze fanned it above the puny figures struggling with water and blankets. From the Parade, no one could see the efforts of the firemen — only that the glow brightened, waned, flared again. In the warehouses, turpentine, paints, puncheons of rum exploded and sent up jets of flame. Brilliant spouts hissed up from drugstores and were visible from the open land. Years of accumulated capital and careful investment riddled the sky with light.

Against this latter-day scenario of fire, ruin and despair, the street preachers gesticulated in triumphant frenzy. The Bedwardites knelt in a circle around their cross, a rough contraption of broken wood jammed crookedly in the earth and casting twisted shadows on face after face. The smoky glow of kerosene lamps silhouetted the swaying, chanting figures, and against the low rumble from the city there beat the persistent heady rhythm of their chorus and impassioned clapping. Abe felt the power of the circle. Its white-clad figures rocked in and out so that it closed and opened, sucking at him as he passed. He shrank as the image of their cross started and danced across his path and the shrill disharmony of the chant swelled over him. Suppose it was the end as they said? How could one be sure? And, even if the end were in sight, meanwhile... yes, what of meanwhile?

Something took form in his mind as he searched the dislocated groups in the darkness. A strange man passed, eyes locked to the earth and arms rigid at his sides. Abe remembered him, an inmate of the asylum, one whom Abe had seen sometimes being driven out in a family buggy. Then he noticed others, drifting among the dazed, the hysterical, the heartbroken. Lunatics had escaped the tumbling asylum into a broken world. With a struggle he composed himself. He walked the Parade determinedly, and at last a lone, slight figure sat with head thrown back gulping the night air. He sank to his knees and she lifted from her lap a shapeless wad of fabric and laid it on the grass.

He held her wordlessly, almost fiercely searching her face, which was remote and unreachable.

"When I couldn't find you," he breathed at last, "I wanted to die."

"From the boat, it was so hard."

Somewhere near the asylum, she thought, they had been put ashore. Out there was damaged too and no one had time to help, but there was a driver coming in to look for his brother. When she eventually reached Parade, she could find no one in the crowd.

"Ben is at East Street with Sarah," Abe hastened, and her strained mouth relaxed and quivered. Then her face tightened again.

"Mama."

He grew very still but tightened his grip and her reserve broke. It all tumbled out disconnectedly.

"I haven't found her. And worse, you know, she hasn't come.... Under the desk there and through the dust, I knew you would come, and she was there, I tell you. She said *Stella*. Not calling, only calming me. Then when you took me out I didn't see her. So I ran all the....

"It was a furnace, but I... searching for a way through the smoke, the screaming. But it's all gone, Abe.

"And she didn't come. When I tried... only a wall of fire. She was not in the boat. But I had to, the baby was choking too. No, really. Look, a baby. She just threw it to me, this woman all alight. I don't know, another burning house. God knows how to find out.... Abe, Mama wasn't in the boat."

"How you reached Parade?"

"The driver talked and cried all the way. I don't know what he said. I couldn't listen."

"You're safe, and Ben. I can face anything else."

"Where we'll go? What about Sarah?"

"Safe. We're to go to her. Icelin is coming to help you find the place."

"I'll come with you."

He held her, whispering that he must not stay.

"Listen. We have nothing. I've thought of a way we can live, but I must start now. Now."

She searched his face distractedly.

"Coffins, Stell. We going make coffins."

He tensed, fearing she would shrink away, but she tightened her fingers on his shirt. Glad, so glad he had thought so fast. So practical. And oh, his poor hands. She laid her cheek to the bandaged fingers. She would help him too, she would do anything. Only first she must look again. She must *know*. And of course he must go and find workmen at once.

"How I can leave you like this?"

"Must. No use unless you start now. And Icelin is coming."

But he clung to her in the open Parade ground until she pressed him to go.

"Or it will be too late, Abe. Someone else will think of it."

"Wait for Icelin."

Then he was gone.

The little that was left of the darkness seemed cruelly long and painful with uncertainty, yet somehow it protected her. Beside her an old man coughed and muttered, and a few dim, hunched outlines were reassuringly near at hand. Further away were little splashes of flame, blacked out at times by shadows crossing in between. Above, the vastness of the fire-torn sky was immediate and pressing, blotting out from her mind the realities beneath it, so that thoughts related to her mother only flitted through her. In the darkness floated sounds of grief or madness, but disembodied. A child sobbed here and there on a questioning, disconsolate note. Adults called to each other, to their children.

Their cries were muted sometimes, respectful of the sleeping or the dead, sometimes with shrill panic, sometimes with a tremble of relief. Voices rose only to melt again into the general disorder. Beyond Stella, the darkness was audible with a low tense humming. Weeping and complaint, pain and anxiety struck their separate notes but together merged into a strange monotone, deep, taut, rushing all around, between her and the thunder of the fire.

At night it seemed that all that was necessary was to wait for this humming darkness to clear. It seemed that if only the sun rose — and there was no sense of certainty whatever that it would — if the sun rose at all, the fire would be controlled, damage could be established, the lost found, the dead buried. She sat in an agony of waiting, but in expectation that when morning came she could search out the pieces of her life and fit them together, however jaggedly. It had seemed so to her under the pall of darkness.

As the night thinned, the shadows about her took form and substance. On her right an elderly woman, crouched, half-lying, across her bundle. It was large and heavy for a woman of her age to have carried; perhaps it belonged to someone else. She moaned, but no one came forward to comfort her. Stella's eyes strained away into the dimness. She gathered closer to her the baby that had come to her in the fire, and she eased herself achingly to her feet in the grey light before dawn. She reached down and touched her feet, peering beneath her hem. They were swollen tight but she forced them into her shoes and stood.

It was brighter now, and the circle of figures extended further than she had expected. She took a few cautious steps and stopped abruptly. She stood at the centre not of a circle but of an indefinite mass. The elderly soul near her still clutched her bundle and moaned, and it was not a bundle but an old man, lost and ill-looking. Stella took a step closer and saw that he was dead.

The sun rose and the horizon slid back to uncover more and more of the Parade and its crumpled occupants, fifty, a hundred, hundreds of the derelict.

Icelin found her. She had followed the directions Abe had wrung from the workman. After salvaging what she could and trundling it up East Street in the wheelbarrow, she had left Ben sleeping, exhausted by his hilarious ride to Goddie Sarah. Icelin had brought milk and a little bread, and Stella unwrapped the grimy bundle with the strange baby, who swallowed greedily the milk that they dribbled into her mouth.

Icelin talked as they fed her. They were to go to East Street, Icelin said. The house had fallen but Miss Sarah and her mama were safe. The fire had not touched them and the wooden coach house was standing, so Miss Nana had coaxed Miss Lynn there somehow. Miss Sarah could hear little or nothing, but she was calm and — look, she had dressed the gash that cut across Icelin's hairline. Mr Abe and Miss Nana said they would all stay together in the coach house. Icelin hesitated, then added that there was no other news. She took the baby from Stella and settled it on her own shoulder.

Stella kept a little of the bread and sent Icelin back to East Street with the baby. Then she began to weave through the crowd on the Parade, searching. A woman of her own age pressed her arm, asking in a strained, hesitant voice whether she had seen Lettie.

"Five. With a burn mark...."

She traced it down the side of her face, and when Stella shook her head and tried to slip away the woman's hand tightened.

"Help me find her." Her voice rose in anger, "Wait!"

Stella pulled away hastily, paying less and less attention to the hands that beckoned and groped at her.

"Have you seen.... Do you know...?"

She stopped beside one boy who begged for water, but

when she had filled a tin at the fountain she could not find him again. The Greenidge family huddled together around two crocus bags of their belongings, lamenting their house. But they were all together, she thought furiously. A middle-aged man whom she had never seen before stared at her with the colour rising slowly in his face, and he pointed, hissing under his breath. When she shrank away he yelled,

"You do it! You. Is fe you!"

In and out she wove, and Racecourse was so much wider. Must be thousands there, she thought. But it was further away. Mama would never have passed Parade to go there.

But then. If Catherine had been able to reach Parade, she would have been at the Goldman house instead by the time Abe dug out the desk. She would have met Stella on the way into the city. She would have held her and.... And surely it could still happen.

She was hurt — that was it — not badly, only enough to keep her from finding them. Stella began to pray that her mother was lying somewhere, a little injured. Just enough. A broken leg. She wiped her eyes and held her head to ward off madness.

Then Mama had not reached Parade. And she was nowhere along the way. Unless someone had helped her. Where to?

Stella paused to work out the direction to the hospital. The fire had stopped at the Parade, not affecting the buildings beyond, and these were mainly of wood. As she walked north she saw that they had been little damaged by the earthquake. Before the hospital milled hundreds like herself, exploring the last, slim hope, bodies drenched with effort and anxiety. Pressing into the heat and sourness she strained to reach the porter. It was late afternoon before she elbowed her way into the dim room, which seemed almost clear, apart from a few attendants picking their way among the shadows. Stella touched the sleeve of a nurse near the door.

"My mother," she began.

"Look through, look through!" The nurse indicated the room at large with a broad sweep of her hand.

Something grasped Stella's ankle and she started, gasping, as her eyes adjusted to the dim light. The floor was dark from wall to wall with people tossing, moaning, silent, and among them nurses and doctors picked their way hopelessly trying to distinguish the living from the dead, and administering opiates for severe wounds and burns, for spine injuries and multiple fractures.

"Stella!"

She swung around to the sound of her name. Dr Eliot, who had tended her as a child and delivered both her babies, looked old and exhausted. His left arm was in a sling.

"You helping here?"

"Mama! You seen my mother?"

He stared at her, bewildered for a moment, then answered sadly, "I don't think so." He shook his head. "Try that side. Well. Better look right through." He detached her gently and turned away, leaning over a woman near his feet briefly and drawing the cover over her head. He glanced up and saw her expression.

"This isn't your mother."

When she left the hospital it was night. Kingston burnt on. She found a place, back on the Parade, near to a family that she knew by sight, gratefully accepted a piece of hard bread and sank onto the short, sharp grass. Ben, at least, was safe.

In the second dawn after the earthquake she limped from the south side of the Parade back into the city. Under a dense pall of smoke it lay in heaps of rubble and deserted but for a few forms bending and tugging. Some of the streets were impassable, and soon she could hardly tell one from the other. Against the lurid glow of fires which yet raged in the distance persisted the dark outlines of ragged bands, men and women with children clinging to their hips and shoulders, with their injured on rough stretchers between them, with all that was left of homes and possessions rolling before them in wheelbarrows. By now she had heard that about two thousand crammed the Parade and countless more clustered on the Racecourse. Behind them, the levelled ruins smoked in scattered piles down to the sea and at times the ground still trembled with a sound like distant thunder.

But she must find the place. That much she must do.

To the south though, along what should have been King Street, regular patterns formed on either side of the street, row upon dark still row, strangely neat in the midst of chaos. Then the wind swept up from the sea and she gasped, buckling. The impact of the stench knocked her back, like a physical blow, and she wrenched around, away from the orderly lines laid out for the carts that trundled by. Then she stopped cold under the brilliant sunshine and would have turned back to the search but another, stronger force halted her, a determination filling her inexorably like molten metal flowing and hardening in her — never to look back. Mama, she responded. Go with God, then, wherever you are. Go with God. She stumbled away up the street and out of the catacomb that had been Kingston.

Against a huge, upturned foundation stone she slumped to command her breath and gather her bearings. There was nothing familiar about the isolated arches, tumbled beams, charred brick and fragments of stone and glass that stretched from beneath her feet and away on every side. Fifty acres of blackened rubble extended to the low jagged skyline, broken by thick, dark, smoke columns. Nothing was real about the dusty forms they were uncovering on either hand and dragging to the roadside. Wildly she glanced about for the city, but it was gone.

II
The Covenant

10

The Scissors

THE GOLDMANS were a sensitive, demonstrative family and everything flowed through Grace. Their desires, pains and laughter coursed through her and became her own, and her whole soul was mapped out on her face. Yet she was different from them, soft but unmalleable, fiery but healing. Papa and the boys clung to her despite conflicts among themselves and although Ben kept warning her to stop quoting poetry at him. To Mama she was something set apart, a gift from God.

It was not favouritism. Stella brooded over her sons in fear and laughter. Ben, who was almost nine, pampered through babyhood, grew to a spoilt boy, headstrong and dangerously charming. It was a good tamarind switch he needed, Icelin knew, but his father postponed it. Vern, even at three years old, was obviously different. His bottomlessly black eyes captured and drowned you, yet his attractiveness was unlike Ben's — nothing of the rakishness. But Grace Leonie. She was the comforter. To Stella's mind, Grace had been bestowed upon them in acknowledgement of a wound never to be healed.

Like Ben, Grace noted that they had no gramophone and rarely went to moving pictures at the Palace Cinema. Still she said nothing until the early years of the Great War when she was nearly eight and the house on Windward Road seemed suddenly cramped.

"Mama," she began one day, over a bowl of pimento berries.

"My baby?" For Stella, running her fingers through the mauve beads for the liqueur, Mama was a word of purest balm and scorching recollection. Her long, certain fingers quivered and paused momentarily.

"Mama, you don't like Charlie Chaplin?"

"I find he looks so foolish."

"And why we don't move, like Lisa?"

A pause. Then Stella dipped into the bowl again. "Not yet. We being a little careful now."

Grace knew what that meant. It had to do with the way her mother shared things scien... scientifically, cutting melon lengthwise to give everyone an equal share of the middle, which was sweetest. It had to do with her father working at nights, walking sometimes when he should take the tram.

Stella glanced up and, as usual, the child had everything in her face. Grace's mouth was pursed reflectively, her eyes deep and wide with understanding. Yet what could a child know of fire and ruin, the nights on the Parade, months with Sarah in the coach house at East Street, of years of second glances at older, straight-backed women of Catherine's build. Of hopeless hoping. It had to do with the bitter, useless struggle with the insurance company. All the while Abe had been straining to pull them back from destitution. Stella had helped him hammer together the coffins which kept them alive — and not even one for Catherine.

"We must be careful," Stella repeated inscrutably, "and you must help all you can."

Then Grace began to save. She emptied out her prized collection of John Crow beads, sending hundreds of tiny, brilliant little red and black seeds bouncing and scattering away in the garden, and she began to fill the pan with half-pennies earned by watering Goddie Sarah's begonias. She reduced her purchases of paradise plums from the vendor at the school gate and once even retained half her offering at Sunday School. But that day the lesson was about some man who held back part of the Lord's money and died on the spot (it was a name like Anancy but of course it was not Anancy) so after a nightmare week Grace added the offending coppers to the Sunday offering. Ben found out and laughed at her, but he didn't haig or torment her, as he would haig Vern or his parents at every opportunity. When Ben started to nag he was in your skin like cow itch, but usually he eased up on Grace.

It was a busy time quite apart from school, with cricket in the backyard and dolly house and not to forget to learn golden texts before Sunday School came round again. The Bible occupied a low shelf that any child could reach and it had pictures that Vern especially liked. But he was beginning to learn how to really play and could do clapping songs.

There were many songs. At school, songs were taught to all the children together and there were more at church concerts, besides the skits and dances. It was more pleasant singing at school than memorising verses, not because the verses weren't nice, but because Teacher Mason was afraid of Inspector and carried a little ebony whip in case you left out a line (so it was a good thing that verses clung to Grace's brain like burrs). Besides, everyone was anxious to escape into the schoolyard and play ring games, singing again, *Just Arrived from Colon Bay* and *There's a Brown Girl in the Ring*.

Papa got so mad he said "D—" when he heard Lindy DeLano wouldn't sit beside Grace. What? His pretty baby with her lovely long plaits? He said even if the Miss Lindy's father was blond he wasn't a man of any substance and was drunk as a lord every Saturday night. Papa said one day Mama and the children would have just the house he wanted for them and he wouldn't owe anyone anything and Mama said don't worry we're fine Abe and he said if he had to mix the mortar with his blood — and Lindy DeLano indeed.

Meanwhile the house on Windward Road, though cramped, was pleasant with potted ferns and roses. Edging the foundations of the walls were tiny red ramblers. The neighbours knew one another well, exchanged garden produce and speculated on the progress of the war. Outside came the tramp of soldiers' boots, easy, relaxing from their training. Perhaps, Grace thought hazily, they were going for a swim, for what was there for soldiers to do in Jamaica?

Nearby, Barnett's Beach drew Ben on weekends and afternoons, even mornings when he should have been in school. He just crouched there with his sharp nose into the wind and his eyes straining into the glitter of the ocean. It terrified Nana.

"He will go on. He will go on with it until he drowns," she quavered.

Stella could not bear to hear her. Never say things like that even if they're possible. Especially if they're possible. Words can seal the future. "Shh! Shh!"

"Stupidness!" Abe snorted. "Drown, my foot. Boy will live to be hung."

In fact Ben did not go to swim, only to yearn for the horizon. Ears alert, nose aquiver, Bulla went with him, as he followed him everywhere with his curled-up, white-tipped, brown tail. The dog romped near the shore then shook and settled down on the sand at Ben's feet, wide and round as the tough brown molasses cake for which he was named — or was it after someone in the war? Who cared, Ben thought, scratching Bulla with a grubby toe. Ben wished he were old enough to go to war. Nothing happened here. One day he would go. This island was too small to hold him.

The waves swirled in and out of his plans, swelling and dissolving them. Not a human soul, not even a bird disturbed the wildness of the beach, and the isolation fascinated and appalled him. Nana fretted uselessly that he was headstrong and reckless, but he recognised her secret admiration.

At nights he drew and planned. He was building a model ship, intricately exact. Chip by chip. Maddeningly slow and complex, the task of manoeuvring minute pieces into place, but

Abe had taught him about wood and there was nothing, once undertaken, that Ben would not see through to the end.

For all of them, twilight was a special time. Quite often Goddie Sarah would join them in the evening, but briefly, for she did most of her own housework after office hours. Only on two afternoons Stella insisted that she could spare Icelin to help Goddie with the cleaning, and Nana waddled over to sit with Aunt Lynn when she could. At twilight on Windward Road, everything was suspended for a while; even the conflicting passions of the house had burnt low. Ben settled peaceably with his tools, Vern with his picture books, Papa with his papers. Nana nodded in a cane-seated rocker. Icelin said goodnight, loosening the pins that held on her cap. She tugged it off, exposing the bare scar tissue from an old injury that disfigured her hairline with a glimpse of shiny scalp running jaggedly up from above her temple. Then she stumped from the back of the house down to her own room. This was when Mama rustled out to the living room to sink thankfully into the chair before the door.

"All these boys volunteering, Miss Stell. Thank God ours are young. What do they know? Chat about imperial loyalty. Damn nonsense."

"Abe!"

"I mean no disrespect to Britain. But what we need is federation with Canada."

"Your language, I mean. It's getting worse and worse."

"Thousands and thousands of lads, from a population of under a million."

"And to go so far away. No one knows what goes on until they come back...or don't come back."

"Well, there are the papers."

"Still. So far away it hardly seems real."

Sarah's attention was elsewhere, her good ear turned to Grace and Vern singing on one side, and occasionally to Ben muttering about unsatisfactory grooves and pegs on the other.

It was a reassuring room with solid oak chairs. On one side-table was the jardinière, old gold on deep blue. A second table glowed with the warm sheen of a brass lamp and its deep rose bowl for the oil. An oval, marble-topped table supported the epergne, rose-coloured to match the lamp. The room radiated warmth of polished wood, brass and tinted glass.

Somewhere, it was true, somewhere called Sarajevo, someone had shot a man in a coach (things happened abroad that could never happen here), and from then on in the papers and on their parents' lips were murmurs of turbulent events — the war abroad and, closer home, events remote because they were unintelligible. A man named Garvey and something about Negro unity. (Even coloured people like themselves he called Negroes.) Apart from Goddie Sarah, who never cared what people said, other friends of the family were offended; but Papa only smiled and said Garvey was a dreamer and that the Americans would soon jail him or send him back to Jamaica. Not a bad man, Papa insisted, just ahead of his time.

The rumours were a fourth dimension of family experience and unreal in Windward Road at twilight, for then the lamp lighter passed. Sunlight for sewing or homework had smouldered and flamed, deepening to purple on a cobalt sky still too brilliant for the lamps to be effective. Later Stella would work in the cool silence of the kitchen at night, stripping green stalks for pepper-pot soup, soaking red beans for rice and peas. But just for now, in this briefest of twilights, the Goldmans gathered on the porch to see Sarah leave and then to sit, talking or in silence, waiting for the lamplighter.

Far down the street a lamp would flare and a little satisfied grunt and comfortable current of recognition passed through them. Then flare after flare in the grey half-light would bring him closer, until a gush of flame scattered the gathering shadows in time to gleam along the pole being drawn down.

By now the deep blue calm and grey shades had thickened

through indigo to tangible night. Soft shadows separated from the safety of the darkness and fluttered or darted randomly. Sometimes they swept onto the porch but gradually they congregated further away, wheeling around the lamp. Yet even in the house the light, by now, drew all manner of flying things into its inevitable, fatal whirl. Sometimes a great moth would come lumbering out of obscurity, flapping heavily but secure in its clumsy, aimless movements until it saw its destiny and swooped with one graceful fascinating, fascinated act of commitment into its own torment. Then Stella held her breath as it rose again, knowing that it could only be safe if it made its way back to the shadows yet realising that it was fated by instinct to the circle of light which had claimed it. So with heady, flattering approaches and with soft retreats and delicate circling in and out it would make love with death. And if for some reason she could not turn out the light and slipped cowardly from the room, yet the consummation of the terrible wooing followed her with the acrid scent of singed dust and the prolonged last drum roll of its wings.

Yet minutes later, the obscurity, the cruelty, the perversity were all forgotten and the next morning would be as brilliant and tender as any other. The children would laugh around Icelin's tolerant discipline broken at times by her, "Riddle me dis an' riddle me dat. Guess me dis riddle an' per'aps not."

"Does everything have an answer, Icelin?" Grace asked, wriggling in delight at a hearty helping of bammy and pear.

"Nah!" Ben objected. "You don't hear them say, jackass battyhole round but him doo-doo square?"

"Mama! Mama!" Grace wailed. "Ben say a dirty word!"

Icelin smothered a smile as Ben vaulted through the low window and was gone.

Occasionally Mama was ill — asthma, as usual, but sometimes with what seemed a touch of indigestion. Old Dr Eliot said he was beginning to wonder about her heart. Persistent coughing tore her breathing into ragged gasps. Icelin beat a teaspoon of sugar into egg white with Canadian Healing Oil and, yes, better, Stella nodded, but her words came shallow and laboured. Yet, grey and fragile as she was at such times, she answered Grace's thoughts with calm accuracy.

"Almost over. Don't I always have it? Frightening... I must look awful... but not dangerous. Breathing better now. Listen."

Grace leaned to her chest. Mama only wheezed now when breathing in.

"You can't do anything to stop it from happening?"

"Hmm. Well, from I was a child Nana wanted to take me to the physic nut tree."

"What?"

Mama's eyes sparkled from the pallor of her face. She would get better, Grace thought.

"You have to go to the tree and stand 'gainst it and ...when they pick the bush... then... they chop the tree near your head. After that you just make tea with the bush and drink it." She paused thoughtfully. "They say if you chop it Good Friday, it bleeds."

"The tree?"

"Hmm."

"Is true?"

"Don't know. Old time people say."

After a while she reflected, "Plenty things I take. Medicine from doctor, bush tea—Nana give me cow-foot leaf once. Try one thing, try another. Different ones help. Always come back though."

"You ever had a really bad one?" Grace whispered, eyes fixed to her lips.

"Once."

"When?"

"Ben was small. Bad day. Running, running. Nights out in the dew. Smoke, dust everywhere."

Grace waited but Mama grew silent and her face distant. It

was not a story she would tell today.

Grace quivered to see how pale her mother lay on the white sheet. Maybe they should well call the doctor, she thought. Just in case, Grace rubbed her duster over the silver plated knobs at the ends of the curved four-poster and searched out a new nightie and bedjacket. She stroked the duster around the high mirror above the drawers, for Dr Eliot was so tall. Most important was the washstand. Pretty too, Mama loved it. Scrub the whole set, carafe, soap dish, chamber pot. Bed slipper dusty. Rinse it. Fill the goblet and hang fresh, hand-embroidered towels on the rack. Aah, the rocker. Grace settled into it, poking the duster among the bentwood swirls, tipping back and forward gently with her eyes fixed apprehensively on the still figure in the bed.

The afternoon was restless, cough-racked, then quieter. Wearily, Stella sat out for tea on the back porch of the house.

"You should have good bread, Miss Stell," Abe grumbled, "not this foolishness they selling now with the cornmeal. Why you don't chase them when they come to sell you it?"

"But they can't get the flour, Abe. The war...."

"Well, when the cart come, tell the breadman I say he should feed it to his mule."

"Abe!"

Grace rocked forward. "But I like this bread you see, Papa."

He pinched her nose. "Greedy Grace like anything name food."

"Going be fat favour hog," Ben crowed. "Nggh! Nggh!"

"Mama!"

"Speak decently, Ben!"

"Children, you Mama not well," Nana fretted. Her attention wandered to the laundress who waited at the back door for Icelin to take the enamel mug from her.

"Miss Stell sick all day you know, Louise," Nana quavered, "sick bad."

"What do her?"

"Asthma, Louise. You know 'bout it?"

"Hm! Well ongly one ting good fe dat, and she nah take it."

"Tcha! Miss Stell will take anything, man. Why? Is so bitter?"

Getting no answer, Nana leaned her head persistently to the woman. "But it really good?"

"Done with asthma."

Stella and Abe stared at her. Icelin came slowly to the door of the kitchen and watched attentively. The children stopped bickering and leaned forward.

"Then talk, nah?" Icelin snapped.

For an instant Louise hesitated, then shrugged contemptuously.

"Nuh ganja? Boil it mek tea."

She swung off into the yard without bothering to wait for their reaction.

Stella sat in stupefied silence and Icelin said hesitantly, "Me really hear dat already, Miss Nana. Miss Stell, it nah do you nothing you know. Dem give me it aready fe belly-ache."

"Yes," Nana agreed. "I know 'bout that. Never know 'bout it for asthma though."

"Me hear 'bout it, Miss Nana."

They stared at Stella regretfully. After a while she went back inside to lie down.

"Mas' Abe, sah," Icelin addressed him boldly without glancing up from the chair she was wiping, "if it was you, sah, you would take it?"

"Take it yes," he snorted. "But you know Miss Stella by now."

Icelin sighed.

Over the wide, grey metal wash tub in the backyard, Louise shrugged. She had known the Goldmans for years and the Stollmeiers since she was a girl, but they did not know her. If they wanted to die unnecessarily of asthma... well. Her eye caught the lignum vitae tree and she recalled that the sailor-man had asked her if none of her bushes could help him with syphilis. Let the Goldman-dem stay with dem white doctor and dead.

Icelin understood the Goldmans. She would pray for Miss Stell in August Town that evening at the duty service. Her mind skimmed to rows of white-covered tables with their bread and healing water. She would pray for Mr Abe too. There were little economies in the kitchen again and he was working late.

The war had ended when a notice appeared in the *Daily Gleaner* that the house on Windward Road was up for public auction. The Goldmans moved to a house only a few doors down the road but the place was older, meaner, rented. For four hundred and twenty pounds they sold the house with the wide double doors, the cool porch and the street light directly before it. The epergne and jardinière went in the auction. So did Mama's mahogany bed with the silver knobs.

Papa's ironic smile crinkled, the little lines growing in the corners of his eyes. He sold the store downtown and moved his business into smaller quarters on a side street.

"No coffins this time, Miss Stell. Not even coffins."

His face narrowed, and his skin became dark and sunken around the eyes. Ears and chin sharpened, whitened.

"We've always bounced back," Stella reminded him steadily, and he rubbed his face on her hand gratefully.

Then the baby came. Quietly, properly, unannounced. Grace had no basis for linking her mother's thickening frame with the discreetly mysterious arrival of Les.

To Grace at twelve years old, it was incredible how something so inopportune could give such joy. Then Nana fell ill shortly after Les was born and it seemed, even as she lay fading, that they were laughing and crying at the same time.

"Cathy, Cathy," Nana called deliriously, "he going leave you, I tell you." And later she breathed, "Sis will take care of you, Cathy."

Stella sat on the edge of the bed sopping Nana's face with white rum and paused reflectively.

"Icelin, you used to work with Miss Lynn before I knew Nana. She knew Mama then?"

Icelin regarded her thoughtfully. The ignorance of employers was an eternal source of amazement. "You know Miss Nana real name, 'M?"

Stella was startled.

"Well. I suppose I... Not her surname."

She was embarrassed to acknowledge that she did not know her by any name but Nana. Still it was not hard to admit to not knowing her surname, for servants never seemed to have surnames. Nana had grown to be so much more than a servant, but who would have thought to ask at that stage.

"What Miss Catrin call her, 'M?"

Stella thought. "Was it Cissy?"

"Sissy, 'M. Miss Nana name Adella Donalds."

"Why, but Icelin, Donalds was Mama's...."

Icelin was silent because there was nothing more she could say without seeming to forget her place, and in any case Miss Stell was far away, studying the drawn face on the pillow.

"Sissy," she pondered. "Mama never talked about... those days. Yet I've known Nana almost all my life and never thought to ask her name." And Stella had followed strangers in the street, furtively, postponing each moment when she might catch up and see the face that was not Catherine's, yet she had missed the resemblance, right here, now unmistakable, even now drifting out of reach.

Icelin averted her eyes discreetly and melted out of the sickroom.

Nana never regained consciousness. After her death, eighteen months passed as Abe recovered financially from demands that had converged on him, but then he announced triumphantly that they would move again.

The new house had four large bedrooms, which was important because Grace was fourteen and needed her own. The house had cedar floors and a front door they could polish. The front door had a fine brass knob and clean new hinges. There were more windows, looking out onto a bigger garden. For a while, however, Stella explained gently, money would be shorter than ever. The laundry had diminished when Nana's illness came to an end. So they could save money there. To the children, who had nothing to do with the woman anyway, the loss of a laundress was no momentous change. It meant more to Icelin, but she only muttered inscrutably, "Is a ignorant woman dat, Miss Stell. Well hignorant," by which she meant that Louise Haynes had an ancient, deep-rooted grudge against the world.

It would have been surprising if she had not, for the world had made no arrangements for Louise or her children and frankly didn't care quattie for any of them. She had come to Stella, whom she loathed, as a last resort when she had been a long time on the street. Stella remembered her vaguely as a dim figure, perhaps at King Street. She had seemed to drop out of their lives, back into the unfathomable and unreal level from which she came. Then she had seeped up again into the life of the family. Someone, Nana or Icelin, had said she had a child or children to support. Of course, all of her type did. Poor woman. Stella couldn't say she took to her at once. But. Give her a try.

Louise worked well enough, not more or less than she was paid to. On weekends she hustled as a higgler and at nights she entertained sailors on the dark back streets near the waterfront. Now and then she plied a more shadowy trade learnt from her grandmother, Cassie, the obeah woman who had reared Louise before she ran away to Kingston.

Nana had known about Louise's children; the older boy was mentally an infant. Nana had understood Louise, remembering her from East Street and Catherine's backyard and realising that survival was all Louise could afford. Now Nana was gone.

That was the morning Louise crept unsteadily into the

tenement after a night on the wharf with the wrong sailor. He had savaged her like an animal, ripped from between her breasts the paltry sum she had had from the man before and kicked her in the groin when she protested. Then he had driven her away bruised and penniless. She longed for her cot, for two quiet hours before beginning the day. But inside she found the older child dead. The little one had tugged and tugged at him without response and at last bawled himself to sleep and there he was, wet and coffee coloured, bundled up against the rigid, wasted frame on the filthy ground. She scraped the door to shut out the world and set about what had to be done. No outcry, no commotion. It was a fact, simple and cold as a hard round stone, and no more surprising. She had expected to lose. Failure had become routine.

Louise disentangled the living child from the dead and later, when he woke up yelling for tea and bread, she wound his lead to the bed leg and silently went on with her preparations. That day she was away from work but next morning she tied her son to the bed leg with a bowl of milk, some bread, and a few boxes to play with, and she turned out for work without comment.

Stella came down the steps and picked her way delicately across the back yard. Louise was tall and broad-shouldered. She might have been fat had life been reasonable to her, but there was not an extra ounce — only sinewy muscle rippling on sturdy bones. She bent over the tub with a tense power that drew forehead and jaw in taut lines and overcast the brows. She barely glanced at Stella, her deep-set eyes shadowed with dark memory and bitter expectation.

As Stella talked the woman's expression grew turgid and obscure, like a deep pool stirred and muddied.

"But plenty people need a laundress, Louise," Stella ended lamely. "I going ask around, eh?"

Abruptly the woman swung back to the tub, squelching Abe's

shirt against the scrubbing board. Stella faltered, shrugged and turned up the steps. No helping these people.

But to Icelin, Louise muttered, "Im wi' sorry though. Me going make im sorry."

Icelin bristled. "But after she cyan't do no better. Save she have fe save."

Louise laughed mirthlessly. "Dem say brown man wife nyam cockroach inna corner fe buy silk dress."

"Dat not your business. Once you know she no getting nobady 'stead a you. Is me going have fe wash and Miss Stell same one going cook."

"Unno chat 'bout wash an cook. Fe-me pickney dead. While me looking likkle quattie a wash for Stella Goldman fat-battam gyal-pickney, mine dead. Dead 'pon ground."

Icelin froze. "Lahd Gad. Me sorry. Sorry fe hear. Is which one?" She waited. "What do im?" In the thickening silence Icelin stammered, "But nobady here do it."

Louise stared at her with her eyes dry but dark with congealed resentment and her lips pinched together with threat. "She wi' grind."

Icelin's sympathy evaporated without trace. "Woman, what you chatting? Is what you a go do?"

Louise heaved the tub effortlessly and watched with satisfaction as the rinsing water crushed fresh buds on the ramblers Stella had set in the new garden. Two upended as the brown water ripped away the tiny roots.

Icelin turned away, muttering contemptuously, "Full o' mouth. Is what you tink seh you can do?"

Then she paused and regarded the other woman for a second or two to murmur softly, almost gently, "See 'ere. No try put nothing in dem food, eh? You goin'? Walk you maaga foot go with you mirasmi pickney. Make me see you in me kitchen one time — you dead."

Louise's nostrils flared.

"After me no pay no taxes pon me foot. Make sure you no get inna me way." And the afterthought hissed, "No need go in no kitchen fe drop cassava juice in tea. Not even fe go inna house self. Burn wangla where de child a walk and the woman go see im pickney skin rotten off with cocobay."

Once, as a child in St Thomas, Icelin had seen a man decaying with cocobay, the Jamaican leprosy, and now she grew still, still, staring at the woman from a cold black calm, her voice just a conversational whisper. "You want see you blood run like syrup?"

Talk, only talk. Maids always wrangled among themselves. The days passed and Louise worked quietly and seemed uninterested in the household as usual. She rifled through the rubbish finding nothing but odds and ends the children had thrown away, but she had often done that before, looking for anything she could use. Once though, Icelin caught her scraping up the tiny, white slivers which had fallen when Grace trimmed her fingernails.

"You dutty black nega bitch!" Icelin boxed the fragments from her hand savagely, "Where you going wi' dat?"

The woman shoved her aside wordlessly and hurried outside.

Icelin began to follow her after work. Her path lay through the meanest city streets, among the sex-starved sailors after nightfall. The tenement was closer than Icelin would have thought. Not far from the house on Windward Road a path along the drain and a short-cut across scraggy open lots led swiftly to it. Near too was the grave of the older child where Louise squatted to gather a handful of dirt, and there was the other, a thin and surprisingly light-brown tot, swollen in the belly but sturdy and alert. Strange, gold-brown eyes rested on Icelin as she peeped at them from around a wall and he cried for his mother, pointing at the jagged mark that branded Icelin's scalp, but Louise brushed him aside. After that Icelin shielded herself from those eyes.

It was only a night or two before Louise left the Goldmans that Icelin discovered the source of the woman's confidence. That was when Louise stopped at the edge of an open lot and paused for a moment under a ceiba. Icelin crouched behind its huge buttress roots and gazed up to the spreading branches of the silk cotton tree — the god-tree her grandmother would have called it, for it dwarfed the mango and poinciana nearby. The branches, bare at this time of year, spread a hundred feet above her head and perhaps twice as wide. In the yawning darkness between those roots that harboured the duppies of centuries gone, Louise's lips moved soundlessly.

Icelin's devout Bedwardism trickled coldly away and deeper, more ancient sensations stirred in her. True then. True 'bout Louise. The black twigs of the ceiba reached for Icelin's mind, whirling it back to half-forgotten tales and wild rumours tangled with the image of the giant silk cotton and the name, whispered even in her imagination, of Sasabonsum. This was the lore of Louise's grandmother, Cassie Haynes, but even this was recent past. A more deep-rooted anger lay far beyond the time of the Goldmans, the Stollmeiers or any conscious recollection of Louise herself. Pain had seeped down forgotten generations locking the present to a past that could never die.

In the sane daylight, Louise finished her time with the Goldmans expressionlessly. Mid-afternoon of her last day she announced she would go early. Stella paid her and she left. The children slept unknowing in the long hot hours after school. Then suddenly Grace burst into the kitchen sobbing violently. One glossy braid frayed raggedly beneath the shoulder, mocking the other swinging to her waist.

Ben, of course. Stella routed him out and he denied it, but with Grace hurt and sobbing, Stella bristled with accusation. He slammed out of the house, yelling that he would sign up with the regiment and that if he got shot in the war it would be their fault. Stella called after him coldly that the war was long over but he snapped that there was always one somewhere and he would find it. The front door shuddered behind him on its brass hinges. He didn't care a damn about Serbia, or France, or England for that matter, and he would have supported the Germans anyway. Grace crawled back to bed with a headache and dull, secret pain which woke her in the night with her fingers crooked stiff and her mouth numb. Stella found her vomiting secretly and dispatched Icelin with a note to the druggist, while she herself made the cerasee bush tea.

And only today Louise gone, Icelin reflected. Nah. Just hold druggist note carefully. Dark so.

Down the back step, picking her way and her foot bumped on it. Cool, soft, bloated. Hard to see in the dark yard, yes. Eh, eh! Big bullfrog, flopping like he... maim and overbalance forward 'pon him face. Night dark though. Make me see, closer.

Her face inched lower, nearer, eyes groping — then she sprang back, nausea flooding thick in her mouth and she spat, gasping obscenity. A small brass padlock clamped the toad's mouth raggedly together. She grabbed the broom handle, aiming for the swollen, padlocked grin and gagging again at the soft thud as she whacked it far out into the night.

Time. Lahd Gad, time.

Her room door yawned ajar and it was there with the oil lamp's reflected gleam. Steel glinting on the table and then cold between her fingers and the night black, the path uneven. Gnarled branches of the ceiba unclenched above her, reaching for her mind as she pelted out of its reach and ducked into a dingy back street, with a voice sneering, woman whe' you running going, when you going stop, when you going stop...?

The tenement hunched black and still but for the lamp by which Louise worked tirelessly. The mean, sour-smelling room reeked of its smoky lamp and unemptied slop pail. A plate of brown rice and stew peas perched on the edge of the table, cold and untouched, and the gravy had begun to dry in a grainy film over the enamel. Behind it the table was cluttered with rags, feathers, bones, parrots' beaks, teeth, egg shells, hair and broken glass. Tucked safely to the back squatted a flask of rum and small damp container of fresh grave dirt. Above drooped two flags, red and white. A black one in a small jar presided over the end of the table where she worked.

The rest of the room was little different. A narrow cot had been the children's but she shared it now with the little one. Yet this was so piled with bags, boxes, bottles and bundles of cloth scraps that it was difficult to guess when last anyone had slept on it. A few faded clothes hung limply from a bent nail by the door. A rough plank supported by two bricks formed a shelf for a scattering of provisions. In one corner stood a coal pot stove and pitch-oil tin, in another a rat-trap with its square of green-flecked cheese.

The table where she worked was relatively clear. The lamp was pushed well aside and underneath spread a few scraps of material brought from the other table or the bed. She had tied the pickney again because he was meddling in everything. She hated to tie him except when leaving him alone, so she tried to make up for it by answering his chatter although it broke her concentration.

Neatly she stuffed small fragments of cloth into the narrow tube of cotton then tacked down the opening. She reached for a larger object and began to stitch onto it the portion she had just made. It was nearly complete, a small rag doll dressed with blue and white cloth strips to give a rough but recognisable impression of a school uniform. And now the lid of a jam jar carefully pasted over with straw to form the jippy-jappa hat was gummed to a thick plait of black hair, real hair, still with the sheen of life upon it and longer than the doll itself.

Louise worked at an even, confident pace, unfraid of her power. Back, far back in her childhood, she had got over the sense of weirdness that accompanied the dances and choruses, the sacrifice of fowls beneath the twisted, groping branches of the ceiba, the shadows they had locked inside its massive trunk. Now she was rid of the external flourishes of her trade and worked coolly, at her own pace.

When the broken door handle rattled she was just attaching the hat and its hair to the head of the image. Louise rested the doll in its protective circle, muttering the traditional command, "Tan dere till me come!"

To the intruder, her voice raised in irritation. "Eehi?" Then she grumbled, "Who fe me dis hour a night!"

She scraped back the chair, stumbling over the child. Righting him she rubbed his head briefly. She opened the door without lighting the boundary candle to control the doll and after that there was no time, no time even to see more than the brief gleam of cold steel as the kitchen scissors plunged down into her breast. The child cowered on his lead in the corner, whimpering,

"Mumma! Mumma!"

His gold-brown eyes dilated with terror as the scissors that gleamed down lightning bright, raised dull and dripping red and plunged again. He screamed and screamed, struggling to free himself from the cord that fixed him to the bed-leg, tightened noose-like, jerking taut so the floor tilted slimily underfoot. So he skidded and ploughed face down into the slippery pool that spread widening, thickening crimson from the inert body of his mother.

"Mumma!" he whispered with his lips dripping her death and his face shock-grey, murder-stained, as the intruder slammed in the door and backed away, and the sound of running, crunching on gravel, faded into the blackness. Then he fell silent, blank-eyed, seeing only within. Over and over. The hag mounted his mind and whipped it to remember forever. Sharper and clearer. The steel pierced into his soul as his own humanity seeped away with his mother's blood.

11

The Goldmans

I⊤ WAS two days before the John Crows circled, flopped dow.ı,
fluttered and consulted over the zinc roof in the tenement,
stretching bare, withered, red heads and scratching their vulture
claws against the metal till the tenants gathered, pounded on the
door and wrenched it open.

Stella pieced together fragments of the *Gleaner* report and
connected the description with Louise, and the fishman confirmed it. A small child, huddling speechless on a lead, had been
discovered with the remains. And perhaps he had cried before
they came, other tenants in the yard shrugged. He had often
cried before when left alone. A woman took him in but no one
knew his name for although he was big enough to talk he would
say nothing. A doctor had examined him and said he was in
shock.

Icelin could shed no light on any of it.

"Me just see her come work and go home, 'M. But me work
with her long time. Here. East Street. Me cyan't feel good 'bout
it,'M."

"You don't look well, really. How you look so?"

"I fall down, lick me head, Miss Stell. When me done this
fowl, me going a me room go lie down."

"Go now, make me finish it. You don't stay good."

To Stella, the news of Louise had come as a bleak wind,
whispering of a world harsh with raw, dark passions beyond
comprehension. The grey, lean world was peopled with other
anonymous images, faceless like Louise, different in outlook

from anything Stella could conceive of, lacking values to which she had been born and affording only basic commodities like hunger and hatred. In Stella the wind of rumour stirred sharp doubts and misgivings about her relationship with Louise, about her lack of relationship. But then, what was she to have done. Faint sensations shivered along her skin — curiosity, guilt, helplessness.

To the children it was unreal. Oh, exciting, yes, to hear Mama and Goddie Sarah going over the mystery in shocked whispers, and it put one in a special position, knowing someone who had died, especially someone who had been murdered. Well, not knowing her, of course, but acquainted with her. It lent one a certain stature, a certain drama. But the notion was remote, indistinct. Of course no one would discuss it with them. Although Grace was in her teens and almost ready to leave school, she was to be sheltered from the sordid, from the details of evil.

She probed for news of the outside world, but even Icelin put her off abruptly. "Miss Grace, 'M, what you want to know 'bout dem kind a people for? It don't do to know too much 'bout Louise or where she come from or where she gone. She was a bad woman and she live in a dutty place. By-m-by she dead and all now so her spirit a fry. Best you put dat one out you mind."

Icelin swung back to her soup muttering about the okra seeds taking long to turn pink and saying how this soup reminded her of her grandmother and the old ways that were gone. Now pepperpot was a soup made up anew on each occasion.

The murder required thought though. Not the sort of thought possible in a drawing room hazed by Papa's pipe smoke or restless with Ben. Grace retreated to Goddie Sarah's grape arbour.

All of them had their refuges. Vern's peace lay within, while Ben plunged out to lose himself in the tumult of the street, so that Mama cried at night, muffled, into her pillow. It was to

Grace herself that Les came for refuge but she did not realise it till years later when some of the softness had gone out of her, replaced by helpless rage, and the arbour was chopped away. They needed these retreats for they were cut off, as a family. They were adrift without aunts, uncles or grandparents. Unfair, she supposed, but what of it. Friends were close with the intimacy that came of having much in common. Friendships extended across families and down generations so that actual kinship meant little. The early lives of their elders were irrelevant to Windward Road and rarely discussed. Mama and Papa sacrificed even the present in self-discipline and hard work to build a future which was not their own, and perhaps that was their refuge. She did not know about Icelin, of course, and perhaps Icelin had no refuge. Yet Icelin, Mama and Goddie Sarah were linked in ways Grace did not understand. All she knew was that Goddie and Mama had planted this arbour together and Icelin pruned it and clipped the grapes.

Icelin had not wanted her to come here.

"What you going heng round in all dat bush for, Miss Grace? Next ting galliwasp bite you."

"What must I do then?"

"Galliwasp bite you, you mus' run fe water and reach it before de galliwasp reach it, 'M. Den de lizard will dead 'stead of you."

Grace's feet stirred up the soft shredding leaves on the floor of the arbour and myriads of tiny silver-grey beetles scurried about. There was no galliwasp and she wasn't even sure they existed. Facts were so intersected by... by stories, and in themselves so unreal. Strange that Louise should be dead. The elusive beetles slid under stones and short flat leaves, leaving a few other darker shadows darting in short random little spurts, changing direction suddenly and slipping out of sight. The earth was soft here, freshly turned.

When someone you know dies you're supposed to be sad.

Yet Louise's death was disturbing, but was anyone sad? Grace was not sure everyone's death diminished her. Of course Louise was no one they really knew. The beetles had all gone and it was just wet, mulched soil again, broken by inconspicuous flat stones. Life was full of commonplace mysteries.

Their lives settled again easily. But so it went on, uprooting, settling, uprooting. Icelin fell ill for a while, and for three months had spells of nausea and occasional faintness.

"Take care she's pregnant," Sarah murmured to Stella.

To Sarah, Stella had to speak more loudly than she cared to on such a subject, and she chose her words carefully.

"How? After we never see her with anybody? She goes nowhere, except church."

Eventually Icelin left for the country to "pick up". She returned months later, plump and glossy.

"Me go bathe in the sea and take de water at Bath, Miss Stell. Just like you tell me. I well now. No see how I get fat, 'M?"

With Icelin back the household returned to normal. Meanwhile, Abe's business became established; it had taken him seventeen years after the earthquake to rebuild it securely, and now he spoke of new contracts to sign. By the time Grace left school, the house fitted them with the familiar snugness of years. They sold its cheap, temporary furniture and replaced it with mahogany. Mama had a new bed, not four-poster but a modern style Papa had made himself to replace the one that went in the auction.

Friends of the Goldmans from before the earthquake or since, through business contacts, from church or in the neighbourhood, visited regularly through the years. They brought starapples, cake, plantains — whatever they had. Singly or in families they drifted in and out, the Fletchers, the Halls, the McIntyres, the Durands.

Angus Durand was a close friend until he swindled Abe in a business transaction and brought him to the edge of financial disaster. The Goldmans reacted instantly, together.

Stella tried to find Icelin another position, but Icelin bristled, "Forget me tell you long time, 'M? Me no want no money."

Icelin cooked rice with pumpkin from the back garden, highly seasoned so they would not miss the meat.

Ben abandoned his arrangements to go to sea on one of the larger vessels of the United Fruit Company. A position in Customs would be vacant at the end of the month and in the interim he took manual labour on the dock. It was brutally heavy work and the men resented him at first. Then he learnt to curse them as freely and foully as they did him and won, at last, a grudging respect.

Grace packed and left for a temporary teaching position in Montego Bay but, despite his protests, Vern was not allowed to drop his studies. Reverend Jackman regarded him as his son and arranged that the church would pay the expenses for his last few years of school. Vern dreamed of entering the ministry, and the family would have starved rather than deprive him. There was no money to keep Les in school that year but he was so young that it probably did not matter except that when he started again he would be older than most of the boys in the class. He went to work with Abe, to run errands, and, although his father grumbled that the boy made a joke of everything, Les was willing and competent.

So it was this that he and Stella had built, Abe reflected as they pulled together around him and the ground settled under his feet and the house stood firm. Grace returned after her three-month job, looking different somehow with her hair trimmed short and fluffing softly under the brim of her hat. For the first time she felt, like conflicting gravitational pulls, the extremes of personality that impelled her brothers apart, straining their parents when there was no crisis that demanded cohesion. At once, unknowingly, she began to gather up their lives into her own hands.

Goddie's life was restricted now, for her mother was senile and incontinent and could not be left alone at night when the day's worker was gone. Grace spent a week with Sarah before going to work again, and Les ran back and forth between the two houses. In Goddie's garden, the arbour trailed neglected and overgrown with weeds and unkempt tendrils. It could not be pruned now for the pearl pale bunches clustered under it.

"But tomorrow," Grace thought, "I going clear it up."

Next day broke cool and overcast. That was good. She had not slept well, what with Aunt Lynn stumbling about all night gathering her shoes and asking when they would send the carriage to take her back to East Street. Cruel, Lynn whimpered, after the life she had known with Jacob to leave her out at night under a guango in the midst of all these lobster shells. Plaintive quaverings and the deeper mutters in which she answered herself filtered in and out through Grace's dreams and she was glad now after a solid breakfast to get out into the sanity of morning.

She propped up the tendrils taking care not to bruise the young fruit. Dead pieces hanging should be trimmed but they would have to stay until the vine had finished bearing.

Near eleven the heat thickened and pressed her down onto a low stool in the shade and she thought wistfully of shaved ice with condensed milk, but she was reluctant to pause and lose heart altogether. She scraped the hoe experimentally over the weeds within reach. The earth was moist so the wiry little stems yielded. Still sitting, she hacked forward with the hoe again, tugging the broken whips and ragged upturned roots towards her.

"Born to be worthless," Papa would have chuckled, pinching her nose.

She dropped the heavy hoe for a light fork and stabbed down, loosening the soil. With the weeds clear, all kinds of odd little things surfaced — old bus tickets and a favourite hair-ribbon of her childhood. She sighed and with her foot pressed the fork deep into the earth, but it rammed into something hard with the dull clink of metal. She unearthed it and shook off damp clods of soil. It was a pair of scissors, long, pointed, vaguely familiar. She held it to the light, wiped it on the grass and spun it over and over. It was locked shut with rust. Funny she thought. Years. And, yes, it was theirs. Mama had fretted over it.

"Nobody but you Icelin," Stella had grumbled. "Is you keep taking it out."

"Miss Stell, after is you same one walk-walk all round de place wid it."

Grace strolled absently from the arbour into the clear hot sunlight. She wandered into Les who was near the back gate with a new friend. Austin was a quiet boy, deeply attached to Les for protecting him from the school bully. Les said that Austin was old for the class too, because he had started school late, but that he was brighter than anyone else. He ate up the work, Les said.

"Where you find that?" Her brother grinned as he turned out into the street, and the other boy's eyes followed her reflectively as he padded after Les.

With one hand Grace waved vaguely to them, and with the other she rubbed the mud away between her soiled fingers and turned the rusty scissors this way and that in half-amused bewilderment.

12

The Balming

ICELIN CASTRIES stiffened on her iron single bed, eyes fixed on the ceiling. Thin now, and shiny tight over the bone, her legs jutted out of the faded skirt rigidly parallel. Her feet, hard and yellow on the soles and splayed widely at the toes, stuck straight up. Like a child's doll overlooked, she stared into nothing. Nothing to live for but the next day's work.

She twitched nervously for there had always been some baby, some illness, some moving from one house to the other — all the emergencies, hers. Well at least they had settled permanently on Windward Road. Mas' Abe pull it off somehow.

No use. Eggs pelted at the ceiba after Louise's wake smashed and trickled in slippery gobs down the gnarled bark and the dark, glistening trunk reflected in her soul and in her belly a slimy, knotted waiting. The sasa bided its time. Unconsciously she hummed an old unpleasant tune that crept upon her now more often than she cared.

She groaned and shifted as the child's eyes peered in and out of her mind. She had kept away from Louise's child these ten years. Tenants in the yard had taken him in and she had sent what money she could till he won the scholarship. Bedward had required his followers to give him everything they had, for he was going to fly to heaven, but she had held back something for that child. By now he was big. She wouldn't know him, she thought. She tried to blot the night from her mind, but it seeped in through crevices.

Path dark dark. Where the man come from? She held her

head to stave it off, but it returned as it always had, as it always would. Iron hands clamping her neck without warning, felling her to the stones. Hot foul breath in her face and her scream choked by the fist clenching her throat.

"I go take what I want. You could dead or live," he hissed as she passed out.

When she had come to, it was dark and silent under the ceiba with the black trunk towering and branches crawling across the sky and the stones beneath slicing her back. She stumbled away, trembling, and clutched the torn soaked skirt tightly around her legs.

All night she washed herself.

Blood, blood. And where him did come from? Cyan't do nothing. Cyan't tell nobody 'bout de path near de cotton tree — next thing she connect with Louise. And what anybody coulda do if she did even tell? She don' even see de man face. And suppose it wasn' man? Suppose.... After all, right there so, by the duppy tree. And who blood she wash 'way so? Her own or Louise? And then how Louise child face mark with blood and him eye yellow like puss. Then she Icelin pregnant and go country have the baby leave it. Cyan't keep baby and work. Too besides, nobody a Kingston mus' know 'bout no rape.

And de balming. For all the wash dem wash her, pour water round the flagpole, dance and bawl and travail round, and warrior shepherd urge dem till one prophesy, and one bawl in tongues an wrestle wid de spirit dem, and Mother Righteous sponge her wid de twenty-third psalm — but no balm could balm dat spirit outa her. And all she follow dem — boil de womb weed and de button weed and the leaf of life and all the other weed dem boil down mix wid Gilbey's wine take her half-glass regular — the darkness only purge out of her womb to full up her head.

And is fe-her own pickney she leave so. Well. Make it stay a country. Grow fat an nice. One day she must see it. But no. Next ting question raise. One nice likkle pickney leave so. And de other pickney with de puss eye and him face mark with blood. All night she did wash.

Outside, the breadfruit tree dripped with a hollow pop, pop onto the roof, bringing her back to the Goldmans. That roof, she thought. Zinc loose, and what 'bout hurricane season. Mas' Ben woulda see to that. Mas' Ben. Is a good woman im need. Miss Nana woulda know what to say. Well, Miss Nana gone. And now Miss Lynn too, so tiny, like a child in the coffin. And what a way Miss Lynn did los' without Miss Nana. Both of dem gone now. And now Miss Stell, crying, crying over Mas' Ben.

Icelin rolled off the bed onto well-worn knees and prayed for Mas' Ben.

The brothers still argued interminably. Ben annoyed Les, partly by smart comments about Vern but mostly by his contempt for Les's friends. Les was always running out to meet some boy named Austin for football or hiking, and Austin was always in Les's conversation. Stella begged Ben not to bait Les, but he scoffed and called them the little lovers, and made a vulgar noise between his teeth when Abe said Les should be able to bring his friends home to meet them and that they must honour the stranger within their gates.

"But where the Austin im come from?" Ben demanded. "We see im at school and in the street, but all the dress-up im dress-up don' fool me. He don' look like he have no background to me. But is your business. Anyhow, you know what them say. Lie wid dawg, you get up wid flea. All I say is, im is a jinal."

Les shrugged it off with an irrepressible twinkle. "Jealous Ben jealous," he chuckled. He said Ben didn't have Austin's brain and wouldn't get as far.

"He is jealous," Grace agreed softly, "but not of Austin's mind. You know Ben's bright, just didn't settle into the books. No, Ben's grudge is he just never managed to get as close to you as Austin has. You're always off somewhere with your friends and Ben never sees you."

"Tcha! After the old Ben don' have no feelings."

But Grace shook her head, knowing them. They were sunlight and storm.

"You're right, Grace," Vern's hand alighted on her shoulder like a benediction. "When we were little Ben plagued us and we turned away. I hardly know Ben."

"It's not your fault," she insisted. For who among them knew Vern, the mystic.

"Rev. Jackman says it is not enough to love God. There must be enough to spare."

Ben scoffed at Vern too. "Thank God for old Jackman, or parson Vern wouldn't have nothing but his prayer book to talk to."

Ben was twenty-five when he met Belle. He was dark, with chiselled features like an East Indian, cool-skinned, capped with black, glossy hair. Mas' Coolie, his friends hailed him through his office window on the waterfront. Ben was an expert with girls, especially those who were soft and pretty and helpless in beads, wide-brimmed hats and large floppy bows. Belle was fairer than he was and her hair a mass of thick, red-brown waves. She had no family whatever when the Goldmans met her, and Ben was stunning.

Year after year Ben had drifted, for only a strong girl could hold his attention, and no strong girl would put up with him. It would take a saint, Abe said. Ben knew no saints at all though he knew women of different concentrations. Three strong ones had raised him — Stella frail but enduring, Goddie outrageously honest and tough, Icelin intimate and possessive but still a stranger. None were saints.

Then he met Belle and perhaps she was a saint. Actually, Goddie thought her a bit of a fool, but that was a little unkind for Belle was a competent nurse at the orphanage and Matron said they would be lost without her. However, Belle had obviously nowhere else and owned practically nothing. She had no one but her mother, who wrote her from Cuba once a year and sent her a handkerchief at Christmas. Matron had whispered that the mother had put her in school thirteen years before and left for Cuba. No fees, no explanation. The orphanage had taken her when she was nine. Belle Flannigan grew up to idolise her mother and still wept over the emptiness of Mama's life, alone in Cuba.

When Abe fell ill, Belle was the rock they clung to.

"You must watch Papa Goldman," she remarked, "and that trouble you see him 'aving. Is his liver, you know." She enunciated the words carefully.

"You think so, dear?" Stella too articulated clearly and carefully, concerned that Belle could not slip in and out of educated English with the ease of the Goldmans. She hoped Belle would be quick enough to pick up the correct pronunciations so that there would be no need to be direct. Belle was a good girl and Stella so afraid of offending.

"What about your own father, Belle?" she enquired.

Instantly the soft green-grey eyes melted and overflowed and Belle shook her head. She was pretty in a soft way, like the lady on the label of Lydia Pinkham's Vegetable Compound for the relief of feminine discomfort.

"Long time now he gone. They had a explosion below deck and was weeks before we hear. They did... they bury him at sea."

For a while Abe improved, and Ben and Belle married. It was a simple, devout ceremony, rather like first communion, with Ben's rakish good looks slightly out of place. From Cuba, Belle's mother sent a blue and silver card with a long prayer.

They lived within walking distance of Ben's family, so while Ben was at work Belle was in and out of the house on

Windward Road. She was happy. She adored Ben and worshipped Stella.

So when Abe collapsed it was Belle who worked tirelessly to
ease and support them. It was a slow, internal trouble which no
one including the doctor understood. After a time Belle read
aright the greyness of the mouth, which Stella refused to see.
Meanwhile Abe himself, when the morphine worked, let go and
wandered alone in the back corners of his mind.

"Hear, O Israel. What is to go by fire and smoke... will go."

Of course, it was not until after the funeral service, when
even Augustus Jackman had left, that Stella crumpled. It was definitely her heart, the doctor said.

Smoothly they slipped into the groove of nursing her; but
now Belle's baby was almost due. If only Papa could have lived
to see it, Ben brooded. Sarah kept talking of it to Stella, bribing
her with it. Get well, she said, so you can see the baby.

Icelin knelt on the hard wooden floor of her own room,
crouched over her bed with the household crumbling around
her and it was all she had. Even her soul she had sold for it.

As for Stella, she knew old Doctor Eliot came and went —
hobbling now, but she would have no other doctor. Sarah was
there in the day and Grace by night.

"Mama," Grace pleaded.

"Mama," Stella whispered.

Belle was always there, big as she was, sponging, fanning
Stella or just sitting quietly in the armchair. Then it grew quiet.
Too quiet. They were waiting. Not for Belle's baby; that was a
healing thing they would have told her at once. They were protecting her. It must be vast and terrible. Their faces told nothing
of catastrophe, but at nights as Stella dropped off to sleep something momentous brooded over her. She asked nothing, grateful
not to be told. But she knew it was something to shake the soul.
A heaviness in her chest grew hard and piercing and she went
down again into oblivion.

It took time for the bed to settle again solidly to earth and for the fixed lines and surfaces of the room to spread flat and unwavering towards its corners. The angles made by walls and ceiling had become distinguishable in her mind from the sharp wedges of pain which each breath drove between her and her life. But now she caught the tinkling of the chain switch against the light bulb and the occasional knock of a wooden dress hanger behind the door. A bright pinpoint at the end of a dark tunnel grew and became a shape like a small, white, star-shaped orchid, almost within reach. Then it dwindled and brightened to a glowing point in the dark room, a night-light with a few tiny flies and small moths around it. Through a blur of voices she distinguished Grace.

Only Grace could tell Stella about Vern without killing her.

Vern was dead. A minor accident; then tetanus. Always he had been different, filled with a glow they did not comprehend, and they had had to give him back. He had said strange things before... before his jaws locked. Before they could even see him clearly he was gone. Yet it was as if he remembered centuries, and had seen the world through a hundred faces. Strange, Grace reflected, how she had always thought him the adopted one: before they told her about the earthquake. They had had to give Vern back.

"We picked your best roses, Mama." And she held out her hand with a pool of light in the centre of her palm. It was a cross. "Rev. Jackman said that he had meant to pass the cross Papa gave him to Vern, and you should keep it now."

The baby came in time to save Stella. Ben insisted on naming it Vern, despite all the others said, and he never forgave himself, for now he became afraid for the child. To Sarah's annoyance, Belle called him her angel and it made a chill creep along even Ben's skin, but the boy grew into a warm, playful little creature of flesh and blood, sweet-natured but spirited, and wonderfully, reassuringly healthy. Slowly, by fixing her heart on the baby, Stella recovered. In the afternoon when she rested he curled near to her in a tight little lump, bottom pointed hopefully at the ceiling.

Belle was a nest builder, whose contentment lay in eternal work and sacrifice. Her garden was knife-edged lawn, bordered by brilliant, short-lived flowers and shrubs that flared in brief riots of colour and disappeared abruptly. At the back, tomatoes which Stella had long dismissed as too miserable to be bothered with, grew to silky, breast-shaped perfection. It was a small house of highly polished furniture, stiffly starched crochet and bleached linen. Heavily spread in white chenille and veiled in spotless mosquito netting, her bed was immaculate as an altar. Bathroom and kitchen gleamed with scrubbed porcelain and enamel and, at any hour, smelled of disinfectant.

Belle sewed clothes, embroidered Ben's handkerchiefs, stitched his shirts and delicately hemmed by hand each shift, receiving blanket and crib sheet for her nursery. She would have sewed for Grace and Stella too if they had let her. But the kitchen claimed most of her time. Ben stormed out in the morning and returned at night hungry and insulting rather than eat breakfast without a butter knife or grapefruit spoon. He had soup before supper and cheese or dessert after main meals. Grace was impatient with the whole thing. She wouldn't have put up with it, she assured Goddie. Grace was furious when Belle slipped in the bath and fractured her arm yet still produced ham and stuffed turkey at Christmas, only for Ben to pick at his plate because the white meat was dry.

Yet Belle's devotion was unshakeable. She gave all that was required of her as if it were Ben's due and followed his every movement with adoring eyes. Even at night she performed the ultimate sacrifice with the same expression of unflinching, devout submission as the marble saint in the chapel of the orphanage.

Ben found it convenient living with a saint, but boring. He knew his wife's heart to be a sanctuary but its walls could not contain him. For a while he resisted the urge to find other women and threw his energy into extending the house. He measured, whistled, sawed; and beside him Vern fetched, tugged and chattered away. Then Belle worked happily, singing hymns over the kitchen sink and stirring her pots.

Stella watched Ben plunge his soul into the room he was building for Vern, and pin his heart to the child who laughed and tumbled around his feet in the wood shavings. He scattered the crumbs of his contentment for Belle who glowed with love and gratitude for it. And Stella went home with a glimmer of hope that perhaps Ben's life was settling on firm ground; but beneath the hope were surges of pain and compassion for Belle that one feels for a child who is beautiful and blind. Still, after the pain, when it seemed to the family that there was no suffering left untried, there was Vern. The child lay warm and healing on them. Ben was steadier — never like the others, never still or predictable, but quieter. Vern had become his soul.

Still Ben wandered out sometimes to sit beside the sea. The dream of going to sea had receded as he grew. Yet even now something of it still flowed through him, lapping, swelling, eating away at restraining rocks and boundaries. He sat one Sunday morning on a low worn stone that jutted out stubbornly from the shore which claimed and bound it by innumerable years of shifting, settling sand. He rubbed his fingers on the nub blown shiny by millions of stinging particles on the wind. He sifted the warm, gravelly sand between his feet and through his toes and worked them down till they felt cool and wet. Behind him the sand sprawled back amid a tangle of coarse weed and rubble till it disappeared beneath the tall rough grass, the thorn bushes and scrappy sea-almond trees between him and the road. Before him the sand seemed different and alive, clean and loose at the water's edge, not earth-bound, but moving thinly in the wind like a veil skimming the surface. Further down it was flat and glittering dark where the water had recently swept over it. Little runnels lingered where the wash had sucked around stones and larger shells, pulling at the land as it went out again.

The water itself was a strange grey-green under the slightly overcast sky, not rough but restless, curling and foaming around the rocks and tugging at the shore. Most often it was like this, unsettled and unsettling, shifting grey and green and glinting blues further out and, nearer, cut by currents of disturbed brown and ruffled into foam.

Above, it was unquiet, yearning for land and horizon at the same time. Beneath lay the real turmoil, swelling and churning, driven to the limits of the world and hungry to devour them.

It was a plain, dull day at Barnett's Beach and Ben put on his shoes for home. Then he remembered that Vern was out with Stella and Grace. He could stop at Minnie's house but — poor Belle. Anyway there was Vern. He went to the office with his mind blown clean and sharp and pulled out the ledgers.

Now there was a new face on the waterfront. Paul Cohon was startlingly different from anyone Ben had met. His tall, lean body hovered taut with intensity, yet out of the urgent, dark brown face gazed dreamer's eyes. Yet it was a dreaming devoid of absent-mindedness, an intellectual hunger. Nothing in the experience of Ben and Paul could have prepared them for each other.

Paul had the capacity to immerse himself in a task and concentrate on it instantly and profoundly. He seemed also to divide his concentration between several operations at the same time without loss of momentum. In fact, he was driven by an insatiable need for knowledge, a need so pure and fierce as to spare attention for little else. Women did not distract him.

Only one was real and essential to him — Martha Jane O'Reilly, his grandmother. No one ever called her by her married name, which was Horne; but then no one called her O'Reilly either. She was just Miss Martha Jane. This indomitable woman had buried her husband after the earthquake and delivered Paul. Three weeks later, his mother had died.

After the earthquake, Martha Jane had grasped life stubbornly and forced it on him and now he must know it. It was not enough to be physically in possession of it; his mind must contain it. All. It made life seem so short. He had done well in school and never stopped reading. He read quickly, constantly, intently. His mind devoured the pages. Yet he could not afford a university education in Britain and no job he could find satisfied him.

By the time he reached the waterfront, young Cohon had been from one temporary job to the next, but it was his own fault for leaving the *Gleaner.* Ten shillings a week had not been bad in the thirties for a young man with his Higher School's Certificate, but the job simply made no impression on Paul's mind and he left for a promising offer that fell through, then drifted from one temporary position to the next. He spent a few months in country schools. The first he reached by boat and arrived too sick to teach. The second was better, for he went by rail and arrived in good condition, except for the cinders and ashes blown back onto his white drill suit and for the scuffing of fifteen-shilling shoes Miss Martha Jane had bought him in a fit of extravagance. Eventually he returned to Kingston by *Gleaner* car, but that had its own complications as he discovered while they hurtled around the sharp, twisting curves of the Spur Tree Road with no brakes.

Job after job. Eventually he took a temporary post as an outside officer on the waterfront.

"Mas' Goldman, sah," a clerk grinned as a well-set, cool-skinned man of about Paul's age disappeared through the door trailing a string of obscenities.

To Cohon's surprise, it turned out that Ben Goldman was a great favourite of the men. They explained that they could pull nothing off when Ben was around.

"Him will curse we, sah," they beamed.

One said he had been ill and Goldman put his hand in his own pocket, drew out money for the druggist and swore at him until he went for treatment.

The first time Paul actually spoke to Goldman was when they caught a vagrant red-handed, eating a tin of corned beef from one of the crates.

"Sixpence a tin," Goldman bellowed. "And watch the red salmon. Watch the carton." He pointed to the empty spaces and bawled an obscenity.

The waterfront, however, offered few surprises and was sordid and stultifying for Paul. He came to understand Ben Goldman who physically grasped life in both hands to straighten it out, while Paul's own interest in the world was more detached, more intellectual. Outwardly he searched for a full-time teaching position but really he longed for the means to study continuously.

"Shoulda be a monk," Ben grunted. "Wait. I didn't hear 'bout something? Even government office must better for you than waterfront." He scribbled an address on the back of an old invoice.

Suddenly the four years of temporary positions came to an end. It was 1936 when Paul found himself in a real job.

He pushed the door ten minutes early and spotless to behold in white bag. His grandmother had carefully arranged for the suit. Six grey flour bags Martha Jane had purchased at a shilling each and painstakingly bleached them to blinding white, measured and calculated them to the inch, cut and pinned, fitted, basted, stitched, washed and fitted again. He was weary of it before it was through, but Martha Jane was pure O'Reilly still and she was adamant. Bag was the wear, and Paul would have one for the new job, come fire or flood. Later she acquired a few others, and with two and a half she made extra trousers, but for now only the suit mattered. She had completed the ironing and hung it on a nail beside his bed at four-thirty that morning. Paul was all she had.

He reported to Jennings just as Mr Parker's door burst open. Parker's movements were surprisingly swift and abrupt for a barrel-shaped man, and he was half-way across the general office and roaring at one of the typists before Paul could focus on him. Parker was tense-jawed, and puffy around eyes that were small but inescapable.

Sensing observation instantly, he darted a look over his shoulder, skewered Paul with contemptuously fleeting attention and barked at Jennings, "What's that?"

Jennings shrugged an apologetic shoulder in Paul's direction. "New junior clerk, Mr Parker. Mr Paul Cohon."

Parker's eyes raked him with a pessimistic glare. "You know anything?"

As Paul faltered he turned away in disgust. "No damn use like the rest, I suppose."

His wide back dismissed them as he swivelled round to bear down on a wretched typist.

"What to do with him, Mr Parker?" Jennings's voice bleated strangely through the continuous rat-tat-tat of the typists.

Parker gestured impatiently over his shoulder without looking back. "Oh, take it away and put it to work."

At his desk Paul glanced woodenly around the room. One of the girls nearby dimpled at him. "Tcha! Don't bother with the old Parker, you hear. The others not so bad. Jennings is OK. We'll give you a hand if you need anything."

Paul regarded her stonily. "Rest assured I shall manage."

He settled in among his files but his acute hearing caught a whisper from beyond her desk.

"Not bad, mm?"

Then a voice that must have belonged to the same girl who had greeted him breathed, "But what a *hog*."

He groaned inwardly. Never have happened to Goldman, he thought. Ironically he discovered that she was Ben's sister, reserved, almost painfully proper, yet genuinely warm and helpful. She was also too bright and too sensitive to open herself to further rebuff.

The office was better than the waterfront, but it was still a dead-end. He studied at night and read during lunch time. The silence of the girl nearby interrupted him, for with everyone else she was full of laughter. It sparkled in her mischievous, slightly slanted eyes and rippled over her full, tight figure. The crunch of gizzadas (glossy with sweetened coconut) and the smell of ripe plums from her desk interfered with his attempts to work through lunch, as did her own efforts, as she bustled about the office, to control that suggestion of a wiggle. Paul caught himself more and more frequently in bemused contemplation of Grace from behind. Eventually he gathered his most winning smile and most sociable voice and approached her briskly.

"So," he beamed, "who occupied the position before I came, Miss Goldman?"

Grace did not look up. From above, with her head bent, her face was confusingly heart-shaped, but her voice was icy. "A Mr Louis. Austin Louis. Left for an opening in the bank. Pleasant, polite chap. Gentleman. We do miss him."

Her fingers flew over the keys and her eyes never left the page. After a while Paul realised that the conversation was at an end.

Mid-August days lurked hot and heavy and every night Ben grumbled that the ackee tree outside his bedroom window must come down. It became a ritual in which Belle argued that the ackee tree bore fruit and it was a sin to cut it, while Ben growled that ackee was poisonous and that if he ever caught her serving it to his child she would see what Jamaica man look like when him mad. Belle would sidestep, getting back to the weather and pointing out that there was no breeze to block.

One night the heat broke in a downpour and they curled into bed, grateful to roll a little closer together. When he woke up and turned towards her, touching her arm lightly, she lay with a sinking heart, pretending to be asleep. Then he shook her more roughly so she pulled away involuntarily.

"You know you awake," he muttered impatiently. "Crouch there shrivel up like shame-lady! Listen. Is heavier."

He sprang up to look outside. Rain thundered on the roof, and outside the water rushed along the gutters spilling over, tearing up the flower beds. He tossed her a glance of brief sympathy. She would be hurt in the morning to see her garden.

He roamed over to Vern who burrowed tightly among his pillows, hugging his home-carved truck. Ben fussed with the cover tucking it around Vern's toes. Back on his own bed he hitched on the edge fretfully. Even when he stretched out, branches scraped the window and the nearby gully growled continuously in wet blackness split by sheets and jagged forks of electric blue-white, nagging even his closed lids so that he lay tossing on the edge of sleep.

A grinding bump jolted him to awareness and he sprang up in a cold sweat, wrenching Belle's arm. Through the curtains, incessant lightning whitened the room from the roof to the floor which swirled with brown water. Out of the window, through a sheet of rain, he could see nothing. Water crept up and around his ankles to his calves. Belle swayed groggily on the bed and he pushed her up to the chest of drawers and from there to the wardrobe. The house heaved on moaning timbers and he sprang up to her, tearing the sodden ceiling to hoist her to the roof.

"Get in the tree," he yelled. "I will pass Vern."

The water was almost to his thighs, but the new side of the

house was higher and must be dry. Water gurgled along the passage and down the steps, leaving Vern's room untouched.

"I can come in your bed?" Sleep-blurred baby voice.

"Don't move. We coming in yours."

Through the roof of their flooded bedroom Belle screamed to him for Vern.

"It's OK," he bawled. "Must be just the main, burst on our side. We can go in his room."

She hung precariously on the bending, swaying branch and he clambered up to it to help her edge back to the torn roof. But the thunder of the gully rose to an enraged roar and the flood which had risen like a wall against bush and debris smashed through upon the house, ripping it apart, and swept the room that Ben had built for Vern out to the hungry sea.

At dawn they prised Belle down from the ackee tree. They unfastened her fingers one by one from the branch, easing her onto a blanket. She had screamed Vern's name all night until only a whisper was left, and still she whispered it. And then she cried for Ben — who with a howl of fury had plunged into the towering madness of water that battered his breath away, tumbled him against branches, rocks, torn rails and tramlines and finally flung him in contempt against the rubbish stored up along its path as it tore out to sea. Others it had pounded to death against bridges or simply crushed under its own weight. But among the twisted ruins of houses, exposed water mains and drowned fowls, Ben breathed unwillingly.

When he gathered himself, he would speak to no one, least of all to Belle who had given him a son to lose. He drank for a while, but rum never for an instant drowned the agony of brown water rushing through dreams waking and sleeping. The women he turned to shrank from his black silences. His mind toyed with suicide.

On the beach he hunched upon his rock, studying his hands, almost expecting some visible trace of corruption. Everything he touched rotted, he thought. Everyone. The sea churned, wanting him.

His brothers, rolling and wrestling on the floor, tumbled through his brain, and Les would never forgive him for plaguing Vern as a child, even if he came to understand Ben's rejection of Austin. His father had never seen him do anything worthwhile. Then Vern, his brother, lay in eternal calm among unopened buds from Stella's garden. His mother sobbed through his conscience, discreetly into her pillow, thinking no one could hear — and the baby, Vern, healing her. He pushed Grace to the back of his mind because she was not his flesh and he didn't have to love her or not love her. Then he gave up, for it was no point trying not to love Grace. He looked down again at his rough, workman's hands that Paul Cohon called his disguise. They belied his brain, absolved him of thought, and he must, must escape somehow his own excruciating mind. He got up. Slowly he waded in, resolved to swim out until even he could swim no more. Even his powerful shoulders must give out, his sinews tear, his heart break at last and his mind mercifully dissolve. The sea curled and sucked at him and he remembered the gully and betrayal of rending wood and lunatic water tearing Vern away.

Grace flashed on his mind again and he remembered no beginning of his love for her and could only imagine it from what he had been told — the baby of his childhood, ash-smeared, a toy snatched from the flames. He looked around him in revulsion that he had come so close to deserting her and backed out of the water, cradling her image in his mind.

She was soft and tough. Paul Cohon watched her at work in the midst of her pain and saw that grief and fear lacerated her within but that her spirit was unaltered. There was that kind of awe he had for excellence, and he glimpsed in her, suddenly, a rare mastery over the emotions that tore at her. More than anyone he had ever met she was bombarded from within with intense sensations. Yet she typed on accurately. Shatterproof. Her grief had not softened her towards him either.

Paul steeled himself for a businesslike approach.

"I have some correspondence here, Miss Goldman. I wonder if you could type it for me."

"Doing something for Mr Parker now, Mr Cohon. Miss Gayner may be able to help you." So she refused to budge. Not an inch. Not for anyone. Paul strolled over to a machine that was temporarily down, opened it and made a few swift internal adjustments then typed briefly. He passed Sis Gayner's desk on the way back to his own. "What a good thing you write short letter, Mr Cohon, since you need to type them up yourself."

"Not a professional job, I suppose, but adequate for my needs," he replied quietly to Sis, but he placed the sheet before Grace.

She could not help reading it and was startled into the merest hiccup of a chuckle.

It said, "Won't you at least have lunch with the Hog?"

So it was a year of endings and beginnings. Ben's divorce came through and Belle moved to Canada. Her farewell was a blow to the family and Stella's breathing became erratic again, complicated by angina.

Grace was furious. Ben should have pulled himself together, she fumed as she sat out in the dusk with Paul. Even if, as Goddie said, Belle hadn't much upstairs, she was a good woman, and Ben had chosen her and she had suffered just as much as he had. "And I've no leave now to nurse Mama. I can't give up the job and still pay the doctor."

"Let Les do it," Paul said. "It'll be just a week or two. I'll help him if he falls behind."

So Les sat with Stella, missing classes in his last year of

school, but every day Austin trailed in dusty and loaded with notebooks to keep him abreast.

Ben made no effort now to keep Austin from the house. He wanted nothing but to give his brother a start in life, and he drowned his own self-contempt in work.

"I was a rotten husband anyway," he threw out wryly to Paul.

"Inappropriately matched, perhaps."

"Belle's a saint," Ben objected staunchly.

"Well." Paul regarded him quizzically. "No doubt. Can't imagine anything more unsuitable."

Ben regarded this increasingly frequent visitor thoughtfully. "So is not only book you read, eh?"

Meanwhile, Les made his own observations.

"The old Ben not so miserable again, eeh?" He grinned at Austin, and the other nodded amiably, rearranging his notes.

"I know this part. You can have it now. I going cut the diagram stick it in your book." Austin sprang cat-like from his haunches to the kitchen drawer then settled again snipping.

He would do anything for Les, Stella thought, and it was healing, their friendship beside her.

Between her chores Icelin hovered over Stella, following her gaze. Icelin's own blood-pressure was high, the doctor said, and Miss Stella's illness was perhaps too much for her. The boys looked up together, wide-eyed at Icelin's sudden intake of breath. It was too much, how it had all crept up so silently on her — years, losses, blood betrayals.

Without warning Icelin clutched her head, tugged at the buttons at her throat, ripped off her cap and began feverishly to tear at her dress. The blood rushing to her face would not have shown were it not for the livid scar, and she crumpled, gibbering in terror between the sickbed and the boys who stared up from among their books on the floor.

It was then that Icelin began to wash clothes (even clean clothes) all day, to wander in the night and, in the morning, to cling to her bed. Grace and Ben consulted doctor after doctor but eventually there was nowhere else but the Bellevue Asylum. They begged Reverend Jackman to see her.

"You must get well, Icelin. Miss Stell well wanted you to go down to Goldfields with her. Look, Miss Stell gone down to Goldfields for rest and she say she don't know how to get on without Icelin. Talk to me nuh, Icelin? You can't talk to me? You don't remember me, Rev. Jackman, from Miss Stella was a girl and Miss Catherine living on King Street and I self marry Miss Stella to Mas' Abe? You can't talk to me tell me what happen?"

But in her tormented brain it was a stranger's voice or one tuned specially for her — mad Icelin.

"Make me see me pickney. Make me see me pickney just one time."

"Well that's why you must get well and go. Miss Grace miss you, man. And if you went Goldfields, don't you would see you own family? Don't you from St Thomas? My grandfather used to say he had family there too. Long time I believe we were army people. Your old people mighta know."

Her mind was a rock in time. The present, the past and tales of the deeper past swirled around, tumbling her thoughts.

"Long time, is hog we did hunt," she chuckled. Then she rocked quietly backwards and forwards. "Scissors well sharp." She started up in alarm. "You say you is a soldierman? Come fe me?"

"No, no."

"Pickney eye bright."

She scrubbed at her frock and when he tried to still her nervous fingers she shrugged him away.

"Can't see it have fe wash? Hm. Soldierman don' fraid blood."

"Shh. Is a long time any Jackman was a soldier."

Later, he begged Grace to keep Stella from seeing Icelin for as long as possible. Grace persuaded her mother to spend another week away from Kingston, in the mountains around Mandeville.

"Why?" Stella protested.

"To fleet the time carelessly," Grace shrugged. "God put us into the world to have fun." She alone could suggest such a thing to Stella and escape a sermon.

Stella surrendered, she was tired. But it was Grace herself that brought solace, revelling in the smells from the guesthouse kitchen, gesturing poetically at the morning mist and, miraculously, producing a letter that had arrived just before they left Kingston. Belle had written from Canada, and they read her letter again and again.

"And look, Mama. Written just a few days ago. What a thing this new airmail is."

Ben was settled and had established himself as a customs broker. When Les found work at the *Gleaner*, Ben bought him a second-hand Remington typewriter. Paul Cohon begged their permission to type a note on it sending "his respects" and posted it to Mandeville. Over lunch Grace chuckled to Stella that frankly she was still undecided about him. She had told him before leaving Kingston that she couldn't think how to plan her future with someone so withdrawn and intellectual.

"You'll get fat," her mother warned, for the stew peas had pigtail and the sweetest dumplings. "You going be a little dumplin' yourself in no time."

"Well Mr Paul look like him like dumplin'," Grace retorted with a wink.

The retreat to Mandeville was terminated abruptly by reports of labour disturbances in Kingston. The papers carried news of the charismatic Bustamante who attacked the colonial government on the conditions of the working class. They had glimpsed him from time to time, a striking figure with compelling eyes beneath prominent brows and flying hair, and now he stalked determinedly at the head of a mass of workers.

"Such an uproar, Grace, and the boys all alone. Les is sober but you know how rash Ben is."

"This has nothing to do with Ben, Mama."

"That ever stopped him before? Next thing he decide to take on Busta. That crowd would tear him to pieces."

"Ben's mad, Mama, not stupid. Anyway, *we've* never stopped him before."

"He listens to you. Look here, old man Jacobs can drop us at the station tomorrow, and his boy going to Kingston today. Send make them know we coming."

Astonishingly, it was Paul who met Grace and her mother at the railway station on their return and completely outraged and dazzled them both by executing a few gaily complex dance steps on the platform and singing, oblivious to the rest of Kingston, the most maudlin of popular songs:

> *There's a rainbow round my shoulder*
> *And a sky of blue above,*
> *The sun shines bright 'n the world's alright*
> *'Cause I'm in love.*

"I trust I have put an end to your anxieties about my propriety," he bowed stiffly, "and I assume that exaggerated rumours regarding my sanity are forever laid to rest. Better hurry home," he added, offering them an arm each. "Kingston is becoming an exciting place, and I suspect that civilisation is about to rock."

Indeed, the unrest swelled and erupted in labour riots. The Goldmans listened to the McIntyres whispering discreetly, "Is so blown up, man. Chat 'bout suffering. Look how the Chinese work. And the new Indian people with the jewellery place we saw the other day. Is that why they have likkle substance. Plenty nega people just don' want work."

"No. But still. Is foolishness what they pay them."

"They can all go on stir up hatred see where that get us."

"What going happen if all dem rabble turn on decent people?" Ben demanded.

"Shh! You can't chat that so loud," Stella cautioned.

"Plenty people get take for granted in this place, man," Les grumbled. "After you cyan't get good job if you don't go school. How poor people can afford keep they children in secondary school? I say is long time now dem people waiting on a champion and you lucky is Busta dem get."

"Lord. You can't talk anything but Busta?" Stella leaned forward. "Miss Sarah, you don't hear you goddaughter get serenaded in the railway station?"

"A sensible boy," Goddie Sarah concluded when she heard, pursing her lips. "Can't say I know any of his people. But Cohon is an old Jewish name, I think. Where he's from again?"

"Nothing Jewish about this one," Grace snorted. "And is Kingston he born and grow up in like everyone else."

13
Flotsam

THERE HAD been one though, another Cohon, three centuries before. The Jew had flickered his eyelids briefly then squeezed them tight again straining to remember. Sunlight, sunlight. All about him the black dungeon of nightmare and the blinding sunshine of his tortured fantasies opened into each other without warning and there were long periods still when he was unable to distinguish where reality lay. The filth of the green-black floor did not soil him so much as those few clear droplets of water. And the name. But what was the old one? His mind wrestled with intervening images of priestly robes and iron instruments searching for his name.

Not the new one. That was Spanish and Christian. The old Hebrew name of his fathers' before him, that the priests had tried to wash away. His fingers rubbed weakly at the droplets of baptism. Blowing out the light and bolting the doors had not helped. When he had tried to scrub away the baptism a thin whisper at a chink in the wall said,

"Marranos." Swine.

So they came for the crypto-Jew and his family.

Cohon. That was it. He squinted upwards again but the light and darkness still poured in and out of each other. He listened for his wife then remembered that he had not heard her for... hours? Days? Years?

They had supported her, talking all the time with soft voices and hard eyes.

"We will help you. Soon you will remember everything."

Daniel Cohon blocked out the sound of her screaming and tried to focus on the pale, ascetic face hovering over him.

"Where are my children?"

But there was silence as always. Once they had replied, "You have no children."

But after that there was always silence. Nearby the priest's voice rose in anguish, "Only for your soul, my daughter. Tell us and save your soul."

Then came the creaking of machinery and the sounds that could not be her voice.

Cohon took a deep sobbing breath and forced his eyes wide open so as to search the darkness, but it was hot, bright sunlight. He flinched but kept them open, forcing himself to make out where he was. The dungeon was a deep hole in his mind, into which he fell from time to time. His children had vanished and his wife was silent at last but he was... he was not in Spain.

The sunlight of his fantasies was real after all and piercing. He began to recall that in Europe tales had reached him of Seville d'Oro, the city of fabulous splendour that the Spaniards had built in Jamaica when they abandoned Mellila. And what a pestilential hole Mellila had been. The Spanish settlers had fled it, reporting desperately of ants that swarmed through its houses killing their children by eating their eyes as they slept in their own cradles. A Christian babe, they wrote, could not live more than its sixth month. Rumours of the gracious city they had built instead drew him to the island, but by the time he arrived it had already mouldered under years of decay.

His mind fluttered back to the past, but in trying to avoid the yawning darkness he could not remember how he had escaped. It was always like that. He could not select the memories. Quickly he clutched at the present. This was a new place and free. He might not be liked or even respected but he would not be seized by virtue of race or history and forced into a mould prepared by others. His children, should he ever have more, need never be torn from him again, nor cast away, nor swallowed up by power lust of man or institution. There was a place here for him and he would find it.

From the ruins of Seville to St Jago de la Vega, on the track that led south over Mount Diablo, he had come upon a savannah sudden and brilliant in the dark struggle of greenery. Monesca was ripe and teeming with vegetation and with birds swooping and fluttering. He saw no monkeys, though the guide insisted they were there and that the place was named for them. By the time the area was renamed Moneague, all this would be forgotten. The lake would go and come and go again. Yet Cohon saw it as unchangeable. The rolling curves and fecund hollows, and the lake silkily placid in between, enlivened yet settled him. He felt he would possess something of it if he could. Then he heard there was such land in the south-west, and thought of travelling on to see Morante. Yet he hesitated. As a trader he looked towards the ports, Esquimel and the Cayo de Carina that would become Port Royal. He fastened onto life near to La Vega, although other Portuguese settlers had told him of silver and copper mines between the ports.

Cohon rebuilt himself. There were stronger foundations than silver and copper. The nearest hato, for one thing, was less depleted than others which had been over-cultivated, cleared and burnt. The seventeenth-century shipyard hummed with activity. Vessels towered up on the stocks, hammered together from cedar, and the rest of the grazing ground was thick with valuable timber: ceiba, mahogany, and lignum vitae. He grew preoccupied with a rich, flat plain, overrun as usual by cattle gone wild and multiplied like vermin. He contemplated them with a sort of calculating fondness, assessing the value of their hides. He turned from the unclean spectacle of grey-green iguanas slithering into the bush, but the Arawak name of the plain chanted in his mind like an incantation over the future. Liguanea.

Of course, he was too late for the gold. The Indians had dug for it, dug for their lives. First they scooped just a bay in a clean-swept corner of a mountain stream where the water washed the heavier particles clear and left them behind. Then they had dug the channels to carry the sand down to the lavadero. Basin after basin they chiselled in the unyielding mountain. Down swept the torrent, loosening, washing, scrubbing, precipitating from one scoop of rock to the next, surrendering grudgingly at last the sacred pebbles or masses of shining metal.

Now there were tales only, of a prospector who had spent twelve years and countless Indian lives scrubbing worthless sediment, of another who had found almost at once a lump like a guava. Now there was no gold to be seen except in sacred relics and the houses of the wealthy.

So Cohon accumulated his copper coins. He could declare with absolute truth that he had been baptised. He was fair complexioned with light brown hair, and when he presented himself at the church it was easy to believe that his family had been Christian for generations, whatever his name. He was a reputable tradesman when a new and unexpected source of wealth surfaced, literally from the deep. There was a pearl bed in the harbour. His long, pale face filled and gained colour. He would have liked to grow his sidelocks again and feel them brush his skin reassuringly when he bent over his books, but, whatever he wore on the outside, the Shema echoed through his soul.

The Lord is One, Cohon reflected. For there he was, the Jew, tortured, stripped, hunted to the ends of the earth. The Spanish had broken his wife on the rack and seized his children. Even here they had wiped out the innocent Indians, their memories and precious secrets. Yet here, overhanging the gold, on the very knife-edge of creation, here it was. In the midst of his enemies was a portion of the earth for him and for the children he was yet to have. His mind sped ahead, through and beyond his life and into the next generation and the next. Exactly when it should be perfected was unimportant. What mattered was the personal nature of the contract. It was a matter between him and the Ancient of Days.

Cohon began to think of land, farmland in Monesca or Morante, and something, though he could not quite think what, something on the fine, flat land of Liguanea. But he would need Africans to work it. The Tainos, the Peaceful Ones, were all dead.

The Cohons stayed on in Jamaica even after the English came. In the 1660s they would not have been wanted in Cuba or any other Spanish settlement nearby. As his contacts widened, Daniel began writing to his acquaintances in Europe for news of his children. Again and again there had been no word. He settled down with a well-to-do widow and established himself as a merchant. Their son, Nathan, had no loyalties anywhere outside the Point, nor memories outside the island. Even his father's memories were not his. Daniel had not tried to share them and, anyway, they were not the sort of memories anyone wanted. Young Nathan Cohon's mind held measurements: pounds of tobacco, tons of fustic and lignum vitae, hides and skins and sticks of ebony. Fifty-five pounds a year secured a fine house, one of a couple hundred on the Point — once one seemed Christian. Coinage, bullion and hides there were, enough for export to London. So Nathan had no inclination to seek further afield for a promised land. He was not alone there. Other Portuguese Jews had chosen to take their chances with the English.

Daniel was long dead and Nathan irrevocably severed from Europe when at last a sallow-faced traveller stood on the doorstep of the Cohon house in Port Royal. Sagging under a vast coat rotten with sea water, he introduced himself as Josiah Goldmeer. Twelve years ago, he stammered, Daniel's brother-in-law, Solomon, had handed him a letter to deliver. It reported that

Daniel's first children had been redistributed by the Inquisition to Christian families and could not be traced. His brothers had fled to Germany, and his wife, of course, was dead.

Goldmeer apologised in halting English. He had stopped or been detained in many countries, but he had clung to the letter year after year, even after hearing of Solomon's death.

"I don't know how to thank you." Nathan let in his visitor with some embarrassment, uncertain quite what to do with him — a stranger with a letter from a stranger about strangers, a letter from the dead about the dead. Confusing. Nathan's abilities lay in business letters, orders, bills, receipts.

"Sit down," he urged, ringing for Madeira, pondering his next comment. "Of course, my father was the one, you know."

"Yes, yes." Goldmeer stared at him encouragingly.

Nathan shrugged, trying to be natural. He had nothing to apologise for, after all. He tried to speak simply, and loudly and slowly enough for even a foreigner to understand.

"I've always been here. Never met my uncle. Solomon was his name? Aah. Of course, my father told me all about it. When I was little he told me stories."

"Stories, yes," Goldmeer murmured helpfully, polishing his broken nails on the worn coat. "Children, they love stories." He was losing track of the conversation.

Nathan rose abruptly. Goldmeer was beginning to annoy him. "Well, will you settle here or move on?"

"I have got a little place," Goldmeer ventured, "a valley, in the country."

"Aah?"

"Morante. The house, it is no good. Broken, was never large. Spanish lived there and... but they gone, no one knows." He paused, exhausted. It was a long speech for him.

Nathan's eyes narrowed, searching. "Who were they?"

"Castries, I believe, the name. A man I spoke to think so, but he is new there also, Jackman is. He think it was Castries."

"*Castries?*" *Nathan Cohon turned it over in his mouth, testing it. "Castries. No. Business people?*"

"*Aah. No. I do not know. But I think no. It is a... broken place, the house. Good land.*"

"*And Jackman?*"

"*English. Army people first, I think. The land is good land.*" *Nathan smiled briefly and Goldmeer nodded. " I grow up on a farm. This... will be mine alone.*"

"*How did you get them to sell it to you?*"

"*I travel last under name of Stevenson.*"

Nathan's mouth twitched again, for the last thing Goldmeer looked like was a Stevenson. Still it was a relief— this ghost's discretion. They relaxed somewhat, protected by each other's vulnerability.

"*Sugar, then?*" *Nathan mused. "What is the name of your land?*"

"*Yes, sugar, I suppose. Not... grand. Just small.*" *The newcomer looked away, into the past, into the future. "Goldfields. I have called it Goldfields.*"

This property in the valley turned out to be a losing concern and Goldmeer was torn by creditors. So Nathan Cohon bought it at a good price shortly before he died. Goldmeer limited himself to his store in Port Royal, as the town on the Point was now called, and he struggled there to recover himself by trade. Meanwhile, Nathan's son, Isaac, stood on his new property, staring at the house. It was a damp, vermin-ridden barn of wattles, plaster and leaking thatch, and Isaac Cohon wondered what he could do with Goldfields.

As soon as he had dismissed the bookkeeper, O'Reilly, who was Irish and probably unreliable, it occurred to him to improve this house in Morante, move his family to the country and leave himself free to enjoy Port Royal. For now the town hummed with activity of all types. More women lingered on the back lanes than in the old days, and they were full-figured and firm-fleshed with bold, laughing eyes. One in particular, Hannah Davies, occupied him for almost two years.

In London, there had been sixty-three women for the gallows, Hannah among them. They had huddled in a black pocket of Newgate, yearning for the world and cursing it in the same breath. Name after name had been sent up to the Secretary of State and, for some, the pardons had been granted.

Hannah's name was rejected. At first she did not understand. It had seemed so automatic. If only her name were sent, she had thought. She hadn't been caught lifting the stuff, only conveying it to safety. But a stranger had looked at a paper with meaningless scratches on it and had decided that she would hang after all.

"What is it?" the other prisoners whispered.

"She'll be trining on the clats," one muttered in the cant. This was a burly woman, charged with theft. She had been whipped and would be shipped west. "It's hard, and me just clying the jerk. She ain't no lift, only a santer."

Might not wait for the gallows, Hannah shivered, eyeing the place. They said the plague was there, and the Quakers especially were dying, one after the other.

It became a dark haze except for the awful circle within and through which she saw the walls, the guards, the other women, her bowl, the rats and filth upon the floor. Everything was dark except for these somewhat wavering shapes. Yet even these she saw framed as it were within the noose that grew clearer, brighter, tighter with each passing day until it seemed that whatever her eyes rested upon, or even if she closed them, it burnt like a hoop of fire that threw everything around it into shadow.

When they came for her she walked like one to the gallows,

for the noose had strangled out of her mind all hope of any other destination. Her knees melted beneath her and her vision was dark except for the shadows writhing in and out of the circle. One spoke to her of a paper, of signatures, justices, the king, but it was nothing to her, nothing even while they pleaded the pardon in open court and while the sheriff argued with the merchants.

They were at sea before the circle paled and opened onto the others huddled in irons around her. One or two she recognised but there were countless others. A Quaker from whom she shifted uneasily, though he seemed healthy enough. A gentleman shipped for harbouring a popish priest. (Well-served, she thought.) A few vagabonds, obviously Irish. Her thoughts wandered to the sailors. It would be well, she thought, to run a ship. A profitable business.

Hannah was a business woman. She had sold herself success-fully ever since she was twelve, apart from pilfering, extorting, vending anything else she could. With sudden, almost prophetic, clarity she decided that she would not be indentured long. Her thoughts began to run on capital.

In the third week at sea the squalls drove them between decks. She huddled, watching the Quaker and one of the Irishmen bat-tening down unskilfully, stumbling over their irons. There would be no fire for dinner. Water trickled over the edges of the boards and streamed down the plank against her back. By nightfall she sat in several inches, and the woman opposite hugged her baby high to her shoulder to keep it from drowning. The Quaker fin-gered his ration of raw potatoes miserably and eventually bit one and spat in disgust. But later, in the dark, she heard him munch-ing and a brief low groan of satisfaction. In the cabins, Hannah reasoned, there might be herring or salt beef.

It was dawn when the sailor edged past. Hannah stared till she caught his glance and inclined her head slightly. All she needed was the opportunity to come and go in the cabins, and the sailor was a restless man after three weeks at sea. The nooks where the cabin passengers lay might barely accommodate one body, but there must be dark areas on a ship for those who would find them. Hannah was certain that before next nightfall a walking mort who knew what she was about might have dry biscuit, perhaps even bread. So she slid the torn cloth of her bodice as far over her shoulder as she could to show a gleam of wet, young skin. Then she lived comfortably enough until they landed.

Port Royal had its seamy sides, and Isaac Cohon was by no means as averse to exploring them as his grandfather, Daniel, might have been. Isaac's father, Nathan, had been a businessman day and night and had little time for frivolity; but Isaac was a man of means and some leisure. Years of experience on the streets of London had developed in Hannah a sort of sixth sense about the pox and, directly from London as she was, she knew a Jew when she saw one even without the queer little sidecurls, and she relaxed. Jews were an abstemious lot usually. Good shoes too, she assessed him rapidly, distracted from the mundane and missing the fine lesion that might have warned her.

It was a chance encounter but fateful. Isaac's adventures required planning. The place Nathan had bought in Morante had been dingy at first, for Goldmeer had lacked money even for basics. But when Isaac inherited the building he extended and redecorated it to his wife's content. Now, often as not, she was there, armed with paragon for new upholstery, silk and platillas for her own wear, coarse German linen from Osnabruck for the servants. So Isaac was free to sample the succulent beauties of the Port.

The town was a hive of activity now, with continuous interchange of silver reales and pieces-of-eight, with gold escudos, pistoles and doubloons. Much of it had come in through the buccaneers, together with silk and precious stones, signalled by the great cannon booming at Fort Charles and sending the town into a frenzy of expectation. The Central Market on the High Street rustled and squawked with turkeys, capons, ducks, teal, pigeons, doves and parrots and reeked of their droppings but in places smelled more pleasantly of herbs and fruit.

The road which ran west to the turtle crawls was lively with businessmen and their customers, enquiring for the shoemaker or cordwainer, demanding directions to a storeroom where they could assess calf or yearling skins before workmen conveyed these to the tanning house. Craftsmen like the pewterers, tortoiseshell-workers and pipe-makers conducted business or watched the sea tensely. Here the choppy water churned with the arrival of the wherry and of canoes with good water, shipped in casks from the mouth of the Rio Cobre. But larger vessels were awaited, bearing supplies and raw material. The rougher traders cursed and jostled each other, while the ivory-turners hung back, anxious for their imports from Africa. Then the turtles — loggerheads, green turtles and hawksbills — would be hauled out from their seashore enclosures, upended and lashed back-down on deck for export to England and provision for the sailors.

It was a blazing heat, to be quenched by Madeira, rap or mobbie for those not daring enough to chance the water. The weather and the lawlessness spawned taverns, rumshops, gambling hells. Arguments erupted in the rum-hazed glitter of coin and treasure, resolved often enough by duels, for the Brethren of the Coast were beyond all control and celebrated by the townspeople for the prosperity they brought. On the way to their meeting house, the Quakers threaded their way quietly past the riotous waterfront, and the bells of St Paul's and Christchurch clanged their warnings unheeded. Release exploded in brawls or bloody entertainment like cockfighting, while in and out strolled the strumpets barefooted in their linen petticoats and straw hats, comforted by a cup of punch or clay tobacco pipe. Some belonged to John Starr but others, like Hannah, were independent. They had avoided the cage and the ducking stool in London and could look after themselves in Port Royal.

Hannah was sleek and playful, though of course Isaac lost

*interest when she began to swell. But there were always others; he
had only to send for them. His wife was a strong, capable woman
and stubborn when she had a mind but she was secure in
Morante, on Goldfields.*

*Hannah would have forgotten Cohon as easily as he did her
had it not been for the child and the pox. She held the infant,
cursed it, fed it, shook it at times, tried once or twice to abandon
it, but eventually kept it and began to like it a little. Only she had
not the slightest idea what to do with it. In a fit of bitterness she
called it Cohon, Philip Cohon. She gave it to an older woman to
nurse for her and paid what she could but her means shrank.
The fact was she was less attractive now. Her breasts sagged and
her belly had never tightened after the birth. The pox gnawed at
her. She was sturdy still but not marketable.*

*More and more, she began to consort with the sailors and
privateers who had been her regular customers. She tried a few
short voyages to entertain them in the usual way, and she prospered for there was no competition on board. But then it became
unbearable because of the pox and she began to work among
them on the ship. In months she was as competent as the men
and spied a sail faster than they could. So when the hunter
manned out his pinnace and gave chase they were ready, and
powered on the enemy a volley of short shot.*

*Hannah Davies was the only woman on board among a
crew of fifty Spanish, twenty-four French and nineteen English
seamen. Some of the English were descended from privateers who
had settled in Tortuga after being driven from St Christopher.
They told outlandish tales of hunting wild cattle on the savan-
nahs of Santo Domingo, and gave her tastes of the dry smoked
beef that the Carib Indians had called boucan.*

*At times she saw her child and, once she was sober, hugged
him repeatedly, stuffing him with sweet things and half-true,
half-mythical tales of adventures at sea. She whispered how they
would forbear the enemy from coming on board and how nar-*

rowly she escaped the law when her ship bilged upon its anchor. When she ceased to appear the child was confused and slightly resentful for he had looked forward to her tumultuous visits. Eventually she became a vague memory of cakes and spell-binding stories. For his nurse had the sense and compassion not to reveal to him that his mother, Hannah, at last had been hanged — committed to the custody of the Provost Marshal without bail or mainprise, on several counts of indecency, petty theft and assault, but largely for piracy, and hanged at last.

Cohon, of course, knew nothing of this, and if he had would hardly have troubled himself about it for a strumpet's whelp was not a real Cohon after all. Besides, he was busy with his own concerns. The Cohon house in Port Royal was a fine two-storey brick building, one of perhaps two thousand others in the town on the peninsula. It was unbearably hot in the summer and by early June every year his family moved to Morante.

So he was alone one hot, still, dry day when a slight tremor brought him to his feet, a stronger one into the road outside. Then quicker than thought the earth heaved and split. The house, the town, crumbled around him. The street rippled violently then collapsed sickeningly beneath his feet, and over the thunder of the quake the sea rose to a roar and fell upon him.

He struggled timelessly in the current and was losing consciousness when he broke surface and found himself clinging to a rafter on a boiling sea far above the roof tops, and it seemed to him that the bells of sunken churches tolled eerily through his brain before a massive wave crushed him below again. Then once more he shot up, clinging to the beam but lashed and twirled around helplessly. He was beyond shock when the ship came, driven from the wharf by storm-force waves to plough over the town.

He grasped for the rope that coiled down to him and clung

*obdurately as it was hauled up, and he slid heavily over the rails
to lie gasping on his back, staring from the deck into the midday
sun. The days after skidded by in nightmare. Water gushed from
the dead windows of the buildings that protruded above the sea
near the point of the submerged peninsula. A turbulent waste of
mud and floating debris surged between them and the mainland. The connecting neck of land had vanished without trace.
Hundreds of bodies bobbed on the harbour waters, drowned by
the tidal wave or ripped decomposing from recent graves in the
cemetery. The half-submerged face of his own coachman floated
before the ship then disappeared as the hulk rode over it.*

*Hog Craal, it was called — the place they came to — miser-
able huts that the rain soaked through. It was weeks before he
contacted his family and resettled completely in Morante. By
then all the other occupants of the hut he had shared in Hog
Craal were dead of fever. Even when this wretched place grew
and spread into a city that would replace Port Royal and flourish over the Liguanea Plain that his grandfather had coveted,
Isaac could not enter it. Kingston was nothing to him. The
Goldmeers moved there, bankrupt again, but ready to begin
again from the beginning. But Isaac Cohon stayed in Morante.*

*Stripped of all other property, the Cohons concentrated on
developing Goldfields and they prospered without losing themselves completely in the British ways. They spoke Portuguese
among themselves, showed themselves in church with decreasing
frequency and, privately, worshipped in the Sephardic tradition
late into the following century. By then the green-gold valley had
been in their family for over a hundred years. Their descendants
had never heard of Goldmeer and would not have been able to
identify his family anyway because, somehow, in the process of
settling in Kingston, the Goldmeers changed their name to
Goldman.*

*A few of the Cohons had ties in Kingston. They handled
coinage and traded with Cuba, Hispaniola and the Spanish*

Main. Backed by this lucrative business of money-changing, the plantation spread and flourished. The original patent initiated a venture that would grow to twelve hundred acres. The Cohons accepted foreign coins from soldiers and tradesmen and profited enough on the exchange to sink thirty thousand pounds into sugar planting. It was gratifying, they reflected, that the Africans who worked it were saved from savagery to be part of a thriving enterprise. Elsewhere, a brown Cohon was growing, parentless, as best he could, but he had no knowledge of the plantation or its owners any more than they knew of him.

Meanwhile, each master of Goldfields protected what he had as best he could, for Goldfields forged his mind into a machine for its own perpetuation as it forged the mind of every master that it owned. When, at last, the first Stollmeier gained control, Goldfields would take, make and break his mind in turn by razing the past, justifying the present and blinding all vision of the future. Even Isaac Cohon had fortified the plantation by building a great house on the slope which overlooked the sea, and positioned loopholes from which it could be defended. Inside, he had guns, ready for any emergency. Any possible assistance was a day's journey away, and what God had given Cohon, Cohon would keep. The house was solid. Its walls were two and a half feet thick with brick quoins and brick facings about the windows, and its roof was impregnable with good English slate which had been shipped in as ballast.

For Isaac Cohon knew that there were wild blacks out beyond the grey stone walls around Goldfields. Day after day their power grew and became one with the strength of the mountains, inflexible as the giant arm of rock that stretched its massive fingers to the coast. The wild blacks held the Blue Mountains, from which the streams glittered softly or roared foaming white over the rocks to spread out into sheer green basins. Until these stray negroes could be reabsorbed all of that was theirs; but Goldfields, Goldfields was his.

14

The Garden

GRACE GOLDMAN and Paul Cohon married in 1939, and honeymooned in Goddie Sarah's old house on Goldfields in St Thomas,
but it was nine years before they had a child. Icelin Castries had
been in the lunatic asylum from long before Adam was born. Her
own infant, the legacy of rape, had been born briskly in St
Thomas and left there. Icelin knew no more of it. Vaguely she
learnt from Rev. Jackman that Miss Grace had a son. It was the
first baby in the family that did not meet Icelin in his introductory
moments of life.

Getting out had been awful. The blissful monotony had fooled
Adam, as he rocked suspended in the dark timelessness of pulse
and wash in a world created to cushion him from every shock,
and especially the shock of discovery that eviction was
inescapable.

Its darkness was perfection before it became a trap in which
he struggled blindly for the passage out. Its fluidity preserved and
sheltered him until, with the overwhelming instinct to draw
breath, he found himself drowning in it. Its closeness reassured
and cosseted him until it began to tighten rhythmically, squeezing
him out.

At first he would not. He hung there stubbornly in the past
which heaved convulsively around him, feeling himself dying.
Then, because he was still a part of it and could not act contrary
to it, he began to move with the compulsive shoving force that
squeezed and crushed him forward. Then anything to be out,

even into the nothingness beyond. He broke out into the ghastliness of wide dry space, blinded by morning light and drowning in air. Even as he gasped for breath he was shattered by a new, appalling sensation. Noise. Something enfolded him, and there was the touch and smell of his old world again.

At last the formless brilliance began to take shape, to form sounds and patterns, meaningless at first but sometimes recurrent. Sounds ceased to frighten him and some were a comfort, but it was best to curve against warm contours and feel the security of another's breathing, rhythmic, rising and falling, lulling him to the half-remembered semi-sleep in which he had hung before the period of becoming.

Independence began for Adam when he gained dominion over the floor. At first he was set down on a blanket and, when he found himself at the edge of it, he wobbled to a standstill, rocking slightly as he balanced to stretch across a hand and test the shining brown surface. It was smooth in a bare, cool way. He crawled onto it and found it steady, slightly uncomfortable on the knees where the planks joined but otherwise reassuring in its resistance to palms and legs. He waited, patting it, to see what it would do. Then he rolled up, onto his bottom and balanced there with his back straight while he rubbed his hands on it, learning it. He bent forward cautiously for a brief lick of a dark streak in one of the boards, then straightened again, turning the taste over on his tongue. Suddenly, impulsively, he flipped forward and was off in a straight line for as far as he could go. Retrieved and returned to the blanket he sank gratefully down and fell asleep almost immediately, but it was only the first tour, and so he came to know the house, its shape, taste and texture, grain by grain, from the floor up.

The house was at one end of a cul-de-sac with the Deitrichs opposite and the Andersons on the right hand side. There was open land and a small gully on the other. Further up the road lived the Roses, the Halls and the McIntyres. At the corner, the Shermans had recently moved in.

It was years before Adam saw the house as a whole, though, let alone the road that they called Oxford Close. At first he understood it vaguely as we might imagine the earth hanging in the wilderness of space. But intimately he knew it. The smooth brown glow of floor reached into nooks under the dressing table, wardrobes, cupboards. The fat curves of dark wood sat solidly at the base of table and cabinet legs. Dust-filled little holes waited for the bolts of the doors to be dropped into them.

For a long time he was unable to distinguish the house from those within it, for no detail of it was unrelated to their lives, and its security flowed through and from them.

Grand's room was most familiar for it was his as well. It was more cluttered than the others because of the two wardrobes. One was rarely opened, so crammed it was with clothes, linen, letters and pictures of long ago, even the corset Grand had been married in. Not that his grandmother, Stella Goldman, looked as if she had ever needed a corset. The years had worn away any spare flesh she had ever had from her erect, fine-boned frame, leaving her not so much thin as fragile. Her eyes were sharp and direct beneath still, dark brows, her head firmly poised and her mouth controlled. She would have looked severe were it not for the laughing crinkles at the corners of eyes and mouth. Besides, now that her silver-white hair was trimmed to a short, manageable crop, it resisted all efforts at discipline and wisped into silk-soft curls around her head.

Grand was strict, swift to raise her slipper in warning, rigid in her notions of propriety, but she was soft too. Her fingers moved with the same gentle precision over roses, Irish linen and cut knees. Quite often she was ill and everyone whispered that there must be no sudden noises, nothing to startle her; but in a few hours she would protest. Even with her voice sounding thinner than usual she would be demanding the baby, and by morning she would be out among the old rose bushes. They were so old that no one quite remembered when they had begun, for many had been transported from some other house. But the notion of another house where the family had lived before was meaningless to Adam. What was real was the garden of timeless roses and Grand snipping away dead leaves and welcoming the waxen-crisp little buds.

Even from inside her room she would begin to greet them, for her window opened over one of the rose beds, and she would stretch out and touch them lightly, drawing her hand in with the transparent skin pearled with dew. Then she would be impatient to go out. She would whisk away the long cotton nightie and make the bed. (Adam's mother said her own Papa had carved that bed for Grand.) From the bed Grand moved to the dressing table, combed her hair and balanced her favourite linen runner crisply in one hand while she dusted with the other. The runner was that strange colour they called écru, bordered with a silky vine of grapes. Grand's Mama had embroidered it and several others for her when she was getting married and it was the only one left after the earthquake because it had been on the clothesline. Soon the cloth would be flat on the polished table again and Grand put back the figurines, pin dishes and hand mirror.

Uncle Les had no time to play before work, and there was little left around in his room to meddle with. He was neat. Perhaps it was because he had no wife. Everyone except Les seemed to think this sad, though Adam could not see why. After all, Les lived with them and they were all happy.

"He should get married and have a child while he can," Adam had heard his mother say. "Look at him with Adam."

Les's room was usually closed because he was often out and there were things, like the typewriter, that Adam must not touch.

Besides these, there were only the startling ties Grand hated.

"Les is wasting his life here," Adam's father brooded. But what did he mean?

Adam reached his parents' room early. Daddy would have been up and studying for hours, for he was leaving the office to go into the Church.

"Why he didn't settle on this before?" Ben pondered. "Is obviously where he belongs."

"Fled him," Grace pursed her lips.

"Eh?"

"You know, down the labyrinthine ways of his own mind..."

"Oh Gospel, Grace!"

"Exactly."

By the time Adam arrived, Daddy would be stacking away the notes that arrived every month in that big brown parcel half covered in stamps because it came from far away London, the same place where The Exam would be set. His desk was just outside the bedroom on the enclosed side porch that served as a study. Daddy seemed tensely pleased about The Exam, but to Adam it sounded ominous, like a rat trap. Mummy said she did not want to take any exam ever again, though Daddy encouraged her to study with him and get her degree too.

If Adam reached their room early he could get at the pencils his father kept on the desk, except for one actually chained on a little screw at the side. Or Adam could dip into Mummy's big jar of vanishing cream. There was always a little scuffle over the pencils and the cream but they all enjoyed it really and it became a recognised part of the morning ritual.

Mummy dressed so carefully that Daddy was constantly muttering dark predictions about the final day when all flesh, as he put it, would gather before the Maker and be asked what they had done with Time. Mummy would emit a brief snort of laughter and eye him over her powder puff as she dabbed at her face, apparently quite unmoved by his dramatic upward gestures.

She chuckled. "What I have done with Time is to get up early and make cake. You wanted to do without it?"

"And are you suggesting that I can't bake cake? I learnt early not to be helpless. Miss Martha Jane would not have put up with it."

It was true. He even mended his own clothes — to the horror of Uncle Ben.

All the rooms pulsated with activity. Even the bathrooms were busy all day with bathing, cleaning, hand-washing of underwear, filling the fat enamelled goblet for watering the house plants. Friends and neighbours dropped in and sat a few minutes or just kissed and handed over a brown paper bag and left again. Others tramped straight through to the kitchen, tasting while they chatted. Even the spare room was a vital thing, always containing some aunt or uncle, not necessarily related but distinguished from the rest of the family only by their rate of turnover. Once the room had belonged to an Auntie Belle, whom Adam could not remember.

There was no separating one room from the other. They all poured, bled, chuckled, tumbled one into the other. Each room had at least two doors, often three so that each lay on the way to some other part of the house. Grand's room had four doors and it was almost unthinkable to walk from one end of the house to the other without threading one's way through it between the bed and the wardrobes and taking care not to step on the cat.

There were enclosed porches on each side, and several doors opened onto the porches and into the garden, doors which were little more than polished frameworks set with panes of ornamental frosted glass. Friends as intimate as family drifted through any door. The McIntyres, a huge, rollicking family, passed through individually or together. Uncle Austin came once or twice a week. Uncle Ben was there almost daily. (Ben should go back to church, Paul insisted, whatever people said. Chat nonsense about denying divorcés communion. Who needed it more? Grace fumed in agreement.)

Everyone who came was the common interest of the family as a whole rather than the special property of just one member. Parents had been in school or church, or had worked together, so that children were born into ready-made friendships. To Adam it seemed that everyone had known everyone else from the beginning of time.

The garden diffused away from the house. There was a wide lawn and low border of blue plumbago. At the back ruled the old rose bushes, and beyond spread the mango trees, except for the one Grand called Number Eleven, which was close to the house. Away in a far corner rose the gaunt stub of a coconut tree struck by lightning from before Adam could remember, and a short stretch from it crept a dying grapevine transplanted from some previous existence. At the side of the house was the opening to a path through an arbour of trailing allamanda flowers that Grand said she had known since she was born, for she had transplanted these as well from King Street to Windward Road and then to Oxford Close; but the old garden bench beside it was crumbling and unsafe.

Into the remotest corners of the garden a few members of the family rarely went. For years Uncle Les had not wandered under the back hedge which was overhung with trailing orange puffs of Smuggler's Pride, and he could not have found the leaf of life plant in an emergency. Grand, on the other hand, had planted almost everything, fertilised it with guano, the bat-dung they had bought from a workman near Goldfields where there was a cave rich in the valuable droppings. Uncle Ben cackled when he heard. "Rudy Stollmeier legacy turn bat doo-doo. I not surprised. He was always full of...."

"Ben!" Stella withered him. "And a little child right here."

"Sorry, Miss Grace," he muttered penitently. But he was not in time, for Grace eyed him caustically.

"Don't forget yourself again and trifle with me," she snapped.

It was Grace who had had this house built, for Paul thought little about property, but Stella's garden it remained, and she knew it all stone by stone and leaf by leaf.

By the time one reached the hedges on the outside it was all finished. Whether it was the gaily untidy hibiscus or bougainvillea or whether the darker, more severe wall of privet, it made no difference. The borders of the garden were the outer limits of life. There was only one gate after all and although it was kept open it was sealed with an invisible line. Once his parents had driven out across this, Adam could only wave to them. No child could pass over it without permission. Grand did not cross it in her garden shoes. The jowly old dog that Ben called Churchill would tear back and forth along it snarling at the postman but never break through the physical emptiness of the gateway into the street.

The world was marked out by invisible lines that defined its boundaries. So it seemed to Adam.

He was the first and last child, the pivot in all their lives, the deciding factor in every calculation. The house was full, not just of toys from his uncles and books from his father, but of plastic cups and cardboard boxes, of cloth scraps from Goddie, little patches of sunshine on the floor, sheets being shaken and bellying up and a myriad of fine shining specks of dust which danced where the light beamed in past dark mahogany furniture. From up on the dining table, if no one caught him in time, he could glimpse the new picture Paul had brought for Grace, a crowded view of animals huddled against exotic leaves looming vividly from a dark and hazy background. Stella and Les thought it ugly even if a Jamaican had painted it, but they kept their silence for Paul was excited by this local artist. The painting was

precious and Adam was not to touch it, but they placed a strong
box for him to climb on and stare as long as he liked.

In the evenings it was important to be tidy early to make sure
that Daddy took them for a drive. Green lawns with the hills pre-
siding over them and the ancient arches of an aqueduct fixed in
his mind as Paul pointed out the University College which had
recently opened and where Paul said Adam must come to school
one day as he would have liked to. At bedtime Adam had to turn
off the mahoe lamp, and then Grand must be patted for as long
as possible. Otherwise, she said, she could not sleep. It was a
time of great responsibility.

Grand was frail, strict, warm, playful. He slept best curled
against her, especially when breathing was hard. He followed
her through the garden, underfoot in the kitchen and played
beside or under the bed when she rested. He wriggled over her
and combed her hair. The maids bustled in, pulling their work
clothes out of the bankras and whisking on starched caps and
aprons. Then the higgler would come, with the wide flat market
basket with the concave bottom cushioned on its cotta to balance steadily on the brilliant bandana tied at the back of her
head. Easily she swung the basket onto the landing of the back
step and Grand drew her chair to negotiate for breadfruit, avocado pears, corn, sweetsops — all Adam's favourites. The maids
shared out tastes of everything and good strong soap mixtures to
blow bubbles. The house bustled with preparations or repairs,
news, laughter, anxiety, protest, celebration. The air was
flavoured, now with food, now with baby powder, polish, disinfectant or flowers.

Sometimes they went on long drives over the mountains, perhaps to Dunn's River, where the six-hundred-foot series of water-
falls foamed down to the sea. The car crawled carefully back
through dim, fern-encrusted rock walls and he drifted off to
sleep as the adults talked of how things had changed since this

last war, of Busta and Manley and of the new bauxite mining. He smelled the red earth, and the cake in Grace's basket, and the huge ripe fruit of a jackfruit tree along the way, and he slept drunkenly from the seabath.

Uncle Les was his idol, plaything and confidante. It was Les whom Adam told about Joseph, the gardener. Joseph, Adam explained, needed new pants. The front of his was torn and Everything was out. Uncle Les should give Joseph his old pants, Adam advised. Les's subtle investigations showed Joseph's pants to be intact when he wanted them to be and he advised Grace about the gardener. So Joseph was gone. In a way it was a pity, Adam thought, for Joseph seemed to like him a great deal. Joseph had called him to show him all kinds of things in the garden and petted him with soft quick strokes that made the child want to wriggle away. A day or two after he left, Les remarked that Austin was trying to find some sort of job for the man, to keep him out of trouble, and Uncle Ben shrugged significantly, "Austin would."

"What's wrong with that?" Les snapped.

"Nothing, if he has the time to waste on scum."

"Well, well," Grace intervened, "he's trying to prevent him from going to the bottom."

They stared at her for a moment in disbelief and she returned their gaze in bewilderment. Abruptly they plunged out of the room together and Grace sighed and shook her head at Stella.

"Those two. Lord, Mama, you don't get tired of the bickering?"

"Well. They are both right in a way. Sometimes you turn someone away... later you hear. There might have been something else you could do... but..."

Grace knew she was thinking of Louise Haynes.

"I can't say," Stella went on, "that I feel to do anything for Joseph. But I suppose honest work, on the road or something..."

Grace nodded. "And I suppose Austin is so aware of hardship."

"We don't know what he might save the man from."

They half smiled at each other, puzzled by the shadows of another world.

Adam burrowed into Les's things, stole his slippers, sucked his shirt sleeves and tickled himself with the points of his uncle's collars. One day he awoke to see a dozen faces grinning and peering at him under Les's bed and Petrona reaching a tight shining arm to pluck him out.

"Eh! Eh! But look Mas' Baby asleep ya under Mr Les bed. Afta Miss Grace all out pon road a look fe him."

He wriggled away and crawled out feeling small and prickly from being stared at and laughed over, and when the story was recounted to Les and Goddie in the evening the child grew quiet then sullen. Unaccountably he erupted into tearful screams.

Grace picked him up at once, murmuring promises of the fun they would have in the next few days.

"Hope Gardens, with his best shoes. Shh! Who will look so smart?"

"And go downtown with Goddie," Sarah put in, "go to Nathan's."

Adam dried his eyes and sniffled. "Walk 'treet?" he bargained.

They saw their opportunity and pounced on it. "Yes, and drink Coke."

"And then," Grace reminded him, wiping his cheeks with the back of her hand, "then remember Aunty Belle is coming?"

He stared at them seriously but fascinated. He did not remember this Aunty, but such visits from abroad inevitably brought untold surprises. Gifts, treats and country outings and favourite dishes.

It seemed as if the day would never come. When it did it blurred past in a haze of activity. By afternoon he was overexcited by the laughter in the kitchen and the new colours in the spare room. Early that evening it became meaningless to him, a promise not materialising, and he lay across his father's lap on the porch, watching the cat stalking crickets on the lawn. Quiet, ever so quiet, then a brief wriggle of her hind quarters and she sprang, settled, munched briefly, then straightened herself to sight and pounce upon another. Dusk fell and she became part of his uneasy dreams. Beside the rocking chair, night-blooming cereus began to open, petals unfolding almost visibly. He stared trying to see the actual movement, mesmerised by the huge magical white blooms and heady perfume.

Late that night soft, excited voices hummed in the doorway. Briefly he opened his eyes and cried out then dropped asleep instantly again in the certainty that someone would hurry to him. But in the morning he started up, aware of a difference in the house. He whimpered, searching for Grand, then a movement reassured him and he rolled over to her burrowing close and reaching for her face.

She washed and dressed him early. He wanted to go in the spare room but they refused and he waited tensely for the door to open.

When it did, he started away in shock for it had never occurred to him that she would look... new. They had talked so much of Aunt Belle that he expected to recognise her but she was a stranger, in different, foreign-looking clothes. Her voice reassured him but still he retreated, deprived of that thrill of recognition he had expected.

She sat at the table, talking, laughing, glancing at him — quick, hopeful little glances, almost birdlike in their bright darting; wanting him to notice her.

After breakfast, he followed cautiously and stood outside her door, watching her at the dressing table. They were going out and she picked up her comb to redo her hair. His mouth puckered in surprise as it tumbled around her, glossy, red-brown curls. He rubbed his fingers together longingly. In the mirror she smiled at him, her strange, greeny-grey eyes lighting and snapping.

"Come, come to Aunty," she begged.

He touched her hair experimentally then held and rubbed it between his fingers in satisfaction. She took him around the room showing him her things. One was a picture of himself, no, not himself, but so like him he was confused and flattered when she said it was her own baby. He scrambled up into the armchair and watched as she darted around, chattering to him continuously. How long she had wanted to come, how she had read the letters over and over, longing to see him. But now with the war over at last she was here. She had brought shoes for Grace. She knew it had been hard to get a good pair because of the war, but now she heard they were making them here, and clothes. All sorts of business growing up growing up. She had brought him a little pair too. Try them and see. Never mind he would grow into them.

For three weeks he followed her about, hanging on her skirt. He was caught by the longing which she betrayed with every look and word to him, curious about the feelings that ran high in the house, the love and regret in Mummy's attitude to her, and in Grand's. She talked about Canada in a funny way, triumphant and critical at the same time. It seemed she would never come back to Jamaica to live.

"Nothing for me to do here," she sighed. "Canada now, you can do anything honest and you still somebody." She stared at the garden. "When I'm old I suppose if I can save enough I'll come back. But I don't see how. I buy my plot long time though. When I die is here I must be buried. In God country."

That evening Grace said to Paul, "What about taking Belle to the country for a weekend. What about Goldfields?"

"We could," he admitted, scratching his chin reflectively. "The

McIntyres just returned the keys, and I haven't passed them back
to Goddie yet. Sam says his whole contingent camped there up to
last weekend. Would be in order."

"Westward Ho, then? Don't pinch me, you vermin!"

"What all this plumpness make for if not to be pinched?"

"Shh! Too out of order."

They left early in the morning, so early that it was still dark
and cool among the first hills. Then, as it grew light, there was
the sea with the foam white and silky looking. It didn't matter
that the car was crammed, for Adam shifted easily from lap to lap
and they broke the drive from time to time. They parked on the
way and ate the boiled eggs and soft rolls that Stella had brought,
and they waited for Belle and Sarah to wash their hands in a
stream that sprayed down from the rocks almost into the road.
Every now and then they paused to buy fruit, and munched as
they drove.

A gnarled old man lurched by on his donkey and nodded
pleasantly, raising his hand with two fingers forming a V.

"Labourite," chuckled Paul.

"Ben don' like Busta at all, eeh?" Belle laughed. "He sound
like he would dead for Manley."

All the way they talked. It was true that the country was
polarised between the two parties. Grace said that Les sym-
pathised with a large body of the working class that saw
Bustamante as its saviour, but Ben admired the educated and polished leader of the other party. Norman Manley had the class
required to run a country, Ben said.

"Actually," Paul mused, "if the workers understood Manley
they might like him better. This socialist philosophy is a disturbing thing for us middle-class people, you know. But the workers
might accept it."

"But what would happen to us, Mas' Paul?"

"Hmm!"

"Maybe bungo people won't understand?" Belle pursued.

"People may not be educated, Miss Belle, through no fault of their own. But they not necessarily stupid."

"Tcha! Stupid yes. Just as well too."

"Well Manley is a brilliant man. Outstanding lawyer. He will work out a way of making himself understood."

The canefields flew past, such a gentle green they could have rolled in them, Adam thought. Then they drew alongside the old grey stone wall and turned in and up the road across the estate and towards the house. Both Stella and Sarah were quiet, Stella brooding on all her mother had been denied, Sarah remembering briefly, wryly, that she was to have honeymooned there with Jonas.

It was funny about Goldfields, Adam thought. Goddie Sarah said it was rightfully Grand's and Grand said that of course it was Goddie's, but they all agreed in the end that, anyway, it was for Adam. So it was a special place to visit, though some storm had damaged it badly and they had never fully restored it. Mummy talked a great deal of all that could be done, but said that it took money and honest labour which there was no one to oversee. They had repaired the original square centre of the building, and closed off one of the wings for the time being. The other was in ruins anyway.

People who lived around simply worked the land and took the produce. And why not, Goddie demanded, when she wasn't around to use it herself. When she came with Stella and the Cohons, men loaded the car with breadfruit, plantains, coconuts, ortaniques and sugar cane.

The trees opened and the grey stone house stood out on the green rise of land before them. They unloaded the food, but inside was linen and cutlery and it was completely furnished with old four-poster beds each with a funny roof of cloth. The table legs were dark and twisty and the front walls had curious peepholes looking out to sea.

Later that day they went to the beach but the next morning Grand stayed at home because the others had something entirely new to show to Belle, and it was a steep walk.

"Mama has never seen it, but she couldn't take the walk now," Grace said. "A maid we had long ago showed it to us when we were children and came down with Mama and Goddie for a weekend in Bath. You'd remember the woman, Belle. Icelin."

"Whatever happen to her?"

"She got queer in the head, poor soul, and had to go to the asylum. But when we were little she showed us this."

It was a waterfall that tumbled into a bathing pool, jewel green. Adam lay on the bank staring into it incredulously. His father dropped down onto a low rock beside him and waited.

"Icelin said when she was little they used to climb down there," Grace pointed. "Her brothers knew a cave somewhere. Behind the falls themselves."

Adam stared down and the green light made strange patterns on his mind, and he thought God's eyes must be like that — bright and bottomless.

All too soon the weekend sped past; they were back in Kingston and Aunt Belle was gone.

In August the days were slow and still. On the swing that hung low from the mango tree Adam rocked slowly, watching the patterns of sunlight through the mango leaves and occasional shadows of heavy fruit. When these were ripe they were sliced and shared scrupulously for these were Julies, but the black mangoes were eaten at random. Petrona had sliced away the stainy, unpleasant stems of a few, and she had placed the saucer nearby on an old *Gleaner*. So he sat, hardly swinging, feeling the thick juice running down his chin, hypnotised by the dragonflies aimlessly shimmering back and forth and a shiny black bumblebee whirring among Grand's roses. The leaves hardly moved and the afternoon sank down heavy on his eyelids.

"Inebriated," Paul crooned.

Paul had driven in and found him there sleeping with his sticky face against the rope of the swing and the half-sucked mango on his lap.

"How?" Grace gasped. "We've been watching him there, swinging and eating so quietly. But sleeping? How he didn't fall?"

They wiped him and laughed over him and put him to bed. This was what it had all been for. Grand had planted the mango trees for him years before he had been born.

Grand was beautiful, frail with a sort of brittle gracefulness like the china figurines on her table. Her hands were rich brown from the garden but her face coffee cream from the protection of her broad-brimmed straw hat. She seemed not so much old as different, scrupulously tidy for the afternoons in soft floral prints with rounded collars. Her shoe-heels were actually rather high, but thick. Her hair was cropped short but was fine, soft, silvery, wavy, a delight to play in. She rarely bent, and lifted nothing heavy, yet she ran the house all day, revelled in the garden and in the afternoon she and the baby, as she still called him, sat fresh and tidy on the porch waiting for everyone to come home from work.

This was the vision of Grand that would stay with Adam until he died, a sketch in fine lines, delicately coloured in pastels, of a lady from another time. She sat on the porch in a high-backed rocker among her huge pots of maidenhairs. Her feet were set firmly on the tiles, modestly together, her shoulders frail but thrown back and her face raised above the lace-edged collar, surveying the garden. It was a face never to be forgotten, clean-cut lines, planes and angles that should have made it hard and

246

unyielding were it not for the tenderness with which the mouth curled and the alternating lights and shadows of her eyes.

But far from Stella's garden lay another yard, and the home of another boy. The yard edged the junk heap with its piles of trash, filth and potential loot, with its rooting dogs and flapping John Crows. As the stench of the dump steamed up, the huge black bare-headed vultures swivelled raw-red wrinkled necks in search of intruders, then stabbed again into the piles, hobbling and stumbling over them, lifting clumsily into the air and flopping again lopsidedly. A boy stoned and cursed them and they shuffled aside. One pecked out but hopped back as the boy swung his stick, and a dog nipped in boldly to snap at the prize.

"G'way, maaga dawg," bawled the boy, hurling after it a stream of abuse.

He grabbed the greasy bag with the half-eaten patty and dropped it into his sack.

It had been a good morning and he had more than he needed. He always took more. Eye bigger than belly, his elders grumbled. But he did not care. He had learnt early never to pay attention to adults. He kept away from the white-garbed pocomania women who clapped and swayed on the street corners, from the healing balmyards and from the Baptist church with the black parson who preached about eternal bliss when he was poor and hungry like the rest.

The boy lay in his packing case on the edge of the dump and savoured the patty. He had no business with a parson who preached about happiness to a congregation in which no one made more than ten shillings a week. It was not that he didn't believe in spirits. Everyone knew they were there. (Plenty time him have trouble with duppy, one time even with coolie duppy, the wo'st kind.) Suddenly he remembered dreaming about his mother last night, and wondered whether she was dead. The thought made him uncomfortable and he put it away. His life was better now that there were no adults in it, he decided. You did what you must to stay alive and that was that.

A pair of magnificent legs, lush and glossy, passed in front of the packing case and he deepened his voice as best he could and rasped,

"Eh! Eh! Nice woman come in ya nah! Me waan' give you one pickney!"

He was gratified to hear her good-natured kiss-teeth, but huge puss boots directly behind the woman stopped at the packing case and to his consternation a brawny arm shot in and plucked him out.

"But is what dis?" The man with the dark glasses dropped him in disgust and pocketed his knife. Then a slow grin spread across the man's face. "But is a likkle nasty nega boy and me nearly cut him. Trying fe play man. Look ya, likkle whoreson pickney, respec' nice woman or I go cut it off gi' maaga dawg fe nyam." He kicked him gently and strolled on.

The boy crawled back into his case, gripping his shoulder ruefully. He didn't like what the man had called him. If he had had a gun he would have shot him. He rolled onto his side and drew his knees up to his chin, squeezing his eyes closed.

His earliest years had moved him from one squatter camp to the next in West Kingston. His earliest memories were of Kingston Pen, with his mother, Isildor Castries. Of course there was no kitchen but she had a coalpot stove and cooked food on it. He breathed deeply trying to recollect the smell of her food but nothing came but the stink of the dump. There had been other children but he was not sure now whether they were hers or not, for they had left early.

At night when it rained so hard that she did not go out because the streets would be empty, she had nothing to do and she talked to him. She grew up in St Thomas, she said. "Me mumma ongly squeeze me out and leave me go back to im big job a Kingston, never even send back fe say 'dawg'."

Now she thought about it St Thomas was a comfortable place. Plenty food. (Deacon son at the church did like her bad, and him people did ha' likkle money.) But she said the country was quiet and she went to town as a schoolgirl to work for a brown woman who taught her nothing but expected her to mind the house.

"Cuss she use to cuss me, box me up. I find one sweetman and run 'way from her."

After he dropped her there was man after man, beating after beating. "You 'member Red Man, Victor?"

How could he forget? Red Man had kicked him and pitched him out the house.

"I couldn't do nothing for you, you know, not before him leave for himself. Me never 'fraid any man like me 'fraid Red Man. You know why him combolo did call im Icepick?"

It was after Red Man left that they moved to the Trench Town camp and lost themselves among its twenty-six hundred inhabitants (in case Red Man change him mind and come back, his mother had said). There was still no kitchen or toilet but she brought in more money here and they had food. ('Nuff provision an even likkle saltfish.) But then came the hurricane.

Hurricane Charlie, in 1951, was nothing for which residents of Trench Town could prepare. Victor remembered that when the sky changed his mother hurried him to shelter in a big building. It could have been a church or school. He spent the hours crouched against her wet body with his face buried in her bosom as the wind came screaming for him. Water poured through every crack and washed under the door. Above them a window crashed as a tree branch drove through it, then the wind knifed in and the other panes bulged and burst, and the glass flew wildly as the pressure built. The door ripped in and the wind roared and grappled with the roof, mad as a trapped beast. He wriggled against her, squealing and covering his head to silence the noise. Whup! Whup! And the grate of tearing wood. But it abated before the roof went, and in the sodden aftermath they returned to the piles of splintered wood, soggy cardboard and twisted aluminium sheeting that had been their home. They struggled for a while but then she was pregnant again and the new man was not about to feed an extra mouth.

"You big now can see 'bout youself," she explained, crying but firm. "I cyan't manage widout the likkle help. Him say him going America, going take me."

Victor was ten then. She may have been twenty-seven, he thought. Not old, not thirty.

So now he shifted for himself in the vast complex of the ghetto, part of no household, spiralling away from the mother-centred rule of the limited family life he had known. A grant from the British Government was devoted to rehousing of storm victims but the dimensions of the task were of a magnitude few understood.

Kingston was growing. The middle and upper classes spread from the Liguanea Plain upwards to the hills, but below the poverty line the growth was cancerous, physically contained in spaces that grew more and more crowded before the outside world sensed threat or registered pain. Young migrants poured in from the country obsessed by dreams of success in the capital. As few returned, the myth lived on, swelling new waves of migration. In Jamaica the birth rate rose; the death rate fell. The camps swelled. By the time the boy was grown the population of the city would have increased since his birth by over eighty-six per cent. Poverty teemed in its narrow confines.

The boy walked briskly away from his packing case, past the fence of ragged aluminium fencing and hedge of macca bush.

Spotted mongrels dodged him and a goat fled bawling into a drain choked with stinking garbage in black water. He knew the ghetto and its surroundings well, every rum shop and ganja den. He ran errands for other scufflers like the basket-makers and ganja pedlars and gathered and sold firewood, but he had little to show by the end of the day. In irritation he hurled a stone into a small shop window and fled as the owner rushed to the door. Fun fe bwoy a death fe bullfrog, shrugged a drunk slumped at the root of a blasted cotton tree.

Several of the men did better with gambling or by begging with intimidation than by occasional carpentry and garden work. The knife flashed easily but their violence was communal and provided it remained among themselves the outside world cared little. A pedlar collecting bottles swerved his rickety wooden handcart around the boy, cursing his intelligence and ancestry. Victor's mother had sent him to school but that was one problem he no longer had. Still he didn't want to live in a packing case all his life. He made up his mind quickly, as he had few alternatives to consider. What he needed was a gun.

Pants of expensive material, smooth and seamed, brushed his arm and he leaped aside to see better. Polished shoes, so soft-walking they had surprised him. A starched shirt. He hurried forward. "Glad fe see you again, sah."

The brown man paused and regarded the small coal-black face tilted eagerly at him and the boy struggled to maintain his composure as the astute gold-brown eyes impaled him.

"Again? Where I ever know you?"

"You don't mean you don't 'member me, sah? An' we chat so much time?"

"I chat? Wi' *you?*"

"When me fada did work for you, yes. Bass, I fall 'pon likkle hard time since. Puppa dead, Mumma sick sick. Know you wi' want fe spare me likkle help, sah."

The well-groomed brown man smiled faintly and looked around at his two rough companions.

"Is a jinal," he purred.

They snickered, and the boy felt his danger. One of the men was huge, marked by a twisted scar that wormed its way from ear to chin.

Quickly the boy returned his attention to the brown man.

"Please, sah, after you should help poor black people, sah, a rich brown gentleman like you."

"Why on earth?"

The child edged forward and lowered his voice. "Can sell you something, you know, baasman. What you like? I have de good stuff. I have everything." He ran backwards in front of the man. "Good weed. Can get nice woman." Desperate, he added, "Or if is not woman you like, sah..."

The man with the cicatrix lurched forward threateningly, but the sleek brown man waved a vague hand, lit by a gold watch and ring. "Give the pickney a money."

And the bossman strolled into a rumshop as the coin tinkled on the ground behind him.

The boy hesitated on the other side of the street, waiting for the bossman to come out. The two stalwarts leaned at the door. Victor decided suddenly, strolled unconcernedly forward then dived unexpectedly between their legs into the ill-lit room. Between the startled voices and cigarette smoke and the hands grabbing at him he rolled nimbly and accurately for the polished shoes and crouched with his arm raised to ward off whatever might come, searching the face of the bossman.

"But what de likkle mad rass tormenting me for?" the brown man breathed. "Boy, what de hell you name? What de bumbo you want?"

"Gun, sah."

"What!" The explosion of rage was interrupted by a shrill

whine from the boy.

"Waan' work fe you, baas. I see you is a real baasman. What brown gentleman doing in ya? Me waan' better meself, sah. I begging you set me up. Gimme one gun, make me help meself, sah, I going work fe you good."

The thick, pungent air of the rumshop was electric with tension and the child smelled his danger and turned over on his tongue the taste of fear, but the chance of his life had come and his lips, numbed with terror, stumbled on.

"You wouldn't be here, sah, 'less you could help me. Gun, sah."

The brown man leaned back in his chair and the room waited. He was powerful, confident, smooth. His strange eyes held the boy's, not unkindly, subdued by an expression of remembered pain. The child felt his fear trickling down the sides of his face, pouring down his sides from his armpits, and his hand went involuntarily to his groin to prevent his bladder giving way.

"You want work for me, eh?" The ghost of a smile hovered at the man's lips. "You is a real man, man." He signalled into the dark recesses of the shop. "Bring a drink for me colleague. Not that, bring the real thing." He accepted the unlabelled bottle and poured it into a fresh glass. "Have a drink wi' me, man."

The smell, the style of the bottle, made it unmistakable. It was not just white rum, it was the unofficial, highly concentrated version they called 'jahncrow batty'.

The child's eyes locked with the brown man's gaze and the thin black fingers curled determinedly around the glass. He flung back his head swiftly and gulped it down. Flame blazed down his throat and licked into every tube and crevice of his chest, searing away his breath. He gagged, struggling for breath and the brown man lunged forward, tilted back the boy's head and forced a tumbler of water to his lips. He swallowed somehow and gradually caught his breath, even as vision blurred and his bladder gave way at last. As they carried him to the door and he lost consciousness, the bossman's voice faded in the distance.

"You is a brave boy. Look fe me when you done grow."

When the child opened his eyes, he closed them tightly again, tormented by even the fading light of sunset. His head threatened to explode. The lurching movement of the beast under him was intolerable and he tried to slide off but he was tied to the narrow ridged back of a mule. He vomited and lost consciousness again before he could struggle further.

He awoke to cool night with the smell of vegetation and the glow of a kerosene lamp on a table. He stared around the small, incredibly clean room and sniffed again. Food. Cooking food, like his mother's.

"Him wake up, Puppa."

A boy of his own age tugged the arm of a tall man of straight, proud build, with heavy, hanging matted hair and beard.

"Where dis?" whimpered Victor.

They leaned over him and the man began softly, "Shh! Don't move yet. You don't know you nearly dead? Who give you de jahncrow batty? What you name? No have no Mumma?"

"Dem call me 'Nancy Boy."

"Dat not name fe man. What name you Mumma give you?"

"Vic." He strained to recall the whole thing. "Think is Victor Castries."

Everything poured out mixed almost unintelligibly. Red Man and the hurricane and the packing case and the brown bossman who would set him up with a gun and his mother squeeze out in St Thomas.

The other child stared at his father incredulously, but the man just listened quietly, nodding.

"Dis pickney name Matthew," he remarked, when Victor stopped. "You can call I Pa Leon. Drink likkle tea. When it safe fe eat I going give you food."

Pa Leon kept Victor for five weeks. He administered leaf of life to ease the child's head, and dosed him regularly with cerasee bush because boy live in packing case beside dump mus' have thin blood. He questioned him repeatedly about his Mumma, until he was convinced that there was no way of locating her. Pa Leon fed him with the food he and Matthew ate. Real food cooked on a coalpot, fresh from the plot he called his vineyard. It was a dense mesh of coco, melon and pumpkin vines with provision foods of all kinds underneath and fruit trees emerging from the top. Victor ate mangoes and bananas till his bowels worked regularly and painlessly for the first time. He and Matthew played and hoed as if survival were possible without chicanery and violence. They drank the ganja tea Pa prepared every other night by boiling the leaves with two teaspoons of sugar.

"It brainify de yout'," Pa explained.

He did not share the weed he smoked, however.

"When you big," he promised, gathering the sensemilla, high-grade marijuana in which the female flowers had not been fertilised by male pollen. He inhaled deeply, closing his eyes in thanks. "Holy weed," he intoned, squatting in the fragrant twilight before his door.

In the mornings Victor stroked the fat nanny goat as Pa Leon milked her.

"Tomorrow we going on a likkle trip," Pa informed him. He glanced at the boy's face and added gently, "Not to frighten, yout'. No more packing case fe you. Me no waan you chase no more brown man fe gun. But I is a poor man, though you wouldn' tink so how you suffer a Kingston. Nothing I eat dat I don't plant Iself in de virgin eart'. But still I is a king." He shook his head gently at the startled expression of the boy. "I a king dat wear no crown. Black Judah. Selassie smile 'pon I. How beautiful my skin an' how perfec' de labour of I hand. Look how you get fat an' nice now, how you clean and you face shine. You use de chew stick dis morning?"

"Yes."

"Yes, Pa."

"Yes, Pa."

Pa Leon would take him to St Thomas. It was far but the Israelites had journeyed across the desert and when Pa and Matthew returned to Africa there was no telling how far they might have to walk. If he could not find the Castries people or if they did not want the child, he would keep him somehow. Early in the morning while the mist curled up the narrow path, the three trudged down the hillside from Pa Leon's vineyard.

15
Verandah Talk

IN THE other, parallel world of the Cohons, it was years before Adam saw Aunt Belle again. He was thirteen.

When he glimpsed her it was with a shock of familiarity. She was unchanged, it seemed, a timeless person.

"You look so different," she gasped.

"You don't."

Still she followed him with her eyes but now he recognised that the longing was not all for him. He knew that she was think-ing of her own son and what he might have looked like if he had lived, and he pitied her. She talked of Vern as if he were still alive or had died only a matter of weeks ago. She spoke of her mother sympathetically as a woman of many sorrows, again as if she had spoken to her recently. Stella she treated with an adoration that bordered on worship.

"And what 'bout your old lady, Mr Paul?"

"Aah. Struggling along, Miss B., struggling along."

"Struggling!" Belle's ready chuckle lit up the eyes so recently misted over. "Well, if Miss Martha Jane is struggling what can the rest of us expect to do?"

They grinned, Paul's habitual tension breaking as he rumbled into a deep, satisfied laughter, for he was proud of the grand-mother who had brought him up.

"She'd be delighted to see you, Belle."

"Well, I'm ready to go anywhere. I don't know when I'll be back, God willing."

So on Saturday they set off to see Grandma-on-the-Mountain.

It was a frequent outing for Adam but never lost its savour. Always there was a last-minute scurry in the kitchen to find something to take for her.

"Well, she will have cake, depend on it," Grace fretted. "Still I suppose she might taste a piece of this."

"Lord, Miss Grace! The raisins fell," Stella demurred.

"Tcha! Never mind that. You put it in. What 'bout the pork? Too heavy for her, eh?"

"Here. Here. You know what she will be glad to get? Look a bottle of lemon wine, Miss Grace."

"Aah!" Grace pounced on it triumphantly and held it up to the light so that the sun winked pale gold through it.

Paul nodded his agreement. "She'll enjoy that. I'll offer her a little support."

"Now just you don't drink it out."

"Come on, come. Time is trickling away."

It was always like that, Adam reflected gladly. The ritual was reassuring. The road curved up steeply into the hills. It too was always the same and would always be the same. The world was warm and solid beneath his feet.

They were through Bog Walk and over Diablo early, even while the mist was curling away from the river. Moneague was deep green wet countryside, rich in provisions and overflowing with fruit trees that bent laden over the fences. When they passed the special bend in the road where the air changed, everyone remarked on it. Suddenly it was cool and heady with the smell of rich soil and vegetation; they were almost there. Like magic, Adam's sinuses cleared and his chest felt dry and open.

At the foot of Irish Hill, Paul blew the horn, one long, one short. Adam jumped out to pull back the three heavy bamboo poles which served as a gate. He waited till Paul drove in before shoving them back. This was harder because they had to fit back into slots which were surrounded by bullgrass and tangled yam vines. Paul forced the car up as far as they could and he began calling as soon as they abandoned it. It was a wide drive, slick with wet grass and bordered with bearing citrus trees, tall corn and sugar cane. They hiked up it slower and slower, Belle chirping happily, though intermittently, through laboured breaths, the others nodding and smiling though mostly intent on their own thoughts.

She should have responded by now, Paul's mind raced. Suppose she's fallen? Unless she has the radio on and she can't hear. Of course she was getting on. He must remember that. So were they all. Only yesterday he could have scampered up the hill like Adam. He watched him scrambling along heedlessly, beckoning impatiently, running hack to meet them, making little forays into the trees in the hope of ripe tangerines. Paul inclined his head to the boy and shrugged at Grace. "Where does the energy come from?"

"More important," she gasped, "where does it go?"

Belle wandered back to the path with a few tangerines and hailed Adam, who came leaping and skidding back to them. They stopped and called again and this time a response came from a few yards ahead. Paul smiled but was panting a little and did not call back.

One day, Grace thought, it will be too much. Why in God's name don't they sell it? He's young still, but one day he will be labouring up it.

She halted and tried to catch her breath, looking around and wondering to herself for the hundredth time, Why would somebody want to cut herself off like this. In God's name, why?

In a few seconds, Adam thought, disciplining himself not to look back too early, I can turn around and see the whole world. Then I'll stop and sit on that old stump where the pear tree fell down.

When he got there he paused and turned around slowly. The land slid away green and wet towards the valley which he could just see between the fruit trees over high stalks of cane and corn. He could glimpse the road, and a thin dark line of water materialised then lost itself in bush. He took a breath of satisfaction and grinned at the rich earth smell and the pungency of wet greenery and fallen fruit. Then he heard the scraping of the gate which kept the chickens reasonably near the house and he glanced back to see his great-grandmother listening for him expectantly.

Grandma-on-the-Mountain was a short well-covered woman in a cotton print dress with an apron, black laced shoes and white socks. Her eyes were hazel-brown and her hair, whatever colour it once had been, was silver-white. It was long and thick still and she wore it braided and lapped across the crown, a striking contrast to her sunburned skin. She walked as firmly as ever but carried her crooked stick everywhere, partly for security on the slippery hillside but also to reach for fruit or part the tall, razor-sharp grass that grew off the path. Today, mindful of a bunch of bananas that might be fit enough to collect and of ripe sugar cane along the path, she gripped her cutlass sturdily in the other hand. They walked down together, talking about the animals, especially that thief of a dog, Chappy. They met the others standing arm in arm and laughing in short gasps about the slope.

"Then you not coming up?" Martha Jane demanded.

"Oh no! Why you come all the way down?" Grace wailed.

"Well, after I wait and wait and don't see you, I say you change you mind. Gone home and don't come look for the old lady."

They chuckled and gathered round her.

"And what a greeting!" Paul waved his hand at the cutlass.

"That nice bunch you saw the other day, boy. I was just going to nick it off."

Distress etched little lines around Paul's mouth and eyes as he took it from her. "Oh now, good Lord. Dearie, how often I must remind you? Jus' avoid the machete for me."

"Miss Martha, you still using you cutlass?" Belle's eyes were wide and bright with admiration and amusement.

Martha Jane responded with a sort of good-humoured impatience. "Eh! Then child, is old woman you take me for? What happen to you?"

And she set a brisk pace up the hill.

By the time they reached the house they had several ears of corn and long, bowed purple-green stalks of sugar cane. The bananas were cut but left on the hillside. Paul would change into an old shirt before cutting off what they needed and bringing the rest of the bunch up to the house. Miss Martha would have had them take it all but Grace insisted that it was too much. When Paul had changed, Adam would go back with him, carrying a bag for the oranges.

The house was a wooden structure, raised on stilts for ventilation and the ducks and chickens ran this way and that in and out from between the supports, nesting in the warm dry area beneath. Along the outside of the porch, on the white-painted wooden rails, roosters would perch to survey their domain or a hen might flap up in search of grain that Martha Jane might have spilled on the way out. At one side, under one of the tangerine trees, stood a trough of clean water and around it there was always a huddle of activity. The ducks were in and out so it had to be changed regularly. Fights would break out and occasionally Martha Jane would burst out with a bucket of water and slosh it over the rail at them so the hens fled in startled little spurts of half flight, barely lifting off the ground, squawking in alarm. Then the ducks flapped their wings and glided away low with their bumpy yellow feet trailing the ground. The gobbler, of course, would shuffle hastily aside, raising his head with an expression of great offence, but he never actually seemed to run. Martha Jane said he was too lazy, but Adam was sure it was beneath his dignity.

For Adam this porch was the best part of the house. He hung over the rail, popping his thumb into the centre of a tangerine so that the rind made his nose tingle, and he spat the seeds as far out as he could for the hens to argue over. Normally he liked to eat the whole pegs, but here was a patchy brown and white dog who sat attentively upright, staring unwaveringly at his mouth. So Adam was forced, when he had sucked the juice out, to toss Chappy the little skins which he caught adeptly and swallowed with one gulp, his hypnotic eye still fixed on Adam's lips and his ears rigidly laid back.

Inside, the others wandered through the bedroom to a window that opened over a washbasin and was partly obscured by branches. On the other side of the room a door led through the small sitting room. Here was Paul's old day bed, desk and bookcases. Here, on one shelf, were the volumes collected year after year with the insignia and motto of the old school, and the inscription, *Presented to Paul Cohon for Excellent Work.* They were clean but tunnelled here and there with worm holes, as were the Latin dictionary and crumbling algebra texts. On another shelf were Teach Yourself books, everything from ship-building to butterflies, and nearby Wodehouse rubbed shoulders with Virgil, Molière, Gibbon and Hornblower. On the bedside table, still ticking, was the clock Martha Jane had given Paul when he entered school.

The air was fragrant with newly-baked bread. Adam hurried into the adjoining kitchen to see the others slicing into the fresh loaves and spreading them with home-made pineapple jam.

"You didn't tell me!" he wailed.

"Boy, in this world you have to see about yourself," Martha Jane advised roundly, and sawed off the crusty end that he liked. She whisked a yellow checked cloth off a dish at the centre of the table to expose generous slices of cake, dark and sweet by virtue of brown sugar and raisins. She halted abruptly as a thought struck her.

"But stop! What about the dills, Paul?"

"That's right!"

"Big Massa here," she inclined her head to Adam, "he going love see them. We have to lock them up," she explained, " 'cause of the puss."

"That cat will slaughter anything," Paul agreed, then doubled up. "Tell them the saga of the mongoose!"

Martha Jane took it up shrilly.

"I come out one morning and see this thing lying on the step. And I say, No, something kill the puss. When I look, is a mongoose the puss kill come bring and leave for me."

They chuckled till Belle wiped her eyes and queried, "Then Miss Martha, you don't get lonely sometimes? I mean, you never feel to come and stay in town?"

Martha Jane stared blankly through the window, her feet planted firmly apart and her head thrust forward stubbornly.

"You see the grapefruit tree? My husband and my one daughter bury right there. Me same one close the hole for Luke. When I come down from this mountain it will be in a box. An' I prefer the box stay here too."

Paul shifted uneasily and got to his feet. "Well, well. Time marches on. We better retrieve those bananas, eh, Adam? And look lively too," he added peering out at the sky. "It's setting up to rain."

"We can stop at the spring?"

"More fish? Mm! Upstairs is gloomy and muttering, my boy. Let's postpone extension of the aquarium to a subsequent expedition?"

"Eh?"

"Next time," Grace explained.

Indeed it was black and thundery and Grace bit her lip apprehensively, but it held up until they reached the car and Paul inched cautiously down the drive.

"My Mama," Belle sighed, "she was a strong woman too."

"The stream, Dad?" Adam urged.

How long, in God's name, Grace agonised silently. How long does she think she can stay here?

Don't they see? Paul turned the wheel rather far to the left but righted it instantly. Telling her to move only makes her more determined.

Martha Jane listened to the sound of the engine dying away and turned back up her steps, running her fingers along the rails. At the door she paused, reached for the cutlass and took it to her room to lay it flat under her bed. Chappy followed her but kept away from around her feet until she was seated. Then he wiggled closer on his stomach till he could rest his head on her instep. She grumbled but was content. She heard the speckled hen cackle from beneath the house and knew there was another egg. She smelt the rain but as yet there was no sound of it on the roof. She stretched for the plate Paul had left beside the radio. Paul didn't make a bad cake at all, she thought. The bread she had kneaded herself, and they had enjoyed it. Poor little Adam. It seemed they only bought store bread. A rooster crowed and she chuckled in satisfaction, knowing Paul would be there again before the next weekend. "Sing while you can, old boy. Sunday coming."

She passed her hand over the slim prayer book Belle had brought for her and drew comfort from the smooth leather binding then laid it gently aside. Indoors, on an overcast day, she was almost totally blind.

It was raining when the car reached the stream, and Paul promised to bring Adam back another weekend.

But on the next weekend they drove instead to Goldfields for the first time since Aunt Belle's last visit. Grand was frailer and could not travel. Adam missed her but took guilty pleasure in the fact that without her they could drive on to Boston Bay before taking the road home. They wound slowly back on the coast road with the jerk pork still stinging their eyes and his sinuses clean and clear after the pepper.

They had slowed down by the bridge before they saw the man who turned out of the narrow path immediately beyond. He was tall and so remarkably erect and proud in his bearing that they would have noticed him anyway, but from the instant they became aware of him they were incapable of taking in anything but his head.

He was black with rather slanted eyes and a face overshadowed by masses of heavy hair. His moustache grew into his beard. His beard, black and shaggy near to the skin, browned and separated into uneven fingers where it hung upon his chest. His hair too fell well beneath his shoulders, matting like the beard into long, reddish-brown locks. A boy walked with him, shaggy too, and with the same eyes.

When the pair paused on the bridge, the car could not pass.

"Good morning, son," Paul smiled at the child.

The child stared at him, curiously uninhibited. "Not your son, Puppa, only your bredda. Is Natty dem call me," he added. Then, proudly, "But Matthew Leon I name which mean Lion in foreign tongue."

"Pleased to meet you, Matthew. Beg you little pass?"

The father drew Matthew back out of the way politely and continued his haughty passage over the bridge, leaving room for the car to overtake them.

"Who is he?" Adam breathed, riveted to the outlandish figure striding alongside them, head triumphantly held high.

"Shh!" Grace warned.

They speeded up and passed hastily before Paul undertook an explanation. "A Rasta."

"Eh?" Belle was obviously at a loss.

"Rastafarian. It's a cult, Belle. You don' remember hearing about Howell? Went to prison years ago."

"What he did again, Mas' Paul?"

"Preaching a lot of blasphemy about Haile Selassie. They say he's God. Howell was just a troublemaker."

"So what the government doing about them?"

"Oh, the police raid the settlement and they had a big flap over it and the whole thing was shelved. The Rastas themselves aren't so much the problem. The trouble with this sort of thing is the types who use it to camouflage all kinds of skulduggery."

"But why they have to keep they head so?"

"Scissors and comb mustn't touch it."

"Then what 'bout water. That is sin too?"

"But stop! What is this?" Grace squawked.

Adam had parted his hair randomly all about and pulled it into little peaks which wilted slowly back towards the scalp.

"Rastafari!" he pronounced solemnly.

They laughed and Grace ran her hand through it rumpling then smoothing it with her palm.

"Don't you bother with it," Paul snorted. "This is just the type of madness some of these empty-headed young people will take up."

"Tcha! No man," Belle demurred, "not decent people children."

"Mm!" Paul was not about to attempt a debate with Belle.

"How you know about it, Adam?" Grace's eyes sparkled curiously.

"Grand and Goddie talking."

"I'll be glad to see Miss Sarah," Belle reflected.

When it was time for Belle to leave, the house grew quiet.

"When next you coming?"

Grace and Belle hugged closely, lingeringly.

"Lord knows, darling," Belle sighed. "Every time it's harder to find the fare. But I have nothing else to save for. I coming. Sometime."

She glanced at Stella and a shadow passed over them swift but unmistakable. Inexplicably Belle remembered the filigree jewellery Abe had liked to buy for Stella. Then she realised, yes. Stella is like that. Cobweb fine, with a soft gleam. There was no one, she thought, no one she had ever met comparable to Stella. And every time she saw her the threads of the filigree were finer, almost transparent. Fear and longing surged and tumbled in her as they held each other.

"I'll be back soon," she whispered. "I'll be seeing you, Ma."

"Yes, yes," Stella comforted her.

So they clung, rocking gently to and fro and lying to each other and to themselves.

Uncle Ben came regularly after she had gone and seemed closer somehow. He collected Goddie every evening and brought her to Stella.

"I'm a tough old brute," Sarah sighed, "but Stella was always delicate."

The McIntyres, the Gayners, Miss Minnie from Dad's church, even Austin came more frequently now, as though they sensed a gap to be filled.

It was months before a tapping at the gate roused Stella and ushered in a robust black woman leading a boy of about Adam's age. Lively, bright eyes darted around the garden and assessed the house.

"Please,'M, me asking you help dis boy with likkle yard work, sweep yard. Long time him grannie did work fe you, 'M. One Icelin. Yes, 'M. Is she granpickney self, name Victor. Rastaman find im a Kingston, bring come a country fe we, and we want im go school a Kingston, make something of imself for im teacher in St Thomas say im well bright. Im win free place to Wolmer's, yes 'M, im do well even though im did out of school fe a while. We board im out in town, but if im could sweep up fe you Saturday it would help im, 'M. Many tanks, 'M."

Victor was quick and willing. His eyes ranged everywhere. He saw that, while he swept, the boy they called Adam rocked on the porch reading. One day Mr Paul stopped beside him.

"How you doing in school, Victor?"

"Aalright, sir."

"Raise you face when you talk to people, son. Look up. You have a nice bright face. And you understand so quickly. What you want to be when you grow up?"

"Don't know, sir."

"You get ideas if you read. Do you read, Victor?"

"Not plenty like Mr Adam, sir."

"I don't suppose you have as much time," Paul acknowledged gently. "But stick to the books, you hear? You could be a doctor, you know."

Victor looked up startled, then his face fell. "Science book too expensive, sir."

"Let me have the titles," Paul murmured. "I'll see what I can locate for you."

Stella watched from her window. Paul again. She too wished the boy well, although she couldn't figure out how Icelin could have had a child without her knowing. Then again she could not decide whether to tell him about his grandmother who knew no more of his existence than he did of hers. She would visit Icelin first, she thought, and see her condition. No point burdening a child.

So the next morning Grand had to go out. Someone she knew was ill, she said, and she must see her. Grand didn't feel so well and she wanted someone with her. Adam was big enough, she reassured herself as they sat jolting from side to side in the bus.

It was a long, white building. Walls, ceilings, people's clothes, trolleys, they were all white. Adam greeted Matron politely and saw that Grand was pleased.

"If she recovers from this she'll go back to Bellevue anyway,"

Matron murmured. "Whatever we do means nothing to her. Well, see if she knows you."

Through the crack between the hinges Adam could see part of the bed. It seemed flat, white and clear except for a worn black face. Grand stood over the bed.

"You know me, Icelin? Miss Stell? What 'bout Miss Sarah? Miss Grace, who you used to call Miss Baby? Aah, yes, Miss Grace. I don't know if you can hear me, but Miss Stell come to see you, Icelin. I have Miss Grace little son too. Miss Grace baby. I wish I could help you, after all you have done for me."

Icelin's lips moved irrelevantly. "All Miss Grace pretty hair fe make obeah doll," she moaned.

"Eh?" Stella sank into a nearby chair.

"Miss Baby hair," Icelin's voice rose angrily, "fe obeah doll. An is Louise leggo de spirit 'pon me by de cotton tree." Then she grinned. "But de bitch dead," she crooned. "Bring de scissors come. But watch im pickney dey inna blood." She stared blankly into Stella's whitening face. "Is dat why Bedward couldn't fly, you know. Is me. Hold back money to help de pickney. But de bitch dead."

"Oh Jesu, Icelin. God have mercy on you."

The woman's voice hissed in an urgent whisper, "Watch de pickney."

Outside Matron spread her hands helplessly. "She will probably get better, you know. She'll leave here and just go back to the madhouse."

All the way home Grand was cold and still. That night she fell ill. Adam wondered if she had caught anything at the hospital, but Mummy said it was her heart. Perhaps the bus ride had been too rough.

The house was quiet in a tense way now with an anguished business under the surface. The doctor emerged from the room, talking in a low reassuring voice, washing and drying each finger deliberately in the spotless white guest towel and leaving it wrinkled but still spotless. By evening Grand sat up and the next morning her familiar outline moved beyond the windows, pruning and snipping. But she was pale as the old rose she had set from Lynn Stollmeier's bush.

In the evening Goddie Sarah came and sat on the verandah, talking in that clipped, downright way that Adam loved, but her mind was full of evensong with Catherine and Stella. Everyone had come. The McIntyres had brought hot cornmeal pudding for Adam and Miss Gayner had dropped off a bag with mackerel, a hand of green bananas, two dry coconuts and a couple of scotch bonnet peppers. They had not stayed. They had just walked through the house that was always open.

Mom, Dad, Uncle Les, Uncle Ben, Goddie and Austin sat with Grand on the porch in the twilight. They sipped Coke, nibbled cake and recalled stories from strange eventful days. Their voices rose and fell over the hard time after the earthquake, the repairs they had made to Goldfields after the hurricane. They hurried over the flood, but Adam remembered hearing once that the next morning, walking along the beach, they had passed people who had been washed away and half buried in the sand and wreckage. What had looked like a rock jutting up through seaweed was a head left sticking up. Or a face only, adrift in sand. They spoke less of the flood when Ben was there because of a fury in him, never stilled. Shh, they had said, for his little Vern had disappeared without trace and half the house too. It couldn't, Adam thought, have been anything like this house, strong and sure.

They talked of strange people like Bedward who had planned to fly to heaven but died in the madhouse. Yet Stella said, no — not Bedward please. She didn't want to be reminded. When they argued over Busta, Adam's father grew silent. He hated politics. But Uncle Les was impressed, enthusiastic; Goddie suspicious.

"No, Sarah, no." Grand shook her head faintly but definitely. "He's not just a dreamer. Busta will change this country."

"I'd like to see him hold office," Uncle Les said. "I'd support him."

Ben snorted and waved his tinkling, frosted glass contempt-uously. "An uncultured hoodlum?"

Austin shrugged. "The poor will be heard," he said.

"They don't want to work," Ben snapped.

"You might be better off with Busta than you know," Austin's eyes were reflective. "Someone can use their poverty and make them an offer they can't refuse. Then the whole place can blow up."

"Who you think can make wo'thless people do anything together?" Ben sneered.

"I could. I could make them riot; I could make them work."

"Yes, Busha."

They chuckled. Austin was commonly called Busha at work.

"Wait now, wait," Grand waved her slender, almost transpar-ent hand for peace. "Don't start."

"No, Miss Stell," Goddie Sarah interrupted her. "Give them a chance. You don't remember that holiday at Goldfields when the children caught fight and were tearing the place apart? And how Abe would quote Garvey? 'Leave them alone, Miss Stell, they will eat each other!'"

Then Grand laughed and cried a little at the same time. But mostly she laughed and laughed. Who would have thought that she was dying?

But the laughter caught in Sarah's throat for Stella was filigree frail and so much was unfinished between them.

"We have to fix up Goldfields, you and I." Sarah caught Stella's fingers and felt them slipping away. "For the children."

16
Trailways

THE OLD *Goldfields had spread down towards the coast with level land where sugar cane swelled thick and sweet and provisions could be cultivated with relative ease. The pasture land flourished rich and juicy to the point where the estate sloped up into rockier more hilly terrain. This was still passable woodland and offered most of the timber for maintaining the estate buildings. Even in the eighteenth century the great house was an unplanned conglomerate of large rooms around a vast central hall but it looked down towards the sea across a vista of lush cane and further out beyond a deeper green belt of coconut fronds. To the left, a stream bordered with dark plumes of bamboo cut the canefields. Inland, near to the spring, clustered the huts of a hundred and sixty-five slaves who worked the twelve hundred acres that was Goldfields.*

But beyond rolled the sea and beyond that an ocean vast as death and further yet the afterland that the slaves whispered of, the shore of beginnings and returnings.

There a girl jostled for her chance on the roadside. She was in her early teens, tall and powerful for her age but playful, inquisitive, wilful. Her eyes were still, but more searching than was seemly. Their intensity made her conspicuous. In the end her curiosity betrayed her as the elders had forewarned.

A ransom of two hundred souls had been dispatched by the

Dagamba people to the Ashanti and news of their passing whispered through the village like wind in the millet fields. She craned forward above the shorter women to see the coffle pass and only for a second she met the eyes of the scrawny driver who followed it. Instantly he sprang forward and shoved her in line, unchaining and flinging a sick one out into the dust. Rough hands closed on her, stripping, shuffling her into step with a brutality that wrenched her ankle.

The heat. The halter. She sank under the hours, and the flies buzzed and landed more boldly. Her ankle swelled, hardened and throbbed until the faintest pressure on the foot became unbearable, and the men began arguing among themselves whether to carry her and gain what they could or slit her throat and be done. Faintly she signalled to them that she would walk. Her ankle sharpened to a blade beneath her then blazed to a flame. She marched through a haze of pain muttering feverishly. They shunted her from the interior to the midlands and eventually to the Gold Coast. So the group was delivered to the English fort, Cape Coast Castle, and the Ashanti received their value in firearms.

Neither the coffle nor the hold prepared her for the terror of arrival in Jamaica. She gazed from the deck in relief at the grey blue mountains and the green tangle of solid land, but a gunshot split the air and the crowd on the shore heaved and burst into small groups. Men leapt aboard, shoving each other madly for first choice. A thin man with a long white face and shiny black hair seized her shoulder and panic rose and burst in her. Her grandmother's tales surged up, and old rumours returned to her of famine in the white man's country and of his insatiable appetite for black flesh. She had never believed the ramblings of the old ones but they must be true. She had come through the filth and torment only for this.

One or two women broke away screaming and leapt into the sea. In a flash she saw it. Die, die! She too struggled to reach the side and destroy herself rather than be devoured by savages. But the pale fingers bit into her, unyielding as iron teeth, and hauled her away.

At the plantation a long silver brand thrust deep into its pot of spirits, and the girl shrieked when the Goldfields mark burnt into her. Still the terror of imminent death abated and she began to think her fear of being eaten was ridiculous. After a while she learnt that her name was Cleo.

Instinctively she sensed she would control only what she could understand and she grappled with fragmented impressions. Of stone buildings and demonic captors, pale and lank-haired, outlandishly garbed in tight wrappings at the leg, issuing commands unintelligibly. Of blacks of all creed, language and custom, herded together indiscriminately. Of monstrous interbreedings of both species. Stamping horses, snapping dogs. Whites who were servants of whites. Blacks who were drivers of blacks but servants of servants of whites. Huts and ox-carts. Hoes. Backbreaking labour. Structureless village of unravelled lives.

The seasoning period yoked Cleo into the routine she was to share with countless others, but she was quick and cunning. Others talked of running away, but she sensed the bitterness of escape to a life fraught with tension and discomfort. Besides, where was there to escape to? Others lived from day to day and schemed only to avoid the whip but she dreamed out beyond her own life and down the generations. Panic had passed and left her coldly watchful.

Others whispered that in the fields the easiest lot fell to the young and beautiful. It was hard to grasp, at first. It meant judging beauty through the eye of the stranger. But Cleo saw that, as an African, she lacked something that the creole women possessed. Then she recognised her purity of blood as a disadvantage. Just so much she could achieve for herself then. But for her children....

Cleo began to hold herself separate from the pure blacks except for the driver whom she dared not reject. A Scottish bookkeeper noticed her at about the same time so her first pregnancy was taut with suspense. Eventually her daughter was born — a mulatto.

It was agony to neglect it those first eight days but essential in case it proved to be a ghost child, born-to-die. On the ninth day the wet nurse informed her that it lived. They could change its clothes, bathe and name it.

Cleo gathered the fragile little limbs together and slipped her hand under the baby's head. Conflicting emotions swelled and churned in her. The child's skin — soft, like some rare and precious fabric. Unbidden and with a rush of hatred came a vision of the whip and in her mind the tender back was seamed with bright wet red and nausea rose thick and bitter. But her mind sang out of possibilities, for the baby was brown. She had clothed her in a sort of armour. She gathered the infant to her in relief and triumph and named her Princess.

Later there were other babies but none like Princess. Last came Phippa, fathered by the unwelcome but persistent black driver.

By middle age, Cleo reaped other benefits from her careful choice of partners. She was set to assist the midwife and from this position she operated as procurer. There were five men to every woman on Goldfields and she could afford to be selective. When a new overseer arrived she arranged at once for Princess to be his housekeeper.

Still it was not enough. Massa Cohon rode by with his tiny son perched on the horse before him and Cleo stared thoughtfully after them. Mentally she gathered the strands of her future and tangled them with the masters of Goldfields.

In the mesh of vegetation beyond the plantation the lines of descent interwove as irresistibly as within the grey stone walls. Like leaves of the forest the years drifted down covering the generations. They buried the virgin wilderness of the valley some Taino

*had found long ago and all recollection of that shambling barn
and useless, sprawling farm that the Spanish owners, the Castries,
had eventually abandoned. Even the bankrupt operation that
some other proprietor, Goldmeer or Goldman or somebody, had
fumbled with for a while sank deep into the past. Now, open to the
sun was the massive enterprise of a successful sugar plantation.
For the Cohons who owned the plantation in the early eighteenth
century the valley had turned to gold.*

*Even as old families blended into their surroundings, new
faces flashed with pale clarity on everyone's attention. On a ship
recently docked, one countenance more sallow than usual was
startling with its great beak of a nose and sunken, intense eyes.
The German Jew Stollmeier was desperate for work and hoped to
find it on Jewish property.*

By the time Stollmeier had sailed from Bristol on the Catherine
Brown *he was capable of halting English. That was two years
after he had followed the Rhine down to Rotterdam and found
himself without enough money for the passage. He worked his
way across the Channel and, in Bristol, he relinquished his freedom in return for passage to America. Somehow, the merchant
contrived to ship him to Jamaica instead.*

*Stollmeier proved an unsatisfactory investment. In Kingston,
one by one the planters passed him over for other servants displayed on deck. A few planters walked up and down for a while
feeling muscles, enquiring astutely about intelligence, docility
and morality, and carrying home their purchases. But there were
relatively few buyers. Business was failing.*

*When the Captain gesticulated, the planters shrugged, snap-
ping that everyone knew it was negroes who were in demand
these days. Some disorder on the dock heralded a different band
of clients who elbowed aside the well-dressed planters that paced*

*in methodical analysis and comparison. These new buyers of white
cargo were less discriminating, rough cold men who invested in
groups and drove them mercilessly across the country selling
where they could. The white servants huddled together when the
soul-drivers passed trying not to catch the eye of any of them.*

*Eventually the Captain stood beside Stollmeier trying to stir
some interest in him.*

*"But a strong man," he insisted. "Eighteen pound you paid
for the last one and 'e broken down with fever. Fifteen," his voice
rose to a shriek, "you paid fifteen for even the cursed Irishman."*

*"An Irishman's trouble, but he's still a man," a planter
growled. "This here's a Jew."*

*The Captain gasped and stared at Stollmeier, whose hair was
as scraggly and unkempt as the rest of the cargo. His clothes were
as foul. There was no discernible difference in cut.*

"A Jew! Ye filthy swine, you niver told me you was a Jew."

*"You never ask. You ask only if I can read the Bible in English
an' I can."*

*The customer spat in contempt. "Never told you. What of his
nose, for God's sake, his nose now?"*

*"Oh, Christ, man." The Captain grew red and choleric. "How
many men have great noses? I should turn away a man for his
nose?"*

*"Well truly his is not much more than your own. Perhaps
you're a Jew too!"*

*The Captain flung himself on the buyer and as they struggled
Stollmeier slid quietly overboard and disappeared.*

*Only briefly he stayed in Kingston, cheap labour at a board-
ing house run by a young woman named Anna Cohon.*

"Jewish?" he inquired.

*"No!" she grunted in distaste. "Anna for my grandmother. She
was Anna or Hannah or something. Davies her maiden name
was — no Jew. She die when my father Philip just a boy. He*

barely know her. Philip Cohon come to Kingston just after the
Port Royal earthquake with his nurse. The mother dead long
before, he say. Was a fine English lády. A great traveller."

"*I hear there's rich Cohons in the east. In sugar.*"

"*Hm. Well, no money in my family I know 'bout.*" *She moved*
away from him irritably. Trust a Jew, she thought — want fe
know 'bout you money. "*You better find something else,*" *she mut-*
tered. "*I don't need no man here no longer.*"

He stared at her, struggling for control. "*You know of any-*
where?"

"*No.*" *She swung aside. But her voice trailed back to him.*
"*You best try the army. They go take what they can get. All them*
Africans in the mountains, and the plantations to protec'. Slaves
to think about. Army, I suppose... Or maybe some Jews will take
you. Try them rich Cohons you hear 'bout, nah?" *she cackled.*

So he was in the street, with the fowls squawking from the
shadow of carriage wheels, with the mule droppings and brown
whores. He knew the Cohon woman sent for one of her black ser-
vants at night, for all her feistiness. He grinned sourly, raised the
lid of her water barrel and spat as copiously as he could, then
trudged off.

Stollmeier did find his way east but it was all for nothing. He
saw managers, owners, overseers, but there was no work and
indeed scant respect for one whom even the negroes dismissed as
a walking backra, a white man so destitute that he owned no
horse. At last, on Goldfields, an underling was ordered to give
him a meal and a night's shelter, but there was no employment.
Stollmeier resigned himself to the idea of joining the army, and
in the morning he prepared for the return journey to Kingston.

It was a glowing green in this valley he had come to, not the
deep ancient green of the forests but the tender glow of fresh
shoots, young leaves and infant cane. The lower slopes of
Goldfields lay filmed with carefully cultivated provision grounds,

and above them waved woodlands regularly thinned for timber. So even the hills were a softer green than in other areas. They rolled gently between the fields and the hazy sweep of the Blue Mountains beyond.

In the early morning the sun was gentle and the mountains still dreamed in their mists, but the valley brimmed with light. The birds had rustled and twittered among the leaves and hushed, and in their pause passed a few moments of unnatural silence broken by a swift whistling rushing sound. And a scream. And again the sound of the air sliced by a whip. And a scream. And again. And again.

A rustling above him indicated that the birds were stirring again. Twelve. They were accustomed to all the sounds of the valley now. Eighteen, nineteen. They fluttered down and began to pick at the wet soil. Twenty-nine, thirty, thirty-one. A quick stab and a worm writhed and was swallowed. One of the screams rose unusually shrill and the birds swirled away in a blur of white and grey, soared and settled again. Thirty-nine. It was over. Some new African was wild and hardened. He was one of the few they might never break. But they would try.

Inside one of the huts, Cleo peered at her granddaughter, Crystal. Cleo had consented to see the child but was by no means sure that she would do. Grannie Cleo's time was valuable. She motioned the girl's mother and aunt out of the room; and so Princess and Phippa waited nervously beyond the opening. They were half-sisters and as suspicious of each other as they were unlike. Princess was Crystal's mother, brown and almost middle-aged. Phippa was younger and black satin.

Crystal stared at Cleo wondering how this shrivelled woman could possibly instruct her and Grannie returned her gaze narrowly, evaluating the girl's creamy, oval face and the curve of her mouth which was parted in astonishment showing the pink moistness inside. Her hair was neatly arranged in long, black braids and her nose tolerably straight. Cleo's eyes returned to the girl's mouth, which was full but not heavy. Crystal ran her tongue over her lips nervously but her eyes were irrepressibly playful.

"Is what?" Cleo's voice was a broken flute. "Is learn you want fe learn?"

Crystal gathered her thoughts with difficulty, unsure of what was being offered. "Yes, Grannie." It seemed the safest answer.

"Pickney, you know seh what Massa want?"

Crystal stared again. Everyone knew that. She smirked. Grannie continued. "One ting im don't want is no fool." She paused to let it sink in. "Is one ting in life im want you for. If you nah can do dat im nah go keep you. If you can't do it better dan next woman im nah go keep you long."

Crystal's gaze flickered at the thought of Massa Cohon turning her out of the big house to return to the hut.

"Grannie," she faltered, "me will do what you say."

Cleo shuffled out to the doorway where Crystal's mother hovered tensely, and she paused impressively.

"Is a good gyal," Grannie pronounced. "You could see im want fe better imself."

She glanced scornfully at Phippa who had proved too guileless and too black to draw the attention of anyone worthwhile. Phippa had shown preference for a wild salt-water negro above creole men who might have been interested if she had asserted herself. And the Guinea bird would die, Grannie Cleo noted, mentally recalling his threats after the whipping. The fool would force them to kill him.

For Phippa, Cleo's route to escape through her children was not only too abstract for comprehension but repellent in its practical details. Phippa required happiness in her own flesh, and

*freedom that was physical and immediate. Few in fact could con-
ceive of the future with the breadth and cold appraisal of Cleo.
Into the grey future she saw her offspring as masters of Goldfields,
her ultimate triumph, freedom and revenge. But Phippa loathed
her for breeding them to pleasure the whites and for discarding
any like Phippa herself as black and discounted.*

*Crystal preferred to live in the great house and wear fine
clothes than to struggle in the huts. She was not a rebel like
Phippa, but she was ignorant.*

*"Grannie," she fretted, "nah you same one tell me lie pon
floor, say bed ongly for wo'tless."*

*"Floor yes. But me nebba say you fe spread out like you sick.
Not you shoulder me say, Crystal? Not you heel dem? Not fe drop
down pon de ground like you dead make Massa see you sprawl
off. As im come in de room make him see you ready one time.
You weight pon you shoulder an heel, pickney. Make de rest can
move."*

*Under her instruction every muscle inside and out came
under Crystal's control. On the afternoon of Massa's return, the
old women gathered and muttered over their herbs preparing the
balm bath. Little by little they filled the great tub of water hot
from the fire outside. Crystal felt the herbs drawing from her the
tension, anxiety and reservation. Her muscles loosened, pores
opened, mind soothed clear and calm. As she rose they bundled
her in warm clothes, and she was composed, passively waiting.
When she had sweated enough they soaped and scrubbed her
and returned her to Grannie for the massage. The odour of khus
khus filled the room and lay heavy on the air. Grannie rubbed
her arms, legs, ankles, reached between her toes, everywhere.
Everywhere but her breasts, the fingers worked over her in circular, rhythmic movements.*

When all else was done she turned to work on the breasts.

"Bring de feather come," she commanded.

Crystal wondered vaguely about the feather but under Grannie's hands her mind spun in ever closing circles towards an unidentifiable focus. Grannie began to flick the feather lightly and Crystal gasped. Again and again till her breasts were tight and her limbs loose. Grannie turned back to the rest of her body massaging in the mixture with the khus khus and the girl twisted in its sweetness impatiently. She felt a cup at her lips. Rum, she knew, feeling the sip she had taken burning through her but there was something else she did not recognise.

The drink lapped about her mind and she felt her life flowing in her. Her pupils dilated and she began to hear the swish of the feather and to... to see Grannie's voice soothing and urging her. The cloth was blindingly white and the billowing folds when they shook it coiled and swelled around her.

Grannie wound the fabric round and round her loins sealing her away from everything she had promised. The constriction was unbearable around the fluid she had become but, unhurriedly, Grannie Cleo continued the massage. After an immeasurable time her mother entered with her new clothes and escorted Crystal to the great house. As they left the house Cleo glanced contemptuously about for Phippa, but the daughter who most resembled her was gone from Goldfields.

Phippa stumbled to her feet and found herself in a vast dark emptiness of trees — nothing in any direction but a green gloom broken by wet, dark columns and twisting grey ropes of vine. And silence. She stood bewildered as if by a failure of one of her senses, waiting for an essential part of her to work again. But silence. She strained, for in the distance surely she must hear something of life. No.

Absence of the grinding of equipment, trundling of carts, cackling of fowls, dull thud of the hoe on damp earth, brief whistle of the whip. Absence of voices calling, commanding, muttering, laughing, crying. Emptiness of silence.

It came upon her that she was alone with two small girl children in the wilderness, and her heart died in her. She stood for seconds or hours before she was aware that the pickney hanging on the left side of her frock was in tears.

"Eh?" She knelt and regarded her fearfully. The faint hiccupping noise was startling in the bush. "No bawl make noise. Soldier-dem."

The child's eyes widened with a faint catch of breath and the noise stopped but she clung to her mother's legs wordlessly. The woman detached her and stooped, searching her face.

"What do you?"

The response was a subdued whisper.

"Me belly."

Briefly the day spun through Phippa's mind. Nothing since tea, the first meal.

The African's death had numbed Phippa. He had gone too far and they... She leaned forward to vomit, but her mouth flooded briefly with acid. Her mother, her sister, so engrossed in serving up that stupid little fool, they hadn't noticed Phippa. All day food had been unthinkable. When she had found herself she had taken the children and gone. Nothing since the morning meal and now the bush was growing dimmer. Food. They must start.

Where to? She stared around. The bush was identical in every direction except for a slight incline of the ground. Up, she thought. Away from the plantation and from the soldiers. Away from the scorn of her family and the whip and the lust of the head driver. But then. A trap snapped on her mind locking it. If she turned down the incline they might be found. If she turned up, they might never be found.

A whimper at her hip forced her into motion but in a carefully level direction, neither up nor down, suspending choice. Then she was forced uphill, further and further. Underfoot the leaf mould was centuries thick and her wide flat feet left dark patches of crushed vegetation and ruptures in the moss covering on the tree roots. One of the children saw bright berries on a shrub and pounced on them but Phippa boxed them away for fear of poison. As their hunger grew the children became querulous and unpredictable. Then far off, as if only in fearful imagination and then with terrible certainty she caught faint shouts and barking. A search party.

Before her the mythical darkness of tree trunks wavered and formed. It was a man, tall, bark brown, clad in leaves. She stilled a scream. Automatically her mind rushed back to old tales. Then she steadied. He was a living legend rather than a dead — a Maroon.

He hurried them deeper into the bush. They were higher than she had ever been when they reached a ledge and he dropped on his belly to peer over it.

With the flat side of his cutlass he swept aside a curtain of vines to expose what appeared first to be a wall of smooth rock. Then she saw it was broken at the extreme right by shelves jutting at intervals of a foot apart from top to bottom and that each brief horizontal was rivetted by stunted shrubs and low tough grasses. The children started at a bright flurry of movement. A parrot flapped squawking away among the treetops. With a shock Phippa heard it — a window on the brain flung open. Leaves rustled, and somewhere over the nearby rocks, water grappled eternally with stone. Under her feet and the children's, twigs snapped explosively and they panted audibly. But the man, Quao Castries, slid silently beneath the trees, a shadow among shadows.

He signalled her to climb down first but it was impossible, not knowing where to put her feet. So he began easily, steadying himself with thicker roots and glancing up anxiously, whispering

to them not to grasp at the smaller, shallow-rooted vegetation on
the rocks. At the bottom he reached up to land the children safely at the base. At last she lay sweating at the foot of the rockface
while he shifted nervously, prodding her toward the bush.

"Soldier," he breathed. "Soldier a come!"

He led Phippa and the children further down, into a gorge so
treacherously deep that she cried they would be trapped. She
pulled away, struggling to turn back. The dogs were yelping
behind them now and a warning shot ricochetted at the opening
of the gorge. He boxed her and tightened his grip, grabbing the
younger child under one arm while she tugged at the older.

The far side of the gorge was closed by a waterfall roaring
down from a tremendous height of rockwall and forest, and he
drove them under the edge of the torrent. The children screamed
when the icy force of the cataract smashed down on them. Then
suddenly they were crouching on a dry dark ledge behind a veil
of tumbling water. Now they followed him unquestioningly and
he led them through a dark passage in the rocks to a fissure
through which they watched the soldiers clambering in bewilderment along the gorge.

When the hunters abandoned their search, the Maroon put
an abeng to his lips and threw back his head for a long resound-
ing note while the whitened jawbone that dangled from it jerked
lightly back and forward against his face.

"How you know 'bout here?" she breathed.

"Fe-me father. Fe-im fader. Always know."

"From when so?"

"From time."

That evening, Phippa and her children ate as they had never
eaten. Land crabs and fish with yam, plantains and alligator
pears. Thick slabs of cured meat hung over the fire, tantalising
her with a smoke so savoury, peppery and succulent that she
dribbled inadvertently. Then Quao Castries laughed, human
and relaxed for the first time that day. He rammed a sharpened

stick into a sizzling brown chunk and handed it to her.

"Eat good while nyam last," he rumbled, watching her tear into it with watering eyes.

The drums talked all that night, relaying the progress of the soldiers, the ambush, the number of the enemy killed. New rum from the still licked into their brains and ignited them to resist as brutally as they were hunted. It was a night to remember.

But there was no real escape. Never. Not even when they joined Quao Castries's village and settled into his hut. Memories inherited from Taino and African ancestors burned deep in Quao and guided him from within. Instinctively he knew the tracks, streams and caves. He eluded the authorities. But there was no escape, no way to evolve beyond the prehistoric battle for survival in the dim days and misty nights among the towering tree ferns of the Blue Mountains.

Year in, year out, they fled the soldiers and hunted them. They knew it was so in other parts of the island as well. News reached them of daring exploits and the name, Cudjoe, seized on their imagination. But it was a life of slow starvation broken by the brief exhilaration of near escape or of some fortunate opportunity for vengeance on the soldiers. Then the drums exulted and their triumph throbbed in the darkness. The fire of resistance ignited the spirit of the drummer and he flung his head back in ecstasy of the words pulsing from his fingers. The message blazed into their blood and they erupted in dance, pounding the rhythm of their survival into the rockbound heart of the mountain.

But routine existence passed under the pursuit of bloodhounds and under obstinate commitment to their hard won insecurity. Phippa immersed herself in this deadly game of survival and when the time came for the village to be abandoned she too left it and merged into the forest, not walking through it or hiding in it but giving herself over as they did finally and completely and becoming one with the bush. Their movements gained meaning and direction as a new collective urgency drove them from familiar trails. Their meagre possessions lay smoking behind them and they were searching for a leader.

They gathered leaves and small branches and bound themselves with vines, winding themselves in greenery. They no longer moved independently among the trees but branched from one shrub to the next, rooted motionless beside the boulders when the forest was disturbed, swished faintly along the riverside like a thin dry wind in high grass. In the steep places they crept hand over hand from one jut of rock to the next, passing the children over carefully where the shelves were far apart.

On the second day of the great trek a young woman miscarried but they made a litter and carried her till she could walk. Phippa could not tell their number for they clustered in small groups, aware of larger movement that she did not actually see. Quao and the others had different ideas of what the route might be but they shared one common goal — to find Cudjoe, a figure as real and legendary as themselves. For Cudjoe they must go across the island into the mountains and through the mountains. For years they had celebrated in song Cudjoe's struggle with the soldiers. Now they would join him. They glimpsed each other in small gatherings on and off, but they knew themselves to be a force of hundreds. Individual groups wended their way, meeting only occasionally but somehow drifting, drifting towards Cudjoe.

From the village they had followed the river towards the coast and then east and parallel to it. Swift River was dry and low where they found it and they cut across. Then they swerved as the terrain forced them. North, south, north again by the hills. At least there were no soldiers to contend with.

Weeks must have passed when they turned inland for fear of being blocked by the mountains and missing Cudjoe. So they

came to Moneague, which the Spanish had called Monesca. They
gasped in relief at the soft, green, rolling hills around the lake.
They had heard that the lake occasionally disappeared and they
had been afraid of missing their way without the landmark. But
there it was, with little fingers of grassland reaching into it to be
cool. Moneague was inviting, but they must not rest for there
were sure to be soldiers. They avoided settlements where they
might have been able to find food and were desperate with
hunger by the time they came to the O'Reilly property on the far
side of the lake.

They seized what they could find. The fat woman O'Reilly
kept there bawled and bawled that she would call the soldiers for
them till one of the men kicked her to the floor and chopped her
into silence. They torched the house and left.

So they forced on, swung hard south by Grierfield skirting a
range of mountains which were scattered about in conical
humps. These opened up at last, but Lluidas Vale was too
exposed an area to cross so they wound around it keeping to the
foot of the mountains. They found themselves in a land cut
again and again by rivers which became increasingly difficult
to ford. Then Quao said that the River Minho must be near and
they grew wary, travelling parallel to it but northwards, per-
plexed by swollen tributaries near to the main stream. Tension
tightened as the land herded them nearer and nearer to the
Cane River barracks.

Near to the barracks they glimpsed an army scout safe on the
rocky hillside. Before he could raise the alarm they signalled
urgently to offer him a woman. Quao Castries was ahead with
their own scouts so the group turned easily away and left Phippa
for the soldier. Now if she followed them they would kill her and
if she left the party she would die in the wilderness. But then, she
thought, he might torture her for information on the rest. And
what of her children?

When the soldier came she was ready for him in her irre-sistibly glossy and muscular nakedness. Under her unfastening and teasing fingers he sank beneath a tree where she delayed, satiated and exhausted him until he slept. Then his knife, smoothly from leather and sheathed again as effortlessly in flesh and sweeping open his throat, swift certain movements. She wiped the blade on his pile of clothes, grabbed his gun and dived back into the bush. For many hours she trailed the group before overtaking them.

At first they were dangerously suspicious, but when she showed them his ears and the gun she had taken from him they welcomed her exultantly. Then they were merry with tales of Cudjoe's exploits and expectations about the welcome they would receive and commendations they would gain on account of their feud with the whites.

Under the dense cover it was hot and thick with buzzing green-backed flies and nervously darting striped butterflies. They broke a path over bedding planes of limestone that slanted almost like steps beneath their feet. Ferns and wandering jew cleared briefly to expose a city of red ants and the trees closed again. It grew shady, dark, then pitch black in areas. When it lightened two women cried out almost simultaneously beneath a looming tree with heavy fruit. They looked inedible Phippa grimaced, but the women laughed and shook their heads. Not food, not food. Antidote. Strip away the pith and grate the fresh pods to make tea. They pointed out a thick three-inch centipede on a slab of grey stone. Cock-pit, as they called it, was harmless, but was only one of a myriad of crawling things that teemed in the fallen leaves. They gave her a pod to travel with.

By now they had lost a few of the company. Two children were gone; Janie had plunged into a ravine and Manboy drowned in crossing a river. Suddenly they realised that no one had seen for hours an older man who had complained of chest pains the night before. All of them were bruised and stung and their feet itchy and bloated here and there with chiggers in pearly bladders under the skin.

Still there came a night when they stumbled through the grey entrance to a dry cave, empty and clean but for a scattering of bones at the entrance. The next morning brought certainty that they were in the Cockpits at last.

This was a vast region, its surface area magnified indefinitely by miles of strange straight-sided hills of honeycombed rock, detached from each other by deep valleys gouged over millions of years by water percolating through limestone, riddling the land with caves, some a mile or two in length. Because of the water, the escarpments were forested with vegetation so dense as to resist penetration even of light, so dense as to imprison the uninitiated and reach its dim loops into the spirit to throttle the will. Fragmentary groups of the wanderers merged and split again in the defiles between the mountains, even as water dripping through the ages of the earth had trickled and accumulated into underground streams that wound through and around the base of eerie hummocking, plunging landscape that haunted their every turn. Numbers grew even hazier but remained an impressive certainty that had become charged with almost religious awe over the hundred-odd miles of their journey west.

So Phippa was with Quao and the rest when they joined Cudjoe's Leeward band. Now she had four children, the older two fathered by her rebellious African and two more by Castries. For a while, vine-wound and leaf-clad, they persevered in the dream of merging with the guerrillas of the strange eastern mountains. But they never settled in Trelawny Town.

It was a gruelling freedom of stalking and hiding, of terror for her children and of hurried munching from gourds and pods like the chocolate brown seeds of the cacoon. Worse, it was devoid of fellowship between the groups or of interest or acceptance by the heroes they had sought. Phippa was with remnants of the original Windward group when, after scant welcome and a couple of years of disillusioned drifting, they prepared to march back.

It was different now. The march west had been fearful with uncertainty yet hopeful. But now they turned east again knowing the punishing path ahead and at its end only the empty village they had left and could not retake. Yet they longed for the straightforward hills and undeceitful valleys of the Windward mountains and they had their pride; they had lived without the energetic, barrel-shaped presence of Cudjoe before and would again. They would be happier with the legend than the man. But, for Phippa, recollections of the return march hazed with pain for, on the day after they left the Leeward group, Quao Castries was sighted on an exposed knoll of rock by Private Stollmeier and two other soldiers, and shot through the head.

Slowly and randomly strangers fall together. Purely by chance it seemed lives quite irrelevant to each other met in a common time and place. A young Stollmeier, from an army family, had done well and eventually bought a modest property of his own. Then he found himself attracted by Goldfields and, conveniently enough, by its master's only child, Clare Cohon.

Crystal's daughter was an ambitious girl — fortunate to have the same surname as the master of the house, to bear a strong family resemblance and to look white. Her lack of education and refinement did not distinguish her from the creole whites. Her father, Edward Cohon of Goldfields, was a vast shaggy man, crude in his manners. In fact, to the contempt of his foreign visitors, he spoke rather like his negroes.

Joseph Stollmeier was unperturbed by young Clare Cohon's inability to speak like an Englishwoman. His fortune did not establish him as one of the elite, and his background was

Jewish. His German lineage conveniently separated him from the rest of the Jewish community, which was largely Portuguese in origin. Yet Clare's Jewish background, however slack, attracted him. Stollmeier would have to raise his family in the island, for he was not an Englishman who could just ship children home to school. In all of these considerations Clare's legitimacy hardly mattered. After all, she was white, wasn't she?

Edward Cohon was coarsely amused and did not bother to disillusion anyone. Young Stollmeier was rather an upstart anyway. Cohon tolerated him for the sake of the Jackmans, whose land neighboured Goldfields. Perhaps because of their own distant background, army people always interested the Jackmans, and they introduced Joseph Stollmeier as a promising young man whose father had done well in the army.

Stollmeier was frankly surprised at Cohon, who carried himself sloppily for a man of his means. Stollmeier himself did not affect European fabrics but was coolly attired in kerseymeres. Most of the other guests wore the light English broadcloth. It fitted less slickly than it might, perhaps, being unlined, and it would no doubt have cut rather more dash with a bit of lace, but there it was. The tropics, after all. Breeches of Russia drab were durable, neat and not unbearably hot and the waistcoat and stockings were as light and cool as could be found. Stollmeier cared for his appearance although he was not a foppish man. It seemed to him that Cohon carried comfort too far.

Cohon's daughter was quite another matter. Of course, she was not oppressed by the heavy brocades of the two English women present. One of them seemed likely to sink at any minute under the thick white cap that had been fashionable in the British winter and was now in summer just arriving in Jamaica. Her face was startling with the fine red pimples of prickly heat that marked her as a newcomer. In the thick August afternoon Clare Cohon moved with a pleasing ease, sensibly attired in fine lace-trimmed linen that showed up her figure, modestly laced about the breasts though she was.

Dull afternoon it would have been otherwise. His eyes darted after her. He had seen her driving out and stared at her as he stared at all women. Normally he did not care for white girls but she was not the washed out white of most. Creamy skinned she was, flawless in texture and features, and her eyes snapped challengingly under the pert, starched, mitre-shaped cap. When he had tipped the brim of his white hat she had glanced at him as if in amusement, yet somehow calculating. The English women seemed pale and sick beside her. She had something more.

Besides there was Goldfields, a good venture to marry into. It was a fine house now. Cohon had added a verandah so that the solidity was relieved by turned columns and wrought-iron balustrades.

"You cyan't drink the cider," Cohon was explaining to the newcomers, "cyan't touch butter for now either."

"Well, but what is there to eat?" the woman with the prickly heat fretted. "The flour is certainly alive."

"Oh well, biscuit and flour — you know. They come all the way from North America." The Reverend William Jackman chuckled, secure in his well-established knowledge of the island. His people after all had come across with Venables.

Cohon shrugged. "You just open it in the sun and they walk 'way."

"But so many of the local foods are inedible," Prickly Heat gasped. "There's one they gave us with green vegetables, okra-pods and peppers — mainly peppers!"

"That not for you," Cohon smirked. "Pepperpot for locals, only locals." He grew serious. "You husband him musn' touch it." He glanced at Stollmeier. "Husband have the bilious fever. Orange juice." He nodded rapidly several times. "Seville orange juice for the bilious. Well." He eased himself to his feet. "Make we walk

then." He saw Stollmeier's eye on Clare and smirked spitefully for a moment, then his expression softened. He pinched the girl's cheek absently.

"No sons, no sons," he commented irrelevantly. "And de mother dead too. Poor likkle thing. Pretty child, eeh?"

The English women hastened to agree politely. Privately they thought Clare's complexion awful. The sun, they supposed. Or, with sly amusement, was there something more?

Princess shuffled painfully onto the porch and handed Clare her parasol.

"Nuh go in hot sun an forget i'," she muttered and turned in.

"The child's Nana," Cohon chuckled. "Think she own her."

"Nana?" Prickly Heat queried sharply, looking after the elderly woman questioningly. Princess's brown face was crumpled but expressionless as old paper.

"Nurse her from... oh... before she born. And with no mother, you know."

Stollmeier offered Clare his arm and led her down the steps of the piazza.

"If you were to leave Goldfields you would want to take your Nana with you I suppose?"

"No have to," she responded thoughtfully.

"I thought you might be attached to her."

Clare smiled at him inscrutably. "She wouldn' want come."

"She has children?"

"After slave no have family. Is only me she have. Me one she live for."

"Yet...?"

"When me leave Goldfiel' me go leave Nana."

"Why is that?"

"Oh she old an' talk-talk too much." Clare waved gaily towards the neat row of huts beneath the bamboo. "We goin' de wrong way. Make us take this path with the others."

"What's along the other one?"

"Just the nega house dem."

They turned onto the other path and he began to tell her about Kingston. Briefly he paused to stoop among a cluster of tombstones. They traced the progress of Cohon's children: died at two years old, 1718; died at eight years old, 1719; died at seven years old, 1719; died at twelve years old, 1722; died at nine months, 1723; died at fourteen years, 1723; died at five years 1723; died at three weeks 1724; died at nine years, 1730. And then his wife, died in childbirth, 1734.

"How sad for you," he commiserated, "losing all your little brothers and sisters, even your mother. You must be so lonely."

"Not again," she responded mischievously and with the hint of a dimple.

William Jackman viewed them with mixed amusement and irritation. His people, though originally army folk from Port Royal, had been residents in the area for generations. One had even been overseer on Goldfields briefly but had eventually been dismissed for incompetence, and Jackman found a peculiar amusement in chuckling about Cohon and Stollmeier with his friends.

"Young Stollmeier's grandfather should have visited the Cohons in the old days. He could have had Clare's great-grannie free. Part of the hospitality of the house. People take care of their brown bastards eh, but damn it all — marriage!"

"You sure what you saying, man?" his friend, da Silva, chortled over the jug of sangaree.

Jackman nodded his head vehemently. "Forget I born and grow up here? Anyway. Don't they're all heathens together, when you think 'bout it? I won't be here. Retirement coming up. Going home in a few years."

He looked around at the riot of colour on the hibiscus bushes, at the deepening blue of the evening sky and the ferns fluttering *lightly on the porch and he began to wonder how it would feel to leave after all his life, and to wonder what England was like. He had never been home.*

Stollmeier found his father-in-law, Cohon, an indolent man and careless of family responsibility. At times he would take offence over trivia, erupt violently and embroil Stollmeier in a quarrel he did not understand. Stollmeier told himself that he came to Goldfields only because of Clare. In fact she had little interest in Goldfields and would sooner not have come. But Goldfields after all was going to be his eventually.

Stollmeier grew haughty and fancied himself a man of property. He lived expansively. He dressed, equipped himself and entertained lavishly. He was in debt, of course, but so was everyone else of note. Some farmer named O'Reilly pestered him for money to rebuild in Moneague after a Maroon attack. Stollmeier owed him of course — a trifle. But it was outrageous for O'Reilly to keep reminding him of it. Upstart Irishman.

The creditors flapped around Stollmeier, pressing their claims but maintaining his obligations among themselves to preserve him and fatten their inevitable shares. Stollmeier was unworried by them because when he sat on the porch sipping Madeira with old Cohon, he knew Goldfields was going to be his.

III

Rapture

17
Warner

AUSTIN LOUIS was big-boned but lean, bronze and tight-fleshed. He walked lightly in his well-cut suit, but was muscular, with short, padding steps, giving an impression of power tightly reined. Beneath his sleepy playfulness lay restraint, unending patience and relentless persistence. His word carried weight, unquestioned by those above him or below. Busha, they called him.

His was a square face, wide at forehead and cheekbones, casting in shadow eyes that were lively but inscrutable, watching and filing. His mind caught and recorded limitlessly. Les said Austin heard every whisper on the wind.

"Those people in the banks smell things before they happen, you know. Austin has some account abroad now and I can't help wondering what it means."

It was Saturday. A cut-glass bowl that had been Stella's favourite sparkled with fruit salad in the middle of the table. Grace fingered it wistfully as she rested a dish of grated coconut beside it. Then she paused, apprehensive. "Why would Austin want money outside?"

"Don't know. He says it can't last forever."

"What?"

"He just say so."

"He offering to carry out ours for us?" Ben demanded, his ham-like arm reaching for the salad. "What interest he has in what we do with money? All right!" he grumbled as Les bristled. "But ratta no play a empty loft."

"Well I don't know 'bout anyone else," Paul chuckled, popping into his mouth a pinch of coconut between tapering fingers, "but my resources are too limited to export."

Les leaned back and regarded Paul quizzically. Smile lines were beginning to etch their way into the corners of Les's mouth and eyes.

"Austin must be have it." Grace glanced at Les.

Les shrugged, but Grace thought, Tcha! Les must know. After he and Austin were so thick. She twitched and rubbed her arthritic shoulder as she lowered herself into Stella's empty chair, filling its corners as Stella never had.

Mama gone, she thought. Well. We sleep to wake. Yet when, Grace wondered, had she begun to replace her mother in every way, dispensing calm, restraining anger, and salving wounds with laughter. She shifted as the nerve in her shoulder lanced again.

Ben's voice broke in, "If you would rub with the blasted liniment, you shoulder would get better. Chat 'bout the smell!"

That day it rained. Bright blue thickened and dulled to a dark line blurring to grey, moving in from the sea, rushing over the backyard to patter on the window panes, overtake the roof and front yard, and to drum with gathering momentum until, all around, the hills melted into cloud. Grace and Paul were in their Saturday huddle over the *Gleaner* crossword puzzle.

"You don't think Austin is getting a bit mercenary, Miss Grace?"

"Well, remember you just don't like money and property."

"It's not that I don't like them. You handle these things better and I leave them to you. But you want them for what you can do with them. He wants them to have, to use them to get more."

"He's a practical man, with his head well screwed on."

"And I'm not practical?"

"No. Not at all. But good. So good. Paul? Paul, for God's sake, is the middle of the day. What would people say?"

"I had not envisaged a notice in the *Gleaner*."

"Scamp."

Outside the sky was blotted out and water pounded on the roof and spewed off its corners.

In the heart of the city, Victor Castries shrugged his school bag more securely onto his back and flicked the water from his eyes. He would arrive at extra lessons soaked, but he knew now that there was no other way out for him. Since the days of his packing case on the edge of the dump he had glimpsed the brown boss-man occasionally but never attempted to contact him. Now Victor wanted respectability as well as comfort. He lost touch with his barefoot contemporaries from Trench Town and forged other friendships.

The myth that was Kingston continued to weave its spell on the youth of the country and draw them from the timeless round of garden plot and Sunday meeting. Now one quarter of the island's population lived in Kingston, and still the city grew, adding twenty thousand souls each year. Victor made friends in Harbour View, the first suburb growing up outside the Liguanea Plain, but mostly the growth of the city was internal, squeezing the poor closer and closer. More and more Jamaicans emigrated to Britain but the growth continued; the constriction intensified. In West Kingston, the population in Moonlight City doubled.

Walking the fragile causeway between the classes, Victor sensed the turbulence growing visible, audible, palpable. Black activists urged resistance.

The squatter camps had regenerated, swelling and pressing the city's back to its wall of mountains. In Trench Town there were more one-room huts, more packing-case and fish-barrel dwellings than ever. It was a community of strangers. Now half of the inhabitants of Kingston had been born elsewhere and the recent migrants concentrated in its yards and tenements. Independence came — whatever that meant. The rhetoric associated with Independence fired pride and determination — but to do what and how in West Kingston? It occupied Victor's mind considerably as he moved towards his final year of school. All he could think of was to get out of Jamaica altogether. That meant a scholarship.

He arrived at Oxford Close and asked for Mr Cohon, then explained that he had saved for extra lessons on Saturday and could no longer help with the garden. He was startled at the spark of admiration, flaring to enthusiasm in the lean figure, tensed above him.

"And you mustn't on any account give up your studies. I want you to promise me. If things get hard, come and see me."

Victor wondered what image this man could have of hard times, but beneath the automatic resentment something jolted him — a current of enthusiasm that was instant, real and powerful, charging him with determination. He was shaken by recognition of Cohon as an actual person, who had glimpsed him as real and separate from the rake and wheelbarrow and garden hose. Victor parted with him more gently than he had expected to, nodded as briefly as was polite to Adam, reading on the porch as usual, and vanished from their lives.

On and on the rain beat, a continuous low growling above Oxford Close, till the water cascaded off the eaves into widening, frothing pools that spread and joined, drowning the Cohons' backyard. The grass blades quivered in patches and tiny streams cut their way through the flower beds and among mango trees, following indentations from the last rains and washing down them towards the back fence and along it into the Andersons' yard. Another of Stella's rose bushes was uprooted and the pale bloom drummed into the earth. Water flooded down the window panes, sprayed in through the wooden lattice around the porch and rippled over the tiles and white enamelled chairs. Overhead it rolled with low thunder, continuous but urgent, as if there might never be a chance to rain again.

Grace paced, window to window, restless with thoughts of Sarah. Goddie should not be living alone, she fretted. Especially not now, not any more. Ben must bring her for tea and they would talk. It would be too much for Goddie to move into Mama's room, but Adam could, freeing the room that had been his since Miss Martha Jane died. Paul would not mind. The intertwining of their many lives into one added to each of them untold dimensions, and each new arrival fascinated rather than threatened Paul. He thought with amusement that Grace saw every space in the house as a gap to be filled, but it was her house. He never owned things, though he cared for them. When he tired of a house throbbing with activity he withdrew into some book. Grace followed him into his mind if he invited her, but otherwise she perched outside knowing he would return. Goddie would never intrude on him, Grace thought.

Goddie Sarah had narrowed considerably but could never be frail, even in old age. Proud and erect as ever, she had not stiffened, not even now. Grace watched her with almost tearful fondness as she collapsed on the sofa with a belly-laugh that would have put a higgler to shame.

"Goddie!" she gasped.

"Ah, Gracie, Gracie my love. And what a noise in your house."

She choked a little and fumbled for the hearing aid she had somehow disconnected. Then she sat up rather more dignified and fanned her face with her inevitable lace-edged handkerchief before breaking down again in a deep gurgle and stamping her feet rapidly in their polished high-heeled pumps.

"Why, you fiend from hell," she shook her head affectionately at Ben, "look how you've made me conduct myself. Out of my sight you... ruffian."

"What did he do?" Grace laughed in quiet bewilderment.

"Oh Gracie. Can't tell you that, man. A good girl you are, like your mother. Blessed Stella. Good, good woman." She wiped her eyes again, from Ben's mischief or Stella's memory, it was hard to say. "Where she got this Satan from I will never never know. Oh well. Stella. Gone years ago. Who would have imagined the world would go on without Stell. I have never missed anyone like I miss Stella, I have never missed anyone so. Jesu. Stella, Stella." She wiped her eyes again. "But if you know what times we had," she chuckled, "how we played pranks on Nana, poor old Nana. And when it was time for Stell to go home we hid in the garden behind the lions — we had these big stone lions, you know. Then when Stella got the typhoid I knew if anything happened to her I would die. I made sure I was going to be buried with her. Don't laugh, you fool. And Jonas courting me — I could tell she didn't trust him and so angry with her because I knew she was right — not that we quarrelled, never. Stella was worth ten of Jonas but I wondered whether she would find the right person how things stood with her and such a particular girl, stupidly so. Old Jackman was such a fool to make her slip away."

"Jackman? You don' mean Rev. Jackman?"

Goddie stared at Grace. "You didn't know? Yes. Augustus Septimus Jackman same one — that Ben used to call Septic Jackman. Jackman same one. Poor brute. Probably still in love with her, old and dry-up as he is. Anyway, I was afraid she might end up alone."

She pondered a little and shook her head with strange, awakening eyes. "Yet look. She had everything in the end... a rich woman. Even when they had to auction her bed and turn away the washer-woman. All I ever really had was Stell." She sat nodding into the twilight and added, "And Stella's family. And it's been enough. All I need."

Grace stretched forward and linked her fingers in Sarah's. "Goddie, live with us. Wait." She gripped the older woman severely. "Things are different now. I can't sleep at night knowing you alone in that house and can't hear tief breaking in if the hearing aid battery gone dead."

"Woman, who you talking to? I have money now to pay my

own private army to protect me."

"In Switzerland, Goddie. You are here. Now."

"And the last thing I'm going to do is to bring it back here."

"Why? You plan to go Switzerland?"

Goddie shrugged. "Not impossible. But, no. It's for Adam. Make it stay where it is. All my life I never had it. My father lost his... poor old Jacob Stollmeier. And his brother's family over in Germany. Jesu, Gracie. Auschwitz. Poor people. I never knew them. Rudy Stollmeier kept in touch with them but they stopped writing my father when he married Maman. I hardly ever heard of the German cousins till they were gone. I never thought of their money till that lawyer contacted me. But Auschwitz, Gracie. Well, I'm an old woman now. Better off in my own house."

Grace shook her gently. "Hush you mouth, too hard-ears. You know Paul adores you. And Mama would have wanted it."

Sarah slapped her thighs and guffawed again. "Rough me up! Just because I'm old and broken down? Forward pickney. Just for that I will move in on you and give you all hell."

Adam was sixteen when Les began to caution them about being too free. Television had arrived in Jamaica and Les had bought one for Adam but he insisted that the back and side doors be locked before they sat down to watch *Bonanza.*

"Nobody should turn their back on a door now," he warned.

"Nobody should turn *his* back," Adam corrected righteously.

"Or *hers,*" Grace grumbled.

"I've never approved of generic *he,*" Paul snapped in agreement. "Damn feistiness."

"But you don't remember when Mama was dying we fell asleep with the front door open?" Les insisted. "When we were children — no, only recently, and you two had just got married ('39 that was) — we would walk street any hour?"

"All down town," Paul agreed, "to the cinema — eh, Miss

Grace? And then for patties." He ran his fingers up her neck and into the hair she had just combed, rumpling it, but she relaxed under his hand like a cat, sinking back against him on the couch and bumping her head against his shoulder.

"Busta," Ben pronounced, "and all de ruffian-dem. Is they spoil it up."

For Paul the thought was a lonely cliff to which he withdrew, and from which he overlooked the abyss. Grace felt the pause and gathering tension in him, and she turned her attention back to the others.

"Whole pack of them," Sarah fumed. "A perfectly lovely little country before the politicians started tugging it backwards and forwards between them and tearing it to pieces."

The McIntyres would join in and soon they would all be in it. Paul would weary first. "Anyway," he sighed, "must life revolve around the wretched politics?"

Grace would say, "You like to close your eyes to it. Pass Sam those nuts."

"My eyes are wide open," Paul would remark with dignity. "I merely intend to outlive them all."

"You better," she snapped.

"Miserable girl," Sarah chuckled. "Never mind, Paul my boy, you're perfectly right. Nuts at this hour, woman? You anxious to bury me?"

Les leaned forward and spread his hands. "The only crime Busta ever committed was to insist that men who work should be paid."

"The whole of them are a parcel of crooks," Sarah snapped.

"Manley is a gentleman," Ben protested.

"Parcel of crooks everyone," Sarah's voice rose shrilly, "and whichever one you all idolise and put into power will make mincemeat of us."

"Mincemeat," Grace agreed.

"Then how we vote, for God's sake?" Les yelped.

"Oh, vote as you like, you fool. Just don't make a god out of a politician." Sarah sighed and her face grew sad, reflective. "When I think what it was like here. I don't know what's to come, but thank God I won't be around."

"Oh, cheerful one," Grace groaned.

Politics meant nothing to Adam. Outside of his schoolwork he immersed himself in foreign novels. He danced ska at parties but his own collection of records featured American and English groups. Dance, painting and sculpture meant little to him and though he enjoyed the occasional play at the Little Theatre, local talent flowered around him unnoticed. Still, he liked the current movies and went often with Les. One evening, Adam waited for Les outside the cinema till the show was halfway through, then trudged home anxiously.

It was ash-grey evening, purple-streaked, when Les finally slammed in from the *Gleaner* office, shouting about the *La Coubre*.

"Munitions. Whole ship blow up. What Castro going do now? Make me see. Whole dock gone up. Hours they working on the fire. We wait to hear. One heat. Rescue-team couldn't reach into the wreckage."

"What was on the ship so?" Grace gasped.

"Grenades, they say, and tons of explosive loaded at Antwerp."

"Deaths?"

"Twenty so far. But that goin' double or even triple."

"Jesu. Weapons and explosives. So near, all this violence?"

"It's all over the world." Paul pronounced. "I don't know why you think violence is a local invention. We just been living so good...."

Certainly it was within weeks that Les brought news of riots in South Africa over government pass laws requiring Africans to carry identification cards. Police had opened fire in the Johannesburg area.

"But imagine shootouts in your own city," Grace protested.

"Now is those people have a problem," Lisa McIntyre remarked, depositing on the kitchen table a brown bag with the unmistakably round bulges of Bombay mangoes. "Thank God for a free country."

"Miss Lisa, we could develop our own problems," Paul ruminated. "The Federation is the thing we need."

"But we not like South Africa and all those places," Grace protested.

"No. But we're a small country and a touchy people. Security could just..."

"Now Williams saying Trinidad going secede," Les grumbled. "What sort of federation we can have now? Where we going from here?"

"Must be to Canada," Ben chuckled, "like the Gayners."

"For what?" Paul snapped. "What they all want, or think they want and think they will get if they go... away... somewhere... it's all in their heads. They may as well have stayed. The paradise is only in their heads."

"From what the Gayners said in that last letter, paradise is in Canada."

"Well I'm not prepared to go one place," Paul sulked, planting his feet stolidly on the polished tiles.

"You can't say that, darling," Grace remonstrated. "You don't know where we going be in ten years' time."

"Well, I shall be right here. Probably in this chair, pegging my orange. Of course," he offered helpfully, "I may be in my grave."

"Oh, vile." Grace flounced away and switched on the TV.

Sometimes only Grace, Les and Austin sat listening to Sam McIntyre on the porch. "I just don't understand why people like Clem feel threatened."

"But what foolishness you talking, Sam? You don't hear someone hold him up with a gun? Austin, you know everything. What the police doing? And where people like that get money to buy guns? Is a business, or what?"

"Grace, is an incident, man. Is not some type of flare-up," Sam intervened. "What wrong with you? You don't drive through the countryside? You don't see the love our ordinary people have for each other? Watch Lena. She not just Jamaica white, she obviously white. Cyan't hide. Nobody ever rude to her about it. Because she is a Jamaican and like any Jamaican. However poor they are, Jamaicans basically all the same. Warm, hospitable. You don't find so?"

"All right. But you can't ignore what's happening."

"Like what? Is what? Don't people happy in this country?" Sam insisted, turning up his broad pink palms.

Les stared incredulously then glanced away, catching Austin's eye. Austin listened to them talking in circles about shadows while he saw it sharply and felt, almost smelled it, on every wind — a quivering tension, a fractional shift in that huge, seething, faceless mass that was unreal to everyone else on the porch. Only to him did that quarter of the population of Kingston have reality. Paul might suspect. Les might hear say. Only Austin tingled wide awake beneath his sleepy, half-smiling yawn, sniffing the evening.

Austin followed Sam's gesturing palm, pink and vulnerable, and a door sealed in his mind for years creaked open. It was the door to the latrine in a yard. A yard with a hundred and fourteen tenants and one toilet. They ate mainly on weekends, what they could scuffle from the market. In between, children had little handouts from one adult or other, provided by ganja peddling or prostitution. Apart from these sales, most of them had never worked and never would. At night when it rained the cardboard huts soaked, stank, sagged and finally collapsed. Aunt Lettie had sagged too, her face seamed, and her bust and arms hung baggy. She had less and less to offer and one day she carried him to another woman who was poor but employable, and just handed him over. The new aunt worked as a maid somewhere in Half Way Tree. Day in, day out, she reminded Austin that he was brown and she beat him to do his schoolwork in addition to the chores by which he earned his keep. Then he had met Les — Les who had gained a bloody nose fighting for him when no one else ever had.

The cool lively faces on the porch in Oxford Close were of a separate existence, unsuspecting. Austin stretched for one of Grace's cheese-paste sandwiches and turned it over in his fingers. Slim ribbons of soft white bread alternated with pastel green, cream and pink cheese filling. One day, he reflected, he too could sit on his own porch and serve three-toned sandwiches. He had bought land in the hills overlooking Kingston where among the older smallholdings, farms and nineteenth century houses, fine new middle-class homes were sprouting up. The foundations had cost the earth, but now he could build, landscape, furnish and seal off with walls and electric gates.

He glanced across at Les and a comfortable warmth spread through him, so that he didn't even notice when the door to the latrine closed again in his mind.

Les had no idea where Austin had been or where he came from, and Les did not care. He had understood as a child that Austin could visit him but that he would never visit Austin, and Les had kept their friendship away from home for a long time, so as not to embarrass the other boy. It never occurred to him that Austin could resent the kind of life the family took for granted, and, far from resenting it, Austin basked, learning, absorbing.

Les, in his two-toned shoes, stylish ties, upper St Andrew manners and Sunday School morality was an obvious type for Austin to despise, but Les was impossible to resist. Everyone knew and wanted him. Wherever he went arms waved, hands beckoned. He was solid, but light; serious, but attuned to some hidden hilarity in the ironies of life. He had a wicked humour, startling, almost cruelly keen in its perceptiveness, but irresistible in its truth and total lack of superiority. Les was warm, devoted;

310

down to earth, but playfully so. His affection was a sort of gambolling that made his name a greeting on countless lips and no one of his family or friends knew the whole range of his acquaintances.

The strength of his connections fascinated Austin. Les treated Paul with combined awe and frivolity. For Adam, his confederate, there had always been a new trick or queer gift. The favourite present had been a turtle, half-crown size with moss-green medallions on his gold underside and with scarlet sideburns. The elegant little beast wallowed in his wide dish beside the dining table throughout Adam's childhood, and now, after eight years, warranted a spacious tank in the backyard. Les was bound to Adam by an odd welter of sensations, pally and protective, because this was Grace's child. His connection to Grace was different to anything else on earth — a sacredness. Les would have died for Grace.

Austin tensed against a familiar pang. How did it feel to have been cushioned from childhood by that certainty of devotion? It was a defensive passion they all had for her, almost sacrificial. Sacramental. A mischievous sparkle from Les relaxed Austin again and warmed him with sensations of amused tolerance.

He could rely on Les and for this reason Les moved him more than anyone else. Then in a split second of searing clarity Austin realised that only Les moved him at all, and vaguely Austin hoped that the two worlds of Kingston froze permanently and completely apart for all their sakes. Certainly Austin was never crossing back. And if the crunch came he would save Les if he could.

"Claudius Henry?" Sam scoffed. "Who he think he is and any African Reform Church? Regiment soon round them up and shoot dem."

"You don't shoot people like that," Paul objected. "Charge them with treason felony, yes."

"Then you shoot them," Austin agreed affably.

"Thank God for the regiment," Lisa sighed confidently. "Should just clean up the Rastas too."

"Yes man," Sam settled back comfortably with his second helping of fruit cake. "They can't pass an opportunity to settle that. Decent people must able walk about, man."

Grace was silent. But no wonder, she thought anxiously, there are some who hate us. For a giant was stirring. Grace held back waiting to see where it would all lead. It must be hard to be poor, she reasoned, groping in her mind for images that weren't there, yet there had been poor people all along, in the old days, and without all the hatred surely.

"I can't think past the blasphemy," Paul shook his head wearily and propped it on one hand. "The politics of the thing is important, I suppose, but the blasphemy is horrifying."

"But, Miss Grace, remember Papa and the coffins he said he made after the earthquake? If he were alive must be guns he would make." Les contemplated the idea and chuckled. "There's money in it too."

"You could be put away for a statement like that," Austin reflected, with a little gleam of amusement lighting his eyes.

"Oh, come on." Sam leaned back and passed a hand over the thin hair on his crown. "Is blown up out of proportion. Little scuffle between some hooligan-dem and the police, and everybody susuing 'bout rebellion. Jamaicans have been murdering each other for centuries. Every country man walk with him machete the way my grandfather carried a cane. In town some people have gun. You don't have a gun, Les? I don't, but my brother has. You, Austin? No? Ben, you must have."

They all laughed and Ben pretended outrage.

"Well, if I were a couple of years younger I would certainly have one," Sam remarked. "As I am it would be more of a threat than anything else — just for someone to lick me down and go with it. But the point is Jamaicans quarrelsome as individuals. As a group — they not doing nothing."

312

"Well, a few are moving out. I heard from Belle in Canada. She says she's met some old friends from Jamaica, just moved into her neighbourhood."

"Let 'em go," Sam shrugged. "Lisa and I are here to stay. Bungo not driving me outa me own country."

"What's to come, Paul?" Grace rubbed her head on his shoulder when everyone had gone.

"I don't know," he sighed. "But *après nous le déluge.*"

They pondered it on and off through Adam's last years of school.

Les had been out one morning and dived into the office only briefly in the afternoon. When the phone rang he glanced at his watch irritably. A typist came in with a message from the editor and he motioned her quickly to a seat.

"Yes, man," he grinned briefly into the receiver. "Customs? I'll call Ben for you."

He dialled a few times till he got Ben's number, but the line crackled and they could hardly hear each other.

"I want you speed up something for me," he bawled. "Boat in with a car. Cyan't stop now man. Papers on the way." Joan was signalling furiously that the editor was waiting. "Call you back later. Eh? Cyan't stop." He dropped the receiver into Joan's hands and shot out.

Ben's voice shouted thinly from the other end and the typist put it cautiously to her ear.

"Mr. Goldman just left the office, sir. Joan here. Can I have him call you?"

Ben grunted ungraciously and hung up.

It was hours before a messenger handed Ben the papers and a container of gasoline. He turned the papers over uncomprehendingly.

"Who this Warner?" Ben stared at the Bill of Lading then

313

shrugged and pocketed the lot. Nobody knew all Les's friends anyway.

In a couple of hours he was on the dock looking over the car. He had had one of the men gas it up.

Warner, whoever he was, had sent back his messenger for it, a weedy looking youth plastered against the gate.

"Wouldn't be my brand new car," Ben scowled inwardly, "any little ninepence-in-the-shilling-boy driving it through Kingston traffic."

Ben decided to take it across the cluttered dockyard himself and hand it over at the gate. The messenger had shown little interest anyway. When Ben passed him, coming in, he was just staring away vapidly with his mouth open wetly to one side.

"Better get it through the open yard myself," Ben concluded. "Next ting the moron mash up Les friend car in front me eye."

He touched the handle and the lock released lightly, softly. It was a sort of balm to Ben, the smooth, easy movement. It was a long time since he had handled a new car. He thought of his old Ford with a wry fondness. With one finger he drew the handle, but the door was heavier than he expected. He felt a little wave of disappointment and chuckled to himself, pulling harder then settling himself inside. The ignition clicked and the warm humming reassured him. He moved slowly, smoothly from the dock.

Crates everywhere. He turned the wheel gently to avoid them and listened, startled by a heavy thud somewhere beneath or behind him, he could not tell. He listened for it again but there was nothing. Then, when he swerved lightly at the next obstruction, there it was. A thud. Hmm. Tyre loose? Could even be the gas tank. Well. Bad enough fe that jackass a' the gate steer battleship like this through Kingston, but if gas tank loose... Hm! Not his business though.

But then a shudder confirmed that there was definitely something wrong with a tyre. Mind you, nail and tack all 'round the dock. He pulled alongside the building and walked around the car.

Flat. Blast. Tyre fe change now top o' everything. He glanced towards the messenger. Time it take fe reach gate and rouse that dead-and-wake, the tyre would change done. Besides, don't is Les crony own the car? A bright stud of metal gleamed against the back tyre. Tack, yes. He stopped and started on the lugs. To his surprise they were tight. There was no connection between this tyre and the first noise he had heard.

He had to drop the tools to open the trunk. It was heavy and didn't stay open without his supporting it, so he looked around for something to prop it then leaned in and pulled at the spare. Didn't budge. He grunted in annoyance, thoroughly sick of the car, and searched around for a catch of some sort. What holding it? But after nothing holding it how it don' move? He sucked in deeply and tugged so that it crunched down onto the floor of the trunk.

Ben stared at the spare for a long time. Eh! Eh! He shoved it again experimentally. The thing weighed a ton. Ben strolled away from the building, glanced towards the gate again and went back to the trunk. Is what sort o' car this? He hoisted the tyre out and had the floor of the trunk clear. He unfastened it and peered down at the gas tank. It was secure enough but something caught his eyes. He raised the door of the trunk higher and propped it to get more light. But. Is weld it weld. New car gas tank weld. Then the thudding. What the hell in it make it have fe weld?

Suddenly he straightened up, so sharply that he cracked his head on the metal and held it dizzily for a few minutes. If the gas tank had something in it there was nothing particularly strange about the weight of the spare. He braced himself and raised the tyre again, depositing it heavily in the trunk. Then he pulled out his knife and began slashing at it savagely. He was red hot with rage. In a short time he had butchered it enough to reach in and tumble out handful after handful of cartridges onto the floor of the trunk.

Gas tank weld, eh? Wait. He slammed the lid of the trunk and tugged open the heavy door next to the driver's seat. The upholstery gleamed satin smooth on the inside. But is cartridge cram up in it. Fury gathered to a throb in his temples. He didn't even bother with the door. He stabbed his knife into the back of the seat, slashed it down one of the seams in the upholstery, then reached in and rattled them through his fingers.

The workers unloading it had shouted, "Mas' Goldman, sah? Is what you have here, sah? Steam rollah?"

He slammed the door, locked it and the trunk, and raced into the building. "Gimme a phone and get out."

Unceremoniously he evicted a clerk who allowed himself to be shoved out with the door kicked behind him. The clerk grinned and emitted a genial obscenity over his shoulder. He was accustomed to Mas' Goldman. Ben grabbed the phone and tried to dial, messing up two calls before he got the *Gleaner* office. Les's voice sounded on the other end and Ben gasped into the mouthpiece.

"Who de hell is Warner?"

"Eh?"

After a spurt of obscenity Ben collected himself.

"One hell of a car. Hell of a car."

Les's voice grew breathless.

"What wrong with it?"

"Cartridges like shit! Through and through. Spare, door, gas tank, all over."

"How you mean — cartridges?"

"Oh God, man, you is a fool? Cartridge, man. Fe shoot gun."

The line was dead still. Then Les whimpered like a dying man, "Christ, Christ. Gun, Ben? Gun? Aahm. Call you back."

"But this have fe report. Now."

"I going call you," Les screamed into the phone and dropped it.

18
Maroons

SOMETHING WAS gathering, though still remote, leaving the family intact in the late 60s. Adam felt a vague unrest, yet still it was just conversation for the classroom or front porch. Gradually though, it dawned on the family that about them was a transformation. Slowly, almost imperceptibly the details were accumulating to massive change.

Little things were lost, gone so gently Adam had hardly noticed. Doors closed earlier. The range of cinemas in which he felt comfortable narrowed. Imported foods grew rare or expensive. A friend disappeared and wrote home from Canada. A house on Oxford Close was let for rent, and still another family was gone. Address books and Christmas card lists reflected the Jamaican diaspora. A tightening circle of anxiety pulled together those who remained, that concern for stability that acts on a middle-class community at gut level. Remote classroom terms like social and economic change had washed past Adam in sixth form, but his home and immediate circle were still all he properly understood.

Even then, with school past and adult life unfurling about him, evenings on the verandah were beautiful as they had always been. Mom bustled in and scurried about until Dad arrived. Then, as late afternoon wore away, one by one they gathered to exchange the day's events. Then Les would rattle the gate irritably, muttering that he hated anything requiring a knack. It was twilight that drew the day together and gave it shape and meaning.

That evening Ben had phoned from the dock in foul temper after waiting hours for Les to return his call. Austin dropped in and sat with them anxiously. Then they heard the Chevy screech angrily to a halt and the door slam.

"Mercy. Must Les destroy the motor car, man?" Paul looked up from a toaster that he had disembowelled and was probing with a screwdriver.

"Provoked about something," Grace shook her head.

"Les always slams doors," Austin grinned.

"Nothing lasts if you don't care it," Paul remarked austerely.

They chattered on, knowing, without seeing him in the dusk, that Les fumbled for a moment or two with the catch on the gate. Across the road the children played more noisily as if their racket could postpone bedtime. Inevitably the idiot dog next door growled and snapped at Les from behind the hedge as if he were a stranger. A gardener strolling past stoned the animal idly and the snarling grew louder. A car coasted by and up the road, and they jumped as it backfired sharply before sliding away with increased speed. The snarling rose for a second to startled fury and then the dog turned away carelessly, raised its leg, scratched the grass towards the hedge in a brief dismissing scurry of its back legs and scampered towards the house.

Paul grunted. "Lost interest already? You mean it actually intends him to get in in one piece?"

They glanced towards the gate expectantly but now it was too dark to see Les past the bougainvillea bush.

"Must be having trouble with that catch again," Austin muttered.

Grace gestured vaguely at Paul. "Darling, when you going to fix it?"

Adam slid to his feet and bounded down the steps.

"Coming!" he sang out but his voice came thinly for he was halfway to the gate.

He couldn't see Les and spun around sharply in his tracks,

certain that his playful uncle hid behind the gatepost to startle him. He called out crossly as his foot skidded on the slippery concrete and he stumbled over something at the top of the drive-way. And it was Les, sprawled in a dark puddle with the top of his head blown off.

The twilight disintegrated into a haze in which the days slipped by. Questions, platitudes and condolences jumbled into bewilderment. Steadily friends trickled through, talking in shocked tones that hushed when anyone new came into earshot. Worry lines grew at the corners of eyes and mouths and between brows. Faces that had seemed timeless were crumpling. Grief etched its network into skin that had been smooth. But there was more. Friends entered into their sorrow and passed beyond it. They not only consoled, they consulted. They not only mourned, they whispered.

The whispering.

When it began, it was the end of one era and the beginning of another. Gradually Adam came to understand that a new factor had entered and lingered on in their lives. Fear. Grief, anger and bewilderment fused into fear. His chest tightened and a familiar itchy sensation drew at his throat as he breathed.

"Why... Who would want to... ?"

Another sensation began somewhere in his chest, a rising, swelling, strangling sensation of pressure. Resentment. A blunt, directionless pain crushed its way upwards.

"Everybody liked... Everybody...." His protest was interrupted by a brief rasping cough. "And the police can't say anything? Why?"

His whisper was like a scream, but Grace only stared back at him. What could she say? The laughter was gone and they did not know why. Only suddenly they were hurled into the wilderness of this world. Ben's mouth set murderously and Paul, inwardly sifting a maze of dead ends, had no explanation to offer. Fear bred in their silence.

Everyone was at the funeral, even people they did not know. It had not been like that for Stella or Martha Jane. It was as if Les's death had signalled a change that made it a personal event to complete strangers. Yet it was a quiet, tightly controlled gathering. The family were too disciplined to weep openly.

In the cemetery the rain trickled down their backs, made little runnels of water through the freshly turned earth and ruined white shoes unnoticed. To Grace there was something obscene about putting Les down in all that mud. To Adam it was meaningless. Les with his mischievous humour, gifts of may bugs, peanut brittle, old shoe boxes, the turtle with the red sideburns — Les living, romping — what had he to do with slow organ music and eulogies and a dark wet hole in the ground. People like Les did not die. But then, superimposed on that was a different Les. Shapeless form in the night, bringing you down with bruising shock on the hard ground. Les you know nothing wrong with you. Pretending again. Turn make me see your face.

But no face. Never ever again.

He stared at the faces around the grave, his father's unseeing, inward turned, unaware that the shoes in which he had been married and whose very soles he cleaned each weekend were sinking slowly into the mud. Ben stared incredulously at the casket, teeth clenched and the thick tendon taut at his neck. Adam avoided looking at his mother and glanced further to the background, to the McIntyres, clustered tightly for mutual support. Then there was Austin. In his eyes, above the determined set of his mouth, the light had gone out. Grace. Adam glanced away again quickly, to Austin, at the empty holes of his eyes where the grief should have been and at the cold bitterness of his mouth; and the dark place in the ground seemed to yawn and superimpose itself on everything else. He stopped looking for faces he knew, because everyone was there.

Adam walked out of the cemetery into a world of sharper lines, deeper perspectives. All around him now men on the street had faces that crinkled into laughter, sorrow, fury. They were people who lived and would die or would be left by those who died. All around the thousands who were and would remain invisible to him became a presence, not so much felt as speculated upon. The island became not merely the place where he lived and might die but a living and dying entity.

He felt some irreversible process to have begun and the country heaving in a sort of semi-consciousness on the threshold of life, dying and being born at the same time. To him all this was a vague sensation prickling under the surface. On his mother the little details made a deeper, more intimate impression. Ben seemed to sink for a while into deep, almost suicidal depression. Goddie receded sporadically into a world of silence as hearing-aid batteries became unobtainable. Grace coped in the day, crisply practical, but at night she began to have nightmares, always the same.

Pregnant again, but not with the gentle expectant fullness that had been Adam. This time she was squeezed and torn by massive organic change. Love strained by fear. Year after year she grew heavier with waiting that sagged from promise into threat. Then. A twinge, rumour of discomfort, intensifying to dull pressure, constricting to secret pain. Then. (Always a taut foreboding of that reality which still found her unprepared.) The time was on her slitting her open, that rending apart of vital organs — abnormal convulsion of nature — God could not have meant to hurt her so.

And the weight that had built imperceptibly shifted in preparation.

Probably this was the point in her dreams. This sinking perception of inner movement, slight but uncontrollable, triggered her total breakdown of reserve and hurled her from personal unease into open panic. For only now came a rising knowledge of what must be borne. Must. Dread replaced by tormenting certainty. Must.

Its huge mass shifted and settled again in a new direction with a dull, sickening thud in the gut. The unrest increased and with it the pressure against the bowels intensified, slackened, and gathered again until the thud became a slow and heavy pounding from within, a torment in her most private parts. The force within absorbed her as it grew, and grew as it absorbed her, struggling and ignorant of the way out, meeting resistance head on and shattering itself and the exhausted tissues restraining it in frantic, frustrated shock after shock until at last she was only an exquisitely thin-stretched membrane of purest pain.

Then her own screaming woke her to the knowledge that she would dream this, always as if for the first time and yet always with the secret dread of familiarity. She would dream it again and again and again.

Yet in the morning she slipped naturally into the surface routine of letting the dog out and the cat in, rattling the breakfast things around and putting aside scraps of chicken gizzard for the turtle. In the mornings, in her mind, Grace knew it was true her way of life was gone, but she was busy in the way she had always been. Only at night, in her gut, did it get personal.

She studied the newspapers and talked to friends. The fabric of their life was wearing thin and fragile at the ends. One familiar business after the other went into shreds. The Gayners had moved to Canada leaving a hole in the Thursday evening, and now the Halls were selling their appliances. Yet, torn as life was, the Cohons determined to wear it still with decency, covering the sore and naked places by drawing it tighter and tighter.

Grace and Paul began gently but relentlessly to pressure Adam into leaving. Apply for a job in Canada, to a college in England, for a visa to the States. But move. Move now.

However, Adam refused to leave Jamaica. He had no reason to give but the sea and the mountains and the emerald pool near Goldfields. He entered medical school and would spend the rest of the sixties and the early seventies there, at the university Paul had promised him from his earliest memories.

It was rigorous training, broken by retreats to the eighteenth-century cut-stone chapel that had been relocated block by block to the campus; and though students in other faculties debated issues of social justice and grumbled about the banning of books by black activists, Adam remained largely untouched by the world. His courses were all-consuming and he would have had no time to read the publications of Malcolm X or Stokely Carmichael, had he even known who they were. Outside, Rastafarians, police and civilians clashed at Coral Gardens and eight died by the gun and the machete. Adam vaguely heard talk of anti-Chinese riots, some political conflict about the growing violence, and outcry about the appearance of teenage gangs.

His first year was undisturbed by the general elections. More confusing to Adam was an encounter in Tropical Plaza with an old school friend who was growing locks and who sported a Rasta queen in a red, green and gold turban. Yet Adam heard of the business places that burnt. Machete attacks and knifings ceased to be reported seriously as guns, revolvers and automatics became common. Molotovs were used in gun attacks. But at last the election passed. The family followed the news reports and Ben sighed,

"Labourite victory. Les would have liked that."

Donald Sangster, quiet successor to the dynamic Busta, was to head the government; but he died within two months. The television showed long lines of his supporters snaking past the body. The Cohons' maid grinned that she done gone to see Mas' D body twice and mus' go again. Uncertainty stretched beyond the election and exploded sporadically in gunfire and arson. Then as the political climate became more settled the family breathed relief and waited.

As far as Adam was concerned, he was in med. school and

politics was the concern of a different faculty. But the next year brought the Rodney demonstrations. News of Guyana was peripheral compared to news of Britain or the States. Adam had no idea why Walter Rodney was denied entry into the country, what he stood for or even who he was. Many had never heard of Rodney before the demonstration erupted. Certainly Adam would never have been involved in the march if it had not been for Pearl Durand.

It was equally possible that Adam might not have been as involved with Pearl Durand had it not been for the march.

Pearl was a stunner. A dreamy-eyed literature student had composed a poem for her and it had been published. She had posed for one important local artist and was said to be considering an offer from another who was looking for a nude, but Adam knew that could only be susu. Beyond the occasional date, he had a friendship with Pearl that had begun when he found her weeping in the Students' Union because her parents were moving to Canada and insisted that she finish her degree before joining them. (And how she could ever finish get degree anyway with all the blasted book these people expect her to read?)

However, her romantic conquests were impressive. A sociology student who had been merging into his own research project on vagrancy was struck by a stray smile from Pearl and evoked a thunderous greeting of soup spoons pounding the tables at his arrival for formal dinner in hall, bathed and properly attired in the red undergraduate gown. Final year students stood the best chance of a date with Pearl, but one of the finest potential scientists among them faltered to a halt and failed his examination when Pearl dropped him to date a besotted Visiting Lecturer from an American university.

"But he's old," her roommate objected.

"And sophisticated," Pearl mused, sweeping aside an unfinished essay to set up curlers and bobby pins. "He makes me feel beautiful and exotic."

"But you *are* beautiful and exotic, you jackass. Why do you need a creaking professor to teach you that?"

"Older men are just so cool," Pearl shrugged. "Why you don't read those damn notes aloud and buy me a little time?"

It was in the following term that the news about Walter Rodney came, strangely disconnected. Students who knew nothing about him learnt vaguely that their academic freedom had been assaulted when the government rejected him. It seemed to Adam that on the residential blocks and in the passageways of the halls they jostled together, the determined and directionless. An informed core grew more committed, more vehement, and drew around them layer after layer of others hazily neutral like himself. Parallel to anger churned curiosity, exhibitionism and bewildered loyalty, and in its midst Adam wandered exposed and lost. Here was something that he did not understand but he was supposed to care deeply about it.

When he arrived to collect Pearl and take her home with him to Oxford Close, her roommate explained wearily that Pearl had marched off with the others. In this way Adam, the reserved, the sideliner, the uninvolved, found himself among a swarm of demonstrators when the tear gas attacks began.

Why Pearl? There were all kinds of girls in hall. The reserved, balanced, single-minded ones suited him, suited his past, suited his future. He had recognised them and filed them for when he had the time. Now Finals were almost upon him and Pearl, roguishly outfitted in a tilted cap and snug Wranglers, was marching into Kingston.

Her lack of inhibition blended her into the group. Adam was conspicuously reserved but Pearl glowed with audacious vivacity that passed for fervour. He shouldered his way behind her, struggling to keep sight of the shapely jeans and quick, shiny boots.

Pearl had always been different, free, shifting, untameable as a sea wave. In the beginning a date with her had been a rare splurge, when she had time for him, when the situation demanded. He had coveted her at first as a stunning accessory, and for Pearl a final year medical student was an item for collection. Then, unintentionally, they became inseparable.

She was a gorgeous girl, pulsing with life and laughter. She danced him off his feet, sharpened her wit on him and startled him out of his life-long assumption that middle-class existence was necessarily a sedate and eternally responsible business.

Unknowingly, he wove his own spell. The swingers in hall were fun for a while, but strays. Adam was the future, the sure thing. Improbably, inevitably, their differences drew them together.

They did not always agree. On Mona Road he tugged at her again and again and she shrugged him off. If he left her he might lose her. Besides, who knew how the situation might turn out? She might need him. His throat flamed and tightened against the dust, but he trudged furiously after her, phrase after phrase slipping through his head. How would he ever explain this?

Adam recognised fewer and fewer students. The crowd swelled, and the heat and noise thickened and crushed down. On Duke Street, the march dissolved into chaos. Strangers jostled him, seemingly aware that he was irrelevant. A Rude Boy sauntered past flicking a ratchet knife arrogantly. Then everyone was running. A bottle whipped past his head. Someone screamed about an ambush. He forgot himself, forgot his anxiety about Pearl's opinion. One thought leapt out, blotting away all others. Neither he nor Pearl belonged in this. He grabbed her and dived aside, along a lane, away from the sound of running feet and tinkling glass, praying, incoherently even to himself.

"Not to be arrested, not injured. Then perhaps no one will ever know."

Chants of "Black power!" broke out, but the shattering windows and windscreens receded as the mob moved off down

Church Street. The rest of October 16 Adam knew only by hearsay. It was a blot of humiliation on his memory. He had been part of a rabble. He might even have been seen in it. Worse, Pearl recognised his embarrassment and was amused at him.

It was part of her excitement, part of her seduction, the wilful independence with which she gave rein to curiosity. She was as inquisitive as a kitten and as rarely damaged by mischief.

He stopped for breath on a low wall and she ran her fingers through his hair and cradled his head against her and she laughed at him.

"Nothing you wouldn't do for me. Eh, Doc?"

Then she smiled ruefully, really smiled with her eyes and the tilt of her chin and bare lift of her shoulder.

"Nothing," he gasped.

There was not a strap mark on her shoulder and his mind swam at the notion of her being copper like that all over, all smooth, moist copper.

He forgot the thousands of unemployed youths who had swarmed around him in the street and the million odd pounds' worth of destruction behind them. Downtown Kingston was halted, looted and fired by the strangest assortment of youth gangs, intellectuals and Rastafarians. They could have turned on persons instead of property. If they had been organised.... But he did not grasp it. He could not spare it attention. Only Pearl was real, and glowing copper. Gladly he sank back into his fragile world and let the molten sensation of her form and flare over him blinding him to the darkness beyond.

Each new excitement was analysed on the porch.

"Then Mas' Paul," Ben boomed, "they don' have enough uprising? Haile Selassie mus' invite to drive the Rasta dem crazy?"

"An' Marcus Garvey an' all make National Hero!" Sam McIntyre interjected.

"Shh! You will make people hate you!" Grace protested. "An' you can't see the government just trying to make peace with restless people in the society? Besides, what you have 'gainst Marcus? He gave people a feeling... a feeling of worth, man."

" 'Restless' is what you call thugs who mash up this city? An' what Marcus ever do for you, or me?"

"We didn't need Marcus," Grace snapped, goaded. "Others did."

Yet the anxiety drew middle and upper classes together. They greeted each other at performances of the Jamaican Folk Singers or of the National Dance Theatre Company.

But Adam had no time. The rest of his course was a grey haze of books, rounds, clerkships and examinations streaked brilliantly with Pearl. His parents were troubled. Pearl was too much for them. Too hot, too fast, too magnetic, too shiny, too everything. These were dark times, Paul cautioned, but he did not explain what he meant. Adam would hear nothing. He knew Pearl best. When the family had had time they would understand. Between his studies and Pearl, Adam had less time to spend at Oxford Close. He visited briefly with her. It was years before they stopped to sit and linger on the porch at sunset.

Then the older ones sat on into dusk, after Adam and Pearl had driven away. The McIntyres came mainly on Sundays now. Now, on other evenings, there was hardly anyone outside the family on the porch with them at twilight. Pearl was a rare event.

"Times have changed," grumbled Paul, with the sourness to be expected of a disappearing species that has glimpsed one of its kind determined on adaptation and survival.

"You just sat like a block," Grace chided him. "The poor girl must have thought you so morose."

"Well, so I am, and with good cause. This is how it feels to go extinct."

"For all of us," she shrugged. "Times always change."
She just couldn't believe the speed at which time passed.

"Imagine," Grace went on, slapping her hands on her knees, "this medical degree seemed such an everlasting thing when he began. I was sorry at first, you know, that he didn't feel to do the law. Well, not sorry, how I could be, but you know this seemed so long."

"I never expected to see him graduate — I mean, to be alive when he did," Ben pondered heavily.

"Ugh! Morbid!" she grimaced.

"What rubbish!" Sarah put in. "Something must be wrong with me. I certainly never had any doubt."

"Well, that's different," Ben spread his hands, "I mean, you're just a girl."

Sarah emitted a screech of laughter so that Paul too shook with a deep chuckle and Grace reached over and grabbed her hand, twining their fingers together.

"We'll have something," Grace gloated, rocking back and forward, "something to celebrate your century when it comes. Lunch, eh! Or you think tea?"

"Tcha! Tea's a women's affair." Ben flipped a hand dismissingly.

"Well! What do you take me for?" Sarah turned on him. "I may not look like much now, but I was hot stuff in my day."

"And talk about hot stuff..." Ben began, smirking and looking from one to the other and angling for their reactions.

Grace compressed her lips and kept her eyes blankly ahead. "Adam is a big man now. He must know his mind."

Ben's mild ridicule crystallised in sharp recollection.

"Is her uncle, Angus Durand, nearly ruin Papa... " He polished his thick, gold-rimmed spectacles savagely.

"Not her fault," Grace quelled him.

"I don't know," Sarah fretted.

Paul shook his head. "Well I don't think much of the outfit, for one. I mean, you're going to visit the chap's parents — granted, a set of old fogies. But still."

"It's a different age," Grace sighed sadly, "a different age." Then she looked up brightly, hopefully. "Of course she's a pleasant girl and interesting. Her eyes are full of... fire."

"Hmm!"

"I mean, nowadays a woman has to have spirit."

"Aha. Then you don't have?" Paul's eyes wandered up to the ceiling. "I think coming here in that get-up to see you — that was poor."

"Well, well."

It hurt him though. It seemed to Paul that beyond Pearl's glamour lay a great emptiness waiting to engulf Adam, and he could not believe his own son could be so blind.

"You will come around," Grace patted Paul's arm as he huddled in their bed, a lump of depression. "She'll grow on you. Like Mrs Whiskers."

"Merciful peace. You comparing daughter-in-law to puss?"

It was true that Mrs Whiskers was by now in charge of the family. She had begun somewhere on the far side of the garage, a bawling scrap of fluff, lost or deserted, and bold with hunger. Thin fur matted with burrs seemed attached directly to the bones. Then there was a scramble of tiny feet behind a cupboard, and Paul poked around underneath, muttering darkly about rat poison. But with a soft thud, out skidded a minute black and white kitten, plump now and vigorously at home. It scuttled across the floor, skidded under the table and dived out to spring ferociously on a mango leaf strayed in on the last breeze. The enemy subdued, it leapt high into the air, feet spread stiffly, fur on end as if electrified, landed, levitated again in the same attitude of shock, then flattened and slid under the original cupboard leaving silence as if it had never been.

Paul, who had remained frozen on his knees beside the cupboard, gradually unfolded, tiptoed to the kitchen, and made his enquiries in an appalled whisper.

"What was that?"

Grace shrugged matter-of-factly and rattled the Pyrex dishes about.

"Thought it was not to be allowed in?" he growled.

She raised her hands in self-sacrificial tolerance. "What I was to do? Bawling for hunger under the window."

Paul raised his eyes upward for deliverance. "Another mutt about the place."

Yet, as months passed, Whiskey grew plump and stately enough to be renamed, and even Paul, the cat-hater, had been found contentedly asleep in his armchair with Mrs Whiskers curled on his lap and with his fingers spread reassuringly over her warm and rippling belly. And from them both a deep and regular buzz of satisfaction rose and mingled in the still afternoon.

So it was Paul, Grace, Ben and Sarah left — getting to be in their dotage, as they chuckled together cheerfully with another Easter approaching. Here they were, stroking stray cats, pandering to every whim of the dog, Captain Morgan, and worrying over the great cold-eyed, mossy-backed turtle in a tank in the back yard. Old Lurch, as they called him, had shuffled turgidly now through thirteen years and grown to the size of a breakfast plate.

With Adam's marriage there would soon be something more worth the fuss, Paul said. He unfastened the case of the electric fan he had bought for Grace when she was expecting Adam, and oiled it as he had done every Holy Thursday for twenty-six years — "Which is why it works today," Grace used to reply sharply when Les had laughed at Paul. But the evening grew dark as Paul grappled with the concept of Pearl — it was all so nebulous. She hated books, she had said. For a while his mind was a crag surrounded by desolation. But Ben sat watching Grace's secret smile. Everything they had was for Adam's children, he thought.

Everything they or their parents had ever done was for that.

No one put it into words for fear of bad luck, but it was rarely away from any of their minds. And even the puss grew fat and proud as a side effect of their expectations.

"And we must really fix up that old house now," Sarah murmured as she nodded off in Stella's rocker on the porch. "Work it out, Paul. But let me know the figure in sterling, eh? I can't take on this new dollars foolishness."

19
Treadmill

TIME HAD *always skirted Goldfields, and at the turn of the century little had changed. In late July the men plodded, weary from the holing. This was the meagre period between the yam crops — the old ones all eaten and the new not yet in. At four-fifteen the head driver had blown his conch and the men had turned out for before-day jobs. They separated to ready materials for the tradesmen, to cut up dung and shift mould. Then they hustled back for tools and breakfast provisions to reach the fields on time.*

Like one or two other planters, Mas' Cohon had taken it into his head to buy two camels. They were stubborn and short-tempered.

"Weaste of time," gasped Jessica's father, panting in late from the pens for Busha's roll call, setting in motion at once and automatic-ally the machinery of plantation discipline. Seized, stripped, pinned to the ground. A new driver, anxious to prove himself, wielded the whip with unnecessary competence. Cupid was middle-aged, creole but pure black, and his skin, sweat-glistened in the morning sun, raised a pattern of new welts between old scars.

"Busha," he gasped, "no floggee, Busha. Cupid good nega, Busha. Nebba come late again. Come force haste fe Massa wo'k. No floggee, Busha, no floggee."

His voice shredded to a squeal and sliced off, answered by a razor-thin line of crimson on black that dribbled across his buttocks and down into the dust before a gush of urine flushed it away.

When it was over it was good to be paired with a younger, stronger man like Cuffee Castries. Cuffee's sister had children for Cupid and the men worked well together. Cuffee was powerful but nimble, a descendent of Maroons, so they said. The two pulled together at the roots of tough old ratoons and opened wide holes for new plants. They moved quickly in the cool before sun high, knowing that by sunset each must have opened a hundred holes. Ten o'clock was breakfast, and by ten-thirty the conch summoned them back to the lines which the tradesmen carried to guide the holing straight.

Next shell blow was afternoon, but the men were still satisfied from the ten o'clock meal, so they ignored lunch and hurried to their own plots and animals. Every spare moment was for the provision ground, for without excess plantains for market there would be no salt-kine for the stew. Now that plantains were twelve shillings per hundredweight it was worthwhile for Cupid to carry the forty-five pound load on his head to market each Sunday. So he worked his ground for the few extra minutes that were his, knowing himself better off than slaves on other plantations whose provision grounds had been destroyed by hurricane after hurricane. But in no time at all he was drawn again by the conch to toil over the ratoons under the blistering afternoon sky.

Sundown brought relief. When the evening flamed and dulled again they turned back to the cattle pens and the stables, trashing or bringing in grass. At last came roll call and by eight they arrived at the cluster of huts. One or two brought home members of the jobbing gang. Two, who would otherwise have slept on the roadside, found space with Cuffee, for his wife was an indulged slave and had already passed them on her way to Busha's house. She had not noticed them as she walked mechanically to the overseer's bed, for her mind was routinely engaged in blanking itself out.

A few huts away, Hecuba Castries tended Cupid's back and wearily dragged out what sweet potatoes and fruit she had been able to find. Now she was relieved of field work and set to grass-cutting, yet even this weighed on her. Well into the seventh month of another hopeless pregnancy, she could hardly force her sagging figure through the long day. This sixth child, if only she could bear it, would free her of labour on the estate and bring security to her old age.

And, oh God, is eight pickney push out living into the world, but three had fe dead. Tetanus, white doctor call it, but is not stupid she stupid — when pickney born to dead dem born to dead.

There was nothing to keep her daughter at the hut. Young Jessica's mind shimmered with magic and old tales, so the elders drew her to them on fine threads of memory spinning into yarns that meshed the centuries. So too the generations interlaced, and it was time to seek out Phippa, Jessica's grandmother and the Nana of countless others. Up to a few years ago Phippa had been a midwife, for she had acquired the lore of her African mother, Cleo, and learnt much from the wild blacks of the mountains with whom she had roamed for a while. Then for a few months she had assisted the nurses in the hothouse, as the slaves called their hospital, but now she was useless.

It was just another plantation. Massa did little for the aged, yet did not actively ill-treat them. On Hilly View, only a few miles away, decrepit slaves with no family to provide for them were limited to a small area of canefield with a few plantains per week. And of course there was the famous old Bedward, notorious in their songs, the Massa who threw away old, broken slaves into a stony ravine. Jessica had often heard Phippa croak out the familiar verse, stamping her foot on the trampled earth around her door.

"Oh! Massa, Massa! Me no deadee yet!
Take im to de Gully! Take im to de Gully!
Carry im go long."

"Eehi. Fe-wi Massa not like some di' deh." Phippa said it over and over.

335

Well, Phippa was fortunate too. She had children and grand-children and she was oddly sacred to them, considering the frailty of family ties. She was sheltered and fed.

Jessica paused at the outer limits of the village, where Phippa lived. Like others, Phippa's was a hive-shaped hut, wattle and daub, with palmetto thatch almost to the ground. But hers was almost twenty feet long and divided into two, and it boasted a bed. Jessica caught her breath at the thought of sleeping on the raised wooden platform with its mat of plantain trash. Bound fe drop off 'pon dutty, she thought. She was relieved that she slept on the safe, firm earth of her own hut.

It was a fine night, cool but dry under the coconut trees bor-dering the clearing, and old Phippa sat out on her tree stump. She still held her calabash loosely in one hand but the other lay idly on the bent end of her stick so, likely as not, she had finished her ration of vegetables and was ready to talk. Phippa was tall and gaunt, for the flesh had drawn down upon her broad frame and withered onto the bones. Dark hollows in her cheeks had sucked deeper and deeper over the years until now they were almost like pockets over the jutting bone of her lower jaw. She was mash-mouthed too, like many of the older women, and apart from the lack of teeth her lips sank in, working tremulously upon the gums. But her eyes, far receded into their darkened sockets, flashed with recollection.

Jessica quickened her step unconsciously to join the other children gathering around the old woman. Older people laughed about Phippa and said she remembered everything, even things that had never happened, but the younger ones she filled with dreams, strange collective fantasies that bonded them even with-out their consulting about it. And the older ones came too, just three or four perhaps, sitting on a tree root or on the ground, recalling a name, perhaps breaking into a chant.

Sometimes Phippa talked about the days before she met the Maroon, and about her first husband and how she had scorned him when he arrived straight from Africa.

"One wild-man," she cackled, "nebba know what him go do nex'. No want food, no want woman. Sit down quiet-quiet one minute, ready fe broke down everyting de nex'."

The older ones around smirked and nodded derisively. New, they sniggered. Salt-water nega.

"Well," Phippa shrugged, "is so Guinea-bird stay. After a few month im settle. Well... dat one nebba really settle."

Her voice sank down as she spoke of the Ashanti's death. The busha had accused him of plotting to kill Massa after a whipping. They had burnt him. She had run away from his voice roaring in the flames — not a voice at last but an unearthly howling, and she had run clutching her two children. In the interior, Maroons harboured her. One she lived with for many years before she returned to the plantation and gave herself up.

Now, withered as she was to a collection of dry sticks, the memory of the Maroon stirred her. Quao the warrior. He fought with tense precision yet revelling somehow in his own skill and flaunting it in lightning feints and swift backlash of vengeance stored and concentrated into one brutal downward chop. Then away again and circling slowly, gleaming sweat on rippling brawn. And all the while the cutlass like a merciless extension of arm and thought swept open the blood path into freedom.

Eight years Phippa had lived in the Maroon settlement with Quao Castries, and she talked more of that eight years than the rest of her life put together. He had never taken another wife, never been harsh to Phippa. A box, perhaps, now and then. But only, she chuckled toothlessly, only when she did well look fe it. And later she would become aware of him standing in the door of the hut, holding out something he had brought for her, perhaps two of the ring-tailed pigeons that she enjoyed. The years had been tense and lean, but she had lived them.

"*But is why you lef', Nana?*" *the children would ask, especially the Castries grandchildren.*

Always it returned to that. Why indeed? Phippa could never explain. It had been a gruelling life and when he died she grew afraid. Afraid of the soldiers, of the dim, slippery paths in the forest, of old age overtaking her in the wilderness, of becoming weak and sick and dying alone under some bush.

"*Bush not easy, pickney,*" *she would mutter.* "*If we did have a regular place, safe... me no know. Hmm! Nanny Town, now. Well, if it was Nanny Town....*"

Her voice trailed off and they clamoured around her as she expected. They had heard the tale of Nanny Town a hundred times, each with its own embellishments, but they could never tire of it.

"*Nanny Town!*" *they squealed.* "*Go aan 'bout Nanny Town!*"

"*Hm?*" *She pretended to be reticent and they pressed her obligingly. At last she relented.*

"*Nowhere 'trang like Nanny Town,*" *she would assert.* "*Inna dem dere Blue Mountain, way, way top o' rock wall. All-you,*" *she looked around contemptuously and swiped a clearing around her with her stick sending the cheekiest of them scuttling a respectful distance away.* "*What all o' unoo know 'bout bush? Unoo ebba see rock-wall?*"

"*Yes, Grannie,*" *they would chorus. Then she would flourish the stick again.*

"*Unoo no know nothin',*" *she spat.* "*Watch!*" *She indicated a point far in the sky above them.*

"*Nanny Town dere. Top o' one t'ousand foot o' rock, middle o' Blue Mountain dem. Carrion Crow Mountain over the town. Fast water on two side and mountain 'pon de oder. Nanny Ribba, Stony Ribba flow pass de town and drop ober de rock into Nanny Cauldron. An' is de soldier-dem Nanny make dat cauldron for. As dem pass an lagga-lagga look in, she catch dem so pull dem down. Nebba see de light o' day again. And so de caul-*

dron bubble, so it frot'. Nanny keep im boiling night and day.

"Nanny," she sighed. Then she glanced up, eyes flashing. "Ashanti woman. Strong obeah. No warrior like Nanny. Round im neck string wid white man teeth and round im middle a belt wid nine, ten knife.

"Dem coulda nebba catch Nanny Town. One way up it have, one likkle fine track, and Watchie sit 'pon it all time. As im eye ketch soldier, abeng sound. Eehi! Ebery man hold im cutlass. Who have gun find im place. Soldier fire gun? Eh! Eh! Tink say Nanny 'fraid soldier? Eeh?"

"No, Grannie," the children chorused.

"Nanny?" the old woman cackled scornfully. "Nanny ketch dem bullet and fire she fire back 'pon dem. Soldier-man pull foot and down de mountain wid im."

The children jumped about her squealing and snickering, making obscene gestures.

"How she fire it, Grannie?"

"After she nah have gun!"

The old woman shook her fist at the world.

"Nuh she rass-hole?" she screeched.

After a while she slammed her stick on a nearby trunk for the disorder to subside.

"Soldier an dem like tell people how dem take Nanny Town and kill all-we. Nutting go so. Nebba see de day. Soldier no match for Maroon. No hear seh how Maroon chop off soldier head an stuff it up im rass? Hear wha' 'appen.

"Sun goin down, a lookout come in. Soldier-dem a come one-one 'pon de path. Woman take pickney, man take cutlass; leave de town clean an hole up inna forest. Soldier pass dere-so from me. Dem no know we all round dem close enough could spit 'pon dem. Dem reach de town. Empty. Search dem search, dem no find nobody. Up to puss-pickney clear out. Well. Dem tired. Dem gone inna house fe sleep. When dem good an sleep, fe-we man dem send for candle. We bring de cangle come, light it and

*throw down 'pon de thatch. When fire ketch all round, fe-we
man come down 'pon dem. Laad! What a night dat! Soldier
runnin' round like ants. Dem run mad and jump off de rock.
Some mash up a bottom, some dere inna cauldron. What a
night.*

*"After dat no one live a Nanny Town. So much a man die
dere, spirit round de place. Spirit-dem burn in a green fire
under de fern 'pon Candle-fly Peak. Spirit-dem tek feather and
fly in and out like seabird, ya-pa-pa-pa. But at night you could
know de difference. At night not even hunter safe round Nanny
Town. Dog wid no leg float over de waterfall. Whooping Boy,
him name. Floatin' in de mist. When him howl, hunter run
home and hide. Spirit-dem.... "*

*Everyone was quiet for a while, then perhaps the older ones
would go on to speculate about the long trek, the wanderings in
the hills, the feats of Quao Castries or the tales they had heard of
Cudjoe's Maroons abandoning their town and hiding in the
Cockpits. But for Phippa the loss of Nanny Town was the end of
the story and she sat staring out into the night.*

*Jessica began strolling back to her own hut, but somewhere a
gombah throbbed low and insidious. She began to walk in step
to it, then to breathe in time. Faster and more insistent it
throbbed in her until it became her heartbeat and she could no
more deny it than stop her own bloodstream.*

*Soon she was at the clearing among the huts. Two dancers slid
around each other jerking their limbs so that the rattles on their
wrists and ankles mocked the drum and the moonlight gleamed
over rippling damp flesh. Somewhere beyond them a woman's
voice raised a challenging invitation and others echoed her.*

*Out of the shadows the rhythm drew them one by one, man,
woman, child. They fell into a circle around the two and the
woman stiffened her torso, the drum throbbing her hips into*

violent pulsing that subsided to slower, more sinuous winding then exploded again in hot, compelling spasms that jerked her hips independent of her upright back and still, chiselled, mahogany breasts. Around them the others were stamping and winding, the women slower and suggestive, the men wildly excited, and old Thomas beat his soul out upon the skin of the gombah.

The circle opened and closed compellingly and the plumed darkness of bamboo and palms wheeled round Jessica. She fell into step with her drumming heart and the rhythm beat hot and sharp in her so that she coiled and thrust around it. Her back stiffened and her shoulders spread, tilting her small breasts up, but at the base of the rigid torso her pelvis writhed independently. The women were challenging each other now and one of the central figures gasped out the "Hip saa!" which was taken up from one dancer to the next. And now she heard her own voice, challenging and inviting.

On the path beyond the clearing, the visitor from the great house paused to take note of the savage customs about which he had heard so much. Jessica Castries's skin rippled in the moonlight. Cohon grinned as he noted the young manager of the Haynes Estate running his tongue momentarily over his lips.

"Ripe likkle ting," old Cohon agreed, as they left the negro huts again for the main path, and his visitor breathed harder in the tropical night as its heat flared through him a returning glimpse of shimmering, excited young flesh.

Next morning, Jessica's mother woke ill and vomiting and she turned out tardy getting to work. This Hecuba was a frequent offender and it was necessary to make an example of her, pregnant or not, so she was dispatched for correction, one week's hard labour in the workhouse and to walk the treadmill daily. She had barely descended from the mill when the pains which had begun two hours before culminated in a spasm which seemed to tear her open, and the infant slid out dead upon the ground. The driver saw her swaying upon her feet and motioned her to work, but the overseer pointed out the bloodstained mass upon the ground and waved her away to the hospital.

"She can't work now, anyway."

"Massa," Hecuba whispered, "fe-me pickney dat. Me cyan't lef' it 'pon ground so."

The overseer wandered on unresponsively and she groped for a hoe, scraped a shallow hole in the workhouse yard, drew the infant in and covered it with earth before she dragged her way to the hot-house. At the foot of the steps that arched over the round tunnel-like entrance she crumpled face-down on the hewn stone. It was weeks before she recovered, determined to try once more for the sixth child.

Of all this Jessica knew nothing. Nor would she. For Jessica was twelve, plump and well-formed, and the overseer had excused her from the work-gang to entertain Mas' Cohon's guest. By evening word came that the visitor had been pleased and had persuaded old Massa to sell her. She spent the night at the great house to leave for Haynes Estate at daybreak. She would never see her mother or Phippa again.

Jessica sat alone in a small room with her food untouched before her. The paths that led from Goldfields were many and twisted. Most were dead ends and others turned back upon themselves and deposited you where you had begun. In dance and song and story it was possible to escape, but only for a while. She had always dreamed of leaving and now she was to go indeed. The disastrous finality of it shocked her beyond tears and she stared dry-eyed into a future empty of every face she had ever known.

Someone, perhaps it was the great-grandmother they called Cleo, had come from Africa. Perhaps she too had longed for a way out. But then, she had known another life. Cleo's mind had had images of an outside world to cling to. For Jessica, departure from Goldfields was a journey into myth.

So she embraced those myths that were her own. She sat, rocking backwards and forwards, first in pain and then in solace, recapturing old tales. The hunter and the leopard. Ananse, weaving a hundred tricks. Cleo manipulating her daughters into the Cohon great house, into the family itself. Phippa and the Maroon. She gathered the memories about her, and they were all she took with her from Goldfields.

Out on the verandah, Cohon poured sangaree for his son-in-law.

"I sell a slave today," he cackled, nodding rapidly a number of times and carefully lowering his bowed frame into a chair. "You woulda like dis one."

Stollmeier was preoccupied with other things. He was worried about the blacks and even more about the mulattoes. There was that damned Durand too.

The Durands and the Guillottes had fled the revolution in St Domingue together. The Guillottes, thankful to have survived the blood bath, merged into the fervent Catholic community of Louisiana. But the Durands had lost their faith. They were stunned by the loss of their property and the plantation into which they had recently sunk much of their capital. The two families had parted awkwardly, their connection by marriage having made them more than acquaintances but less than friends. Vaguely they were aware that the parting was as momentous as the destruction by fire and cutlass behind them. They knew they belonged in the same world, but their world was gone.

In the midst of the nightmare a dream formed, of finding it again or perhaps recreating it for a little while. Elsewhere. So while the Guillottes found their way to New Orleans, the Durands had resettled in Jamaica.

Their slaves came with them — out of loyalty, fear, or the urge to spread dissension, who could say. They reiterated their love for

343

the family and could not be torn from them. The Durands sold none of their slaves in Jamaica. There were jewels and gold enough to sell. Besides, the last thing Jamaicans wanted were slaves from St Domingue. Jamaica had half a million of its own slaves to control.

"It will happen again," Stollmeier muttered darkly. His whole life was invested now in maintaining a sane attitude among blacks. "Madness, letting a horde of revolutionary negas into the country. Watch. Listen to them. You ever hear them?"

"You speak French then?" his father-in-law quavered in surprise.

"I don't need no French to hear they impertinence. They tone, they eye, they movements. They not docile like our people. They don' have no respect."

Cohon nodded slowly, staring down the avenue of coconut trees from the porch which looked out, secure on its stone supports, towards the sea. Stollmeier glanced through the spyglass then shoved it away, pleased again that he had married Clare, Cohon's only child. Goldfields would be his soon and Cohon was still making repairs, improving, fortifying. He strolled proprietorially along the porch, running his fingers along the thirty yards of railing. In the corner of the porch sheltered small, sturdy plants of ackee and cinnamon, recently arrived. Leave it to Cohon to acquire breadfruit as well; he kept his slaves well fed. But Stollmeier knew food was not enough for them.

"They will spread it here," he growled.

Stollmeier was tense, but Cohon more complacent. After all, he was eighty-seven now, an unbelievable age for a white resident as it was. He would be long dead when it happened.

"And the mulattoes will help," Stollmeier continued. "They have the intelligence for it."

Jeremiah padded out on thick bare soles and held out to him a silver salver Stollmeier dabbled his fingers impatiently in the rough earthenware bowl on it.

"How many more them wi' let in?" Cohon's mood had changed abruptly with the realisation that it could happen in his lifetime.

"Till we're butchered in our beds!" Stollmeier snapped.

His mind ran over the arms he had purchased in the first heat of news about the revolution in St. Domingue. "They not going get into my property."

"Mine neider." Cohon pondered a while, looking past Stollmeier into a future for Goldfields that did not include owners with tainted blood. Then he continued. "Mustn' get inna country part at all, you know. Kingston one thing, but country... one step 'way from plantation-dem."

"But the mulattoes going move up, out. Everywhere. A matter of time. Look. You know Durand?"

"No."

"Durand, man."

"Oh. Yes."

"He make his will. Will, mind you. Provide for his mulatto woman. He have a boy by her and he leave him everything. No, everything. The Kingston house small but what 'bout the place in Clarendon, cost him twenty thousand pound. Slaves and cattle, credits, titles. Oh, the dry goods place too in town. All to go to the bastard. He have a girl too, but going take the veil, they say."

"No heir?"

"Younger members of the family went back to France. One set, Guillottes or something, went west to Louisiana. The ones gone to France, well them didn't satisfy with they reception here. They keep sending for Durand, but... "

"Well but Durand not a bad fellow himself, 'cording to what I hear say."

"Not Durand self, not Durand. But the mulattoes, man. Consider if the mulatto-dem intrigue with the blacks. And then if the mulattoes back with property."

Cohon regarded him from under furrowed brows with a

queer light in his eyes. "I see is the mulattoes worry you."

Stollmeier shifted in his chair and stared out beyond the grassy patch where his first grandson rolled and tumbled, tawny in the molten evening.

"I don' trust one of de bastards," he growled.

20

The First Stone

GOLDFIELDS WAS of no interest to Pearl. She said no Durand had ever left Kingston except by plane.

"What they keeping that old mausoleum for?" she shrugged. Even the Cohon house on Oxford Close seemed ancient to her.

The trouble was that the house Pearl wanted was in Beverly Hills. Here the homes of the affluent overflowed from the densely populated Liguanea Plain and inched up the hills that rimmed and looked down on old Kingston. Beverly Hills at any cost, she decided, but preferably a mansion on Montclair Drive. They had been married for two years when the right thing came on sale. She heard about it at a party at Morgan's Harbour. (Nice, select little gathering. Everybody mixed well.)

The problem was how to get Adam to the house and convince him he had discovered it for himself.

It stood well in from the road above a lawn that scooped up from the scraggly rocks which were softened by Wandering Jew and plumes of deep pink bougainvillea cascading from behind them. The roof too curved rakishly up and out like the brim of a saucily tilted hat, and the upstairs verandah looked out over swelling wrought-iron railings to the city in the valley. Apart from the retaining wall, the grounds were enclosed by a neat rim of concrete. This rose on either side of the gate into cut stone pillars topped by black metal lanterns and obscured at their base by fountains of pale cactus. Even from the road one could glimpse the pool at the side of the house, particularly at night when it was floodlit. It was precisely what she needed.

"Don't you love it!"

"Mm. Nice." He stretched across and squeezed her fingers dreamily. "Imagine that kind of money, eh?"

"Well actually is not all that much considering everything."

He chuckled. "How you know how much it is?"

She was careful. Playfully she countered,

"People anxious to sell now, Adam. They just running out of the country. They abandon what they can't sell. People taking next to nothing now for mansions."

"Mm," he agreed with her but his attention was wandering and he drove slowly on. "Look at that top-heavy thing up there. Lord. Gross, eeh? People build some monstrosities, boy."

"Well that one we saw back there was nice."

"Yeh. Let's have it," he chuckled.

"While we're up here, why don't we walk through?"

"Oh, come on."

"You don't know the price."

He pulled to the side and stopped, looking out over Kingston. He seemed to have forgotten she was in the car till he said suddenly, "But you do know, don't you? How much is it?" He turned and his mouth smiled at her below unfathomable eyes.

"Oh forget it," she shrugged. "I just thought we were here anyway."

"Were we here anyway? Or we come to look at that house? Is you wanted drive in the hills."

"Oh come on, Adam."

"Don't do it so again." He said it quietly. "Come straight with me next time."

"You wouldn't listen. You never listen when I come straight."

"Lord, God, Pearl, even if we coulda buy a place so we couldn't maintain it. Is a army of servant we would need."

Silence.

"Is a small place we need. Accessible. Nice area. Hope

Pastures, if we can afford that. Next to people like ourselves."

"Near people like you. Near you family."

"We no further from them up here. Anyway. Is going to help to be near them in the long run. Your folks in Canada. When we have children... "

"Oh, Christ!"

"Pearl, don't say that, darling. Don't."

"We can't live now? We have fe wait live through children? We not going have no time then. I going have no time. I tell you I want a chance."

"You going feel different then," he reassured her.

"I not in no hurry to feel different. We only marry couple years."

He grew quiet, waiting for her to come out of it; but he tensed, sensing that every second of silence brought him nearer to disaster. What she needed was a baby. It would settle and transform her. He was ready now to lay aside outgrown fantasies for dreams of work and family life. He had loved all that Pearl was and now he loved what she must become. They could not really afford a child yet, but he needed her to settle down. It was baby time.

Not yet, she insisted. Besides, she wanted to leave Jamaica. Didn't he see everybody else going? What they were going to do here without their friends? Pure buttu fulling up de country. He wanted a nice carpeted, air-conditioned office with nice patients, or what? Is what im really want to specialise in? Pure rude bwoy and gunshot wound?

"I have patients of all classes. Besides, there are honest people who are poor," he reminded her mildly. "Someone has to treat them."

"But why you?" she spread her pretty hands reasonably. "And if you even get a practice going, how they will pay you if they don' have job?"

It was certainly true about unemployment. More than two-thirds of the workforce of Kingston was unskilled and even the most competent scuffler might have difficulty finding a doctor's fee. Certainly Pearl would not take kindly to the fowl or ground provisions some doctors accepted in lieu of payment. Yet Adam was just as stubborn.

Eight months later Pearl stared into the mirror then closed her eyes and turned away, summoning up her slim image in a bikini and superimposing it on the swollen reflection that was really there. Why couldn't she have been born a man, with a life of her own to keep? Adam found her crying in front of the mirror.

"I young, and my life over," she whispered. "I've missed everything."

So she was at that stage. He ran his finger along the tearline understandingly.

"Oh, who's nervous now. Hush. Little hysteria 'round now normal, you know. Come, little Mom, you life just beginning."

She stopped crying abruptly and stared at him, shocked again at his unique combination of awkwardness and innocence. How sheltered he was and, as a result, how chronically clumsy. No matter how sound a doctor he was, he would never grasp what it was to be so filled with new life as to feel your own over-powered and finished. He was too blind to see she was trapped in his miracle, and that for her it would unfold precisely, pitiless-ly, irresistibly. The uselessness of all his education to her problem dwindled him to a remote, irrelevant point. Only women, she thought, should be doctors.

Under her distancing glance that appraised and dismissed him, Adam fell quiet. The silence between them began to tick in his chest.

Between the pains it came to her that she should have listened to her parents. If she had finished the degree and got a good job he mightn't have pressed her so hard for the baby. The girls who had graduated from her class had choices now that she... but then the pain clamped down again and there was no thought but the end of it.

When it was over they brought the baby to her, but she was tired. Glad, so glad it was all right. Normal and healthy, they said. And over. They brought it to her to hold, strange and wrinkled, wrapped up in an unbelievably tiny bundle.

"Tired, tired," she said.

"But you want to see him," they insisted. "Of course you do."

Nurses and doctors leaned around her. The room was full because everyone knew Adam. It was like giving birth at Cross Roads. They peered at her, nodding and congratulating, "It's a son, first try."

She took it to quiet them and looked at it. It was still smeared from the birth canal. Hers but smeared. She gave it to Adam and rubbed her fingers off weakly on the sheet.

"I want to sleep," she said. "Make me sleep."

When she awoke, Adam was there. They could bring the baby any time she wanted, he said at once. He had arranged everything.

"They don't take care of it till I'm well?"

"Of course. Till you're strong," he corrected. "You not sick, you know. You can come home as soon as you want." He hugged her. "You're wonderful."

Yes, yes. He was lost in the wonder of it. Inwardly she searched for an answering revelation of motherhood and shrugged. Perhaps it came in with the milk. She closed her eyes and patted Adam's hand. His clumsy admiration made her a little impatient and contemptuous, having just followed the whole thing through in its messiest details.

Fleetingly he glimpsed the polite but weary interest of the spectator; there was no mystery in it for her. And his heart sank. More than ever he determined to make her understand how precious she was to him because of it.

For days they fussed over Pearl till she was irritable and resentful. The family came to absorb her into their cosy circle of devotion. The hospital and steady trickle of admiring visitors bored her until she felt every nerve raw and exposed. Then she was home and the thin, breathless wail of the child sucked at her sanity. Every morning she opened her eyes from shallow, apprehensive sleep to the same preemptory whimpering and fumbled wearily with the bottles and the diaper pail.

"Yes, bottles," she snapped. "I not going be swollen and leaky all over the place like some milch cow. Breast feed is for bungo who cyan't wash bottle clean and who live back o' wall where water don't run from pipe."

But, however she resisted, some transaction was complete, and her life changed beyond recognition; uprooted, harnessed, bartered. Yes, there was a maid, for housework. But Adam and his family all expected Pearl to be continually plastered over the child. Grace would have helped of course, but Grace in the house with her lips forming words like sweet, precious and blessed all day — oh God.

In the evenings when the child was eventually lying quietly in its crib, Adam would come in and pick it up. Then the phone would ring and he'd be gone, leaving it fussing and squirming again. Of course Adam was all gratitude and adoration now.

"Like I marry him to be some blasted Madonna," Pearl fumed.

Within three weeks of Gerry's birth, her life had become a silent scream. Nothing of it was hers.

It might have been different in another time or place. But now everything became entangled in arguments over Gerry's care, the demands of Adam's work and, above all, over money. Things she depended on grew scarce or obtainable only on the black market. Others were available but exorbitant. Cigarettes and imported clothes were a way of life to Pearl. Excursions to night spots, brilliant dinner parties, mushrooms, sparkling wine and lobster cocktail — and oh, she had dreamed of a low, sleek sports car and receptions with Adam poised at her shoulder, intellectual and distinguished.

Instead the baby burped and weeweed on her and Adam was tired and preoccupied with shortages of drugs and equipment. She hated the karibas that men wore at official functions now instead of suits, and the hors d'oeuvres were pure buttu food. So the teasing began in her head, echoing whispered promises of gaiety.

"Is only uptown party you know about. You never feel hot party yet. Make we go a downtown dance one night. Make we dance downtown dance."

"But is safe? Brown people can go? How downtown dance different from uptown dance — apart from the buttu?"

"Don't 'fraid, man. Nobody going do you anything if you with me. Besides, brown woman well sweet black man. Anyway, is not safe you really want to safe, eeh? Watch the downtown dance now. Woman 'gainst the tree and the music in the man a rub 'pon her… "

"Stop, stop."

"You know you don't want me stop. Watch me. Nothing I can't give you. Nowhere I can't take you. I have a house in Miami. Apartment in Manhattan. Business connections all over the world. Bank account a Switzerland. And I can take you downtown and bring you back safe. Safe from everybody but me. Come nah?"

Long after she had flounced away from the conversation, it went on and on in her head.

One evening Adam came home to find her curled up in bed and the baby bawling in his crib in the next room.

"What's wrong?" he gasped.

"I tired," she said quietly and coldly. "I tired and I not getting up now."

Adam fretted over her for a moment then turned into the baby's room. Gerry was stiff and purple with rage. Cautiously Adam leaned across and picked him up.

"He's wet!" he called.

No answer. Fat mosquitoes perched on the wall over the crib and Adam scowled at them suspiciously. The child was too upset to be put down so Adam gathered him against his white shirtjack, soaked nappy and all, hugging and rocking him until the screams died to a plaintive hiccup. He carried the baby in to her with a clean nappy over his arm.

"See, he's quiet now," he whispered through the safety pins between his teeth.

"I said, not now," she turned her face away without opening her eyes. "If we were in the States, Pampers would be affordable and he wouldn't be bawling."

When Adam reached Oxford Close, Ben opened the door with his usual solemnity until he saw the carrycot.

"Grace!" he yelled, "Goddie!" He fumbled with the keys for the wrought-iron gate. They had resisted grilling the porch for as long as possible, but Adam had insisted. Ben knew the boy was right but he hated the cage.

"Could dead in ya, hunting for key," he growled. "Goddie!"

Sarah had been ill and had not been to visit Pearl in the hospital or in the house in Hope Pastures. Grace eased the baby out of the cot and gave him to her in the rocker.

Ben hung over her, nodding and smiling. "If Stella were here, eh?"

But really it was the anguish of his own Vern receding at last, ebbing wave on wave. Adam had come within the years of rage that stretched for over a decade after Vern's death — too soon to lull the pain. But Gerry purged Ben of the fury.

Grace crouched down, rubbing her nose along the incredible velvet of the child's back.

"You know I used to think it was the Pears Soap that smelled so, but we can't get it now. It's the skin, you know." Her hair wisped in dishevelled curls, slightly silvering, around a face in which laughter was reborn. "How Les would have romped with him," she crowed.

"Pearl's tired," Adam muttered. "Thought I'd bring him out, give her a break."

Grace glanced at him and said quickly, "You see, I had Mama. And of course servants were different in those days."

"Two maids, Grace, and a nurse," Sarah added.

"And Belle," Ben reminded them, "she helped too — later."

Paul shook his head. "Nowadays, you know, it's a different story." He slid his homemade bookmark into the concordance and reached out to run his forefinger over the silky head on Sarah's arm.

"Different, different," Grace confirmed.

"Yes," Adam sighed. "Nowadays is a very different story."

Grace took the baby from Sarah, smoothing her finger along the transparent pink skin of his hands.

"Quiet with you," Adam said.

"Quiet with anybody at this stage, once you pick him up."

"Mm. I suppose he spoil a little."

"Eh?" Ben said sharply.

Sarah made an abrupt, contemptuous noise by chirping air in through her teeth. Grace smiled reprovingly at Adam and rocked softly.

"What you mean? You can't spoil a baby."

Goddie Sarah spread her wrinkled hands impatiently. "Come, give me the child here. I come through fire and flood into my nineties and I have too little time left in this world to spend an evening arguing with a moron."

Ben cackled with delight, but Grace ignored her dreamily, eyes half-closed. "Sugar. Little sugar."

Sarah slapped the handle of her rocker violently. "Woman, stop your infernal mutterings and hand me the infant."

Grace started with a guffaw. So they spent the evening, passing Gerry back and forth.

"He will be a big boy when your century comes," Paul reflected.

"Where we'll get food for a lunch though?" Grace pursed her lips and her brows furrowed.

"Well, you still have a few years to plan," Ben erupted. "Or you going finalise menu an' all tonight?"

"You'd better," Paul snarled, "if you want to track down the food. Whole of you think is so easy." He glared around him accusingly as they grinned at him. Paul was the expert at finding things in short supply. They called him the Scrounger.

"You research five different places to pick up four items, and every little clerk and cashier is too busy being delicious to attend to you."

The new year came without the changes they had hoped for. The *Gleaner* proclaimed a spate of violent deaths, homes and public places robbed, women raped, children kidnapped. The country tensed in its State of Emergency. The family's circle of friends shrank smaller, tighter.

One evening Adam drew up at the McIntyres as he turned into Oxford Close. He parked at the back and skipped up the kitchen steps as he had from childhood. Jewel waddled past the window, greying now. She grinned and called out as she shot back bolt after bolt, "Is Mas' Adam come, Miss Lisa."

"Jewel, I smell something and I see ackee seed. Don't tell me Miss Lisa have saltfish? Where she get it?"

"Saltfish yes, Sir. Mas' Tony sen' parcel wid a friend come from Canada."

"What! Saltfish from foreign? But you people not easy."

He strolled out from the kitchen into the dining room and froze, jolted into a vacuum. Bare. The sofa, the beer mug from the trip to Brussels. The picture of Lisa's mother with Grand. Everything was gone.

Lisa emerged from a bedroom grinning. "Who smelling out my big Canadian saltfish?"

She paused, following his glance. In the bedroom the mattress was on the floor. Dressing table, wardrobe, everything else had vanished.

"Canada," she whispered. "Is all packed off to Tony. We go end of month."

Adam stammered into an apology for not coming to help but she touched his lips.

"Nobody knew, Adam. Not even your folks." Lisa took his hand and pulled him to the old lounge chair, brought in from the porch. "We never told a soul."

Of course. One never knew. Sometimes just passing a house you would notice that it was empty. Families went away on vacation and never returned.

"Is no point now, with the children gone. Things as they are." Her voice pleaded, "I had nothing left."

What to say? Her fingers tightened on his.

"What 'bout you dear? When you going? I know Pearl wants to."

He forced a chuckle. "We must be staying to turn out the lights."

It was a stale joke. Friends had said, "Last one to leave Jamaica, turn out the lights."

Now those friends were gone.

Lisa sighed and squeezed her plump, freckled arm around him. "Well, for this evening anyway, stay and eat Canadian saltfish and Jamaica ackee."

He hugged her but he was angry.

"Is not you," he laboured, "not because I didn't know. It's... that you have to go. Everything just... breaking up. Soon nothing will be... worthwhile. I hate them for breaking it up. I've never been violent...."

"I know."

"But I could fight. I could hold a gun and kill. I hate them for making me feel... I could kill."

She sat holding him and rocked slightly. His breath was fast and shallow and his throat tightened.

"Everything is different now. I feel so locked in. Everyone... Things that used to be important... Pearl doesn't even seem to... well, the baby. Things were never that way before." He was ashamed because he had talked about Pearl and because he sounded like an old man.

You weren't supposed to talk. Of course you couldn't help it, so you whispered. Fear whispered things along the street, around the dining table and in the living rooms, in markets and government offices, in school classrooms and supermarkets, on street corners and in letters abroad.

"Don't come home now," the Halls had written to their daughter at a college in the States. "No one knows what may happen. Can't you do a postgrad or something?"

Jessie Dietrich wrote her nephew: "How can you think of moving back when you have a job in Toronto? What's the future here? (It's all a communist conspiracy you know.) Bertie is going through hell, fighting for import licences. My dear, it's only higglers prospering in Ja. now. And don't ask about raw materials. This is no place for a businessman.

"Anyway if you do come, dear, you won't find us. Our trailer will be at the gate by month end... P.S. Don't mention in letters to anyone else here."

Pearl was shrill when she heard about the McIntyres. "Well, she's right. When are we going?" she demanded.

Her hair, scraped away into a scarf like that, hardened her face, especially when she felt too harassed to pencil in eyebrows she insisted on plucking out.

"Go with what? You can't understand? Sam has his children to go to. Others have bank accounts outside they been feeding years now. Hundreds of millions of dollars trickle out in the past few years. I never send any."

"Well, more fool you."

He turned away, provoked. "After I didn' have none to send. You not exactly frugal."

"Christ! Don't start."

"Well, how in hell I can get money outside the country if I can't keep none here?"

"You don't have to get it out. People our age go over and start from scratch. You not a doctor? You can't done tell me so! You degree not worth nothing outside of here?"

He yanked angrily at his shirt buttons and said nothing. She lowered her voice and went on more reasonably, "Honestly, Adam. Think of your parents if you won't think of me. The McIntyres have their children to go to. What about your parents? Don't they'll be stuck? Because of you."

He paused at the door and glanced back contemptuously, "Your sudden concern for my parents is touching."

He was gone before she could reply, and she walked over to the phone and snatched up the receiver, dialling furiously.

When Adam came in, Pearl was dazzling in a bouffant ribbon blouse and three-tiered black cotton skirt. Her hair swirled loose and silky, obviously relaxed and highlighted, parting softly in the light breeze that turned the leaves of the starapple tree outside, to show glimpses of contrast. She extended her hand with a flash of iridescent nails and he melted instantly. Apologetic and flattered at once, he reached for her. She whisked the car key from his fingers and drove away.

So it was not for him. He stifled a ripple of disappointment.

After all, Pearl deserved a night out. If the girls were having something, why shouldn't she go? He sank into an armchair to wait up. Under the sofa he glimpsed a toy that had been his. He bent and picked it up, turning it over and over, fingering the familiar grooves. Surely he had just finished playing with this himself.

He remembered it all with aching clarity. The dust giddy in the sunbeams that riddled the open house, Les's laughter and the smell of cornmeal pudding with raisins. The sensations of his childhood pierced him with their immediacy. It was more than nostalgia. More excruciating. In no time at all he would be old. He thought of his parents and looked around baffled at the empty house. He could not say when everything had changed. Only suddenly he had woken up into a bad dream to find time mocking him, with little shocks of realisation shooting through his head.

Pearl clung to her parties, her filmy negligées that the baby must not touch, her Waterford decanter. She was afraid too. Everybody he knew was afraid, he thought. It made it more immense, more threatening. He might wake up one day and find his life had flown by without his noticing. He wiped his face again with the sodden handkerchief.

There was less and less of Pearl. When Gerry was almost a year and "on his own," as she said, she got herself a job. That was no problem in itself; Adam's mother had worked. But Pearl came home later and later.

One day Adam was in by six and fumbling around to find something to eat. It would solve so much, he thought irritably, bashing the egg on the side of the pot, if she would go out early in the morning instead. He was sure even a cosmetics agent could find customers in the morning (clients, she called them clients); but no, at eight, nine o'clock she was still sleeping. At ten, if he stopped home on the way between the hospital and his office, she was still in pajamas. Row after row they'd had about it.

He searched the fridge for cheese. Someone had brought them a hunk from Barbados recently. Must be in the freezer.

(Solid and useless.)

Pearl left Gerry with the maid all day and into the night until Adam came in. The maid, Dolores, simply handed him the baby to bathe and change as he walked through the door, and she slammed out muttering. One morning Dolores failed to return and since then Gerry had stayed at Oxford Close until Adam collected him on the way home.

Often he didn't want to leave and held onto Grace wailing, "Sugar! Sugar!"

Tonight Gerry had not been there. Pearl hadn't even called Oxford Close and the folks had expected him. It wasn't the first time she had taken him along to work, but she could have called. (Christ, no. He understood about cheese and onions, but salt couldn't be scarce. She couldn't tell him salt was scarce.) It was dangerous being on the road later than this in any case, and with the child too. The little hand gun she sported in her purse was stylish but Adam couldn't see the point of it in the present climate. No salt anywhere. He scraped the scrambled eggs into the trash bin and flung the pot in the sink.

The wall of the kitchen lit up with the pattern of headlights diffused through the window. In minutes, Gerry's face bobbed up over the doorstep and he pulled himself into the room, grunting and pawing at Adam until he took him up to watch TV. They stayed there while Pearl showered. After a while, Gerry slid down and began pulling at the things his mother had dropped in the chair by the door. The handbag fell open and Adam bent automatically to gather up the contents.

One was a familiar round, white plastic case. He picked it up, puzzled, and turned it over and over in his hand. Then he sank slowly into a chair. Pearl sauntered out from the bathroom, brushing her hair. She paused with a sharp intake of breath as she saw him with the open bag and the case. Then almost instantly she went on brushing with powerful, angry strokes. Adam held out the case. "What in hell?"

"Is such a long time you forget?" She baited him.

"You know what I mean. In your bag?"

She was furious. "Keep your arse out of my bag. I keep what I need in there for an emergency."

His face was purple and swollen looking. "Hell of an emergency you could need this for at work. What sort of work… ?"

He caught sight of the child's wide bright eyes and anxious droop at the mouth and choked down the rest, coughing explosively. But she started crying, her exquisite little mouth outraged and hurt. "I don't have to listen to your insinuations."

He exploded afresh. "And with my child? You take my child? You bitch!"

"Is yours he is?" She spat it at him, silencing him.

Adam grabbed the boy and the keys and ran from the house.

Slamming the car into reverse he screeched up the driveway. All the way to Oxford Close, he cast covert glances at the child. No, they weren't alike. He hadn't really thought of it but now it seemed so obvious. Everybody must have noticed. In fact, people were always asking, "Who he resembles?"

The child's eyes were wide and brilliant with excitement and terror. Adam swung to the side of the road, crushed the brakes and hugged Gerry to him.

"OK," he muttered. "All right, son. Is all right. We going to Grand and Sugar."

He had meant to leave the child with them and go back, but now he knew it was impossible. It would only bewilder the baby more. Besides, he thought, if he saw her again tonight he might…. He remembered Lisa's voice, "You couldn't hurt anyone, Adam. You couldn't do anything to break the law. Not you."

"Listen," he had snapped. "You not listening. The ones who can't change are leaving Jamaica."

Adam lay on his old bed that night and the baby rolled and tumbled over him contentedly. Gerry didn't seem to miss his mother; she was peripheral to him. He burrowed his nose into his father and slept. But all night Adam lay searching for something that would put his life together again. It was still dark when he dragged himself off the bed and pulled on his clothes. He arranged the pillows about the child and tiptoed out.

Grace was in the kitchen.

"What you doing out here?" he stroked her face wearily.

"Drinking tea. You want?"

"Liar."

She grinned wryly. "All right. Getting you a cup." She fixed an accusing eye on him. "You can't know when your stomach is empty?"

"I can't swallow it. I can hardly even breathe."

"Then drink the likkle hot tea."

He took a few gulps, felt for his Ventolin inhalant and sprayed twice briefly. He was through the door but stuck his face back in. "Thank you, Sugar."

When he let himself in, Pearl was still sleeping, or so he thought until she stretched and opened her eyes, which weren't pink.

"Adam?"

"Who else you were expecting?"

They always said that, but it had never meant anything before. Her eyes narrowed for a minute then she relaxed.

"Adam, don't make us quarrel now. Nice rainy morning and Gerry not here. I mad last night, man. You don't know how suspicious you looked. You never really take me serious?" She stretched again so that the covers slipped.

"Don't worry 'bout your meal ticket, Pearl. Is my child now, wherever you get him."

"Adam." Slight pout and wide hurt eyes he knew so well, and the sheen of her unbelievable skin. Long, silky woman.

He walked over to the bed. "All for me?"

"More." She began to lean back slowly. Too measured.

"To hell with it." He picked up her dressing gown and flung it at her.

The little girl pout vanished and she was coldly furious but it was remote from him now. He was ill with exhaustion and disgust and his senses were numb. The whole thing seemed to come to him from a distance. He heard her leave the house, and he sank onto the bed and slept till afternoon. Strange irrelevant dreams scudded across his mind like fast clouds on a troubled sky. They were pale cream that turned sour and spilled greyly across the day.

More and more she was away. Evenings, weekends, weekdays. Floral tributes arrived. Bills for phone calls to New York mounted up unpaid.

"I tell you is business calls, and they going disconnect the phone, you know," she pointed out. "You self can't manage without a phone."

He shrugged. "I can live at my parents'."

It was as if he didn't really see her. Just the child. He slept in Gerry's room on the single bed near the crib.

Yet sometimes he thought he must be wronging her. He couldn't have been such a fool as to marry a tramp. Occasionally he tried to talk but her face closed and she stared at him with betrayed eyes so that confusion and guilt built in him again until the pain eclipsed itself in numb silence thickening between them. Reality blurred around a few sharp images. The bustle of the hospital, its lights, pungent smells and plaintive noises were relieved by the tumble and cuddle of the child. And so it was for months. He lived in a sort of dream intersected by duty, pain, and brief warm rushes of relief.

One evening he sat on the edge of the bedroom chair not even seeing Pearl dress as he stared into the wardrobe for a clean shirt to wear to old Mrs Coke's funeral. The new drug had agreed with so many other patients. By the time he knew the old lady could not take it, she was gone. The old medication that had worked for years had found its way onto the government's list. Prohibited. Other patients whose medication had to be changed slid across his mind. Michaelson, Thomas, old man Drew. Horror shivered along his skin. If he had his own emergency supply, he thought.

He began for the first time to wonder seriously how he could get money on the outside. His own old people were in remarkably good shape. Goddie almost deaf, of course, but she had always been. Ben's sight deteriorating but... otherwise strong as an ox. Grace arthritic, but stubbornly active. Paul's old prostate.... Of course, Adam knew that in important ways they were in better shape than he was himself. Still. It could have been one of his parents. Or Gerry.

The child rolled around his legs making soft bumping noises on the floor and chirping briefly at each new discovery. Laboriously he made his way around Adam's chair, clinging to the upholstery. Sometimes with an air of intrepid daring he released the chair to lurch off on his own.

Adam held his breath, touched by the brief, ungainly little run and abrupt bump down on the bottom that was so inevitable yet at the same time surprising when it came. He jumped up and grabbed at the child as he lunged at the door. But Gerry wasn't going out, just pulling at it as if he wanted to dislodge it and fussing, "S'ide door, s'ide door."

Talking early, walking late.

"Eh?" Adam encouraged.

"Unca s'ide door."

"What?"

Gerry paused and regarded him solemnly. Ackee-seed eyes, Grace called them.

"Unca. Unca," he repeated, enunciating the word slowly and patiently as for a moron.

"Uncle who?"

"Unca s'ide door."

"Side door, son? What side door?"

"Mummy 'n Unca room. S'ide door open. See pool."

Adam sat heavily back in his chair and Pearl returned instantly to the bathroom. For a strange timeless while he sprawled there watching the child, hardly hearing the words so much as a rise and fall of tone and every now and then the distinct, careful pronunciation of "Unca".

It may have been seconds or hours later that Pearl walked past him with a suitcase in her hands. She didn't say anything to him or kiss the baby.

Gerry tottered from chair to chair until he reached his father and laid his cheek on Adam's bare leg for a while.

"Daddad sick?"

"Mm."

"Here."

He reached into the pocket of his shorts and groped for a minute grunting strenuously. Then he held out to Adam a couple of small, awkwardly shaped objects.

"Taa!" he reminded Adam.

"Thanks, son."

Automatically Adam took them and turned them over vaguely. They were sharp, obviously nothing a child should have. He rubbed them between his fingers absently.

"What are these?"

The reply was unintelligible and Adam bent down to him. "Eh? Mummy? Murray? What?" Again a little nasal babble. They were bone or something. He stared for a moment. Teeth. His mind ran back to biology classes. Shark's teeth.

"Where you get these?"

"Unca."

Adam stared at the pieces, startled. "What for?"

"Unca taa."

"What uncle gave them to baby for? What are they?"

The response was unintelligible. It sounded like "money" but could hardly have been. Adam couldn't make it out. He packed some things and took Gerry over to Oxford Close.

It was days later before he heard the word again. He was filling his gas tank and reached for his cash. Gerry grabbed excitedly at the bills and squealed, "Mo'ey, mo'ey."

Adam stared at him. "Money," he agreed.

And there was something, yes. Shark's teeth as currency in Negril Beach Village. Negril she had been in, sunbathing naked with a set of damn hippies.

"You like Negril, son?"

"No. Unca cross," Gerry pouted.

Adam felt his throat closing and set about wiping Pearl from his mind. He began to talk calmly to Gerry about Mrs Whiskers and her kittens.

Yet one evening when he went home to check the house as usual, Pearl was there. She was beautiful, asleep in their bed. She opened her eyes suddenly and looked straight into his, into him, into the grief and yearning back and wishing it had never had to change. It was true, she said; there had been an affair. But it was over and she wanted them to try again.

"You remember how it was, Adam?" Her face was paler than usual with soft shadows around the eyes, sad and hauntingly lovely. "I know I hurt you and you don't deserve it, but I going make it up to you."

He swung away, seething at her simplicity. Suddenly it seemed as if he had never been angry before. It hit him with the shock of a new emotion. But she hung on his arm. "Give us a chance. For Gerry's sake, nah."

She was crying, so he said nothing. He was confused. He moved back with Gerry and she was there, bright and flawlessly made up in the evenings, alluring and considerate at supper time. But he never moved back into their room.

Once when he was getting ready to put Gerry to sleep she stopped him in the passage with a light touch on the chest. They

were by the doorway of the bathroom, so the light shone right
through her soft, jade-green nightgown.

"Wait up for you?"

Why it mattered to her? Well. One thing Pearl wanted above
all was to be irresistible. Transparent like her nightgown. But
don't he had always known? To be honest he had known Pearl
through and through and wanted her still. And now, anything
was really different? For a second he turned to her, his eyes
lingering over the nightgown. But it was green.

Adam had never liked green. Pearl hadn't bought the negligée
with him in mind.

He had changed even if she had not. Now there was Gerry.

"No," he said, with brutal truthfulness. "Everything spoil
except the child."

"I'll have him if you leave me," she snapped.

Gerry edged against his father and said, "No. Unca lock door."

Adam wished he could take Gerry with him to the States for the
following week. After the conference they could have stopped in
Miami for a weekend, taken in Disney World. But he wouldn't
have enough currency for all that and a sitter too. Adam had forgotten about Pearl before she turned into the bedroom that had
been theirs. He gathered Gerry and walked on up the passage,
rubbing his nose into the child's neck. He wouldn't leave him with
her. He would leave him at home.

When he returned from the States, Pearl was different, less
attentive. She left for work and returned at regular hours but she
was contented somehow, pleased with herself, and now he was
glad she worked and was out of the house.

Yet after his return he was more worn out than he should have
been and he stayed home, troubled by faint discomfort in the pit of
his stomach. All morning he slept.

He woke feeling alert, ready to eat and was searching the
kitchen when the phone rang.

"Eh, boy. Austin here, still at the bank. Listen. I make the usual check on Pearl's account for you. Is overdrawn again. Go ahead and honour it against your account?"

Adam closed his eyes wearily.

"As usual. But how it gone so fast? What's the last cheque?"

"You mean before the hotel bill?"

"What hotel?"

The pause at the other end of the line was eloquent. Austin had approved a large sum thinking Adam had been with her. Adam reassured him. "You know I not going embarrass you, man. Is you help me keep track of this thing all along. But where the hell it make out to?"

He could hardly catch Austin's reply.

"I assumed it was you with her. It.... Well, is made out to a hotel. To Couples."

Adam was cold for a second, then suddenly normal, deadly calm. "Honour it. Any more that you passed?"

"Plenty more, but no others I passed."

"Bounce every blasted one."

He dropped the receiver down on the table, not even seeing the hook, and stumbled into a chair.

He sank his face into his hands and he could see it — Pearl and her faceless, nameless lover sipping drinks at the bar and smoking the complimentary cigarettes. The pool. The tours. Swinging in the hammock and bumping sensuously into each other — she would give a little start of artificial surprise as if she hadn't really meant to touch him. Gerry called him "Uncle".

Uncle. Must be long and lean and sun-bright like Pearl. Not dull and sagging after ten hours at the hospital. Adam could see them across yards and yards of buffet and smorgasbord piled high with everything he used to take for granted as a child, things he had now almost forgotten the existence of, toasting each other with their foreheads almost touching across the table.

Dancing. He knew how Pearl danced. He knew how when Pearl danced you couldn't wait to get her off the floor... but you couldn't bear for her to stop moving against you. There would be a bar too and she would get just barely high. Pearl was never drunk, just high enough to be a little outrageous, just enough. Oh God, he would go mad.

Stop it. He'd have to stop it. Get up and do something. Anything. He looked around for something else to think about but there was nothing.

There was only Pearl, long, sun-coppered all over, gleaming with water and salty to taste. Pearl and the other lean, muscular figure, always from behind, always with his face in shadow. But bound to be white. They turned to each other in a boat rocking slightly off shore, under a brilliant blue sky, under a mist of sea spray. They turned to each other on the hard, sandy ground where they had sunbathed for the complete all-over tan Pearl had always, mysteriously, managed to maintain. They turned to each other in the room that overlooked the ocean and the island with its solitary white tower. And always they were smooth and glossy, sun-brown and sea-wet.

Adam had paid for it. Gerry. Did they let him watch? If not, what did they do with him (Unca lock door.) Had he been... had he seen? Where was he *now?*

When Pearl came in Adam had been waiting for hours, simply sitting. He didn't hug Gerry or even look at him. He just blurted out the question that had tormented him above all others.

"Where you leave him?"

"Eh?" She was genuinely bewildered.

He coughed, a brief rasping explosion.

"When you go out... what you do with my child?"

"You know he stays with your parents."

"In town, yes. But not on a business trip... at Couples." His voice rose to a shriek as he fought for air and the pulse at the side of his head throbbed almost visibly. "And they don't take... children at Couples."

21

Shipmates

THEIR VOICES lapped around him on the fringes of consciousness, just outside his old bedroom in the Oxford Close house.

"Women today are not what they were," Ben grumbled. "No softness in them."

"Or propriety," and Grace's eyes flashed that her mother had been different, and her mother before her.

"Not a matter of softness," Paul snapped, and they knew he was thinking of his grandmother. Old Martha Jane was as tough as they came. This Pearl was brittle stuff.

Grace's face raised, pain-etched. "What were they made of, Paul?"

Dissolving time.

January 1680 — and two days it had been since Owen O'Reilly had had anything in his belly but despair. Now he leaned forward dizzily, propping one hand against the filthy wall beside the notice. Laboriously picking the words out, he read it again. He was too meagre, obviously, to qualify as a first class labourer for six hundredweight of oatmeal and half a barrel of herring. Yet the point was, surely, that there was food. Free food. Food, surely, day after day. And he need pay nothing for it. Work, yes. But he had worked from he could stand. And rare had been the day when he was sure of any more then a few potatoes. Then even those... His mother had lain on the floor and nothing could be done for her, and he had run from the place so as not to see her die.

Owen read the poster a third time, dreaming of a warm cottage, the milk of a cow, a neat plot of his own, bacon.

Priests. He started. They said there were even priests. And one and sixpence a day. Food and shelter free, after all. And what more was there? He would save one and sixpence a day. O Blessed Mother. Save it all, and when he came back.... Then the wind knifed through the threadbare coat — Mary, Mary, it was cold — and he knew he was never coming back.

A week later he was boarding, his hand tight on the papers in his coat pocket.

> *This indenture made the 15th January 1680 between Owen O'Reilly aged 23 years of the one party, and Peter Crutwell of the other party witnesseth that the said Owen O'Reilly doth hereby covenant, promise and grant... such service and employment... according to the custom of the country....*

But something went awry. He never discovered what it was. Somehow, in the confusion on the docks, he had been hustled in with the wrong group.

O'Reilly glanced furtively around at the other ninety-seven penned together under the deck. Apparently he was thrown in with the convicts. There was no one to show his papers to and he was afraid to expose them anyway lest they be snatched. The watch at the door spread his thick legs like buttresses and gripped the blunderbuss. Perhaps, O'Reilly thought, when they let him out to ease himself he might manage to get back into his own group. Then a heavy, balding man squeezed through to the great pail at the centre of the room and hesitated. When he fumbled hastily with his breeches O'Reilly understood that no one would leave the room before they docked. In no time they ceased to see the pail, but as it filled it stank.

O'Reilly and a younger man named Jefferies struck a sort of partnership. They stretched out in turns, each guarding the other's space savagely so that no one lay on him.

Eight days at sea and the food grew scanty, when O'Reilly noticed Jefferies labouring on the biscuit.

"Is it ill you are, man?" O'Reilly stopped chewing and squinted through the gloom.

The other shrugged, flicking away damp hair from his eyes. "Hot in here."

O'Reilly said nothing, but then he saw the lad's skin flushed unlike the pasty yellow common in the hold. "When did it start?"

A sob shuddered through the lad.

"Listen, boy." O'Reilly steadied the thin hand, which shook violently, and shoved half his own biscuit into it. "All kinds of fever there are. Needn't be what you're thinking." He peered into the shadows around the lad's neck and the torn cloth hanging around his calves. "No blotches?"

Jefferies spread his hands, sniffling.

"No, no. I don't see nothing." O'Reilly pulled the clothes back around him. "Keep warm."

The lad's eyes flickered at him uncertainly. "You sure?"

"No blotches, boy."

"The man who died last night... they said it was the smallpox."

"Not a mark on you." O'Reilly punched him lightly and laughed. "You're fair as a woman, boy."

But the fever rose, and around them the sick cried and moaned, tossing and sometimes kicking inadvertently as the lice tormented them. Two days out of his mind Jefferies lay with the fever raging over him; but there were no blotches, and as long as the plague set no mark on him O'Reilly refused to give him up. Water came rarely and O'Reilly tore his own shirt and wet it in his urine to sop the boy's forehead. It was a delicate unlined face. Only a boy after all, the Irishman thought.

The floor pitched steeply jerking them down its rough wooden planks awash from the slop pail, and hour after hour the room sank and heaved violently around them, shattering what little rest the fever and vermin had overlooked. Outside, the guards shouted to each other and one screamed that the mizzen-yard was gone. Hopelessness sank over the prisoners even when the boat lurched more gently, still lapping its excrement and disease into the darkest corners of the cabin. But somehow the lad lived.

"What're you aboard for, boy?" Over and over O'Reilly had pondered it, watching the innocent curve of his mouth and childish, upturned nose. "What did you do?"

"Rape."

"Ye little pig." But there was a hint almost of admiration in O'Reilly's voice. The lad looked such a child. "Got you into enough trouble. Next time, get a willing one, do you hear?"

"Aye." Jefferies grasped his arm and slept.

It was a bond, forged in the seven-week crossing, unlike any O'Reilly had known. But then the ship docked, severing them, abruptly and totally as if it had never been.

O'Reilly slept on the ground the first night in Barbados and in the morning he gathered what sticks he could and leaned together a shelter of plantain leaves laced with withes to keep out the rain.

"You'll make the next better," nodded the man who had advised him about the withes. He spoke like a gentleman.

"What were you?" O'Reilly asked.

"Schoolmaster."

O'Reilly stared, and the other man laughed bleakly.

"Brought to Carrickfergus in '56."

The overseer rode towards them flicking his cane briefly in the direction of the field and they sprang apart. O'Reilly recalled little of Barbados besides the shelter, the schoolmaster, and the whip. Probably he only survived because they shipped him on to Jamaica in a couple of months.

When he had worked out his indenture he counted himself fortunate to find a position of bookkeeper on a small, new sugar estate toward the eastern end of the island. At that time

Goldfields had still been a losing concern and its master torn by creditors. O'Reilly held on for a while, waiting for it to change hands. Working for a Jew did not suit him. When at last the crash came it was another Jew, Isaac Cohon, who bought it from the first owner, Goldmeer, and Cohon promptly dismissed the Irishman. So O'Reilly drifted westward into the centre of the island where he built up a small farm of his own. And for what? His son eventually left Jamaica in frustration after the Maroons burnt the house in Moneague and murdered the housekeeper. They returned to Ireland.

So years later it was in the old country that Owen's grandson, Pat O'Reilly, was born. Then it all happened again. The land cold and hard as stone. Profits meagre or non-existent. The potatoes turned black. His mother lay dying. Pat's father had heard it all from his father, Owen. But it had been only a story. When it turned real on Pat's old man it broke his mind.

The O'Reillys had gone to the Kilrush workhouse when there was nothing left. No work, no food. There had been shelter at first, empty, but between them and the wind. Then the evictions started and in Clare the houses of the poor were levelled one after the other. They had eaten weeds and boiled nettles, day in, day out, until these too were gone. They took the wood of the broken house to make a low cart and dragged his mother upon it with the two little ones naked beside her. Pat and his father pulled it, for the old horse was dead and eaten months ago.

With hundreds of other emaciated poor they clamoured at the door of the workhouse for admission, for a meal and a coffin. Whatever else life had deprived them of, at least they had to claim that last accommodation. They were proud still, too proud to be left for kites and dogs upon the road like the remains of the unburied peasants they had passed upon the way. The O'Reillys had the coffin in time to bury Pat's mother and the officials kept his father and the little ones and let Pat have a mug of porridge. It was a few ounces of Indian meal stirred in an artificial milk made of flour and water. He had no doubt that the children and Himself would be dead within the week, but they had shelter meanwhile and would have shelter beyond. Pat clutched the musty wad of papers preserved from his grandfather's time. They proved his right to a plot of land in the Moneague area of Jamaica. He lied and thieved his way to the port.

Jamaica was a chance for Pat to recapture what his grandfather had built. The first tiny plot in Moneague had been enlarged considerably by a piece bought from a man named Stollmeier. Stollmeier had been disappointed about a plantation called Goldfields that he had hoped to inherit and he had been increasingly harassed by creditors until he sold his Moneague holding.

It was not a large place, but it was prime farmland and farming ran through centuries of O'Reilly blood. Neither the English, the Irish protestants nor the famine could take that away. Pat O'Reilly put his papers before a lawyer and laboured on the docks of Kingston till he could have his land again.

So in the end, Martha Jane could never be anything but O'Reilly. Her husband, Luke Horne, had been a gentle man and Paula had always seemed more his child than Martha's. Neither had Martha's single-minded determination to survive. When she and Luke were running in the front ranks of the crowd with the Kingston street heaving beneath them it was Luke who had looked back — away to the smoke-filled doorway and a woman mouthing, pointing inside. It was Luke who had tried to turn aside. And fallen. Over and over the moment had replayed in Martha's brain. His palm upturned and crushed grey fingers, then the woman's face turning back into smoke.

A resolute woman, Catherine Donalds. Grace knew of her only from Stella. Catherine herself had known nothing of her own parents' past.

One of Catherine's African ancestors, Abū Bakr al-Ṣiddīq, had been nine when he left Jenné with his tutor to visit Bouna, the ancient trading place on the border of the Ashanti Empire. Here his father, Kara Musa, the learned one, had died of a fever while trading in gold and had been buried. Theirs was a prominent family. Several were members of the ulama, men of learning, proficient in Koranic exegesis. One of the ancestors had even been a King's Witness. In these early years the great mosque at Jenné still flourished. The rectangular enclosure jutted upwards like rows of giant teeth, seemingly inviolable. It never occurred to the boy that he would not see the Jenné mosque again or that its own destruction was imminent.

He was a child of promise. His family and his masters had pondered over him and decided. He was still young for more advanced studies in logic and rhetoric, so they introduced him to a school where he could continue working on the Koran under the influence of the Sayyids. These were the great masters, assembled from all over the Western Sudan.

In this way he was not totally isolated from his family. His father, Kara Musa, had had brothers in Bouna and other valuable connections. He had been a man of property whose slaves collected and separated gold for him from the stones of the river. From Bouna, Kara Musa had directed to his wife's father dispatch after dispatch of horses, asses and mules, laden with Egyptian silks. It was Kara Musa's brother, Mahmud, who had remained in the city and received his nephew when the boy came to visit his father's grave. Abū Bakr remained in Bouna for years.

He was there in 1801, a year of revolution for the Ashanti. The deposition of the asantehene led from one revolt to the next as the years passed. Eventually Adinkra, a powerful nominee in Bonduku, sent a demand to Kwadwo, the governor of Kolongzhwi. Adinkra required gold as a ransom for Kwadwo's life. Again he sent, increasing his demands. Eventually he began the campaign. With the support of the Sultan of Bouna, Kwadwo met the forces of Adinkra in battle at Bole and later at Anwiego. But Adinkra took Bouna.

Abū Bakr was fourteen years old when he was captured by the Ashanti. They ripped off his clothes, and bound his hands. Then they yoked him to others, clean and unclean, who had been taken with him. Two hundred miles south they were marched to Tutu Kwame. From there they pressed fifty-five miles south to cross the river at Prasa and in through the land of the Fanti towards the coast.

So at last they came to the place where the world ended.

The boy stared out upon the Gulf of Guinea mesmerised by its vastness and restlessness. There came a man — death white, harsh-featured, his mouth a gash chipped into stone, his body swathed in outlandish garments. A transaction. Something sparkled between fingers gesturing for bargains. The boy shrank away as grimy hands grasped him, smearing his flesh. They shoved him aboard one of the frail craft bobbing helplessly up and down on the heavy water. Further out, a ship waited and there they marched past a huddle of white men around a huge boiling copper. A girl behind him whimpered that they were going to be eaten. He did not know her language but the terror with which her eyes rolled to and away from the copper was unmistakable.

They were taken down and put in storage with countless others who had arrived before them. Interminably they were arranged and shackled into position, circumcised and un-circumcised riveted together. The hold, airless on their arrival, pressed closer with the heat of their bodies, the stink of perspi-ration, urine, and vomit. Night fell, but no one noticed for it was already dark.

In the blackness, the chains grated between the whimpered prayers and queries of the prisoners. An abrupt squeal or sharp hiss of obscenity drew a brief silence that disintegrated again into grunts of discontent as they shuffled and reshuffled their limbs.

The boy lay feeling his bladder full to bursting point until the warm stream of his neighbour spattered over his leg. Then he lost grip and with a whimper of apology shamed himself and disrespected the man beside him. Away in the darkness one cursed but others were silent; they had lost control hours before. Abū Bakr drew his limbs together as tightly as he could and folded his prayers about him, to shield his flesh and spirit from the filth. Then he waited for morning, assuming that even in the hold Allah's sun would rise. After all, he was little more than a child.

It may have been days before the ship sailed. Or weeks. There was no way of telling. By then he understood that he was fortunate to have escaped months of waiting in one of the garrisoned forts on the coast. He grasped a few words of the men around him and learnt that many were prisoners of war. They had been up and down the Gold Coast and knew about the forts. Some of the Fanti had been seized ignominiously and traded by others of their own tribe. The boy whose right leg was fastened to Abū Bakr's left had been sold by his parents when starvation overtook the family. One of his brothers had disappeared, but he had two sisters somewhere on shipboard. He said one was Beneba, the girl who had cried out at the sight of the copper. These were the things Abū Bakr remembered and spoke of later. The rest he lost — mercifully, for in the crossing he slipped from bewilderment to dejection and into the common suicidal despair that was fatal to many of those who were spared disease or suffocation.

He survived the crossing. At first he refused food, afraid lest he swallow forbidden meat. He was force-fed; he vomited, and was fed again. When he was ill they pressed a bottle to his mouth and held his nose until he gulped and felt the fiery liquid sear through throat, chest and limbs and rise giddily to his head. So he survived by such means as were forbidden him by his faith, and he would gladly have died to avoid them. For him the journey was not merely physical torture but a nightmare of defilement, and when he awoke from it he blotted it out.

Jamaica was a long groaning from the port they called Lago. The sailors emptied the filth tubs for the last time and swung the most recent dead overboard before the ship docked. Abū Bakr squatted in the unspeakable slime of the hold in a sort of paralysis. His senses were crippled. Thought and emotion had drained away. The sailors led him up onto the main deck and he blinked rapidly into the white light of the sun, unable to summon the will or interest to avert his eyes. They rolled uncontrollably for several minutes.

A stonemason named Donellen bought him and did business with the plantation owners near Kingston. On the Durand estate, the African encountered a brown mason who had fled with his owner from the revolution in St Domingue. He was a silent man, torn by bereavement. All he had in Jamaica was one daughter of about thirteen whom the master fancied. In a few years there would be a sprinkling of brown Durands on the estate, the shouting and bloodshed would be forgotten and the patois of their mother's country would be alien and unintelligible to them.

The fragile link between Abū Bakr and the workman from St Domingue severed abruptly when the African changed hands again and found himself on the Haynes property. Here his name became Edward Donlan and as he struggled to learn it he stumbled upon Jessica Castries, old Phippa's granddaughter from Goldfields. For a while he lived happily with her and was tolerant enough of her two brown sons by the manager. She was awed by the African's learning and religious devotion. But during the same year he came face to face with a woman called Beneba Haynes who had made the crossing on the same ship as himself.

A face. A ripple on the memory. A shore receding. The great copper on deck was boiling and long faces grinned around it, white, angular and almost lipless, like deathmasks. A face that was warm and soft and glossy black parted at the lips in fear. A cry and a flurry of movement. Recollection flooded through him of a girl powerful but lithe, quick-walking like the great cats who owned the night outside her village. The deck rose and sank beneath him again, the great sea of Guinea tilted up and down and the waves thundered their outrage. She had been there.

Nearly twenty years before, when Abū Bakr had been brought up to the main deck of the slaver, Beneba had stood on the quarter-deck, partially deranged. She had been sold into slavery with her younger sister and two brothers by parents who could no longer afford to feed them.

In a garrisoned fort she waited three months to be shipped, but there she ate better than she had since birth. Her younger brother, the least valuable to their captors, was rumoured to have died in prison. The other vanished on shipboard. All this she accepted once she remained near to her sister.

They came on deck before the sun was high and wandered around until the men brought the pannikins of water and rations of millet with lumps of salt beef. Then the young sailor, the one who tried to touch Beneba every time she passed, would take out the bagpipe and play. Another, more burly, fondled the cat-o'-nine-tails and the girls danced bleakly to the weird wailing pipes and the ominous rhythm of the cat tapping gently on the deck. They danced for exercise only and to give the men opportunity to scrape and swab the sleeping places. All day they dreaded the next meal, soggy horse beans with slabber sauce. Afterwards they were driven down and stowed under the gratings.

One day the sailor played only for Beneba. They made her dance. High, the cat indicated, higher, higher. Suddenly he stopped playing and threw her sprawling on the deck before the rest of the men. She whimpered and clawed the air uselessly. Then the captain shoved his way through the crowd and stared down at them, and he ordered the lad away from her.

But the captain was not always on hand. The men would bend over them, a ring of red faces closing above her, shouting encouragement and impatience. The first time when they took turns they stopped only when it seemed she would die. After a while the bewilderment wore off, and even the anger. Perhaps *one day only the tiredness would be left.*

The best of ships was intolerable when the weather turned foul. The time came when the sailors closed the portholes and covered down the gratings. The air thickened and stank and the fever and dysentery began. They would not leave stowage for the rest of the crossing.

Unfortunately it was a large hold, about six feet high. This meant that two platforms rather than one had been installed between floor and roof to stow extra girls. Beneba and her sister each lay in command of a space four feet six long, twelve inches wide and little over two feet high. They might not sit upright for the rest of the voyage, nor turn more than necessary for fear of pinching each other.

One morning the surgeon came, as usual dropping off his shoes before crawling over them, and he paused at a strange child chained to her left then clapped to one of the sailors. Beneba closed her eyes as the stiff arms were released and the body swung from one sailor to the other till it was out of sight. When she opened them vestiges of skin clung to the boards beside her.

It was bearable with her sister fastened at her other side. But one morning the younger child could not shift her leg. Alternately chafed raw and constricted by the chains, it had turned gangrenous. A strange heat throbbed in Beneba's temples. A man walked through the hold, stepping over them and bending over the girl's leg. He shook his head then signalled to one of the sailors. They poured a liquid over the swollen, discoloured tissue that washed away the seeping fluid and seared down into the flesh, but it was no use. The rot crept up until she stank. When the child was loathsome to herself and those around her, Beneba blotted out her groans with prayers that the ancestors would take her to themselves. But the sailors did not wait for the ancestors. They came for the girl while she had breath to moan and swung her from one to the next with the burst leg bumping and drip-

ping until they dumped her overboard. Then they tossed a bucket of water on the boards where she had lain.

Beneba lay on the soaked board and felt a soft movement at her arm. She glanced over then stretched, peering into the dampness where her sister had been fastened. A pale worm writhed in the dim light.

On the quarterdeck at the end of the voyage Beneba seemed no more sullen or unpredictable than the rest, but she had sealed the rot of the hold inside her memory. Gradually, by excising the unbearable, most of them would heal, but Beneba's mind festered.

Now all the girls were brought on deck again, to be cleaned and fed generously. The surgeon examined the sick carefully and treated them. Beneba herself had been drained considerably by the flux but looked reasonably sound, so there was no point discouraging prospective buyers. Scrupulously the men scrubbed away the traces of discharge and obstructed her anus with oakum. The others shifted tensely for the sale so that all could be over, for the sight of land brought relief. Only the girl with the oakum plug whined and squirmed until silenced by the cat.

On the Haynes's estate seasoning was usually cut short to one year, but Beneba required the full three. She was surly and unwilling, so after a while her back was criss-crossed with scar marks faded to differing extents. No one would buy her. As she grew tense and violent she came dangerously close to being valueless and was treated accordingly. Eventually Beneba Haynes was recorded on the plantation books as being good for nothing.

Then Abū Bakr arrived — intellectual, rational Edward Donlan. His thoughts were ponderings over the past, speculations and calculations about the future. Beneba would never think like him. She reacted blindly to each new pain, while he sat on the outside of his life and analysed it. Still, simply by their contact, her own life changed. He quieted her and she avoided the whip.

His anxiety for Beneba annoyed and bewildered Jessica. She had heard of the ships but they were tales to her, true but distant. She was a creole and would never fully understand the Africans with their strange hungers and affiliations. Sometimes she left Donlan, then scurried back feverishly lest she find Beneba in her place. But it was never so. At last she grew to accept, without understanding, the bond between the Africans.

Of course there were things the Africans needed from her and from the other creoles. The old ones shook their heads and warned Beneba patronisingly. "Salt-water nega tink seh work hard, floggee plenty. Dem no know 'bout long time."

A crone by the fire cackled toothlessly, and the first speaker, a middle-aged woman, prodded her.

"Tell im, Grannie. Tell im wha 'appen to Cato."

The other cackled again mindlessly. "Eeh? Cato come?"

"Eh! Eh! Then, Grannie, Cato no dead?"

"Is true." The old woman slapped one hand on the other and stared down at her nails, ridged and broken as dry tree bark. "One hammering me hear. Well. Dem well spread im out."

She gazed into the fire so avidly that Beneba too stared and seemed to see Cato burning there. Not at a stake, not so quickly, but subtly, blackening from the spread toes and fingers and upward slowly, so that long before the brain died the mind was ruined.

"What im do?" she whispered.

"Want to lick down Busha an' burn de works." The old woman's voice crackled and trailed away.

"But is do im do it?"

Abruptly, Grannie had fallen asleep, the withered flesh of her face sagging and her mouth parting emptily.

"Dem plan it," the first woman responded. "Busha find out 'bout it. Not dis Busha Horne, old Busha."

"How?"

"One of de nurse. Not from de hot-house. Pickney nurse in de

384

big house. She hear seh dem going fire de house an she 'fraid fe de pickney-dem. She tell de housekeeper."

Grannie snored loudly and Beneba stared about her. Most of the slaves were young and strong like herself, for the weak and elderly did not easily survive. But even the old had been young once.

"Why unnu never run 'way?"

A man of about seventy leaned forward and pointed to his mouth disfigured by a spur.

"Me pull foot, yes. Maroon bring me in fe thirty shilling."

A dark mutter stirred the gathering. The Maroons had bought their own peace by agreeing to track runaway slaves. The treaty with the English had come after gruelling years of guerrilla fighting and bitter deprivation. At last they had surrendered most of their independence, little by little, gnawed away by Act after Act relating to the treaty. The slaves saw only the enormous irony of betrayal, fugitives preying on other fugitives.

Jessica looked around defensively. "Long time, fe-me grannie pull foot. Is Maroon take im in wid im children."

She dared not boast, as she sometimes did, that he was her grandfather.

"Tcha!" A derisive ejaculation. "Dat day done wid."

Abū Bakr, whom they all called Donlan now, had listened silently. Now he leaned forward. "Suppose nobody work. Not just one. Nobody work at all. Dem couldn't flog all."

Cunningly the old man grinned at him. "Who go stop first?"

"Me puppa try it once, yes."

Everyone stopped and regarded the speaker, a bald, very black man, squatting slightly away from the rest.

"Was a Guinea man. Dem all say dem wouldn' work. When time come, Busha say floggee. Every man find him hoe. When Puppa ketch himself, Driba have im 'pon ground, fum im till im bleed, and salt im."

"Today not like long time," they agreed among themselves,

"Busha Horne different."

Afterwards, as Jessica and Donlan walked back with Beneba towards her hut, he muttered, *"You cyan't just bust out. You have to wait. Work quiet. Pull youself up."*

Beneba's mind kindled with visions from the fire. Cato. The old man with the ruined mouth. Salt on a bleeding back.

"You don' see? No see what dem do im? Is kill dem a kill we."

Jessica's brows knit in confusion and resentment.

"Maroon help plenty nega run 'way. Years Nana Phippa live wid dem."

Beneba stared at the two with the fire that was locked inside licking away at her sanity.

"Dem eating we fe true."

They were jolted to attention and stared at her uncomprehendingly through the plumed darkness of the bamboo grove. When they parted, Jessica was derisive. *"She mad, yes. No see she mad?"*

Donlan swung away from her in irritation, but the next day he talked to Beneba. He talked about the movement quietly but his eyes gleamed with a vision that was dark to her. *"Dem going free us, you know. Have fe free us."*

"Me cyan't wait pon dat. You can stay do nothing."

"I do all I must," he responded.

"What?" She shot the word at him, an accusation, but he replied steadily in a voice of stone.

"I say the five prayer, care for those poorer na me and fast for Ramadan." His voice wavered an instant. *"I never going see Mecca. But I keep the faith."*

She shrugged.

"And I wait!" he urged. *"When it all come down, what leave going be our own. Is coming down. Is coming down. You can't see?"*

They argued on and on. She had no choice but to wait, yet she could not. The dark places of her memory tore at her. Still, for all

*the years of his presence she was relatively quiet. She even pro-
duced a brown son for Busha Horne. Then Donlan was sold
from the estate and could not write either to her or to Jessica, for
both women were unschooled. When he was gone, Beneba raged
and battered herself against the discipline of the estate, but
Jessica lay hollow with the bottomless vacancy of a vessel that empties and fills and empties again without explanation.*

*He passed into the possession of Alexander Anderson when he
was thirty-three and worked in Anderson's store for eleven years.
Here the African and his accounts, faithfully recorded in Arabic,
came to the attention of a Special Magistrate involved in supervising the Emancipation Act. This Dr Madden, impressed by the abilities of Donlan, began to press for his freedom and moved the public
to subscribe to a donation for him. The people of Kingston gave
Donlan £20 and Alexander Anderson gave him his freedom.*

*For Beneba, there was no smooth way out. Back on the Haynes
estate most of the slaves, knowing her to be unstable, shunned her
lest she lead them into trouble. It was clear enough now that
Abolition was inevitable. The certainty of it grew and pressed on
the landowners and overseers. Fearful deformities arose among
them. Floggings increased in frequency and severity.*

*Busha Horne taunted them as the whip flew and his ridicule
bit into Beneba's flesh with every stroke.*

*"Feel you wi' get you freedom free? Feel seh? Pay fe it. Pay!
Pay!"*

*The public fund raised for Donlan when Madden obtained his
release melted quickly, but he preserved some to take him to the
Haynes property before he left the island. There was an odd turbulence, he thought, when he asked to see Beneba Haynes. He
wondered at it, and a strange fear moved him when the bookkeeper restrained him from going to the huts or the fields in search
of her and directed him to the works to ask for the overseer.*

Hesitantly Donlan made his way over to Busha Horne, who was standing in a clearing by the mill with a bloodied whip in his hand and a dark semicircle of slaves behind him.

"Busha," Donlan almost whispered, "please, I come to see someone."

Suddenly he was terrified that Busha might think him a runaway. "I get me freedom, sah. I going away and I want to see Beneba Haynes first."

Then he was frightened again for Busha Horne had sent for Beneba once and there was a mulatto child as well as a black. The African did not want his interest in Beneba misinterpreted.

The overseer stared at him then laughed.

"Oh, you get you freedom, eh?" He waved his whip hand towards the millhouse. "Well, I give her hers."

Donlan's eyes followed the direction of Busha's whip and he shuddered under a burst of cold sweat. The lacerated remains of Beneba hung by its hands from the millhouse. This way and that the body twisted gently in the wind until it faced him and he fainted.

Jessica tended him. He looked so much older. But, gradually, he revived. He spoke of the journey, of the studies he would resume, of the pilgrimage that might be possible before he died. Madden was arranging for him to assist in guiding an expedition to Timbuktu. His prayers for the magistrate threaded their talk with light. Allah had remembered him. He was going back, he was going back. Even with her arms about him Jessica was already alone.

"When de free paper come," she confided, "I going back to Goldfields."

"If I could only take one person with me," he whispered, "only one..."

"Yes?" She could not wait to hear him call her name.

He gazed at her pleadingly and ran his fingertip down the length of her cheek. "Ratoon," he sighed. "Beneba son, Ratoon

Haynes. The brown child will get work, but Ratoon…"

She allowed him to gather her in his arms for in the very midst of her fury she had forgiven him again for his obsession.

When he was gone, Jessica took the boy he had yearned for into her care, for her own older children were grown. She had always sworn Ratoon was Donlan's, so long ago she had lifted the child from the blood-soaked earth beneath the millhouse where he had taken the habit of playing. Later, when freedom came, she took Ratoon Haynes and her own son by Donlan, and she returned to Goldfields.

At the dock, Donlan found himself a curiosity. At first he thought it was only because he was a negro leaving to take part in an expedition. Then he understood that it was because he was going back. He would leave the new name, Donlan, and be Abū Bakr again. He was a miracle they perceived with awe. At first it had been unbelievable and then he was caught up in delirium. Now more clearly than ever he saw his departure from Jamaica for what it was. Black workers on the docks whispered admiringly, speculatingly, and leaned forward to hold him. Guinea gleamed a promised shore for the blessed dead and he was chosen to revisit it in living flesh. One placed his palm on his and breathed, "Touch de dutty fe me."

The white servants watched them incredulously as if they were a pack of fools. Occasionally they shouted a ribald comment. But some white labourers were brutally treated. Donlan leaned forward and addressed a short thick Irishman who was staring at him in silent contempt. "What 'bout you? You don' want go home? You wouldn' go back Ireland if you get de chance?"

He was unprepared for the expression of outrage that passed over the other's face, followed by a look of naked loathing. Donlan drew back thinking the hatred was directed at him, and it was time to go on board anyway. But his imminent departure made him bold and he insisted, "Eh? What 'bout Ireland?"

O'Reilly answered him out of the past where he had lain on a cold sack in his father's hovel, smelling the smoke settling on the roof and walls, filming their lungs; listening to his mother coughing her life away where she lay on her own bag with the ground hard and cold beneath her, dying, and nothing to look forward to but half a bag of rotting potatoes and the meagre hog that rooted around their rickety table and voided its filth upon the floor.

"Ireland?" he whispered to Donlan almost uncomprehendingly, but his eyes were cold blue, murderously cold and his voice like a knife. "God rot Ireland."

No. Pat O'Reilly was a fragment broken off, like Jessica. He was never going back. The blacks. Didn' know how well off they were. Wanting to go back to Guinea, by Mary. Heaven, they said it was. Confounded Baptists ruining them. And this bloody ass raptured back to savagery. He picked up one of the larger barrels and flung it into place. A rat darted out and scuttled away between the crates. Ye're lucky, rat, he thought. If I was a nigger ye'd be soup this evening. For a month or two he had been on an estate and knew the cane-piece rats were prized as delicacies. One or two of the slaves had even used them as currency. Those were different though, he scowled, fat and clean — not like on a wharf.

He stared around and spat. He had not even seen Moneague, but he knew it was there, knew it was a matter of time before the legalities were sorted out and he had his land. So he bent again, heaving the barrels. The first O'Reilly to come out had been old Owen he had heard tell of. Owen had been whipped in a canefield in Barbados, whipped till he bled. But when he reached Jamaica he had finished his term and worked for money. One of his sons had bought land. Moneague was fine green country, Pat's father had said. He had babbled of little else in that last year as their lives emptied of everything but the banshee wail of the wind and the thin echo of starving babies.

It was a matter of time.

Pat wiped his brow and stared into the distance at the ship the African had boarded. There was no understanding savages.

Back on Goldfields estate, the son of Abū Bakr and Jessica learnt to write, and spelt his name as Donalds. One of his descendants would be Catherine, Grace's grandmother. Ratoon Haynes wrote nothing, for the nights drew circles of children around the cooking fires and the women wove the memories of his mother, Beneba, into indelible pictures crisscrossed by glimmerings of songs and herbal lore, prayers and recipes, and stitched incredibly with the laughter of survival. Old-time people, old-time people.

22
The Elders

"Tears and laughter," Sarah whispered. "When I was young, women were made of tears and laughter. Men might rage at life or give it up. Women stuck it out."

Pearl curled in an armchair at Oxford Close chafing under the anxious murmuring of the family.

"He keeps saying he thought it was only angina," Paul pondered.

"*Only* — what he means, *only?* Good Lord, he's a doctor."

Pearl glanced up. "You mean is more serious?"

"Coronary." Sarah threw the word at her.

"You didn't notice anything wrong?" Ben stared at Pearl. The accusation stung.

"Well, did you?" she snapped. "Don't you see him more than I do?"

Ben's presence thickened and reared, darkening the room like a thunder cloud.

"All right, all right," Grace gasped. "Don't make a fuss. Keep the place calm for Jesu sake."

She bustled back into the sickroom and Paul stalked away — to see Gerry settled, he murmured. But the exit of his straight-backed tapering form punctuated Pearl's disclaimers like an exclamation of disgust. Pearl slid forward for her magazine, skirt riding up briefly to bare at Ben waxed-smooth, oil-glossed legs sleek curving to a jingle of gold-chain at the ankle, soft-buffed little heels creamed velvet like her face, and the toes kissing clean, perfectly cuticle trimmed, passion-rose glossed (with top coat) and one New York gold decal in the corner of a nail exquisite as a child's favourite seashell. Jesus God no wonder the woman cyan't mash ants her very foot too stoshus fe stand 'pon ground.

Ben gathered his dark bulk under control and issued from the room.

Sarah sat still and straight in her rocker, weighing Pearl in the balance of the years. They had never been alone together before. Pearl flicked her eyes briefly over the contents of the rocker. God, she thought momentarily, distastefully, but age made one ugly. Sarah gazed back at her in loathing. One of Pearl's perfectly pencilled brows raised delicately.

"Well? What I do you?"

"You're killing him," Sarah spat.

"What all you want is for me to sit home till I old and dry up like the rest of you, eh?" Pearl threw aside the magazine she had been toying with and wiggled her feet into real-leather shoes. "Well I want a little life."

"Life!" Sarah exploded. "You wouldn't know it if it hit you on the head."

"You're an expert, I suppose." It was no problem being direct with someone who would be dead meat in a couple years, if not months.

"You'd better remember," Sarah snapped in exasperation, "I've seen everything. Everything."

Pearl smiled tauntingly.

"And what have you to show for it? A hotter sex life?"

Sarah's fingers tightened on her cane.

"Hussy." Her voice was barely audible. "Should be whipped."

"And you should be locked up," Pearl yawned over her shoulder and with an extra rotation of her shapely bottom stepped, high-heeled, towards the door.

Let them keep him. Let them keep their perfect boys, babies for eternity. She went home, packed up Adam's and Gerry's belongings and dumped them once and for all at Oxford Close.

Adam mended. The relief sent Grace into an extra fit of activity, especially on mornings when Irene was late. Grace sped through the house mumbling furiously about being done with servants. She moved and shoved things furiously into place.

"Now why the devil they can never put this phone book... hm!"

Bending was difficult for her slightly thickened frame and sore joints but she refused to relinquish any movement, however painful. She dived under the dining table to run a duster along the chair pins.

"Coated!" she barked.

Irene climbed the back step unhurriedly at nine-forty, her eyes straying somewhat for the mango tree nearest the house was heavy with rose-blushed fruit. Grace stared at her as at an apparition. "Wait. Where you come from? Is where you going?"

"Miss Grace,'M?" Irene was at a loss.

Grace swung inside and Irene followed uncertainly.

" 'M?"

"You know the time? You know is nearly ten o'clock?"

"But is walk me have fe walk, 'M. Bus no come. One hour me stan' up wait 'pon bus, it no come."

"Then Irene, you had to walk anyway. You couldn' walk earlier? You think when I was your age I woulda wait on bus for an hour? If I did stand up so long at your age I wouldn' able move at all now. I wouldn' look bus at all for that distance in the first place. Ten o'clock? Lord, why you come at all?"

"Miss Grace,'M?" Irene bleated plaintively. "But is how Miss Grace so vex?"

"O Lord. You can't understand? I don't see you come — I clean, I hang out clothes, I turn in the kitchen. When you saunter in I done bang up me knee and burn me hand."

Grace stared at the woman and Irene glared at the top of the opposite wall, her nostrils flaring sullenly.

"Well don't stand and dream now. Come, give me a hand clean this fowl." Then her expression changed and she turned to Irene with a new tone. "Wait. I hear on the news they had shooting down your way last night?"

"Right by me, 'M."

Grace put down the dripping chicken and moved slowly over to the woman. "Irene? Nobody for you hurt?" she faltered.

"A fellow in the yard did get hit, 'M. Im wasn' in it, but tief running, police and tief shooting. As im open im door, 'M."

"Not...?"

"Dead, 'M. Don' know which one of dem shoot him. We hear gunshot, bladdam, everybody lie down a floor. Voice bawling outside fe come in, nobady move — who go open door, bullet a fly so. Is afterwards we hear 'bout him. Dis marning blood still 'pon de street. Dead im dead, 'M."

"Jesu. Oh Irene. I really hear they have plenty trouble down your way."

"Yes, 'M. After dark we no move 't all. Is dat make me start late sometimes a marning."

"Yes. Well. Be careful." Grace pursed her lips and stared up at her anxiously. "And... you have a way you like talk what on you mind. Is good to be honest, but... don't run you mouth, you hear? Watch what you say and who you say it to. Be very, very careful."

Five days after, late as usual, Irene told Grace that the crash programme workers up the road had stopped her on the way in and asked her if it was the 'ristos she worked for and what party they belonged to.

"Me tell de Crashie-dem me no business in nobady politics, 'M. Work me work, draw me likkle money and go a me yard."

But Irene never came back.

That was the same week They began to steal the deserted house next door. They, of course, were the unknown, the faceless mass that existed outside on the fringes of the world. Bit by bit the house moved. First there was a clink of metal on porcelain as the wash basins and toilet bowls were dislodged from their bases and shuffled out to the waiting van. Light fixtures, switches, electrical outlets. Another night the windows were gently lifted off their hinges. Paul and Grace Cohon peeped over the darkened window of their bedroom in time to see the front door swung lightly into the air and finally to the top of the van where it was strapped ignominiously. Tiles went, one by one chipped out and stacked in boxes, then floorboards were prised up and tied in bundles which were passed out through the gaping holes where the windows had been. At last there was only an empty shell, naked walls weathering into ruin.

All this was over a period of months. Meanwhile the divorce seemed to be coming through and Adam was truly home again, home with Gerry. Now and then Pearl's taunting haunted him and he searched the boy's face for a resemblance that would put his soul at rest. Then he remembered Grace had said she was her mother's child, blood or no blood. Blood, Grace insisted, meant nothing. Certainly Gerry must be theirs and they would fight to keep him. Adam glanced around the garden for assurance, and Stella's old rose bushes bloomed and the allamanda trailing over the parapet was a shower of gold.

When Gerry moved finally into Oxford Close, the lives of the four older members of the family were transformed. Imperceptibly to their friends, unknown to themselves, they had been aging – even Sarah. Now the process was reversed. Ben carved and whittled toys of all description. Each week brought something more original, more complex. Sarah recalled stories that had remained submerged for little under a century. Paul delivered a brief but impassioned sermon on an age when a child could not be left unattended in his own garden; then he swept clear an avenue through his study on the enclosed porch at the side of the house, and Ben constructed an indoor slide. This produced a chaos of books and papers, but no one cared. Gerry climbed and swung from the wrought iron that supplemented the fragile doors of ornamental glass panes and polished wooden framework. Grace all but abandoned house, kitchen and garden to sprawl upon the floor with Gerry among what she described as his taratas.

It was not a matter of spoiling the child, as they understood it. It was a matter of enjoying him, absorbing him with an urgent intensity born of their awareness that time was passing. They had not seen it so when Adam was born. The grandchild was different. All the same sensations were there but more concentrated, more poignant, more urgent, because time was passing. They could afford to miss nothing. Once, in the midst of a conversation on something quite unrelated Grace cried out as if in pain. "Oh, what an ass Pearl is, what a fool."

For Gerry had stacked his blocks together, fumbling, failing, raging, persisting and eventually achieving a recognisable house. Then they stopped everything, congratulating and rejoicing over it and smiling, almost sadly despite themselves, because it would never happen quite that way again.

So they grew younger, or rather they were reborn into a special phase of life where age lay in abeyance and the energy and vitality of the child coursed through them, restoring, recharging, rebuilding.

"I remember when Les was that age," Grace crowed, "tumbling over and over, squealing like that. Full of fun. Rollicking."

"He was something like that even when I knew him," Adam smiled. His face relaxed, remembering Les. Adam looked well now.

"Ah, but as a baby. You can't imagine what a racket."

Friends wearied of the violence, the shortages, the empty political rhetoric, and fled the island. A relative of the Halls was mugged and old Reverend Jackman held up and robbed of his meagre pension. So the tension squeezed close and real. One of Adam's patients committed suicide after his business failed and another arrived at Oxford Close at three in the morning, supported by distraught parents and whispering of rape. Paul conducted the funeral of a church brother who had died of a stroke following amputation of his leg, shattered by gunmen. Ben's office closed under the foreign exchange crisis; he sold his house for what he could get and moved into Oxford Close completely.

"I was here most of the time anyway," he had agreed, when Paul put it to him.

The dollar devalued and the economy caved in.

Houses around the Cohons fell into ruin. In the city, gangs came out and opened fire in the street in broad daylight. The violent death of five men on the Jamaica Defence Force shooting range in Green Bay led into a complex web of intrigue. The family read incredulously of a truce between the warring posses of Western Kingston and studied the *Gleaner* pictures of the leaders, Claudius Massop and Buckie Thompson, embracing over the peace that was reportedly growing up out of the ghetto. It was hard to believe and somehow distanced. The outer fabric of existence was shredding away for, as Grace insisted, every death, every robbery, every rumour diminished them all. But Gerry brought life.

From their widening circle of friends abroad, letters poured in with news of calm and organised existences. There were failures and regrets, but essentially the letters confirmed that normalcy existed elsewhere. Now close friends had homes and gardens the Cohons could not picture and grandchildren were born whom Gerry would never know.

The most extraordinary letter was from a near stranger.

11th January, 1979

Dear Reverend Cohon,
      This letter will come as a surprise to you and I'm afraid it will also occasion you some sadness. I write to let you know of the passing of Mrs Belle Goldman, who I believe was a close friend, perhaps a family member. She was one of the great landmarks of my life.

You may recall that many years ago while working with you on Saturdays I was fortunate to receive your help with the cost of schoolbooks. You'll be happy to hear that I eventually received a scholarship and got my degree in Canada. As you can imagine, there were times of severe financial strain. It was at one of these low points that I was introduced to a group called Friends of the University, who focused on needy students. Many were unmarried or widowed ladies, or childless couples. This was how I met Aunt Belle.

Having no idea of her past, I cannot say why she acted as she did, but the fact is that she almost instantly accepted me as her son. She fed me, nursed me through the 'flu, and almost forcibly took me to church. When I received a grant for a further degree, this time in theology, she visited the minister of our Church and gained extra support for me.

During this time she made several references to her beloved circle in Jamaica. I now suspect, having seen the state of her affairs over the past few years, that she sacrificed the hope of a last visit to Jamaica, in order to assist me. I now know that she mortgaged her house, at one point, to pull me back from disaster.

Aunt Belle died quite suddenly, three weeks ago, of a heart attack. I had hoped to save enough to send her for a visit to Jamaica, but I was not in time.

However, I am returning to Jamaica to live. I left wanting never to see Kingston again, but somehow the island "call 'pon me like duppy." In any case, I hear things are much better there now, what with the rise in minimum wage, free education and so on. There has been a great wave of enthusiasm here and several of my friends returned four or five years ago, anxious to be part of the New Jamaica. I hope the Church will post me somewhere out in the country.

Please accept my sympathy about Aunt Belle and my regards to your family. God moves in a mysterious way....

Yours in Christ,
Victor Castries

"I don't remember the boy at all," Ben pondered, mopping his eyes.

"Yes, man," Sarah objected. "Well-spoken child, about Adam's age? Didn't know his name though. Castries?"

"How like Belle," Grace smiled mistily.

And Paul said nothing, but thought how huge Canada was for the lives of uprooted Jamaicans still to grow towards each other and intertwine. Then he was filled with the wonder of the boy himself. Paul remembered this child with the thin black ankles disappearing sockless into too-large shoes, and now here was this letter, from a man. An unreasonable pride flared in him, lightening the distress over Belle for, at least in some small measure, it was her triumph.

In the midst of their loss and wonderment the family were outraged when Pearl sought custody of Gerry. Yet they were unafraid. What case had she? Adam could argue desertion and adultery. He was prepared to fight with every weapon, no matter how dirty it became. The case dragged, but once the child was not tormented that was all that mattered. In mid-April a new outbreak of violence and looting of business places forced the agency Pearl worked with to a close, but she fought on.

"Where does she get it from?" Paul fumed when Adam was out of earshot. "Decent people don't have money to spare these days."

"Is a boops she have," Ben shrugged. "No woman who love spend money so going leave man like Adam to scuffle a living. Mus' be reggae singer or drug lord or somebody with money."

There was certainly money in some places, they noted grimly. Bob Marley's One Love concert to aid the Peace Fund following the truce between the gangs netted $40,000.

"I don't mind, if it will really reach people who are hungry," Grace puzzled.

Pearl complained to the court that Adam had made no sexual approach to her for over a year. Subnormal, she said he was. Pearl was modestly suited in pastel green and bewitchingly made up. The court found it hard to understand Adam when he said that she revolted him. But he had been careful with his files and produced receipts, hotel bills and bounced cheques. Then she wept bitterly at the notion of being parted from her baby. And who would take care of him? Adam was never home, she dabbed her eyes delicately, and his parents were infirm in body and mind. Adam's lawyer introduced the sturdy, no-nonsense Grace and quietly logical Paul and Adam testified that Pearl had left Gerry in the care of strangers and taken him on outings with a lover.

In September, the court granted Adam tentative custody. One of its reservations was his inability to identify Pearl's lover; the other was the age of his parents.

As it turned out, there was little scandal. The public had hardened under shock after shock of national outrage. Grace read aloud to Ben and Sarah, when Paul was out of earshot, about claims of torture in the army, claims made by a former Colonel of the Jamaica Defence Force. An ex-private, Anthony Williams, insisted that he had been tortured, but controversy raged about Williams' participation in the smuggling of machine guns from the army arsenal. Eventually, by mid-November, Williams' body was to be found, garrotted, but the months in between were crammed with other events that blotted out domestic gossip. After the shooting of a worker in the Jamaica Public Service, a week-long strike crippled the island. Some Albert Robinson, Grace read, announced to the world that the Government had employed him to spy on the Opposition. In the uproar that followed, the Smith Commission on Allegations of Corruption in the Government sifted the evidence. Jamaicans held their breaths as civil servants, army and police officers, Ministers of Government, including the Prime Minister, testified at Headquarters House before the Commission.

Nature itself broke off conventional routines in '79. In Oxford Close pale lemon butterflies fluttered over the wasted gardens. Clouds of them wheeled and fretted about the lignum vitae trees and died upon the road.

"Rain?" Grace shifted anxiously.

Soon there were blackbirds screeching and chattering in dead trees around the looted house next door, an incredible flock, everywhere. Then floods rent the country parts, water, from nowhere, tearing away property and lives.

But the court case ended, and Adam had his child.

The family began to consult occasionally, reluctantly, about whether they should stay in Jamaica, about how they could possibly go. Of course Sarah's money was abroad and she certainly had no intention of repatriating or declaring it (and the new law be damned, she snorted).

"Is it worth it to move out?" Sarah pondered, looking out at the road through the intricate wrought iron casing the porch. "I'll be gone, but you have time before you still. Use it. Use the money. Austin can advise you, perhaps, on how to move what you have, but I can't take mine with me where I'm going. I have no one to leave it for but yourselves. What about the child? The old place in St Thomas now should be worth… oh, what does it matter. No one buying anything now."

At the Norman Washington Manley Airport, the Immigration Officer returned the papers of the Reverend Victor Castries with a respectful nod.

"Good to have you back, Rev. Tings hard though, you see? You cyan't know how life tough now. You really come to stay?"

"Really. Believe me, I tried not to but I couldn' keep away."

"Good luck, Rev."

The battered taxi shuddered along the Palisadoes Road and the man in the back seat closed his eyes and breathed in the sea and the hills, even with their faint haze from the cement factory. He prayed that the Church would post him in Morant Bay.

The driver studied him in the rear view mirror, took in the well-cut suit, flawlessly smooth coal-black skin, wide intellectual forehead and nose haughty as a Spanish conquistador's. Poor Rev, thought the cabman. How im fe live 'pon minister salary in this here Jamaica? Could look 'pon im and see im no know hard-time. The Reverend opened his eyes and met his appraisal with eyes so lively, so knowing, that the driver looked away in confusion, then glanced back and grinned frankly. "Is true you come to stay, Minista?"

"Until they throw me out."

The cabbie cast him an engaging grin, "After dem no trow nobady out here, sah. Ongly shoot dem." He chuckled, then continued reflectively, "Glad you come back, sah. More minista good fe de place. Yout'-dem too out of order."

It was at about this time that work on the house next door to the Cohons was concluded. The walls had stood naked and vulnerable for months, waiting, as Grace repeatedly said, to fall down on someone. Then a truck came in broad daylight and three men began to dismantle it. They took apart what was left of the roof and stacked up the shingles. Then they went to work on the walls. When it was over the yard was practically bare. Grass grew to the edge of the foundations and stopped. There was a raw white scar in the middle where the Andersons had lived, rimmed by a few remnants of wall.

When the owner came back from Toronto he walked all around it shaking his head, kicking at the remains of the flooring.

"Insurance?" Paul asked tentatively. He never liked to seem inquisitive.

"Can't cover this." Jimmy Anderson's son shook his head dazedly, hopelessly. "You know. Theft. You think of furnishings, fixtures even. But a whole house?"

The place opposite to the Cohons was deserted too, closed and overgrown with lovebush. Its owners had migrated. Squatters came and went in the house beyond. Gradually the family found themselves almost alone on the cul-de-sac. They left the house more reluctantly, worrying about the price of gas which was up again, about the effect on the car of widening, deepening potholes in the road, about security, about each other. Early that '79, Massop, the initiator of the West Kingston peace, had been killed. To the family, the country seemed beyond hope.

Still their attention riveted on Gerry and the turmoil around them was only theirs as it would affect the child. They concentrated on buffering him from the present and from the impending future. He could not play outside as much as they would have liked, things being as they were. (There were tales of horrible things happening to children and you couldn't credit half of what you heard but still....) They were determined that life should be as normal as possible. They reorganised the house so that he could romp freely. He climbed and swung with unnerving agility from burglar bars and grillwork, he folded back inexpertly the white chenille spread that had been Belle's and used his grandparents' bed as a trampoline. He dived under beds and wriggled unexpectedly out of cupboards. He became expert at flattening himself and slithering into seemingly unaccommodating places, and he developed the technique of hiding at bedtime into a fine art.

They would have liked to pet him more, but he would not have it. He would not be kissed and gave the impression of only barely tolerating a more distant caress. He was impatient, demanding, persistent. Blocks fascinated him, puzzles, problems. He would sit worrying them out, exploding at times in a frustrated bellow and occasionally hurling his creation to the floor, smashing it. But he would start again, often in tears, but again and again, until he solved it. Neither could they impose their help unasked. Occasionally when all seemed lost he came with the broken pieces for a suggestion, no more. He resented intrusion.

Yet he yearned for company. He followed one or other of them from room to room, inevitably dragging a boxload of his trappings and chattering ceaselessly. Sarah must sit with him while he ate and Grace put him to sleep. Ben must follow him around outside and Paul, morning, noon and night read tales of mystery and adventure. Only in the bathroom he must be absolutely alone or he screamed hysterically.

Only once he asked for Pearl.

"She's away, I think," Grace said carefully. "Miss your Mummy, baby?"

"Mummy have sweetie," he reflected. "Sugar?"

"Mm?"

"Want Bennie beat Uncle."

He was a difficult child to control though they were physically well able to handle him. He was so tough that spanking only infuriated him. Shouting meant nothing either for he faced you fearlessly with an answer for everything. What worked was to talk quietly, logically, to make him think it out. He would do almost anything they asked for them rather than out of a sense of compulsion. Confinement was moderately effective. Humiliation would have been more so, if they had been willing to try it, for he was extraordinarily sensitive about his own dignity. But they shrank from using this.

Gerry was difficult to gauge, a strange, complex set of conflicting qualities and reactions. Still as a stone he would sit, absorbing a story or pushing a brick into place, only the slim, agile fingers moving and coal black eyes darting fire. Yet the next minute he was squealing nervous energy, writhing on the couch with Ben, ricochetting from one room to the next, laughing breathlessly with his shoulders drawn up to his cheeks, head rolling back and soft, curling lips parting, puckering in an effort for control and spreading again helplessly with infectious mirth.

Withdrawn as he could be, violent and demanding, he clung to them with a strange urgent longing as if there could never be enough, as if he sensed a vast emptiness on the outside of them waiting to swallow him. It was odd, Grace noticed, that although you were not to pet him he must sit beside you, holding, leaning, fingering your clothes, curling his fingers in your hair, and, as he fell asleep, tucking his face into your flesh and twining his limbs about you. He was desperate too for approval, indications of pride, interest in anything he did. An expression of displeasure, an imagined slight or ridicule shattered him.

Every aspect of this wild, brilliant, passionate child showed physically on him. By three, his body had drawn from baby plumpness to hard, slim lines, smooth olive, cool but glowing at the same time. His face beneath an untameable tangle of dark curls widened at the brow, narrowed at the chin, curved soft at the cheek for one dreaming instant or so, taut and ablaze the next. It was an elf-shaped face, but deep at the eyes, shadowed by long lashes, surprisingly snub-nosed above a generous and exquisitely shaped mouth and defiantly tilted chin. A mobile, sensitive face of rapidly changing expressions, dominated mostly by the great compelling black eyes, by turn liquid, sparkling, fiery, but lent piquancy by the vulnerable and incredibly sweet curve of the mouth. It was a startling face. They could just sit and look at him.

"Why Bennie watch an' watch me?" he asked Paul.

"His sight is bad, son," Paul explained. "And it's deteriorating, getting worse, I mean. I think he wants... to print your face... like a picture... in his mind. Forever."

Adam was taking Gerry to Miami. First he would buy medicines in New York. His patients had put up the cash and he had arranged for US dollars on the other side. Then he would have his own check-up in Florida. From Miami, if there was enough of his own money left, they would go on to Orlando. It might work out, he warned Gerry, that they would have to settle for an aquarium or the zoo. He couldn't risk an amusement park until the child was old enough to take his rides unaccompanied.

"I'm not so happy about it myself," Paul sighed. "I think it's a bit too much for Adam. Gerry is a handful."

"Exactly!" Grace wrinkled her forehead anxiously.

Sarah emitted a short, hacking laugh.

"Set of hypocrites, the lot of you. Just don't want to let the boy out of your sight."

"Well, I should say not," Paul chuckled, a deep, glad rumble. "And two weeks is bad enough. Can you imagine life without him?"

A pause fell as they considered. They looked away from each other hastily and went on to talk of something else.

In Kingston the truce, if there had ever been one, had fallen through. The family moved about now only by car. Just on the street beyond theirs, Mabel Gray had walked over to Oxford Pharmacy and on the way back, at ten-thirty in the morning, a youth knocked her down and kicked her repeatedly, breaking her hip. The Halls, too, encountered in their kitchen right there in Oxford Close a gunman who held them up and terrorised them for two hours. Enid, the new day's worker at Oxford Close, came as late as Irene had done and more irregularly because she lived on Jacques Road. She said, "Me no come out till de road safe, 'M."

Well, Grace thought, it could be an excuse, but these days there was no telling how much might be true. At any rate, Enid said that they slept under the bed at nights because of bullets whining through the windows. Tales, tales, laughed a friend in the government. Yet more and more of the middle class retreated and even key officials fled.

There was a wage limit now, but no limit to the falling value of the money. Another forty percent devaluation of the dollar was accompanied by a scheduled one and a half per cent monthly devaluation, yet to be applied.

"This is our Jamaican dollar!" Clem Hall exclaimed jocularly to a friend overnighting in the island. "Worth nothing."

Clem's own trailer was en route to New York by now and he had moved out of Oxford Close and was staying with a cousin before joining his family in Florida. But the Cohons stayed on, and Ben Goldman and Sarah Stollmeier with them, tracking the commodities they needed, dodging what taxes they could, sliding into place the bolts between them and the outer darkness. They heard of middle-class Jamaicans living perfectly normal orderly lives, scoffing at the paranoia of others. Yet here was the family in Oxford Close, more and more alone, reading the papers, listening on the telephone, smelling the fear of others, pondering it with minds nurtured in a different age.

"It's Gerry who makes this place bearable now, you know," Sarah mused.

Grace smiled absently, "Oh, he makes up for everything."

Outside, on the lime tree, a horde of blackbirds alighted inexplicably, chattering and screeching.

The Reverend Victor Castries stared in disbelief at the grey-haired minister, who insisted gently but firmly that he appreciated Castries's willingness to serve in a remote rural district but that the Church's immediate need was a ministry to the ghetto. It was the decision of the committee, but of course there would be time to consider.

Victor avoided thinking as much as possible for several hours, though he did try to pray. But he was torn between past and future. He was overwhelmed by the progress of the country in the years he had been abroad — the literacy and school-feeding programmes, the legislation for the rescue of illegitimate children. Now there was a chance for the children of the dumpheap, he thought. Yet a physical return to the places of his childhood was much to ask.

He studied the newspapers for one distraction after the next. Foreign films were no novelty and he immersed himself in the local art that had not been accessible to him before he left. The galleries overflowed with talent, casting the scenes of his childhood in poignant perspectives on situations he had believed sordid, dazzling him with colour he had taken for granted, moving him with depths of character he had never suspected, puzzling him with the complexity of the mundane. Then the dance company whirled before him its celebration of the Jamaican soul, leaped its praise of the human spirit, writhed the broken past upon the floor and with fingers spread taut skyward seized the future.

Then quickly, quickly he must hear and see and taste it all. Bob Marley's face, pain-etched, singing resistance, and the church choirs insistent on Handel's Hallelujah. A vast Baptist sister turbaned and robed in white, wheeled and testified at the street corner, brandishing her Bible. A ragged urchin batted his stolen cricket ball through a store window and cartwheeled down the dusty street over rubble and fragments of glass. And it flooded back, brutal and brilliant, soaring and searing, his own extraordinary progress from the packing case on the junkheap.

Then Victor Castries returned to the church office and accepted his posting to Western Kingston.

On Sunday, Adam was quiet on his way to the airport. He wondered what it would be like if this were his last flight from Jamaica. If he could cash the return ticket at the other end and disappear into the vast United States. He had his child. His mind toyed with it — not seriously, because of his parents, because of all the old people, his patients, the dusty stones themselves and branding sky and trickling water from the hills. But he could not leave the idea alone somehow and he found himself staring at the streets, the skies, the people. What was it like, the Jamaica farewell? To some, an unspeakable relief.

DaSilva had left, the specialist with whom he had worked most closely. For months daSilva had tried to sell his house in Barbican, then to rent it. No one was buying. Eventually daSilva had turned the key in the door and walked away from it. Adam wondered if he could have done that. Could his mother do it? Squatters had moved into the Halls' house already and now it was a tenement. But presumably the Halls were glad to be gone. What would it be like to be going too?

Goodbye, he thought. It was a cruel word. Suddenly everything impinged on him. He saw it all with strangely painful clarity. Like it was after Les's funeral.

He had taken a roundabout route because the regular way down Mountain View Avenue passed by Nannyville and other areas he didn't care to venture through today with the child after what he had heard on the morning news. The city slid past him, its dingy walls messed by unevenly painted slogans in black and red. "The poor can't take no more" bloodied the walls. Was it JLP graffiti or a real cry from the ghetto? There were stories of children fainting in school from hunger, and of a few dying randomly not only by the bullets of the gunmen but by stray ones from the police. Babylon the downpressor, their gardener called the State.

Increasingly militant they had all become. The middle classes moaned now for their freedom as the poor had long before. The rhetoric was desperate, and hollow. Charisma had worn thin and been discarded. Only the gun seemed persuasive.

Yet the churches were full. This was the essence of the place, he thought, sensitive, violent, spiritual. Deep and full from a cracked gothic archway swelled an old organ and voices of a congregation no different from those of his childhood. Lest we forget, lest we forget. Perhaps he had exaggerated the change.

In a way, Kingston had stopped growing; even building materials were short. Blocks were manufactured on a shift basis when cement was available. Manufactured steel accumulated as it remained unpurchased by industry. Qualified builders migrated and professional staff in important government positions drained abroad. Now the inexperienced mishandled contracts, hundreds of workers were laid off and confrontations arose between clients, consultants, workers, contractors. Arson and looting had done their bit. Money was owed, money was owed, money was owed. Firms had closed and equipment rotted.

"I cyan' make the bill, Doc. I could help you with material for any little repairs on you house?"

Where was the remedy, Adam pondered, for a city dying.

Natural disasters too had sapped their strength. The grey weeks of the rains had passed, but the floods in the country had done millions of dollars worth of damage. Forty-one had died and thirty-five thousand were destitute. Thank God Kingston had been spared that much. He noticed the silence of the trees and sighed with relief. At least the weird invasion of blackbirds was over.

Depression dug in its claws. The business sector was the obvious victim among the middle classes, but the restrictions touched all professions and all classes. He had been called into hospitals where incontinent patients lay in their filth because of linen shortages, and disposable equipment had to be used time and time again. Everywhere they were plagued by power outages and one or two hospitals had closed down.

Yet there was money, for somebody. He smiled wryly at the thought of the State Trading Corporation scandal earlier that year. Million dollar rip-off. Hard to believe that people he knew, like Dexter... 'Dextrous', the commentators sniped now. It was said that a ministerial decree had enabled him to slip out of the country. Where was truth? What was truth? Well. No credibility again. With a start he realised how distrust, violence and deception had become routine and worked its way into personalities. Even himself, he thought. He had been... different once. Innocent, Pearl had called him, terminally innocent. He wondered whether he could fully believe in anyone again.

Gerry shrieked with elation and pointed to an army van crammed with soldiers bumping along with machine guns laid across their knees.

"Look, soldiers! Look, look, guns! They have any cannons?"

He was wriggling with excitement. The other day they had passed a tank and Adam had stopped the car to quiet him. How strange to be born to this. He grinned at the child ruefully. Yes. Gerry was a fighter. A survivor at any cost. Not like himself. Gerry raised his arm and levelled two fingers at the van menacingly.

"Braddam!" He swung to Adam, his eyes glowing like coals. "Pass them now. Pass them quick. I shoot them."

Adam smiled, mildly disapproving, as he pulled out and overtook.

"Guns are bad, son. You musn't shoot."

"What 'bout bad men?"

"Well...." Adam sighed. "I suppose sometimes one has to...."

"Well. If I meet a bad man I going to shoot him."

No doubt, Adam thought. Yes. Trust Gerry to take them all on. After all, he smiled to himself whimsically, his heart lifting suddenly at the vague notion of revenge, there probably was a future.

They had reached the parking lot of the airport when Gerry bounced on his seat again and pointed precariously through the window.

"Look! Uncle, Uncle." Then he ducked down to the floor of the car.

The wheel slipped from Adam's hand, whirling, and the car

swung erratically. He hit the brake to avoid the car next to him in the lot.

"Where?" he gasped.

Gerry inched up again and cautiously peeped through the window to point at Austin Louis.

23
Recipe

HOURS OF loitering in Kennedy Airport followed by a bumpy flight to Kingston had left Austin sallow and irritable. Adam shot an incredulous glance at the child but Gerry crouched at the window, staring unwaveringly. Austin padded lightly, boldly over to the car, glittering a grin that did not touch his eyes — which were no longer sleepy but bright now, gold-brown but confusingly cold, fixing in their intensity.

Him? Adam's mind lurched with realisation. Uncle. Pearl's lover? Adam's thoughts spun dizzily. Austin Louis the whole time. And why was he here? They had arranged to meet in Kennedy. The whirling current of thought sucked Adam in. The money, he gasped. He had made a deal with Austin in order to buy medical supplies abroad. His stomach heaved with nausea as the vortex of recognition gaped beneath him. Patients put up the money... thousands and... Austin said he needed cash in Jamaica for a sudden... Austin supposed to meet him in New York with the US currency and... don't Adam know Austin from he born — it was sure, no risk, and thousands and thousands and — Busha, they called him, but... not his money. It was not even Adam's money. And Pearl leave him for this old... His head grew warm and stuffed as Austin Louis leaned pleasantly on the car.

"Taking a trip, Adam?"

Adam stared at him, feeling his throat closing.

"Uncle not going too," Gerry muttered rebelliously.

"Aye, boy. Where you off to?"

Gerry glanced at his father then quieted, suddenly uncertain. He slid back out of range of Austin's glance.

"Nice boy." Austin Louis shifted his attention back to Adam as if learning of the trip for the first time. "Treating him to Disney World?"

Adam tugged at the loose collar of his shirtjack. His neck felt hot and swollen and he could feel something rippling inside his brain. "I have to buy the medicines," he gasped.

"Medicine, Adam? What happen, you sick?" A twitch of ironic solicitude.

"The... money."

"Money, Adam? What money?"

What money. What money.

"Not mine," Adam panted, "is not mine, you know!"

Louis smiled quizzically at the man who doubled over in the car clutching his chest. He blinked thoughtfully as Adam's fingers scrambled wildly in his pocket for the inhalant that wasn't there.

"Where... my money?"

"Your money, Adam? I don' have no money for you. Had a few thousand of my own, you know. I spend it on my shipment."

His voice was a muted growl on and on about the problems of clearing stock, as Adam's mouth opened and closed, opened and closed. Air running out. Time shrinking.

"Nobody want Jamaican dollars again," Austin sighed. "Must be US for every shipment." He glanced away, into the distance, inattentive as if Adam might drive away if he cared to.

But the passage squeezed so narrow now Adam had to pull for a long, long time. A peculiar pressure grew in his rib cage, not part of the asthma attack, intersecting the effort of breathing with a new thought. How Gerry would get home from the airport? The throbbing in Adam's head rumbled heavier, rhythmic, like waves washing to the shore. His eyes riveted on Austin Louis, questioning.

"Shipment?"

Louis inched forward smoothly, locking Adam's mind with his cold eyes that Adam seemed to see clearly for the first time as Austin's breath came quick and warm on his face.

"The shipment of guns, man," Austin purred. "Guns are money."

"God. No. Not my money. You…"

But only the finest stream of air was left and as he sucked at it painfully his chest seemed to be tearing open. He could not afford speech. As he slipped back he shot a whitening forefinger at Louis's face and in the creeping cold he could barely hear himself above the throb of the waves.

"I… have you receipt. Receipt."

Louis nodded, soothingly. "Yes. Show it to the government, Adam."

He lounged through the window blotting out the sky as Adam slumped back onto the car seat hearing the sea pounding and buffeting him from within.

"Only reasonable. Your family owe me payment on my first set of cartridge. Plenty money you uncles cost me, you know. Yes, Les of all people mess me up. Two years it was before business pick up. Thought I could depend on Les. I never expected I would have to take him out, Ben time going come and Grace overdue, but for Les I woulda let them go. But what choice I had?"

Then he growled softly from the frozen wasteland of the soul he bared at Adam through pupils dilated to quench those eyes at last of their gold fire and suck the dying man into the bottomless black holes of time gone by, "And then the other payment. From before your time. My mother, Louise. (For Les I would even have forgotten Louise.) What happen, Adam?" His voice was quiet still, but no more gentle than fang in flesh. "Never hear 'bout Louise Haynes? No. They wouldn' remember her. None of them. But you mean even Icelin never mention her? Is Icelin knew her best. You didn't know Icelin neither? Never mind."

His murmur licked the edges of Adam's blurring mind, whisper-soft but slippery-rough. "I never forget Icelin." He slid smoothly back from the car and smiled mockingly. "I see you going meet Louise soon. Give Mumma my love."

Somewhere a last barrier broke and a flood swept over Adam so that the sea sound roared and smashed its way too vast for his head to contain, thundering through and over him, crushing his chest and ripping his heart to fragments. Austin Louis swept away and the pain and bitterness of Pearl swirled into the darkness as if she had never been. Only Gerry's face... a face... some child... perhaps it was his own face long ago turned up to the pipe organ in his father's church swelling a lament from some Verdi chorus. And all his life rushed in spate around him. Oh Grand, Grand, the rose bushes! There was a garden once where all things grew that were beautiful and fading. Never was a sky of bland serenity as his before the drought, never a sea of confident repose nor wind of quivering tenderness as his before the storm. Never had become his youth, uprooting, tumbling, crushing. Never the dew-slurring twilight silence. Never, never.

After the funeral there was the child, mercifully. Gerry demanded attention and the family clung to him. They needed him to block it all out for them — the shock and unreality. Even in Adam's death, Pearl betrayed him. The deep cut of her neck-line and high slit of her black dress had obviously been selected for another occasion, another man. Well, it made no difference now. Now that they accepted the finality of it, now that they knew Adam was gone, they huddled around the child for comfort and distraction. Nothing else that was real was bearable.

Besides, they were concerned about Gerry because he had been there all the time. Mercifully he understood little, of course. What could a child of his age know? At the same time it was important to find out what he did know. They tried to soothe and draw him out at the same time.

First it was essential for him to realise that his father had not gone to Miami or anywhere else, voluntarily, and left him. In the course of talking they became aware that he wanted to tell them what had happened at the airport. But he was confused about the order of things and assumed that they knew it all already and that they only wanted him to refer to the parts that interested him. Sarah moved from her rocker to the couch to be sure to catch everything, but it was a desultory kind of conversation, broken by little forays into the kitchen and under the couch; it was not the kind of thing they could force his attention on. He had to be allowed to come back to it, and he did.

"Daddy pocket was too tight."

"Mm?"

"He couldn' get the thing."

"When he was in the car? Was Daddy all right in the car, son?"

"Yes. Till he talked to Uncle."

A hush fell. Grace began to question him then. Quietly but constantly, one query after the next.

"Uncle was there?"

"Yes. Daddy quarrel with Uncle and falled on the seat."

"Which seat?"

"The car seat. Uncle come to the car and talked in the window. I don' like Uncle, you know."

"Why Daddy quarrelled, precious?"

He dived between the cushions for a block and began turning it over and over.

"Baby. Why did Daddy quarrel?"

"Daddy was cross 'cause the money gone."

They broke into a confused interchange.

"Eh?"

"What money?"

"Gone where?"

"Must be Miami. All the medicine money gone."

They looked at each other in dismay. Adam knew whoever it was well, to have arranged this exchange of currencies.

"So Uncle is someone he actually knows."

"And he has the money."

They had reimbursed Adam's patients themselves, unwilling to wait for the estate to be settled and anxious that no scandal spread about Adam's compassionate but illegal arrangements.

"Sugar." He tugged at Grace. "Uncle don't have the money no more, you hear?"

"Eh?"

"No. Is all gone."

Their outburst passed as suddenly as it had begun.

"How, baby?"

"I can have a gun too, Benny?"

"What?"

"Uncle say all Daddy's money spend out to buy guns. An' why I can't have no gun?"

Quiet again for a while. His grandfather lifted him onto his knee and smoothed back his hair. They waited. If Paul did not find an answer it did not exist.

"What else about... guns, son?"

"Uncle say, Les... Les stop his... stop... I don' know. Sugar, I want cake. Please?"

"Les?"

"Who Les is, Grand Paul? I don't know him, eh?"

"Merciful Redeemer."

"This man..."

"Les. Jesu."

"Darling," Grace broke in with a still, choked voice, "whose guns, my precious?"

"Uncle."

"Uncle's name, son. Do you know his name?"

The child stared at them puzzled.

"The man Daddy was talking to. What was his name?"

"Uncle!" He stared at them in bewilderment; he was getting angry.

"All right, all right." Ben took both hands and drew the boy close to him, before shifting him back to Paul.

"What did Daddy call him?" Paul persisted.

"Nothing."

"Didn't Daddy say anything to him? Tell me just what Daddy said."

Adam closed his eyes, trying to be precise like Grand Paul.

"Daddy say... said, he has Uncle's... re... reseep."

"What?"

"Recipe?" they wondered.

"Mus' be."

"What you mean?"

"I don' know."

"What else Daddy said?"

"Nothing. That's when he falled... fell."

They shuffled around slightly, wiping eyes, foreheads. Then Paul hugged him, rubbing his chin over his hair and forehead.

"What about Uncle then? Did he try to help Daddy? Did he do anything?"

The child looked at him blankly.

"Did he say anything?"

"He said Daddy must go."

"Where?"

"To see Uncle's Mummy."

"What?"

"Why?"

No answer. Paul took off his watch and allowed the child to wind it. Then he snapped it back on his wrist and caught both small hands in his.

"Now," he continued seriously, "who is Uncle's mother?"

"Louise."

Bewilderment. Still it was a name at least.

"Louise," they repeated it, turning it over in their minds, testing it.

"You know her, son?"

"No. Only Icing... Icelin."

"Who?"

"Only Icelin know her. Sugar, I can have the icing without the cake?"

"Icelin?" Paul shook his head.

But slowly, slowly, out of a tangle of pain and bewilderment the others groped for each other in their minds and back, back.

"I only knew one woman named...."

"That maid, Miss Grace, from when we were small."

"Well, couldn't be."

"No. Obviously."

"Louise. No. But Icelin and Louise. We had two, together."

"Impossible. Still...."

"What happened to them?" Paul watched the others curiously.

"Louise died. A murder. I don't think they ever found the killer."

"And Icelin?"

"Sort of went to pieces, poor thing. She was with us a long time though. All the years."

"Oh, from we were born," Ben agreed.

"Before." Sarah interrupted them decisively. "Long before." She stopped but they knew she hadn't finished and they waited. "I think Louise worked for Stella's mother for a short time before too. In fact... did she work at East Street?"

"East Street?"

"With Mama. At our old house. I think... perhaps."

"But how could this have anything to do with Adam?"

"Impossible."

"But the two names. We don't know anyone else, do we?" They thought for a long time.

"No."

They looked back to the child but he was sprawled across them on the couch in a deep untroubled sleep.

"I believe Icelin is still alive." Sarah's voice came as a shock to Paul in the speculative silence of the room. "Didn't Stella visit her just before the last?"

"What? Where?"

"Bellevue. No. Stella saw her at Kingston Public — some illness, but she was recovering from that. Where Icelin has been for years is Bellevue. Stone mad, poor thing."

"Oh, it's nonsense," Ben muttered after a while. "A little child like that. They make up things."

"He can't make up names like that, names he's never heard," Paul objected.

"We know the people he knows," Ben pondered. "He doesn't know any Icelin. Or Louise."

"Well we don't... now," Grace faltered.

"We don't know Uncle either." A long, dark passage began to open in Paul's mind. "But he does."

They sat gazing down at him, Adam almost set aside. The child was so, so beautiful with his face smooth olive in the twilight and the lashes curled innocently, and damp little tendrils of hair around his forehead. His body rested limply across the four of them huddled together on the sofa and he was utterly, utterly at peace.

"He knows Uncle." Sarah's voice was the hushed, tense whisper of Paul's thoughts.

They sat turning it over silently and the horror of it began to creep up on them.

"And if what he says means anything Uncle is a thief and a... gun dealer, and a bloody, bloody murderer," Sarah breathed.

Grace held the small, damp fist and moaned, "Baby, my baby."

But Sarah's thin, dry whisper went on implacably, "And Uncle knows that he knows him."

It grew dark as they sat there, feeling the weight of the boy on them and the terror in their love for him gathering, crushing out everything, everyone else.

Louise's son. Where to begin?

"The newspapers? Couldn't we work out the date, look back, find a name?"

Sarah shook her head at Paul slowly. "The papers said she was known only as Louise. None of us could remember her last name. A laundress, you know."

"Even if we find him," Paul muttered, "Not a shred of proof. He may be in some high position too…"

"And if we find him then," Grace broke in, "what then?"

Ben's voice cut the twilight. "Kill him."

"Ben! Ben!" Grace gasped.

Ben jabbed a finger harshly in the direction of the child. "Look at him!"

Paul shuddered as a line of Latin echoed spitefully in his mind. Strike him so that he can feel that he is dying. And he felt it too, as much a beast as Caligula. Whoever Uncle was, Paul wanted him dead.

Sarah nodded. She was suddenly composed. "Yes. Yes, if we find him we must kill him. I'd do it myself if I had strength. But I suppose we can find someone… people do."

"Stop. Stop it," Grace sobbed, looking from one to the other incredulously.

"No. There must be proof, there must," Paul muttered.

"Well anyway," Sarah groaned, "we must find out who he is. Uncle is Louise's son. We must question Icelin. Someone must go to the madhouse."

Minutes later, Grace said, "I suppose I'll see her tomorrow."

The early night wind stirred the curtains and made the dry plants rustle scratchily against the bars of iron grillwork.

Victor Castries had laid aside the smart Canadian suit and stripped off his stock. He wore faded jeans and battered puss boots when he caught the bus into town — not into the shopping and business section but to the shattered dwelling places, the grim yards marked by weathered metal sheeting, macca bushes or tangled barbed wire. Here were the men and women grown from the children of the dumpheap. A boy with hunted eyes scuttled sideways into a fish barrel, clutching something wrapped in greasy newspaper. A maaga dog howled in the next lane. This was the city of desolation, and the minister's mind keened, abandon hope all ye who enter here.

As he stood, the boy peeped out like a crab from its hole and Victor looked into his eyes and glimpsed the judgement.

Three men lounged on the embankment of a gully, studying him narrowly and a woman in a tight red skirt and sequined top sauntered forward.

"What me can help you wi' today, nice man?"

"Give thanks, but I press for time today. I looking fe a man."

"Man you like? Can find one fe you easy. Gimme a money I take you to one man you go like."

"No. I mean is someone I want to find. Did good to me when I small."

"What im name?"

"Old man name Leon. Was a Rasta man from de hills. I hear im lose im likkle plot. Did plant ganja an Babylon burn it. Hear seh him live here fe a while."

"Dem have a Rasta man name Leon. Lion him call himself. But im no old. Im your age so. You is a nice man, you know. Like you mumma feed you plenty mannish water when you small? You sure I cyan't help you?"

Victor retrieved her hand which was straying and held it gently but firmly, slipping a few dollars into it.

"You is a real nice attractive woman and I going tell you de trut'. I is a preacherman an if a tek a friend I going get in real trouble. Look ya, you cyan't take me to Leon place?"

"How you know whe' I goin take you?"

"Because I born and grow right round ya so."

"An tu'n preacher?"

"Eehi."

One of the men from the embankment sauntered over.

"What im want? No waan pay you? Make me cut im stingy...."

"Unno clear out," she barked. "Move walk off make de reverend pass in peace."

The man shuffled way sullenly, muttering,

"After me neva know im a reverend. Take care is a jinal."

Victor drew out the battered pocket Testament and crumpled stock and the woman gasped,

"Please to hold me excused, Minista. Me neva know or me wouldn' fast wid you."

From the embankment a youth with a Rasta hairstyle bawled, "Why unno pries' don' go back tell God im forget we. Take you bumbo outa de territory ya before me stick knife inna you...."

The woman cut him short with a stream of obscenity, and turned back to Victor. "Don' pay him no mind, ya Rev. Im no have no upbringing. Me woulda never talk no rudeness to you if me did know. Me self going help you fin' Lion." She paused to bark at the first man. "Speak good to de reverend."

"Cool runnings, Rev," he muttered.

"Seen," Victor replied. "Bless you."

And he walked away from the fish barrel where the little unloved boy ticked on like a time bomb.

The streggae led Victor to a one-room house, surrounded not by bare dirt and macca but by a symphony of pumpkin, cho-cho, melon and yam vines, watered by a split bamboo leading from the hydrant at the corner. And the plants flourished from the drip of stolen water, wrestling and embracing to produce food for the hand that pruned them and fertilised them with dilute urine. Inside was empty but clean with an old bed spring on the ground supporting a burst coir mattress. Plastic bowls drained on a board beside Wray and Nephew bottles, full, probably with water. An infant ackee tree struggled beside the door in its Milo tin. A single can of Betty condensed milk graced the shelf over the coalpot. The Betty was unnatural and forbidden, but a practical precaution against the day when ital might run out.

"Minister, I don't tink I can stop wait wid you, you know," his guide explained. "Have fe look likkle living. Pickney a yard fe feed."

"I understand. Is OK."

But she hesitated.

"You sound like you live a foreign fe a while. Listen, you know seh anybady get ketch killin tief in Jamaica — police no bother with dem."

He looked bewildered.

"I mean, if a man ketch you in him yard and tink you tief, is a'right fe kill you. No understand? Laad Gad, Rev, how you go last? I mean you mus' wait outside. Now when yu see Lion im come back, if is not him one, don't stay. Neider stand outside with man you don' know. Police see a wanted man inna group, dem just spray bullet. I sorry fe lef' you, Rev, but one likkle girl pickney I have trying to grow up good."

She bustled away before he could thank her properly.

It was an hour before Matthew Leon approached. His broad but wasted frame stopped well away, studying the man in front of his premises.

"What manner of man are you?" he demanded authoritatively. "What bring you to I house?"

Victor reminded him of the child his father had found stoned on jahncrow batty and had nursed in the vineyard on the hillside.

A smile of recollection lit the worn face hung with ragged locks, and the Rasta loped over.

"Is you in trut'?" Then he saddened. "Puppa dead, you know." He gestured inside. "Come. I an' I will make known de years."

He perched on a box and gave Victor the chair. As he talked he drew out a rectangular paper, two and a half by six inches, and cupped it in his left hand, packed and folded it. He was handing the first spliff to Victor to seal with his own saliva, but when Victor explained his circumstances Lion nodded reassuringly, "No mind. I self wi' take dis."

"But we was bredda. So much I owe you fada."

"A mystic man, I puppa. A Chief Dread."

"How him die?"

"I self cyan't say fe tell you. Im couldn' take Kingston. Say is only fe Babylon an bandoolu. Im grow thin, im grieve fe de hills. One day im sick an dead. But I feel good 'bout im. Late night I self carry im up in de hills bury him."

Victor's face glowed, "How you manage?"

"Pay one likkle boasy yout' fe tief car. Take him up and when done we run lef' de car. Police find it give de owner." He grinned at Victor, "Fear not, Preacherman."

"I glad you took him back."

Lion walked Victor back past the ganja den and the gentle thud of Bob Marley's "One Drop" towards his bus.

"Is Marley voice keep mine alive when I abroad hearing only Canadian accent," Victor reflected. "Bob, man. Trench Town pickney. Well. I going see you again."

"Serious man dwell hereby, but I going tell dem seh you fe pass in de territory. Nobady nah molest Lion frien'. Another day you stop take ital wid I. But first, say unto I what make you leave Canada an come back a Jah-make-ya."

Where were the words to tell it? Victor gripped his arm and sang the psalm Ras Leon had loved,

> *By the rivers of Babylon*
> *There we sat down*
> *And there we wept, when we remembered Zion.*

Then Lion took it up and they finished together, with the pedestrians at the bus stop grinning, pointing, drumming the side of the bus shelter,

> *Carry us away captivity,*
> *Required of us a song.*
> *How can we sing the Lord's song in a strange land.*

Paul drove silently along Windward Road, taking Grace to see Icelin. Grace had her licence, of course. Paul had insisted on it. Yet she had insisted just as adamantly that she would not drive, and so she never did. At last they drew alongside a stretch of chain-linked fencing topped with three rows of barbed wire. The security man at the gate of Bellevue Mental Hospital lifted the pole for them without a word and they drove in uncertainly. The absence of signs forced them to stop and ask the way. Then they coasted on, circling on the dirt track past dismal old buildings. Condemned-looking, Grace thought, red brick with dark barred windows. Grace came out and beat on the gate. After a while a key scraped on the lock and a nurse smiled curiously at her. A young man, a boy he seemed to Grace, shoved his hand out.

"Beg you a money, Mumma."

Grace shook her head bewildered and he drew back.

"Why?" she asked the nurse.

"Tobacco." The woman shrugged. "They roll it in dry leaves to get a smoke."

"I want to see old Icelin Castries."

"Oh. That's geriatric and chronic." The nurse directed Grace briefly. "If you miss your way again ask anybody for Upper G."

"It's safe... to just stop and ask?" Grace queried hesitantly.

"Yes, man. Is here we have the troublesome ones."

As Grace got back in the car another vehicle pulled up and a middle-aged woman and two youths came out clutching a man who struggled violently, cursing and threatening them.

"Is kill you waan kill me. Is me money you waan. Kill you waan kill me."

Male nurses and orderlies swarmed around him.

"Give him a shot," the first woman directed. "Settle him down."

Paul slid his eyes off the group who had brought in the man. They seemed crushed and furtive.

"Must be a relative. Looks like the father," he faltered as they reversed away from K2.

"And they spoke nicely, you know Paul. Not riff-raff."

They drove back towards the red brick buildings past a woman trudging barefoot on the track. Her tongue protruded and rolled up, vibrating rapidly. At the entrance they stepped up onto a concrete walkway and in through the doors to their right.

People were sitting all about. People their age, older — perhaps younger, but they all looked old. They sat on the step, on the landing, staring into their hands, into their laps, into the ground. None of them looked up as Grace and Paul passed. Others meandered along, loose clothes flapping. One glided past sideways, sliding her back against the wall. Her skirt was tied several times around the waist with strips of cloth and she carried a large piece, of indeterminate colour, wringing it tightly. On a bench to the right crouched a woman propping on her hand a ruined face, lined and sagging from the eyes in furrowed bags.

Out to the left was an open area where one or two huddled under the almond trees, and others lay on benches or on the edge of the narrow porch, their legs stretched out straight on the concrete. On the right, the green-painted doors were cut in thick wooden bars with large keyholes. The rooms inside, hardly more than cages, barely gave access to single beds opposite the doors.

Quiet, Grace thought. She had not expected the asylum to be quiet; but there was no talking except for an occasional request for money. Ward assistants in pink uniforms moved about calmly and patients paced around on stumpy bare feet or sat nodding, scratching, staring away, occasionally wiping their faces — withered and forgotten faces with empty eyes.

A ward assistant led Grace into one of the tiny rooms on the right to a little crumpled heap upon the bed. It bore no resemblance whatever to the woman she had known throughout her childhood. Brittle old twigs on grey cloth. Grace sat down gingerly on the edge of the chair the nurse had set for her and tried to begin.

There seemed no way of introducing herself. She stared at the emaciated creature and said, "I'm Miss Grace."

The shrivelled lids did not flicker. Grace spoke of her mother and of the Stollmeiers and there was no response. Icelin lay shapelessly with her skirt reefed up around her and her withered limbs lying randomly about. Grace talked of Bedward, of Nana, of Ben. Nothing. Icelin Castries heard, perhaps she understood, but nothing moved her.

Eventually, hopeless of a response, Grace mentioned Louise. Slowly, slowly the woman raised her eyes to her. Grace bent forward.

"You remember Louise, Icelin? Is Miss Grace this, talking to you. Miss Stella's Grace. You remember anything 'bout Louise?"

The woman stared at her and parted her lips shakily but instead of words came a high, nasal croaking that startled Grace, made her jump back. Then the words took form and a shrill, discordant tune.

> *Dry bone gone fe me, down de gully road.*
> *Wango wang. Fe go wango wang, down de gully road.*

Again and again Grace questioned her, tugging her hand gently and begging her to listen, but there was nothing more to be had from her but the weird, rasping song.

Grace blamed herself. She could not have done it right, she said. Paul tried to comfort her and succeeded a little for as long as she was awake. But at night, fear flapped in at the window. The outline she could not distinguish but she felt it settle on her chest, crushing her to the mattress. With the labour of each breath she felt its loose, leathery skin clammed cold against her flesh along the little secret crevice between her breasts. Then she was half awake and struggling with reality. Knowledge and feeling grappled together. Her mind said she was awake. Get up. Turn on the light. But her soul, overwhelmed with the subconscious groaned surrender. Now or later. Bear. Then the burden, smothering, pressing in her ribs, seemed to gather mass and darkness so that the room and consciousness merged, filled with a thick, palpable black evil. She knew it was not death (nothing so paltry) that crouched over her, but obliteration. That when it had covered her completely it would be as if she had never lived.

She woke, but did not move. The nights were putrid with all she blotted out of the day, and it seemed to her as if the nights were getting longer, encroaching on the day. What if she should lose her mind? It became another fear she kept at bay. Until the next night.

At last they fastened their hope on the fact that Gerry was unusually aware for his age and that Uncle would hardly consider him a threat. After all, perhaps Pearl had a new lover and the man they heard she was to marry was not Uncle. Perhaps the child might never meet him again. After all, Pearl lived in the States now.

Then Pearl returned. She reopened the question of custody on the grounds that the father of the child was dead and the grandparents were senile. The family knew she couldn't find all that money on her own.

"What job she have?" Ben hammered his fist on the table. "Bringing in cosmetics to sell. Like she turn higgler. Don't is just fancy hustling?"

The court ruled in favour of the mother and Pearl hurtled into Oxford Close in a factory-new, lead-grey Porsche. Gerry did not want to go. He wanted Grand Paul and Benny and Goddie and Sugar. He wanted cake. He wanted Sugar's own cake and if he couldn't have it Sugar must give Mummy the "receipt" for it. Pearl lifted him wailing into the car and drove away.

24
Cul-De-Sac

THE COUNTRY seethed with approaching elections, and all the way from downtown into the suburbs the graffiti battle raged in protest and ridicule targeting Prime Minister Manley of the People's National Party and the Leader of the Opposition, Edward Seaga. CIAga, sniped government supporters. SPYAGA sell black man. PNP Steppin. Third turn for PNP. PNP Zone. But the other side, backing the Jamaica Labour Party, blazed: Vote JLP. Michael is a fruitcake. The walls of the city centre hissed: Deliverance near; Judas in fear. Third term; eat worm.

So there was machinery now to ensure a fair election. On this thread of assurance, frail as a spider's web it seemed to the family, Jamaica hung above a bloodbath. Ballots not bullets, the walls of the city begged.

Grace and Ben whispered between themselves that the island tottered on the brink of civil war. The year dawned dark with power outages and water lock-offs. The women who walked the city streets as their grandmothers had, carrying buckets and washtubs of water on their heads, no doubt recalled the electioneering slogan of years back: Better must come. Now the Opposition quipped: Bitter has come.

Strikes and more strikes. In March, Oxford Close like other larger areas of Kingston lacked water. April brought the Gold Street killings in a commando attack on a dance. Revellers were machine-gunned by uniformed terrorists.

"At least poor Icelin wasn't in the Eventide Home," Grace bawled to Sarah when Ben brought news of the fire that had consumed the home and one hundred and sixty-one old women. And it seemed that the fire raged on in political controversy and accusations thrown back and forth between the parties. But then came the discovery of a Cuban owned trailer with fifty thousand rounds of ammunition for use in shotguns, and the case flared to another national scandal when the manager of the Cuban company, Moonex, was found en route to Cuba, reportedly in the company of the Minister of Security.

"An' who charter the plane?" Ben roared, hands spread, staring them down to silent suspense as they awaited the punchline. His voice dropped to a hiss. "Cuban Ambassador Estrada."

"Yes," Grace said. "I read it."

"Where," Paul gasped.

"Watch it here in black an white. *Gleaner* say so."

"Don't I did always tell you?" Ben threw up his hands in disgust.

Sarah heard little of it because the old hearing aid was just wearing out. She was apathetic anyway.

The trials associated with the Green Bay Massacre and the Massop murder were continuously postponed. Two hundred and seventy-four gun killings had already been reported for the year, and it was said that more guns, and better ones, were available to gunmen than to the police or army. The gun-running trade boomed.

"You don't see where Pearl find the money now?" Ben growled, holding the paper close to his thick, gold-rimmed spectacles. "After no other business can prosper. Half of the country out of work."

It was true that the foreign exchange crisis swelled towards the record deficit for that year — nine hundred million Jamaican dollars. Businessmen from Paul's congregation, who attended the function in honour of his retirement, had shrugged that he was lucky — lucky to be retiring and lucky never to have been in business. They were scaling down their own operations, what with consumer imports cut back and raw material supplies thinning.

It was as well they were all retired now, the family agreed. Manufacture, agriculture — the whole productive sector seemed to be collapsing. From what Ben's old acquaintances said, trade had all but died.

As the economy plunged, inflation soared. Grace confirmed that they were eating into their capital. They began to buy only what seemed necessary for survival, and they were the middle class.

"We better off than most people," Paul muttered. "How they live?"

"Better than we do," Ben scoffed. "Dem can tief."

"Don't be a brute," Grace snapped. "You don't shop so you don't know the price of food. Is serious, man."

In July the city was brittle with suspicion and murderous with resentment.

"It's not just routine crime," Paul pondered. "It's the collapse of politics into tribalism. The savagery is what I don't understand. We used to be civilised. What happened?"

Ben chided him gently, for he was never harsh with Paul. "The trouble with you is that you want to understand everything. Not every riddle has a solution."

Grace thought perhaps Ben was right, for gang supporters of both parties battled bloodily and pursued each other for vengeance. The papers counted one hundred and thirty people dead by the gun in July. They would cite well over eight hundred violent deaths by the year's end. In July it seemed to the family that peace was irretrievable.

Or perhaps it was that Gerry's departure had extinguished hope.

"Me vote, Rev?" exclaimed an elderly resident of West

Kingston to Victor Castries. "How me fe vote make dem shoot me? Then Rev, you no know say whichever side me vote for de other side go shoot me?"

These was no convincing him otherwise.

"Ballot could nameless all you like, Rev. But what you expec' me fe say when dem come an aks me how me vote. Tell each one me vote fe im own party? In de end both side go shoot me." He chuckled. "Dat go bring dem together." He threw back his head and emitted a howl of laughter. "Peace at las'."

A car coasted by and Victor glimpsed a profile from the past. It was the brown bossman. He caught the expression on his companion's face.

"Who de brown man?" Victor asked quickly. "De puss-eye man."

"Now you really want me get shoot," muttered the old man, no longer laughing.

Lion knew, though he would not say how. "Busha dem call im. Name Austin Louis or Austin Haynes. No see de scarface wid im?"

"Seen."

"Im is de devil. Walking de lan', seeking who fe devour. Busha own im, an plenty like im."

"Busha no look like ganglord."

"How you know how ganglord look? Any case, Busha own ganglord. Dem say..." Lion hesitated. "Dem say Busha own politician who own ganglord. Me no know." Lion studied the minister's face with narrowed eyes, startling Victor into the thought that the Rasta looked like a black Chinese. "Why I bredda ask 'bout de puss-eye man?"

"When you fada find me... is dat man had give me de jahn-crow batty."

A pounding on the door introduced the streggae who had first guided him to Lion.

"Rev, beg you look 'pon de school paper!" She flourished her daughter's report at Victor. "Since you get de book fe her, de pickney come out firs' in class." She grinned at him adoringly. "An' now I learning to read in de programme I get de work you send me for. Rev, is how no nice woman don' tie you up yet? How you get 'way so long?"

"I waiting fe you pretty daughter fe grow up. I want you fe me mother-in-law," he grinned.

"You going to de big dance, Rev?"

"Dance again? After Gold Street?"

"I was there, Rev. I see everything. Friend a mine dead. But I cyan' stop go a dance. What I living for? Too besides, I feel fe dance. Laad, Rev! You tink say *mi* pickney could go UWI one day?"

Because the prospect of ruin was imminent and, to the older families of the suburbs, almost universal, it became impossible to speak of anything else. Conversations worked around to it, and stories of the latest murder, rape, fraud or cover-up were passed around with a sort of fascinated horror. Afterwards the mind played obsessively with what it had heard. Fear slipped out of control and rumour ran riot. There seemed no longer any way of establishing truth or maintaining reason. The result was mass paranoia. The truth seemed to be that the city had gone mad.

Only Gerry had kept the family sane. And Gerry was gone. Pearl had vanished with him into the vast haze of the States, perhaps remarried to a man they did not know. Perhaps he was with... Uncle. No letters, no phone calls. Not even a sense of location. He was out there — somewhere. At least, they prayed that he was. Removed from them, Pearl became a dull gleam of hope. As long as she had him, thousands of miles from the only four people likely to understand his story, Uncle might ignore him. Perhaps he had a chance. They prayed he was out there somewhere, but knew that he must never come back.

So there was nothing left for the family in Jamaica. Now it was their trailer darkening the gate, its entrance flanked by the old tree that had stood from before the house was built, so long now that the earth had eaten away beneath it, exposing black, gnarled roots. Vines were overpowering the bougainvillea hedge and pink tails of coralilla waved mockingly.

Up the road, deserted gardens had fallen into disrepair. Love bush strangled the hedges and fine-leafed thorn bushes sprang up in the flower beds instead of gerberas and gladioli. The trees and some of the larger bushes lived on. Ackees were bearing but never seemed to open on the tree. They hung on indefinitely and tauntingly, closed and poisonous. Oleanders dipped and nodded, a mindless, vulgar pink. Under the cassia tree across the way the ground was strewn with yellow flowers, still with the heady glow of life upon them. Soon they would be brown mush around the trunk, but today they were a dizzy, just-fallen yellow. At the top of the road flamed the poinciana more brilliantly than ever, and beyond and above the cruel, rectangular lines of the trailer the land arched into its blue-grey hills, ancient and inviolable.

Their own garden was ruined by the water shortages. A few of Stella's old rose bushes struggled on under the kitchen window where Grace threw rinsing water from the dishes, but they were scraggly for want of pruning and stunted by detergent. The allamanda, descended from the original slip off Catherine Donald's wall at the beginning of the century, rioted wildly over its arbour; but most of the flowering shrubs were dead and what grass there was spread helter-skelter over the flower beds.

Even their more recent neighbours were gone. After Jesse Deitrich's mugging, her son had escorted her onto the plane with one suitcase and her daughter met her in Toronto. Now her house, opposite the Cohons, had been transformed into offices. The pentas was uprooted and lawn space paved with asphalt. It was a good location, abutting as it did on the car park on the other side of the wall that ended the cul-de-sac. The new owners, Presley and De Lano, had arranged to share the car park, and the wall had been knocked down to let the driveway swing straight through from Oxford Close. The cassia survived on a small island at the front left-hand corner of the lot.

The Rose place was never rebuilt after a mysterious fire that had gutted it; nor had the precariously balanced beams of wood and tottering concrete divisions been torn down. Noises came from the yard at nights. Sometimes a light moved, but on the whole it was still.

Next door, the Andersons' house had disappeared. For a while some of the flooring had remained intact with a few low portions of wall here and there, peeping above the grass. But gradually these few bricks were carried away and at last a stalwart couple arrived in a van and dug up whatever tiles remained intact. Now, above and between the bushes that sprang up among the foundations, the open land beyond was clearly visible from the side windows of the house.

The Halls had moved almost a year ago. Yet somehow the family still thought of number three as the Halls's, probably because the quick turnover of tenants did nothing to associate it firmly with anyone else. In June, the police had arrived at the house and found it abandoned although there was leftover food on the table and the stove was still warm. Rounds of ammunition were uncovered in the bedroom and traces of ganja. No rent had been paid for eight months so there was no money for repairs. The new tenants, who looked no more solvent than their predecessors, had insisted that they could not move in until extensive work was done. The garden, which had been obliterated, they offered to restore on their own, and it was planted out in gungo peas. Ben had his own suspicions as to what flourished in-between. In fact the tenants seemed interested only in the garden and there was no sign of them on the premises at night.

At the road-corner in the mornings, children shrieked and

capered in the nursery school which had been the Shermans'
house. At night, of course, like the office opposite the Cohon
house, it was deserted. Across the way from the nursery, the airy
four-bedroom house that the McIntyres had abandoned was captured and the squatters hung over the gate, staring insolently into
every passing car. The first squatters had been a Rasta couple,
quiet and pleasantly spoken, but now, far into the night the
sounds of quarrelling and of shattering bottles were audible even
at the Cohons' end of the road.

By day the road bustled with cars, vans, cycles and consider-
able foot traffic and with the squeals of those tots at the corner.
But at night nothing moved and it was dark except for the oil
lamps of the squatters.

The family depended more and more on their iron grillwork
and on the loyalty of the dog, Sir Henry Morgan. The cornmeal
they had fed him disappeared from the supermarkets and Grace
schemed and calculated over leftovers, which were meagre these
days, and added bread backs and boiled vegetable peel to sustain
Morgan.

"But I feel as if the poor beast is always hungry," she
moaned.

"So much the better," Ben regarded him with satisfaction. "Stay
hungry, dawg, and nyam tief."

Then one morning, silently, inexplicably, the turtle tank was
empty.

"Why?" Grace cried, real tears shining unshed in her eyes.
"Who would want a turtle? And Adam had it... all the years. He
loved it — it was one of the things Les gave him. And Gerry
played with h... him. What use was he to anyone else?"

Paul stared morosely into the empty tank. "Soup!"

"Eh?" Grace's voice rose, not loud but shrill. "No, no. Don't say
it."

Paul shrugged and spread his hand wearily. "What else? He
was a good-size fellow. He would probably have outlived us all,

left alone. Well, we couldn't have taken him anyway."

"But soup, darling? You really believe so?"

Ben shook his head bitterly, "Nothing else, nothing else."

Life brightened when the McIntyres visited their nephew in his suburban Barbican home for three weeks and invited the family to dinner. Sarah would go nowhere and Ben would not leave her, so Grace and Paul set out together. It was a pleasant evening, lively with pictures of the grandchildren in Canada. But it was not easy raising them, Lisa allowed, what with the temptations of the big city. "And some places you working twice as hard to get ahead if you coloured, you know."

Besides, the social life was nothing like the porch at Oxford Close. But there it was. The children were all Canadians now. "I sorry Goddie didn't come, man."

Sam had brought the new hearing aid that they had discussed by phone, and Paul slipped him the package of black market dollars.

"Best thing on the market," Lisa pronounced triumphantly. "You can get anything there."

The nephew wasn't leaving Jamaica, he declared. He was perfectly comfortable, he said. He had moved to Barbican early, when good houses first went on the market at ridiculous prices. Once you were sensible you could live perfectly normally. Three big dawg he had, no likkle mongrel, real bad dog buy from kennel come with papers. Heap o' wrought-iron grillwork and short shank padlock.

"When I go Sheraton or Hilton with the boys and leave Carrie I come home two a.m. and she safe. New car I have, not going bruck down on the road. What I leaving Jamdown for? Children going school doing well, don' need to be white to get big job when they grow up. They happy get they likkle seabath regular and growing good."

Nothing would make him root up himself and leave JA to scrunt in a country dat don't want him, an' inhale winter breeze inna him lungs. Everyting him want right here.

The Cohons were delighted to see the McIntyres again but The Nephew was all brash rhetoric as far as they were concerned. How he made a living was a mystery but he obviously made a good one. And flaunted it, Paul muttered sourly as they turned back into Oxford Close. Tiresome, Grace agreed. For the Cohons the laughter had gone and the rest was meaningless now.

It had taken months, their packing. Wearisome months too, void of expectancy. All they were doing was getting out, getting as far as they could from everything that had been for Adam and Gerry.

Useless, useless it all had been. Even when they were dead and out of Pearl's way, the child wouldn't get anything they had. There were these new laws. He would be a resident outside of the country and you couldn't just take money out, or shift around money in foreign accounts without declaring it. The house that Grace had built, Paul's place in Moneague where old Martha Jane O'Reilly had lived, Stella's garden, Ben's furniture, Sarah's money and Goldfields — they were not for Gerry after all.

Physically they were sound enough, but their minds numbed under loss. They worked mechanically. Grace organised the packing, Ben supervising the loading of the trailer. Paul followed up the paperwork like an automaton. Sarah took no interest, none at all. She was old after all. At last she had surrendered to it. She sat rocking endlessly in the living room, even though the new hearing aid would have enabled her to watch television or talk comfortably with them. She wept all day, everyday, soundlessly, monotonously. There were times when the others went out for no other reason but to escape the house and the sight of her blank, draining eyes.

"I don't even know why we're leaving," Paul grumbled hopelessly. "When did we decide to? What was the reason again?"

"You're the one who organised the place for us. You had Ben

arrange the papers."

"I know, I know. But why?"

"Nothing to stay for."

"But what is there to go for. What are we hoping to find?"

"Oh, anything. Once it's different. It's so awful now. We have nothing."

"Mm. Well we're certainly paying a lot to ship nothing."

"Well, so it is nothing."

Grace looked around at the things they were to carry. The ancient, inlaid desk that had sheltered her mother in the earthquake — it was scratched and battered now, but there was no parting with that. Her mother's bed — Papa had made it. Died in it. It had passed to Gerry. Even the old scissors that Paul was using to open envelopes had been in the Goldman kitchen as early as she could remember. It had been buried for a while then unearthed in Sarah's arbour. Her eye moved to the endless grapevine of Catherine's embroidery, to a bit of china Sarah had salvaged from the East Street house after the earthquake. She ran her fingers over the Bible Vern had treasured, given to him by Reverend Jackman, and over the prayer book Belle had brought for Martha Jane. There, wrapped carefully in some of Adam's old crib sheets, was Belle's silver. They hadn't decided which of the sewing machines to keep, but they obviously couldn't take all four. There were Martha Jane's, Lynn's, Belle's and Stella's. Martha Jane's garden tools lay in a heap at the back door.

Paul slumped his head on one hand.

"I don't want to go. I... don't want to go."

"Oh Lord... at this point..."

"I know, I know. We can't stay."

He forced his attention back to the table. "What are these papers?"

"Family things. Everything. Pictures, letters, school reports. Look at what they say about Adam's Biology, eh?"

"This?"

"Les's appointment book."

"Mm. Put it here in this drawer." Paul shoved it into the battered desk. "Somewhere in it is that name. The man who phoned Les to get the car cleared. The typist saw Les write something."

"The only thing on the page was my initial," Ben reminded him.

"Still. Somewhere in it is a clue to the killer's name. It must be. Les was so exacting."

"Meticulous." They stared at each other for a minute pondering.

"What are the other things?"

"Baptismal certificates. Look Les school report — imagine he failed maths. Bills and receipts. We could dump most — except perhaps the receipts from Adam's patients for the money we reimbursed. How he didn't get one from whoever he was making that exchange with? Then we'd know."

"Would have been pointless. If it had any record of the arrangement, a receipt would only prove he was smuggling money. But, knowing Adam, yes, I'd think he would.... It makes no difference. What's the rest?"

"Belle's recipes. Mama's will..."

She paused at a strange, coughing sound from Sarah. "Goddie?"

Sarah had stopped crying and was still as a stone, staring into the opposite wall. Grace started towards her with a cry of dismay. Gone? But now Sarah gestured her aside impatiently. It was an abrupt, peremptory movement, startling after months of apathy.

"Goddie?"

"Shut up, woman!" Sarah's brows knitted and her eyes strained away from them. "Recipe? Receipt? What was it the child said?"

"Eh?"

"About your cake, when he was going?"

"You mean Pearl not having the recipe? What has that got...?"

Sarah stamped her foot. "Woman, for God's sake, you were never a fool. Don't go senile on us now. What did the child call the recipe?"

The room swam around Grace.

"Receipt, receipt," Paul's voice fluttered through her brain. Already he was unravelling the skein, cobweb thin, leading to the child.

"And Adam," Sarah fired on mercilessly, "the baby said he had Uncle's... recipe."

"No. We said it," Paul corrected her. "He... wasn't sure."

"Receipt, then. Yes. The name. Adam must have had the man's receipt. We never looked... of course we didn't think...."

"Where?" Paul had moved beyond them and paused, puzzled. "We went through all Adam's papers. All. You remember how furious Pearl was... wait a minute."

Ben stared back at him. "You mean whether she knew the man would swindle him?"

"Mm. Well anyway. There was no receipt in his case, or anywhere."

"Do you suppose Gerry...?"

"Yes, he might know where. But he can't help us now." Paul brushed aside irrelevancies.

"But if we could get it," Grace burst in desperately. "The name on the receipt is.... After all, the only way we can secure the child is to get that name."

"And then what?" Ben demanded.

"Anything. Anything."

"Of course, if he's safe up to now, perhaps the man isn't prepared to go to such lengths...."

Paul interrupted Grace. "Couldn't have done much immediately after the funeral and everything. He may have been waiting for the talk to die down."

"We'll do anything we have to... to get him back."

"Stick to the point, stick to the point."

"Yes. The receipt, the name."

Paul said slowly, "He would have had it on him, a thing like that."

"We saw all his papers."

"I don't mean the briefcase. On him, on him."

"They'd have found it, getting him ready."

"But the suit he was to travel in was spotless and you said to tell the funeral home... I made Sam Isaacs's people use the same clothes."

"Still. We went through the pockets. Remember the inhalant wasn't there."

"That's a bulky thing. A small piece of paper...."

Sarah's voice grated on them, pursuing Paul's mind, outstripping his explanation.

"It's on him still. The name of the man is on Adam still."

It took Grace only a few seconds.

"We must have the body exhumed."

But that night the phone rang, catapulting them out of sleep. They blundered towards it, cold with apprehension.

"What's the time?"

"Three-thirty."

"Jesu."

"No. I'll answer it."

They hung onto Paul's voice.

"Yes, Cohon here. Yes, what? Redeemer!"

When he was finished talking he put down the receiver slowly and shot off to the bathroom. When he returned he drew out a chair carefully. Grace pushed the small glass of brandy to him and Ben poured one for himself. It was the last bottle. Only quarter full.

"Well?"

"Pearl is dead."

Thin and dry it sliced the room like a razor blade. They looked at him with wide red-rimmed eyes, faces puffy and distorted with sleep.

"Found in her car. Beaten, raped and shot."

"God. Here?"

"Yes…. They seem to be back."

"All…?"

"They… the police… want to notify her husband if she has one. Her bag was gone. No identification. A ring but no initials. One of the policemen just happened to recognise her because of the court case and remembered me. One of my boys from Sunday School."

"And Gerry?" Grace whispered.

"There were toys in the car. Socks and things."

"He may be… with Uncle then."

"Alone." Paul put the bottle to his mouth and gulped it.

At dawn they were still sitting there.

"Poor Pearl," Grace breathed, thinking of the whip marks the police had found on her. "Poor confused girl. I wonder if I really gave her a chance?"

"What?" The others stared at her in disbelief.

"Well maybe I could have…."

"Could have what?"

Paul gestured Pearl aside almost in irritation. He was sick about what had happened to her. Actually the police had described her as buggered, not just raped, but he hadn't wanted to say that to Grace. It was horrible but finished. Waste of time to think 'bout that now.

"He's making his move. Ready to clean up.'"

"The body," Sarah muttered. "It's the only way we can trace the name and get the child."

"Time, time. The order will take, oh, you know."

"The police…."

"…Will never notice us. A baby babbling about a recipe…. Never."

"The order."

"No use."

447

Ben spoke for the first time in a while, very slowly and distinctly.

"The only way we can get the name in time to have a chance of finding the child is to get it ourselves."

They stared at him for a while, for it took time to penetrate. Sarah's lips were pinched, but she nodded.

"Absolutely, my boy."

Grace was white. "You mean… we…?"

"Don't think about it, darling. Don't think." Ben gripped her shoulder painfully. "I'll do it."

Silence again.

"Well, there's nothing to be done before evening," Paul pronounced. "I intend to sleep a few hours before then."

"Sleep?"

"Sleep." He reached into the drawer behind him, produced a tiny bottle of Valium and counted the tablets out among them.

When last had Ben dreamed? How it started was vague, unimportant, but he was young again and on the eve of Easter it had been a good party in a house perched with a windy outlook to the sea. The maid rested the baby on the sand and it seemed almost in the water for next minute only pastel green bellied like a sail upon the waves. And he saw it, the wide, irritable Atlantic acknowledging a disturbance.

With a wail of fury he plunged into the shallow curl of sea where the women had the child paddling between them and he snatched it back into the house. They were surprised, for the baby had floated happily and safely from one to another. But Ben was blind and deaf with anger. For he could see and hear another ocean on the sea wall clapping, feel the sand shift and the murmur of disgruntled seas. And down the other side of the hill from which the house bared its breast toward the shore, in the sunken plain where Goddie lived, he could see pale trickles pour over the rim, down onto the sleeping town.

All around, nature seemed confused and to encroach upon

them. The sea was high and the sky low. From the damp concrete of the porch he lifted the baby, held him tightly as the flow of water whispered, mumbled, rumbled, flung its inhibitions to the skies, ripping the wall, and in a torrent tumbled past the house, onto the town.

He could hear himself asking quietly in constrained, polite hysteria, "You tried to teach my child to swim in this?"

Then the ocean rose up, went wild, and he heard it growl and hiss as it fell down on them.

He woke and it was dry and the bed steady on the floor. He began to gather what he would need. He opened Stella's mahogany wardrobe and drew out a long parcel, carefully rolled in a dressing gown that had been his father's. Carefully he unfolded Abe Goldman's old robe. Rudy Stollmeier's hunting rifle was a valuable antique now. Ben had kept it well and he had not turned it in whatever the gun laws said. It was all he had ever got from his grandfather. He cleaned and loaded it as he had learnt long ago.

Then he went out briefly to find a man he had known on the wharf.

In the evening, Ben had the back of the car ready with Martha Jane's garden fork and shovel and a borrowed pick axe. Paul came out cradling a Thermos, a short, flat bottle and a crowbar.

"Eh?" Ben regarded him.

"Occurred to me something very cold and strong may prove to be necessary." He shook the Thermos carefully. Then he held out the crowbar. "May need something for the lid."

"Mm. The white rum?"

"Grace thought... you have your handkerchief? Aah. Well. Never mind. I'll tell you later."

"Later?" Ben looked at him aghast.

"Come now, man. You think I'm letting you go into this thing alone? Behave yourself man, Ben."

"No."

"Let's go." Paul slid in firmly behind the wheel. "Come on, man, you can't even see to drive at this hour, let alone read a piece of faded paper. You wouldn't even able find the site."

"Oh no, not you." Ben hung back. "Besides... don't is sacrilege?"

"Time is going, man. Time. Let's go." Paul paused and looked down at his feet shuffling the accelerator restlessly, "I can handle this, you know."

"Mm. Well." Ben got in and slammed the door hard.

"OK, OK, man. Don't break up the motor car."

All the way to Half Way Tree, the streets gaped empty. Strange how wide and clean they lay at night, deserted. The night hung hot and thick. Well before they reached the clock tower, rain drove across the front of the car and the road vanished. A month ago the windscreen had been stolen and replacements were unobtainable, so they had installed clear plastic sheeting. It was inconvenient enough even when it rained during the day. Neither of them had driven it at night since then.

"If this keeps up we going have to cut it out."

"Fogging up too."

Ben jerked his head at Paul's side window.

"That thing opens?"

Paul shoved at it and grimaced.

"Seized up."

On Ben's side the glass had shattered and a piece of shower curtain kept out the rain.

"Well if we don't get some air even you not going able see to drive." Ben glowered at the fragment of shower curtain.

"Bust it."

Ben slammed his fist through the crisp discoloured plastic and wiped away the mist inside the windscreen.

"All this water is not helping me," Paul grumbled.

"What make you go so often? Is the prostate?"

"Suppose so. Thank God for the rain though," Paul reflected.

"Why?"

"Well we in good shape for our age, but how far we could dig if the ground was like stone?"

"How far we could dig anyway by ourselves? I done arrange for a man to meet us." He intercepted Paul's incredulous glance. "I didn' tell him nothing. I did his father a favour once. Kept him out of jail. He going dig, leave and ask no questions. Paul, man, you mus' know we two couldn' manage — and I never even meant you to have to come. And by the way," Ben paused to wipe his fingers scrupulously in his handkerchief, "why you have on the stock?"

"Police mightn't bother with me round the churchyard."

"Tcha!"

They swung past the old courthouse and along the low red brick wall around the church. They could get over that. Ben dropped the tools over cautiously. He touched the wooden gate and it creaked open. They wouldn't even need to go over the wall.

"I come in early and open up fe you Mas' Goldman," breathed a shadow on a nearby tomb.

It should take only a few minutes to find the grave, even in the dark. But they were barely in the churchyard when the huge man with them grabbed them both and pressed them down behind one of the taller stones.

"No make sound," he whispered. "Looter-dem."

The looters worked on a new headstone, knocking the vase of fresh roses aside and fracturing the base of the stone expertly. One stood guard with a long shadow at his chest. One by one others would stop and change places with the watch. At last they hoisted the marble over the wall on the other side.

It was quiet. Paul drew discreetly behind a neighbouring tomb then returned to guide them to the site. When they stood over Adam's grave, Ben hesitated before reaching for the garden fork. His assistant was already steadily at work, and had brought a small ladder to help the older men in and out of the hole. Ben paused and glanced at Paul curiously.

"And the white rum?"

"Later. If we wet our handkerchiefs, tie them across our faces... when we get further down.... It was Grace idea."

"Mm. Little Grace. Well."

Ben passed the back of his hand across his eyes and slammed the fork into the wet earth. "Remember the fuss I made 'bout wanting a vault here? Just as well Pearl was too mean to agree."

Hours later Ben and Paul huddled on the edge of the grave, sweat-drenched. The man Ben had found to dig and to prise the lid grasped Mas' Goldman's arm.

"I dig one up fe you. If you ever need me put one in, make me know." And he was gone.

Now they were alone with the unthinkable and there was no turning back.

The black maw they had opened yawned at their feet, breathing corruption. And within... beyond contemplation. But slide down again. Uncover. Search it. Mind-bending horror sucking at sanity, yet anything, anything for a clue so nebulous it should hardly detain them, only suppose... suppose it could lead to their darling. Anything to find Gerry. Yet Adam. Adam had been their darling too and their fingers shrinking, groping the burst lining of the jacket yielding spongily — then a firm resistance, thin plastic flap. Pull it out. But pulling and, oh God, all loosening under their hands. They scrambled out, retching on the edge.

Weakly Ben dragged himself to where Paul huddled shivering violently against a mound of dank clay. Ben held him tightly, warming him with his body.

"You in shock, man. Here." He raised the Thermos to Paul's lips. "Swallow it."

"No, no. Alcohol makes me go more. We mus' finish."

But Ben made him swallow. "Is finished." He cradled Paul's head and tipped the flask to his lips.

"You have it?"

In the darkness Ben fumbled with the small rectangular slip of paper from the plastic flap. They drew themselves behind one of the tombs and crouched to flick on the torch light. Overhead a helicopter clattered, beaming its searchlight. They switched off their own light and shrank lower.

The chopper passed and they peered again at the stained paper.

"Can't see," Ben moaned.

But it was a receipt for an illegible number of Jamaican dollars, to be returned in United States currency on Adam's arrival in Miami. Paul strained into the gloom for the signature.

"Austin," he breathed. Then, "Uncle?"

A faint animal whimper from Ben, then a sobbing that was question and denial.

"And Les? Les? Is Austin…?"

He wiped his eyes smearing his face with grave dirt and for a moment Paul feared Ben might collapse. But now the hours which had become formless with nightmare gathered shape.

"Go Louis's place find the boy. You can see to drive go." Ben gestured back to the site. "I wi' fix it back."

"No. No time."

"Just leave it?"

"No time. Get this to the house and phone the police." A thought struck Paul. "That letter we thought was your initial — in Les book…."

"B."

They stared at each other and gasped, almost together, "Busha."

"But Les, Paul? Oh God, from they were children...."

"Then Louise?"

"Same washerwoman? Must be that why him name Louis. Papers say the child they find tie up by the body wouldn't talk. No one knew the name. But then, Les. Oh Jesus, Les just meet a boy in school. Is madness. Where it start?"

25
The Spirits

LOUISE HAYNES's great-great-grandmother (the African, Beneba) had left two children for different men. Jamie Horne, the overseer's son, was brown; his children and their cousins never met. Ratoon Haynes was black as it was possible to be. He laboured on Goldfields where he had grown up with Jessica and her son after Emancipation, and he settled more and more into his own provision ground. Three of Beneba's grandchildren by Ratoon were relatively close for a while, until they scattered.

It began even before Ratoon died in 1881.

Cassie Haynes could not settle with any man. Her talents lay elsewhere, in herbs, potions and secret rites for power in another world. It had come to her in fragments from a vast collective memory. Here and there gaped dark empty patches, but scraps of rhythm, myth and ritual clung together in an echoing consciousness where past and present overlapped to become indistinguishable.

Even as a child, when the sugar wain went down to the wharf, only Cassie had stared after it into the night.

"Rolling Calf," her aunts had warned her in a whisper, "Rolling Calf a follow it fe molasses. Turn you eye 'way from de cart."

But she had stared into the night, expectant, waiting on the rattle of a chain amidst the bamboo.

Of course Cassie was four-eyed, born as she had been in a caul. Her mother had been too ignorant to dry and pound the membrane and feed it back to the infant in its milk. Her mother

*had done little for her from the beginning and actually had...
died early. Stomach cramps and an issue of blood. Cassie used
to have to wash out the cloths. Crimson running through her fingers, foul blood-smell heaving from the bowl.*

Then the coffin lid had dropped at the child's feet.

*Better dem did catch de pickney burn her same time only
'fraid dem 'fraid. An' she not 'fraid, not even 'fraid Rolling Calf,
de twice dead. Poison, dem say, poison. Mus' obeah.*

*Secretly, avidly, Cassie had absorbed the mutterings of her
elders and later, in old age, rummaging through her boxes and
vials, she would look for an audience among the young and find
only her grandchild to listen. Louise.*

*Meanwhile, on the outskirts of Goldfields estate, Cassie's voice
murmured the wisdom of herbs and potions and of comings and
goings in the spirit world. She had heard tales only about her
grandmother, Beneba, but the sundering ocean between races
and classes stretched as vast as it had ever been and the hours of
work and violation as futile and grievous as ever. The groans of
shipboard and Beneba's blood under the millhouse haunted the
years; and long after free paper came Cassie lived to see the age
of bondage reenacted through a hundred seasons, settings and
faces.*

*Among them, Cassie's spirit cankered as if the festering pain
and bitterness of Beneba's fate had eaten its way beyond death
into the character of her descendants. Cassie was a woman to
fear, a woman to seek out only in extremity of need, a woman to
avoid when enraged. By the time Ratoon was old, this eldest
daughter was central to the community around Goldfields yet
she was isolated by terror of her unfathomable moods and unut-
terable secrets.*

*Old Ratoon had been ailing long before 1881. His son,
Caesar, had been itching to put the plantation behind him. Not
because of hardship. They knew comfort and security for the first
time. However, Ratoon was helpless now and how could Caesar*

care for him if they moved? (And nub Kingston self im have fe go fe live good, buy shop, work build up imself?)

Caesar was tied to the plantation as long as his father breathed, for deserting him was unthinkable. At the same time, in the waiting, Caesar's life soured. His wife grew sullen as resentment seethed in her against the old man who hung on, against Emmie and Cassie who had built their own lives.

He tried to explain to her that Emmie and Cassie had nothing with which to support their father, that there was no point their waiting on the plantation too. But she whined and grumbled.

Yet it was a good place. Ratoon and Caesar had built it together from sound planks joined neatly and roofed with fan-palms. Caesar and his wife had a room to themselves and one for the children. The old man dozed night and day in his hammock, which swung low from the rafters. Caesar had floored the place, and hung, rather inexpertly, a door at the end of the hall. He had hewn a long wooden bench which ran along one side of the room and made a good-size table. He had bought rush-bottomed chairs with the produce of a garden crammed with orange and mango trees, plantain suckers and coffee bushes. Well away from the house stood the fowl-roost and pigsty, and beyond spiked a border of pineapples. Hard by the door, a tree laden with alligator pears overhung the roof.

One evening the old man hung awake, swaying peacefully in his hammock and filling the room with the fumes of his short pipe. His daughter-in-law fretted over the iron pot of cocos, okra and saltfish. She threw him a surly glance as he coughed slightly, then she sauntered over to the wall to cut off a few plantains which hung there in the company of a large flat side of saltfish over the yam basket. She split the plantain skins, oiled the plantains and returned them to the skins, pushing them over the fire. Then she took a calabash from a low beam and bent over the oil jar which served as their water container. She reached beside it for a coconut shell fitted with a handle and ladled water into the *calabash, then shuffled in her slatternly way back to the pot.*

"Not even likkle salt-pork," she muttered, eying the cocos in disgust as she prepared to tip the water in.

The old man coughed again and seemed to call, and she swung around irritably.

"Eehi! What you want now. Is water?"

She was reluctant to let the pot burn but dared not let her father-in-law complain to Caesar. So she took the gourd of water over to him, mumbling under her breath why de ole wotless couldn' haul him rass out de hammock fe likkle water. When she reached him she saw that he was dead.

When Caesar came in he stared at his father unblinkingly for a long time. As the loss seeped down he stretched out his hand feeling for his wife. Then his eyes riveted on her face. She was dreaming dry-eyed towards the leaning doorway and out past the roost, beyond the sharp spines of pineapple. He yelled and leapt at her so that she stared dazedly.

"You glad! Glad im dead, you bitch."

Fury that had accumulated through the years of her complaints and goading erupted from him. He boxed her once hard on the jaw and then again raising purpling weals across her mouth. Then he caught her up by the loose stuff of her blouse and shook her.

"Get out," he growled. "Get out 'fore me kill you."

She started to face him and he grabbed at the machete on the wall, blindly. Then she ran. Stumbling over her feet for the door, she ran. So they parted.

All the burden of the wake fell on Caesar, but of course the older women came, a distant aunt and two others. They laid out old man Haynes in the fine clothes he himself had long set aside for the purpose. They studied him and discussed the weather. After all, who could say how long it would take to summon Emmie from Kingston, and it was a hot, wet April. They sent for an even older woman who would know to use the pepper elder and pimento leaves to keep the body intact for burial. Caesar himself was dispatched to inform Cassie.

When Caesar returned he found that his wife had come in his absence and taken the children but no one knew where. Neither had she offered to help with the body. But it was all right, the women cackled, arranging their leaves. What she would know 'bout laying out dead fe wake?

Caesar had no time to speculate about his children. He drew out the funeral boards the old man himself had bought from an elderly carpenter on the estate and he sent for the carpenter. Ratoon had intended to be of as little trouble as possible and had saved quattie by quattie and fippence by fippence, and he had left his own contribution to the proceedings. Caesar loathed the practice of carrying the coffin from door to door and setting it down at the dwellings of those who owed money to the dead. High time all that nonsense was done with, he thought. But old Ratoon must bury good, and Ratoon had been a favourite on the estate so his neighbours turned out promptly to arrange the wake. They threw the shed up, laid in the liquor and set about slaughtering and cooking the hog.

By dusk the women were brewing coffee. Then they settled in the shed and near the fire, rearranging their handkerchiefs suitably around their heads. By nine, most of the men had gathered and it was clear the wake would pass well. Caesar leaned on the rough post of the shed while they drank, sang, argued and exchanged old tales. Most he could understand but a few songs were in the strange language of the Africans who had come recently as indentured servants. Everyone was there. His spirit lifted above grief. Old man woulda proud, he nodded.

Afterwards, even as he began to pack his belongings and sell the animals, his departure loomed near but unreal until the third night passed. Then the neighbours gathered again. The plump, glossy fowl shrieked and fluttered desperately as they bound it and Cassie held the calabash beneath when Caesar brought down the machete. Emmie plucked it and the old women gathered the feathers scrupulously to bury them. There was little that Caesar, Cassie and Emmie had ever done together, but now they huddled over the fowl to cut it into small chunks and cook it unsalted with yam.

"Likkle water, likkle water. Next ting it boil over. If it out one coal self, smaddy ya go dead."

As it cooled, they settled comfortably to wait on cock-crow. Then those who had been closest to old man Haynes set out for the grave. On one side Cassie sprinkled blood from the calabash through her fingers. On the other, Caesar scattered the food.

At the end of nine-night, when the black and white candles had burnt out, they turned over the mattress and spilled the water on the ground outside to free the spirit. Then Caesar realised that he was leaving.

"Hold this paper fe de piece o' land me never sell," he warned Cassie, "lest de pickney-dem come back. Me no see how dem wo'tless mother can raise dem."

"Don't go nowhere fe dead 'mong stranger," Cassie warned.

"What you see?" he whispered.

"Blood round you mouth."

It chilled him, but nothing was stronger than the call of Kingston.

Two days later, he put as much space as possible between himself and the plantation life which was all his family had ever known since Beneba, his grandmother, had been bought.

But when the land grew flat and the road smooth and the buildings leaned closely over him he quailed suddenly and the confidence he had always felt about starting the shop trickled away. Still there was nothing else for him now. He tried to find work in the interim but the road snaked hot and dry between one plantation and another and the money shrivelled. Sugar was failing and the labour market plummeting. Now Caesar struggled for a plot of his own — land was all he knew and what

*was left unsold in St Thomas barely accommodated the house
and could not support him. Now, in the new place, the plain
betrayed him; the earth was mean and dry after what he had
left. Now it seemed no one was buying anything. Miraculously,
he had an offer and sold the failing plot at a loss.*

*What was left he sank hastily into his original plan and
invested in a shop in Kingston. When it too failed, no one would
buy it. He folded the deed carefully in his pocket and closed the
door. Like hundreds of others enticed by Kingston, he stumbled
through the maze and dead-ends of her streets and promises.*

Then the cholera.

*Hundreds dying. There had been a hospital on Goldfields
once, but now the blacks were free — free to die indigent in filth
and futurelessness, to huddle moaning in the crevices of
Kingston, clutching treacherous bellies, squatting in stinking corners to spread the plague wider and more surely. Thousands
dying.*

*Work. There was no work. Business slowed and days drifted
directionless, becalmed by labour shortage and terror of con-
tamination. Nothing purged the disease. Not the gunpowder they
exploded, nor the time designated for prayer, nor the bonfires of
dead-clothes. As the city jarred to a halt, convicts were driven
out to clean the streets; but still the rubbish mounted and coffin-
carts could scarcely force their way between noisome mounds of
decay. Then the convicts themselves succumbed and there were
trenches to be dug and no one to dig them. Caesar fled from the
carts and litters of the dead, hiding in any open field he could
find. He starved himself to procure a supply of cayenne pepper
which people said was the only cure for it, and always he
watched for a way out.*

*When the riots began he ploughed through the mob
that clamoured on the docks to leave for Colon. A burly
captain shoved this way and that along the deck of his schooner
supervising the packing in of human cargo and Caesar bawled*

461

above the others.

"Take me! Take me!"

"Full!" The captain flagged his hands in a gesture of finality.

"Take me!" Caesar screamed. "Me can build." He ripped off his shirt and slapped the iron muscles of his chest and arms. "Is brute this, Massa, not man. Take me!" And the harassed captain allowed him to wedge his way in among the other lucky ones.

They squeezed themselves small so that as many as possible could fit on the open deck, and though the sun blazed down and the salt whipped around them, they calmed. As the shoreline of death receded their dreams gleamed nearer, brighter — visions of building, saving. Panama. Not just a railway — what was a railway to them? It was their lives they would build. Behind them the cholera ravaged thousands, tens of thousands, but these few had escaped. Caesar huddled among the others, hardly able to believe his good fortune.

"What fe you a fe you. Is me beg fe come build railway 'cross swamp."

Caesar worked for eighty cents a day while two inches of rain fell on him in an hour and the locals cursed the Jamaicans as antillanos. (And after couple cent can't buy food fe man. Sell me puppa land fe come ya eat snake and green lizard.)

He and a thousand others camped in Gorgona, on the banks of the Chagres. The earthen floor yielded spongy beneath his step and the wattle and daub walls stank of moisture. Then the Chagres flooded them out, but eventually the settlement dried out, crisper and crisper until bamboo walls exploded into flame, engulfing the thatch of his own hut and razing Gorgona off the world's conscience. He moved to a shack on higher ground and it was better going back there after a day's labour waist-deep in the muck. But night and day blended indistinctly as the mosquitoes needled him and chiggers bloated his feet. Asleep, and at work during his waking nightmares, he sensed huge snakes writhing among the coiling vines that looped low round him in a gloom of sleepless, wakeless monotony of dark days tattered with hallucination. Through the drier vegetation, scorpions and tarantulas scuttled nervously between his feet, while the nearby mudflats heaved slithering forward down the riverbank with half-shut, cold-dead eyes and rotten alligator smile.

The heat crushed in. He breathed dry fire of the noonday sun and wet stench of the swamp. Black wet pillars of tree trunks split and twined to spread their dripping pall of vegetation over air close-shrouded and unmoving for centuries. His flesh, born though it was to the tropics, seemed alternately to fry, to boil and at last to melt from him while his claustrophobia among the giant plants gathered to annihilate him. More and more his mind turned to Cassie and Emmie, but particularly to the older, prophetic sister. His clothes mildewed and turned green before the cough started. Then nothing mattered but getting back to Jamaica.

One day after the next the contractor avoided him. The cough worsened but it was unthinkable to leave without his money. Caesar grew itchy and unpredictable. He bought a gun. Again he demanded to see the contractor, and struck the man at the door then languished for hours in the stocks. He refused to work and was lashed. And still the mould-stained, urine-smelling door to the contractor sealed him from his money with the finality of death. Cassie nodded knowingly through his mind. Blood round you mouth.

When he began to spit blood he knew he must die anywhere but in the turgid filth under the giant palm shadows. He pulled the gun from his shirt and fired wildly, shattering the overseer's knee, and he ran. So after three years of labour Caesar escaped penniless and stumbled towards the city of Panama where he met Lee Yuen.

Lee Yuen was a Chinese from the camp of Matachin. From

463

bottomless experience he recognised a dying man. He drew Caesar into the shade of a deserted hovel and spared him a precious dose from his diminishing supply of opium. Few indeed had any opium left but Lee Yuen drew on it only to buy, in modest instalments, his own survival.

Still and patient as a statue he squatted, waiting as the black man shuddered and muttered on the heap of rags. It was a contented sound, for Caesar was dreaming of the clean, cool mountains above the cottage at the edge of Goldfields and of clear water sparkling below.

When Caesar opened his eyes it was dark. He made out the broad, flat outlines of Lee Yuen's face and muttered hesitantly, "Speakee English?"

Lee Yuen indicated a small amount between his thumb and forefinger.

"Is what you bring me here for?"

Lee Yuen pushed a small bowl of grey soup towards him and pointed to the rest of his opium supply. Caesar stared at him suspiciously. "Is wha' you want from me?"

It took time, unstructured and unquantifiable before they understood each other. But then, Caesar had nothing left to do but to try to decipher Lee Yuen.

Lee Yuen was one of a hundred and ninety-five Chinese who stepped off the schooner to Kingston that month and melted into the labour force of Jamaica. He passed several years in the island before locating Emmie Haynes and telling her how Caesar had died. Tuberculosis, but peacefully, with opium. He unfolded the note her brother had written. It was semi-literate and barely legible, but conveyed that Lee Yuen was caring for him and that the shop should be turned over to the Chinese.

Emmie stared at him, not with the hostility he had expected, but with contempt.

"Shap!" she muttered derisively. "After shap no worth nothing. Soso crasses." Her voice shrilled slightly as she threw a grin of

pure ridicule at the Chinese. "You know what name crasses, 'Queeze Eye?"

Lee Yuen considered her for some time before speaking. It was always so before he spoke, a long pause as he weighed the value of the effort. He ran his eyes over her full, tight flesh. He had no capital to send home for a girl and few Chinese women would consider emigrating. He pushed a chair forward, peering at her unwaveringly with his alien, inscrutable eyes and slowly, as if mesmerised, she lowered herself onto it. His face remained expressionless while he spoke and after a time she seemed not to notice his strange version of Jamaican speech, not to distinguish his voice at all, only to see, hear and smell the crowds jostling for sale to the ends of the earth.

At first it was no different to other tales she had heard passed down of sales and crossings. Twenty-five dollars apiece. Eight hundred souls locked in nightmare passage. Death on shipboard. Then docking and mounting fatalities. Bodies thrown away without rites or burial drifted, sank or in some cases bobbed back again alongside, days later, full-blown horrors. Emmie did not understand about Matachin, and Lee Yuen interpreted from his own experience the name of the place where the new imports lodged on arrival.

"Matar mean kill. And Chinos. Matachin: kill Chinee. A so we say."

Work was impossible, circled as they were by death creeping on the stench of the swamp, and as their lives drained away in stomach disorders and evaporated in fever. The Railroad agreed to dispense opium, and the workers' perception of horror clouded mercifully.

Then rumour spread and blazed into scandal. The Railroad was trafficking in opium. The Irish complained and the priests denounced the heathen Chinese and the abominations they practised in a Christian country. Opium was expensive anyway and the Railroad was relieved to stop it.

*Lee Yuen had used little and now he stopped and hoarded all
he had. The others woke up and looked directly on Matachin,
putrid with filth, violence and disease. Typhoid, yellow fever,
malaria, dysentery, smallpox, hook worm, pneumonia, tuberculosis. Those who were healthy drank themselves into oblivion
or slashed out at each other. Inside too, they were rent by addic-
tion. They sweated for the opium, clutched their bellies and
bawled that worms gnawed them within.*

*"You mus' know what 'appen next. Evlyone hear bout
Matachin. Chinee-dem take machete and sharpen stick, trow
demself 'pon de stick. Dey tie on rock, jump in river. Twist rope
an' vine round dem neck and jump. Some hang demself in dem
own hair. All de camp, de ground, de river, swingin' from de
tree — dead Chinee."*

*Opium had never fooled Lee Yuen, and when it stopped noth-
ing looked different. But awakening in the camp to shrunken
feet swaying slackly in loose pantaloons, hanging tree after
creaking tree, and.... Almost, almost he had grabbed up a
machete too, but then he ran. And ran and ran until he fell
upon the road unconscious.*

*"No work 'pon line after dat. Night come, night go. 'Fraid
sleep. Next ting me see foot a heng roun' me head, hundred a
foot in big, dutty pant'lon. Me find me way a city, beg. People
dem help me, but still only beg-beg. Den I hear boat might go
Jamaica."*

*All the Chinese he saw drifted on the street, oozing sores. Then
he met Caesar Haynes who talked, when he could, about the sea,
the mountains and a waterfall at a clear green pool. There was a
shop he had at home too, but here nowhere to die in peace. And
always he babbled of clean water. Rivers and the sea, rain, clean
water. Lee Yuen found what water he could and washed him.*

*"One day when I come I find he take all de opium done and
sleep way clean. So I take paper fe shop and tu'n in meself, ask
go a Kingston. Rai'road glad to trade mash-up Chinee for fresh*

Jamaica nega."

Lee Yuen had been silent for several minutes before Emmie realised he was finished, for his face gave no sign. She was sure he had speeded Caesar by administering the overdose himself, but when she thought of it further she was grateful. Then again, she thought, he was honest about his interest in the shop, unsentimental in his account of Caesar, decent in rendering any account to her at all. Behind his mask of a face worked a quick mind and his tortured past of servitude and survival was not so different from her own. And probably he had feelings after all behind the deadpan exterior. And who else but she would ever know who or what he was?

Speculation lit her eyes with lively interest and, in the end, she moved in with Lee Yuen and produced faithfully, year after year, a succession of slant-eyed brown babies.

Only once she went back to St Thomas to see Cassie on the edge of Goldfields. Cassie was silent and contemptuous for most of the visit because she said Emmie was living with some type of a yellow white man and had forgotten her own people. So Emmie slunk away confused and a little guilty for a while, but then, as her belly swelled again and the children laughed and tumbled around her and the shop flourished so that Lee Yuen hammered on a new wing, then she forgot to feel guilty. She listened hungrily for other tales of Colon. A man named Alexander Bedward had had a vision there that returned him to Jamaica, but she never met him to find out if he had known Caesar.

Her children grew and her grandchildren misspelt their name as Leon. But Emma cared nothing for names. She clung to her Chinaman, as the neighbours called him, she cradled Caesar in sad, but tender moments of recollection, and she pushed Cassie to a far, dark corner of her mind and never returned to Goldfields.

But Cassie never left. Her one child, Rita, ran away and two years later returned pregnant, crying for help to get rid of the pickney. When the child was born Rita deserted it for Cassie to name and raise.

Louise. Cassie had taught her everything and cared for no one else. After Cassie's death, Louise Haynes sprinkled blood from the calabash beside her grandmother's grave, and she would never be afraid of blood again. When she squeezed out the rag with which she scrubbed the Stollmeier library after Joseph's suicide she thought only of Cassie.

But it had been different for Louise's son. Austin had never seen blood until his mother's welled up, dripped from kitchen scissors and gushed into a sticky circle around his feet. And the woman with the scissors had slashed forever on his mind her face — a death mask of rage and terror — and the scissors plunging, spurting his mother's life under his feet, so he fell and lay tethered in it as the death smell rose and swallowed him.

Then there was Les who alone after Louise's death had offered refuge and laughter, and for Les perhaps hatred could be deferred. Perhaps. But then at last Les must be arranged for, Les blown away. And from then the path twisted further, darkened more. Half in earnest hunt, half playful, sniffing after Pearl and trapping Adam (spoilt child of spoilt children). Exigencies of Austin's livelihood in the gun and drug trade intersected his blood trail of remembered pain till greed and vengeance merged in a common odour quickening excitement almost sexual in its urgency. Even as new hurdles rose — competition from foreign posses and international criminals, the dawning suspicion of old acquaintances — Austin padded along paths recalled, lost and crossed again with here and there the smell of the past rising and maddening. And by now Austin had as much inhibition about violence as any predator in feeding frenzy.

After Les, blood meant nothing.

26
Jetsam

WHEN UNCLE had driven out, Gerry tiptoed to the door and drew the latch deliberately. Uncle had ordered him never to bolt it and Gerry sensed a cold rage at the centre of Uncle that punished brutally and passionlessly at the same time. But the notion of locking doors was deep in him from the days with Sugar and Grand Paul, and those were the good days. He set his mouth wilfully and snapped the night lock as well.

Gerry was confused by Uncle. Austin Louis seldom addressed the child but seemed now to listen attentively when Gerry spoke. Then Uncle and Mummy. Pearl. She had said call her Pearl, not Mummy.

Gerry tried to empty his mind, but his stomach churned. If Uncle had whipped Gerry, that would have been painful but understandable. But that he had beaten Pearl unstructured Gerry's understanding of everything. Then afterwards Uncle had stroked and fondled her, his fingers skidding crimson smears on her back. It chilled Gerry because Uncle's smile was still murderously angry and Pearl, speechless for once, froze paralysed with terror. Now she was gone.

Uncle looked like everyone else, but Gerry had lived with him and glimpsed beneath the polish something dark and twisted. In the little messages that Gerry drew for Grand Paul and posted in the cracks of the retaining wall round Uncle's house, Gerry confided that Uncle was a monster in disguise.

Car wheels crunched on the driveway. Then the handle turned quickly and the door bumped as from a confident push.

Uncle's car wheels never grated the gravel on the edge of the drive and the headlamps always reflected in the cabinet when he drove in. This car had taken the bend differently. So Gerry sat quietly and waited. The handle rattled impatiently again, and he held his breath. For a minute or two there was nothing more, but the motionlessness of a dark presence interrupted the line of light under the door. Then came a gentle tapping, too playful for the recent, irritable rattling of the handle.

"Goodnight? Goodnight?"

Gerry flattened himself into the sofa and hardly breathed. Footsteps crunched and faded around to the side door. Gerry crept around to the back of the half-press near it and waited.

A key grated in the lock and the door, swollen with the rain, scraped outward. A thick, clean-shaven man with matted hair put his face in then filled the doorway. He saw Gerry instantly.

"Boy?" he said. "Come. I you uncle friend. He say fe come."

The man himself didn't frighten Gerry; but the lie startled him. Uncle had no friends that Gerry had ever known to visit him in a faded T-shirt through the side door. And a key. Though he had knocked.

The child plastered himself against the wall and stared up unblinkingly.

"What wrong wid you? Nah hear me say come?"

Not a muscle moved on the child.

"Eh! Eh! You cyan't make sound? Dat good."

The man lifted him and Gerry felt a scream of fury rising up from deep in him, but as his mouth opened the man clamped his hand across it and lifted him outside with his feet kicking about harmlessly like a dying roach.

It was a big car, long like the ones in New York. The man slammed him down muffling his mouth and pressing him with his elbow to the cool leather of the seat. With his other hand he yanked the door shut. All the windows were up and nothing was audible but a soft humming from the front.

"Now shut you mout', you likkle bitch, or I go beat the shit out you."

The man released him and Gerry stared up silently. Some of the words were new but what was required of him was clear enough. The dripping trees and the lamp poles sped away, and the car went down, down, swirling around the curves. Soon there were no lights, only black bush on each side of the narrow winding strip and at last just the grey rock of the hillside on one hand and on the other the lights of the city sparkling in the darkness of the plain below.

They reached the bottom and the streets seemed vaguely familiar but hopelessly empty. Then the buildings grew older and dingier with burnt out gaps between them and the streets coiled mean and twisted so that the man drove slower. Gerry had never been this way before and it was ugly and hateful. He never knew when his hand shot out, wrenching the door handle. The man grabbed at him and the child bit down until he tasted blood.

"Claat!"

The shriek warped to a snarl following the boy who lunged out and rolled into the gutter, feeling neither asphalt nor concrete and forgetting his feet, only just slithering lizard-like into a crevice that gaped in the burnt wall and pressing himself into the stonework.

The man braked instantly and plunged out after him swearing. He turned heavily this way and that, rummaged about the rubbish heaps and piles of debris and broken stone. After a while the car started, moved a little way up the road and stopped. It was time to move, the child thought. Get up and run. But he couldn't move. Then there was a soft scraping on the broken pavement near him and he could see the man, first just his shadow, then his arm, shoulder, body, gliding along the wall, his back to it, his hands poised gently, waiting. Soon he slid right past the child, his calves just level with the taut face pressed on the brick. The legs paused right before him. Gerry felt the sob coming up, up. But it never broke, for the man turned away sharply with a muttered curse and in a few minutes the car pulled off and its hum faded into the night.

Five minutes is a long time to sit in a corner, half-an-hour excruciating. Gerry had no idea how long he crouched under the wall before his brain, numbed with the terror of the man, would allow him to move.

When he scratched his way out of the crevice and onto the ground he sat a while, gulping air and sobbing intermittently with a soft hiccough. His shorts were soaked and his knees raw. When he staggered to his feet they seemed fluid beneath him and his body shuddered at every breath. But after a while he began to feel his way along the wall, to the corner of the building, turning, testing his way along the other wall, till at last he stepped out on the far side of the ruin. He moved shakily, hardly in control of his limbs, but quietly as he could. For now he was terrified for the first time. Not because it occurred to him that the man might return. The man had come inexplicably from nowhere and had disappeared again into the dark. But the place was awful. Dirty. Patchy with peeling paint and posters. Rustling with roaches. Stink with garbage, urine and some bloated dead animal. Weird with black, jagged ends of wood and broken beams and gaping holes in the concrete. He placed his feet gingerly, not to touch anything.

Once he stopped, his mouth opening spasmodically and a vast, rushing, straining sensation inside. He leaned forward and screamed briefly twice, three times. When he stopped vomiting he sagged against the wall for a while whimpering hopelessly. Nothing like this had ever happened to him before. It seemed strange to leave it all there, everything that was supposed to be inside him, but what was he to do? It was a terrible choice. He wiped his mouth on his jersey and deliberated. Strangely he was not as weak now.

At the far end of a black, tunnel-like lane gleamed flashes of car lights. Vaguely formed a vision of adult guidance. That automatic know-how. Someone to take him over, take him home. A lady, he thought. That would be good. And perhaps she would take him to the Grands. Sugar would set a warm bath for him. Bubbles. He let his mind play with memories as he wandered aimlessly through the shattered back streets of downtown Kingston.

Outside the Half Way Tree cemetery, Paul and Ben scrambled back to the car and tugged at the stubborn doors. It started easily but there were no lights.

"Damn!" Paul breathed.

Ben sprang out and glanced in front.

"Headlights gone."

"The looters."

They started again and rattled down the road a few yards before the car shuddered and coasted to a halt. Ben jumped out and opened the bonnet, wrenched at a wire or two and slammed it shut again.

"Too dark," he moaned.

"No time for this." Paul looked around wildly.

"You couldn't get it up Jack's Hill anyway."

Everywhere was dark except for a building off to the right. They looked at each other. They were thinking together now, no need to put anything into words. They tried the car again and it moved. They forced it on to South Odeon Avenue and stopped outside the Jamaica Broadcasting Corporation. Beyond the locked gates, the JBC was alive with lights and in the yard a few cars were parked. Paul knocked on the gate with a stone.

'Eehi?"

"We want to request a community service announcement. Death in the family. I have to contact my sister."

He was amazed at his own fluency. Of course he had done all this before, just after Adam's death when they wanted to find Pearl.

The watchman shuffled across, scratching his belly.

"Don't lock up too tight, officer. Won't be long. In fact," Ben wagged a finger authoritatively, "better not lock up at all. We going have to get a tow from a friend in here. You know the car break down 'pon us up the road?"

"No, sah!" The watchie regarded him in astonishment. "Well. Dem no make nothing like long time, eeh, sah?"

"Quite true, brother, quite true."

Watchie nodded respectfully at the Reverend, casting an understanding smirk at the smeared and sweat-stained clothes of the two gentlemen. Their speech had given them away, of course. Even without the stock he would have known they were not supposed to look so.

He watched them till they reached the door then glanced irritably around the gate to trace an odour he could not identify. Must be that old dog with the rotten foot come back, he speculated. He concentrated his attention on the road, his eyes searching a heap of litter on the sidewalk.

Inside the premises the two men dived into the shadow of the building towards the cars. The first had a bonnet lock. Another was relatively new — Ben feared it might have an alarm. The next was a green Toyota, perhaps two years old. Easy. Pick the lock. Paul edged in and opened the other door. As soon as Ben got the starter and the engine turned over he slammed the bonnet and jumped in. They stared at each other in shock for a fraction of a second.

"I didn't know you could pick a lock," Paul gasped as he jerked the car out of the shadows. "And by braille?"

"Papa always said I'd live to be hung."

Ben nodded reassuringly at the bewildered watchman as they squealed past him onto the Avenue.

The Toyota whirled past the Half Way Tree clock tower and sped on into view of Devon House.

"Oh, aahm. I leaving the gun on the back seat." Ben muttered as the car slowed.

"Gun?"

"Same old rifle. Is loaded." He slid out at the corner of Trafalgar and Hope Roads before Paul could protest, and the car swung away past Devon House and along Hope Road.

Grace and Sarah waited. In other words, Sarah sat stiffly in the rocker staring into the lamp and Grace plugged in the polisher. The rocker poised motionless, then Sarah erupted.

"Father in heaven, woman! What in the name of Moses you think you doing in the middle of the night?"

Grace twitched the cord from around her feet impatiently.

"Tcha! Not disturbing a soul. Houses empty all round us. Or you worried about the one-legged gentleman?"

"Eh?"

"Squatter in the garage over the way."

"But what the devil has got into the woman? You're disturbing me, if you want to know, disturbing me. This unwholesome hour, in the middle of all we...." Sarah broke off, shaking her head.

"Well I'm not moving out and leaving the house in this condition," Grace pouted.

Sarah stared at her in disbelief. Was it possible Grace was breaking down? After a while Grace shrilled, "What you want me do, sit and stare into the light too?"

"Well, but pick peas, or read a book or God knows what. But that confounded uproar?"

"I need an uproar. I must have it." Grace's sob broke to a low, suddenly reasonable tone. "I like to do it when Paul is out of the house. He can't stand it."

"Well neither can I."

"Ah well. You are out so often."

"Have patience, woman. I'll be out for good soon enough."

"Nasty."

They bickered on more quietly to comfort each other, though their voices were hardly audible above the shriek of the machine. Grace untied the old cloth which hung through the cord of the polisher. She walked through the house with the duster. It was soothing, rubbing mahogany to a soft glow under the wide hanging lights. She brushed the cane seat of a rocking chair and paused. Imagine that cane still held. Mama had sat in it with Les. She could remember. Stella and Grace had rocked Adam and then Grace had rocked Gerry.

She sat in it again and rocked a little as she rubbed the arms with the duster. She looked past Sarah, rocking in another chair, past the hard sheen of the dining table and into the spare room to the new bed Papa had made for Mama before he died. Irrelevantly she thought, why not run the machine over the floor again.

"Oh, go ahead, girl," Sarah signalled, reading the thoughts printed on Grace's face, "I suppose I want to be disturbed."

Grace guided the polisher along the grain of the wood, watching the floor pick up gold tones among brown, ripplelike markings. The ancient polisher shrieked and shuddered with a pleasing familiarity and little by little the smudges were sucked or rubbed away, fur shed by Mrs Whiskers, bruises or smears from garden shoes, damp marks where Morgan had slumped down immediately after she had last polished. Backwards and forwards. Tiles, ha. They could keep them. The secret, she pondered yet again, was never to use water. Never. For years they had been swept and polished, backwards and forwards along the grain. Every board was good and hard, rippling browns, gold lights and occasional black knots, warm and safe beneath their feet.

She flicked off the switch to wipe her forehead and froze, her ear cocked to the window. The rustling stopped instantly. Mrs Whiskers jumped from the floor to a chair and, unthinkably, onto the dining table. Grace swung towards her with a scandalised gesture then paused, stopped again by a faint but unmistakable muttering beyond the window. She peered at the latches. All bolted. She knew everywhere was locked. Then she saw her own shadow, thrown by the light across the frosted glass of the window. She dropped at once to the floor, kicked off her shoes and skidded across almost on her stomach into the corner by the cabinet. Sarah followed her with wide shocked eyes, but pressed herself back into her chair and said nothing.

Grace thought quickly and coldly of the phone and rolled silently towards it. It was an effort not to grab it but she managed to raise the receiver gently so that the click was imperceptible even to her. Dead. She rested it on the ground and her forehead was damp and cold.

There was muttering outside, then a voice raised.

"Who in dere?"

The women stared at each other. Sarah's skin gleamed paper thin and yellow.

Muttering again, "Dem no answer."

"Dem nah go answer. Just talk."

"A'right. Hear what I say. Unno have something in ya we want.... Give me an we go lef' you alone."

"Tcha! Dem nah give you. Weaste time!"

An impatient exclamation and muttered obscenity.

"One book you have. Notebook. (Is diary im say?) Book belong to one Les Goldman. Push it t'rough de window an we go lef' you."

There was a long pause while the women sat staring incredulously at the dead phone. The voice outside thickened, loaded with threat.

"No make we have fe bruck in."

Grace shrank over to Sarah and gripped her arm. "What we can do?"

"Can't fight. No use talking."

"The book?"

Sarah's mouth barely moved. "If they want it, it must have something. Uncle or.... We must find Gerry."

They stared at each other and footsteps shuffled at the door.

"We go beat it out you."

Grace didn't look at Sarah now for her mind keened, it will kill Goddie. The slightest push would snap a limb, a hip.

"The book?" she faltered.

"No!" Sarah spat. "I'd rather be dead."

Something heavy and metallic scraped on the tiles beyond the door. Inside an idea flickered.

"Right," Sarah breathed. "Try frighten them, Grace. Tell them there's a dead in the house."

"Goddie!"

"People superstitious. What else we can try?"

Grace edged nearer to the door. She was drenched in cold sweat and her feet could hardly carry her.

"Aahm. You can hear me?"

Sudden muttering, then silence. Then, "Eehi. Talk!"

"Listen, I going beg you. I in such a state here. Me mother die this evening. Just a while ago. I waiting on Sam Isaacs's man from the mortuary." She glanced at Sarah. Hopeless, she thought.

"Lady," the voice hissed, deadly quiet, "no test me. Pass out de book."

The two women held each other and Sarah gasped rapidly, "Whatever they do. Whatever they do either of us. When the boys come back make the book be here." Crouching, she crept over to the desk, pulled the book out of a drawer and backed into her bedroom.

But Grace grabbed Paul's diary, rolled it and stretched up to shove it between the bars and out through the three-inch opening they allowed the windows at night. There was a pause, then a crash and tinkle of glass as the book was hurled back through the pane.

"Wrong year, ole woman. Twelve years too late. Me go chop you one chop fe every year."

A crunching thud shook the door, then another and another. Grace edged away. The men worked noisily but it didn't matter for there was no one near on the road to interrupt.

"Eh! Eh!" one shouted. "Is wha' 'appen to Catman?"

"Nah come."

"Come of course. Im gone back fe something down de gully."

"Tell im bring im arse ya wid de blowtorch."

"Eh, woman!" A different voice raised. "Woman! Answer, you bitch."

"Unno bust de door done an beat de rass out a dem."

The chopping at the door went on relentlessly, hacking at Grace's brain.

"If no dead in de house when we come in, we go see dead dey before we go."

Over and over she told them there was no book there.

"Police take it," she repeated.

It was no use. They had been sent for it.

Who knew about the book? The question hammered inside her head so loudly that for a second she thought they had asked it.

"I don't know! I don't know!" she whispered, over and over.

One gripped her chin to turn up her face and she searched his eyes for the answer. He squeezed her and she struggled desperately.

"Frighten, brown woman?" He grinned and looked about him. "Eh! Eh! But look how de brown woman frighten. Wha' 'appen?"

he turned back to her. "Tink say me go lick you?"

He pulled her face to him and kissed her long and wetly, digging his fingers into her clothes.

"Jesu!" she gasped. "I'm an old woman."

He sucked at her mouth again then flung her back against the wall. "You old, yes."

He boxed her, one brutal blow across the jaw that smashed her against the wall and she slid to the ground. Then he hauled her up. "Come, show me you modder. Who you have old enough to be you modder. Poor dead Mumma."

"Eh! Ivan!" One of the others interrupted his taunts with a shout of surprise. "Watch ya!"

Ivan sprang to the doorway where the other man stood, hauling Grace with him. It was a bedroom. On the bed a motionless figure lay shrouded in white linen.

"Is a dead fe true?"

The man walked hesitantly to the bed and took the corner of the sheet unwillingly.

"Lie!" Ivan spat. He shoved the other aside and flung back the covering, than sprang back blaspheming.

The body was laid out, straight and rigid, arms symmetrically arranged, blue grey hands folded around a worn Bible. He stared in horror at it, his eyes travelling uncontrollably to its face, gaunt yellow on the flat white sheet. It looked strained and hideous in death, sunken grey around the eyes and hollow under the cheekbones. The lids were transparent pale, etched with a thousand tiny crinkles.

Shuddering he jerked the sheet back over it. He turned back on Grace.

"How old she was? What she dead from?"

"Nearly a hundred."

He stared at her then he seemed to relax.

"A'right." He shoved her back against the dressing table and leaned heavily on her. "De book now."

She stared at him dazedly as he raised his fist, then she fainted.

Huddled in the corner of Sarah's room where they had dropped her, Grace lost count of time. She twitched her limbs cautiously so as not to attract attention. Her right arm was on fire with pain. Ivan had stamped on it.

The house was upturned, drawers tumbled. From time to time they turned on her, questioned again, boxed her. Once Ivan jerked his thumb savagely towards the still figure on the bed and said,

"Make we chop de Mumma see if de woman wi talk." He swung to Grace. "Chop 'er?"

With a tremendous effort Grace lifted her shoulders a fraction of an inch. She could hardly speak.

"She dead already," she whispered.

They turned back to the search. They began to smash things wilfully. One snatched up a mahogany chair that Ben had carved and smashed it through the glass of the china cabinet. Belle's tea set splintered into a thousand shining fragments. Joseph Stollmeier's antique mirror that had passed through Rudy to Sarah shattered out of existence. They kicked out the glass panels of the front door and sliced sofa cushions and mattresses. Crisply, competently, Ivan capsized the desk drawer which normally contained the diary. He pounced on an old leatherbound volume of Browning with a grunt of satisfaction. It was about the size and colour of the diary, inscribed, "For Grace, How do I love thee. Paul."

"Bumbo!" Ivan pitched it aside in disgust then grinned across at Grace, deliberately unfastening his pants and urinating on it.

"Not it dat?" one called.

"Nothing," Ivan choked, "not a rass!"

"Dem hide it."

"Nah here, man."

"Hide it, me tell you. No hear Busha say is here?"

Through the nightmare it exploded at her. Busha.

The past shattered her mind with a hundred pictures, the faces of Austin Louis. Austin helping them sift Adam's papers and gather details of his investments and accounts. Austin combing Les's appointment book with them. Austin running with them to the gate when they heard Adam screaming, cradling Les against a blood-soaked shirt. Uncle. B for Busha. Austin Louis, Louise's son.

She looked up, shock-riven, as the betrayal shuddered through her with gathering force. The man called Ivan read her face steadily, curiously.

"She hear, yes."

His companion slipped his hand into his shirt and everything narrowed to a tiny point and there was nothing else to see in the room, no room, only one thing left in existence. The small, round black mouth of the gun. Gaping. Filling the room. She tried to pray.

"Wait!" Ivan's voice was sharp and peremptory. "She wi' talk before we done."

The gun wavered and lowered and one by one they faded out of the room. She sank onto the floor again, feeling her bladder give way, and she lay drenched in the darkness.

Then empty of all else, she became possessed by one thought. Gerry. Grace was a practical woman and, immobilised as she was, her mind still functioned. She willed herself to look one by one at the possibilities. Not for herself; she was finished. But for Gerry.

First of all, dexterously she put aside the notion that there were various possibilities. Gerry would be all right. Paul and Ben would find him. Of course they would find him. And he would be... she did not mentally pronounce the word "alive" because of course it implied the doubt, its shadow, running along beside it and stretching longer and longer as the night wore on. But of course they would find him and he would be all right. But she was an honest woman, a clear thinker. Too clear for her own good. She knew she had to face the possibility that when they found him he might be just slightly hurt. Bruised, perhaps. Then, no. No, they would find him innocently unaware of danger, building his blocks with fierce concentration as usual and lift him, perfect, perfect child, safely away. She hugged her good arm about herself, cradling him in her thoughts.

But the fact was that he could be a little hurt, a little frightened when they found him.

It began to flash unbidden at the back of her mind. Not a light, a blackness. (The world without Gerry: black hole in consciousness.) Every time it came she rushed to block it but it was irregular, unpredictable, uncontrollable. A small form, sprawling. She headed it off, forcing in its place the lifting, cradling. But it was there again, a blot of pain at the edge of reason. No, no. Block that. She breathed quickly, overcome by haste. Running, running this way and that in her mind, setting up image after image between her soul and the shadow. Jesu, she gasped, help me.

Then she stopped, cornered by her own judgement. It was there. Look at it. They could find him dead. No. Never, never. But stop. She was dodging again. They could find him dead. Briefly she saw it, brutal in its clarity, little legs sprawling, the gully or the dump heap, and instantly nausea rose in her, a vast sickness at herself for being capable of entertaining the vileness of it even for a second. Blot it out, blot it out. The horror receded draining her of consciousness so that she was left with one ill-formed notion, almost callous. No guarantee that they would find him. It pierced into her deeply, vitally.

Old rumours about Austin Louis surfaced from her subconscious. Les had always scoffed at them but Ben had insisted Les was naive. Ben said Busha liked boys. She had never believed any of it. She had even objected delicately that she had heard of men who were... that way... and gentle. Like anyone else apart from... that. But Ben had said they were all the same and never to leave any boy child with Busha. Then Gerry and Uncle. Suppose. He might want Gerry alive even more than he needed him dead. No, no, her mind screamed. But the dark beast of reason mocked with loathsome insistence, Well but he might. In which case... better dead?

This way and that her mind stumbled till she was dazed and exhausted and a grey heaviness rose around her. She felt herself sinking and grasped from one image to the next, the cuddling unaware child, the child just a little hurt, barely frightened. But it was all too insubstantial to hold onto. She sank, stunned, deeper and deeper into the thickness of it. With a strange clarity she knew herself sinking just as her mind flickered vividly in its desperation. Her sensations numbed under a creeping inertia.

Time passed, then stood still.

She was crumpled in the corner. Physically she had not moved a muscle and she was sure she would never move, and it didn't matter. Listlessly she wondered if she had ceased to care deeply about anything, even the child. She felt her soul grown cold and sluggish. What is this stupor, she wondered idly. Aah, I'm having a stroke. Soon I'll think nothing at all. I'll be dead or alive and not know the difference. The sweetness of the idea began to spread over her, lulling her further. They would say, Poor Grace, thank God she was spared. When they didn't find him — or when they did. Let her go, let her go.

Then she started; something slapped her on the mind. Suppose. No, face facts. Yes, but just suppose. Almost wholly she was certain she would never see the child again. Never squeeze him, hear him laugh, taste his tears, watch his lashes curl in sleep. Better be dead. Spared, they murmured. But suppose they said, Poor Grace, why couldn't she have been spared.

To see him safe, watch him grow, play, stumble, stand again. Help him learn, laugh with him. Laugh and laugh over the past. That was it. Worth risking any amount of horror in the present. Live Grace.

Excruciatingly she forced her attention back to the corner she was in. She pushed at her feet and they moved. She flexed them experimentally and pressed a hand gingerly to the ground to get up. A hot, upward gush of pain made her gasp, test again. Broken, she thought. She tried the other and it worked. Her legs tingled with cramps like a million stinging ants busy in all directions. Her back moved stiffly; her knees were sore. She leaned on the broken cabinet, shifting from one dead foot to the other. The men were outside.

She listened. The silence was appalling. She knew they weren't finished or they would have killed her. She crept to the bed and leaned over it.

"Darling," she breathed.

The still form did not move. She raised the sheet and whispered again, "Goddie, darling."

She stared at her unable to believe it. So it was real after all, the counterfeit death they had connived at. The strain. Her heart. Her eyes flooded over and she sank on the bed gazing at this woman she had loved all her life.

Then she noticed it — her ear. Lord. Goddie, Goddie, darling. She struggled to the dresser and pulled out the hearing aid. Goddie couldn't hear her, of course she couldn't hear her. It would have given her away if she had kept it in, so she had lain down in absolute silence. No wonder her face had been a mask of horror. She had lain in silence all the time with her eyes closed, not knowing when they would lift the cover or what would become of her when they did. Fingers quivering Grace pushed the button into her ear and stroked her face.

"Darling."

Instantly the wrinkled lids popped open and the women

stared at each other incredulously.

"Jesu!" Sarah said. And again and again it was all she could say. "Jesu, Jesu!"

"Goddie."

"When you didn't come I thought you were dead. I just waited and waited. I knew I mustn't move till the boys came. And then I began to wonder how I would know it was them... to open my eyes. And all the while... I thought they had killed you when.... Why didn't you come? You're hurt, Gracie. Jesu. They... hurt you?"

"They didn't kill me. And they didn't find it. So they can't be gone. You can't get up yet. But I don't know where it is. Wherever you hid it they didn't find it."

"Better you don't know."

"They going come back. They wouldn't leave me if they weren't coming back."

Her eyes roved the room and Sarah said, "Nothing here, only the scissors."

"No. Remember the fork?" She felt behind the wardrobe. "Paul made me bring in Mama's little light one."

It was a slender garden fork with sharp, tapering tines.

"I'll keep this," she said. "I pushing the scissors here, under you shoulder."

"All the way up there?"

"You hands going be up at your chest... crossed."

"Oh, yes."

Grace wiped her forehead but the perspiration trickled icily down her back. She kissed Sarah, put away the hearing aid and covered her again. Then she dragged over the armchair and sat down with the fingers of her good hand resting on the sheet over Sarah's shoulder and the other arm supported on the bed. And they waited, for there was nowhere to hide but in silence.

27
The Trail

AUSTIN LOUIS turned from the plains of old Kingston onto the winding approach up Jack's Hill to the massive retaining wall of his house, and he wrenched the steering wheel violently. The men would be out, of course. They had to be out of the way and they were needed at the strip in any case. Illogically, the silence baffled him.

His jaw muscles clenched rigid and his bronze skin washed out to grey. He struggled to get a grip on himself but turbulent sensations churned in him, fury and frustration rising, settling, rising. Hell down at the strip tonight and it was going to get worse. Landing fee gone up gone up. Mus' get worse. Was one thing with police and Defence Force men. Then the regulars — pilots, gas suppliers. All right, all right, must have likkle scavenger-dem hanging round fe pick up a smalls.

But then. Cold sweat shot from him. When the pay-off forge, make one of you own posse wipe off the white man head and make off with half a million dollars gone, drop the corpse down inna sink hole make police find it — is then you dead to rass. No mind what you do to cover loss like that — mix the bottom level of ganja with tanzi weed — no make no difference, for after when the white man come down, him come down with him friends and gun muzzle inna you face.

Get out. The airline ticket in his breast pocket rustled reassuringly. Clean up and get out.

His mind, which raced easily along several levels at once, clicked to the dogs. Mus' let out. Especially with the men gone.

Of course, dog had fe lock up, yes, make what-im-name get in for the boy.

His neck muscles tensed and the years slumped their weight across his shoulders, and he had been the boy's age.... He intercepted the thought with recollection of the fat white man in his big fish-tail car, but then the memory of the white man's six burly friends crushed in on him and his brain raced on to the necessary arrangements. But below his calculations throbbed the yearning to wrap himself in soft flesh. Pearl had got older than he liked his women to be. Shoulda well keep the boy. Not that boys appealed to him, and he had only bided his time in the sullen chill of Gerry's hostility. The child's blatant rudeness had grown on Austin's nerves even as time ran out. In fact, it was when Austin was preparing to vanish from Jamaica for good that Pearl had stormed in, tearful with suspicions and demands. So the boy talk fe true, eh?

Realisation of all Gerry had absorbed and retained had stunned Austin momentarily before he gathered himself and shut Pearl's mouth. But why did it surprise him, for his own memories were sharp as steel. He had been little older than Gerry yet even now the branches of the cotton tree writhed through Austin's mind and, beneath, his mother stooped among gnarled roots, shadowed by the woman with the fire mark that split her hairline. Now, memories of Adam dying at the airport flashed on Gerry more and more with his mother's disappearance. Now he fired question after question and fussed for the old people. Of course, even if he did talk to them then.... Tcha! Year gone by. How they could connect him.... Still, soon the boy would learn fe look up phone number— anyway, im well can talk now tell anybody who Uncle name....

Austin recalled a time without a name, with only insistent, repeated questions that had no answers. His mother's name was all there was. He saw the room in the tenement as sharply as he had suddenly recalled it when he sat on the floor with Les at the foot of Stella's bed and, without her cap, Stella's servant leaning above them was marked as by lightning.

And with that thought dropped the final trap door in Austin's brain. Below the simultaneous and parallel lines of reasoning about travel arrangements and pay-offs yawned a dimension of mind dark and unfathomable beyond control. He glimpsed the Goldmans through a chink in the past that sucked him back into a black and stinking hold gouged in his brain where he was tethered in his mother's blood thickening to slime as her body burst and leaked before him. Then it was Les's blood that cursed and purged him and the clamour surrounded him for the name which was somewhere, somewhere, for Les wrote down every-thing. The book that might name Busha was the one link left, kindling his brain. Burn them, yes. And waste the pickney Waste. Better to have straighten him out but time short....

The chink flashed black again, for Austin had been silenced effectively at that age and he could have broken this boy, used him not from desire but hatred, plunging into his screams and raping his very mind. Comfortingly and fittingly he could have bewildered the child from its habitual rudeness into mindless acceptance fastened perhaps to Austin's bed awaiting his will and then when apathy had settled then to shatter its routine with just such a scissors gleaming its lightning bolt solution to past and future hell and then to lie a while and salve himself in blood. And the fantasy sent shock waves tingling down his thighs and the need for the lifeless blood-drenched body of this child com-posed of all that past grew unbearable as the bottomless pit of his mind shuddered and exploded crushing his foot on the accelera-tor and sending the Porsche hurtling faster and faster into the night.

The stolen Toyota climbed, curving up into the hills directly rimming Kingston, as the road narrowed closer and steeper.

From the rock face to Paul Cohon's right the overhanging bushes dripped on the car and the high grass crowding from the left was soaked. The pressure in his bladder grew but he dared not stop. Palms and bamboo closed him in. Then the bank and vegetation sank to a low wall, offering glimpses down into the valley, black between the hills, and Kingston sprawled out below. On and on the road coiled and spiralled around the mountain. It opened out on the left again and the city glittered at him. At times he swung dangerously near to the rock face and the writhing tree roots and creepers reached almost into the car for him. Cactus and tall green grasses rose on the left, then the high sloping wall of the hill as the valley closed again. He squeezed his thighs tightly and locked his mind against the physical irritation.

When he passed the postal agency he knew it would soon be time. Now the hill was on the left, and to the right of the road was a dark hollow with the city cast in its depths. He slowed down. The car laboured to the ridge where the land slid dizzily away on both sides. In the distance a faint smoke of mist hung over the hills. He passed the wall and its murraya hedge and the Norfolk pine that towered beyond. Well past it, he pulled to a halt and slid out, his fingers shaking with the urgency of finding his zipper in time.

When he walked back he studied Austin Louis's house as if for the first time. It was a modern split-level affair overseeing terraces of obscure flowers and flatter spaces with flares of poinciana. Graceful, but it was built like a fortress out of the hillside. The long cutstone wall marched step-shaped along the boundaries of the land, each step echoed by the dark guard of thorny hedge that jutted above it. He hesitated before the globes blazing on the stone gates and glanced foolishly at the antique Winchester under his arm. Then he peered along the side of the house to the sheer drop of massive retaining wall. Beyond the bars of the inner gate black leggy shadows materialised and paced silently backwards and forwards across the floodlit drive. They could smell him, they were waiting for him, but they were silent. That was the kind, Paul reflected, that was trained to kill soundlessly. For a second he wavered. Supposing, he thought, supposing he was mad and had made it all up. But the lean, restless shadows beyond the gate froze his hand to the gun and shrank him into the darkness beneath the wall.

The gatepost lit up under the glare of headlamps turning into the drive and a long black Buick glided into sight and parked silently. The driver's mouth moved inaudibly before a rectangle in his hand and then he tossed it onto the seat beside him. After a while the inner gate scraped open, then closed again, and there was the clang of a bolt dropping and a sharp command. The outer gate opened and the car slid in a few yards and stopped. Paul pulled himself nearer still in the blackness of the wall, and crouched among the wet green and white leaves of shinensis beside the gate. Water dripped down his collar and leaked onto his back, but he crushed himself deep into the bush.

"What you come back here for?" Austin Louis's voice was blurred with fury. "Don't I tell you I mustn't see you again?"

"Busha."

"Where you leave it?"

"I need a next man, Busha. But I goin' finish." The driver's voice squealed to a whine. "Beg you likkle chance. Goin' finish a tell you."

"What the arse could go wrong?"

"Not de house down dey. Dem cyan' get 'way."

"The child?"

Paul's chest swelled to bursting point in him.

"Well. De boy run."

A choked obscenity, then silence. Then Austin's usual tone, a calm command to park.

"I driving my car. You going search every lane. That chile

491

have to find before morning. Where you lose him?"

"West Queen Street, there so."

A muffled explanation followed, interrupted by an impatient bark from Austin. "No bodder look no money for dis shit."

"Den suppose me find im, Baas?"

A brief pause broke with Austin's voice, cool again, and level. "Then I won't send dem boys for you a morning."

Paul squatted deeper into the shrubbery as the Porsche purred out and turned down the Jack's Hill Road.

By the time Paul reached the Toyota he knew he must chance Skyline Drive, the alternative route. He must get to town first yet he could not afford to overtake them. So instead of turning he pulled off the curb and kept straight, forcing himself to keep a normal pace for a few minutes lest there be anyone around associated with the house. Then he drew a deep breath, leaned forward over the wheel and stepped on the pedal.

Straight ahead, he knew, began a series of sharp curves, but he took them expertly, his mind crisp and clear with mountain air. In and out he wove, rock on one side and precipice on the other. Almost hysterically he remembered how often he had driven visitors here for the view. Now the city reeled madly before his eyes as the car dipped, hugging bend after bend. Wedges of vegetation interspersed with pinpoints of light. Up again to a crest. Clear now. The rain had stopped but the road curved slick with a treacherous coating of fine wet stones.

Kingston spread below, spotted with fires here and there. Night after night some part of the city burnt. Dark patches marked the harbour and Mona Dam. On the left, reddish brown rock crumbled, shelling away to loose gravel in soft showers down the wall of the hillside. Watching them, he almost failed to notice the landslips on the right. Small boulders tumbled for a few feet and were still. Going down, down.

A squeal of tyres and shock of impact shattered him as the side of the car slammed into the hillside, but he had started again and was yards beyond it when the crunch of breaking rock sent a pile of earth, stone and torn vegetation rumbling into the road. To the right rose a massive wall of rock and he swung the wheel to avoid it. Then he was down, out onto the Gordon Town Road. Something moved and he swerved, mashing the brakes. Inexplicably, in the small hours of morning, a cow wandered across the road.

At that hour, cars and pedestrians were scarce, even in Papine, and Hope Road was deserted. Turn into Old Hope Road but continue to Cross Roads. Not Mountain View Avenue at this hour. Along Slipe Road he heard shooting and pressed his foot down harder, thanking God he and Ben had had the sense to steal the Toyota. At Torrington Bridge he thanked God that the hitman had driven on with Gerry and not dumped him over the side like that case Ben had told them of recently. There were green traffic lights at West Race Course and off to Upper King Street. He shot through the red lights at the North Street intersection and relief flooded over him at a glimpse of the Parish Church cross. Then he had reached Parade and the square by Coke Chapel.

Paul abandoned the car, peeled off his shirt and draped it over the rifle. It was a meaningless camouflage he had no time to consider. The stock hung ludicrously on his bare chest, unnoticed. West King Street gaped to his left.

Then he stopped. Realisation slammed down, thumping the wind out of him. He had no idea where to look. The child could be anywhere. He stared around dazed by emptiness and thought to call. Then he remembered Austin and the hit man. They might be at the other end of West King Street now, or on it, approaching him. Then he would be calling the boy to them. He must hide, he thought. (Hide and search at the same time?)

Where? In the park the cassias and cannas were reassuring — perhaps a child might go there, even slip into the intricate rooting of the banyan tree. But then, while he looked there, the men might be combing the other street. And supposing Gerry was still there? Or had wandered round in a circle? And met them?

He forced himself to walk, not to run, close to the walls, along West Queen Street. At the corner he stopped, breathless, and peeped out. Princess Street was clear. He cut across and crouched down between the wall and a couple of old drums that were part of a barricade with which some posse had defined its territory. Wait? See what they would do? No. He was getting to his feet again when a car slowed around the corner.

When they pulled up he was ready. The gunman got out and Austin swerved on. Paul gasped. Of course they must split up. How hadn't he thought of it? The gunman hesitated, outlined in the intersection, and Paul realised that the thing to do was to kill him. Now. He was close. In the back. Paul levelled the rifle and his stomach rose. Only for a second he stopped to empty his mouth, but as he steadied the man slipped into the burnt-out building. Paul squirmed out from behind the drums and followed.

One after the other they slipped among the shattered walls and stinking rubbish of the city. Here the shadows hung thick and silent in every nook. Some were awake though, and watchful, like Matthew Leon, the Rastaman. Lion, as everyone called him now, heard the sob, the stumbling, the grate of heels on loose rubble, then a small brown boy groped into the clearing.

"Sugar?" the child whimpered.

The boy paused a second, panting, then dived on towards the next block.

The Rasta inclined his head thoughtfully and for a moment its shaggy image took shape against the concrete ruin on which he leaned. Then he started back and flattened himself once more into the night. A heavily built man, not from the zone, searched the tumbled piles, kicking aside boxes, poking into corners. His fingers were tense on an M16.

"Hm!' Lion considered. "Him cross dem boundary come test dem? And plenty gun dat fe catch such a likkle youth."

Another man followed, older, weary, frightened, clutching an ancient rifle inexpertly.

Lion lingered for only a moment or two, gazing with interest as they disappeared into the night. Then he nodded decisively.

"A likkle child shall lead dem," he mused.

He peeled himself from the darkness and followed the gunman noiselessly in worn out rubber sandals. In the distance though, his sensitive ears picked up a fine new engine.

Slowly, tirelessly, Austin cruised the streets, searching,

"Son?" he called gently, "Gerry? Son?"

But there was no life, except for the dogs looting the garbage and a ragged drunk sprawled in the gutter.

The gunman moved fast and smoothly after the child once he had picked up the trail, but it was difficult keeping up with the small erratic figure let alone getting him in view.

Lion had dispensed with curiosity and slid grimly after them. After a while the Rasta dived through a hole and dodged across the deserted market and out through an opening he knew on the other side. He sprinted silently along, made a left and tucked behind the barricades at the end before the child drew alongside. Then he reached out and clutched him, one arm circling his waist and the other clamped across his mouth.

He held him still till the man came into sight. The child started and shrank back with Lion against the barrels. When the gunman had passed, the Rasta laid a finger across the boy's mouth and released him.

"You know de rankin'?" Lion asked.

Stunned, the child regarded him from head to foot. Then his eyes travelled up again, inevitably, to the broad face framed with matted locks and uneven beard and the burning, slightly slanted eyes.

"Whe' you come from? Talk boy. You 'fraid I locks? Dem is de strength of de lion." After a while he pronounced, "I know dat man, you know. And dat man know I. You better come wid I, make ah see 'bout you."

The child stiffened and began withdrawing slowly out of his grasp. The Rasta made no effort to catch him again, just opened one big scarred palm upwards and crooned, "Come, likkle yout'. Come unto I."

In Parade, Lion hid the boy in one of the vendors' shacks and hurried some yards away to a dark corner where he whistled cautiously.

"I have a man I want move," he murmured. "Is not one of your yout'-dem. Come from out of de zone. See in de lane dere so. Watch, eeh? Im have one big gun."

He returned to the child and found him quivering with his eyes huge and black with terror. Gerry clung to him and sobbed.

"Why you leave me?" the child choked.

"Nuh cry, likkle bredda. You soon goin' safe."

He sat on a box with the child's face resting on his knee and stroked him tenderly. "Not to cry, not to cry."

There was a whistle, then again, less muted.

"You hear?" he sighed. "You safe now."

He lifted Gerry onto a barrel and studied him. His gaze was not critical like Pearl's nor speculating like Uncle's. He just looked carefully, trying to see what was really there. As he stared his strange face relaxed, little etches of pain or tension smoothed away and reformed elsewhere to smile lines and his eyes, comforting in their admiration, somehow reminded Gerry of chocolate.

"Well," Lion said softly, "well you is a real nice likkle yout'."

Then Gerry noticed that while Lion's face was broad it was delicate and his skin seemed thin-stretched. He breathed quickly for a big man who had stopped running for quite a while.

"You sick?" the child asked solicitously, laying a cool but

grimy palm on Lion's forehead.

The slanted chocolate eyes registered surprise. "Is so you smart too, eeh?"

Lion took the child's hand and turned it over, smoothing away what dirt he could. Then his eyes strayed to one of the buckets of clean water at the back of the shack. He dragged it over, cleansed his own hands, and then awkwardly but with infinite tenderness wiped Gerry's face and arms.

"Brave, sweet, smart likkle yout' like you must clean," he nodded in satisfaction. "Have fe find you family give you to them clean and nice."

An idea formed in Gerry as the kind, tough hands groomed and reassured him.

"Mr Gentleman," he began respectfully, "I don't know you name."

"Lion I name, likkle bredda."

"Lion." Gerry tested it and obviously liked it. "Lion, suppose you don't find them. I can stay with you?"

The Rasta set the bucket aside and regarded the child thoughtfully. "Likkle bredda, you know not what you aks. Hear I. First you is a yout' from a world not like unto I world. I an' I nah have noting and nowhere an nobady. Next ting is, I well sick can't cure. Likkle from dis I can't take care I self, much less.... No. You fe go you own people grow good. But you is de likkle bredda of me heart."

A whistle came again, sharp and near.

Lion leaned around the post at the opening of the shack and muttered to someone. All Gerry could see of the other man was ragged trousers above bright new Reeboks. Then Lion came in again and passed a thick, choppy finger under Gerry's chin.

"A'right. Hear. I going step into a road dey. Wait! Nuh cry. I will never leave you nar forsake you. Tell I. You know a reverend man?"

Gerry regarded him blankly.

"Wear one collar round im neck so. Go church pray and talk 'bout one Jesus."

The child's eyes snapped and life returned to him.

"Grand?" he breathed.

"Grandfada? Eh? Grandaddy? Aah."

Lion hesitated, not wanting to raise the child's hopes, then decided. He couldn't leave him here without comfort; neither could he drag him back into the dark lane where they might meet what was left of the gunman spread out over the sidewalk.

"If you stay quiet here and don't frighten, I and I will go look Grandaddy fe you. You safe here. Ongly stay quiet. I wid you always, even unto the end of the world."

His big bruising hug filled the night with certainty and the child watched calmly as the Rasta set off in the direction from which they had come.

When Paul lost the gunman he lingered in the street for a sign of the child. He waited in a frenzy of inaction, for Gerry could not be still. The child must be wandering further from Paul, or nearer to one of the killers. Paul groped into slow, aimless movement then paused again, impaled on the thought that the child was nearby and that walking on meant leaving him behind. Now Paul slumped against the wall hopelessly, then pulled away again sharply as the image of the car whipped across his mind. At least he could look for the Porsche.

He jerked forward more positively in the direction he expected Austin Louis to take. The walls of the lane were high on each side and only a thin strip along the centre could he penetrate for any distance.

The absence of anything human sent the weirdness creeping along his skin and the strange fiction of the empty city appalled him. He stopped abruptly, straining for some sound on the bare grey road, but there were no feet, only the echoing void of shadows, an almost audible silence. Ahead, the blank lanes narrowed into obscurity. There had been no rain here, for now and then light gusts harrowed up the dust beneath the streetlight at the corner and once, far away, he thought the wind sang with the thin dry whisper of a people who had no tears left.

He had been afraid at first of the loneliness of the road, but now its emptiness reassured him and he trod firmly. Certainly nothing lived for miles around. Yet suddenly, at his shoulder something breathed quickly, softly.

"You walking late, brown man."

He spun around but there was nothing.

A figment of dread, perhaps, at the periphery of his mind. He saw no one. But now the shadows scourged him on for, although physically he had never been harmed in the social disorder of the city, his dreams at least had been raped and it occurred to him suddenly that the emptiness might be alive and waiting to tear him.

The darkness at the corner of Matthews Lane and Beckford Street materialised and a huge yet gaunt Rasta stepped out of the night and bowed graciously.

"Hail, Star. Forward a cigarette to de I, nah?"

Paul stared at him in disbelief.

"Please," he mumbled, his tongue maimed with shock, "please don't... keep me back. There's a child... a baby, in trouble."

"No have no cigarette, Puppa?"

Paul wiped his forehead. "Sorry. I don't smoke."

"Don' mind. Don' mind. Come sit in de dust a while an reason wid I."

Paul glanced around wildly.

"Cyan't sit wid I? Don' frighten so. De yout' safe."

Paul gasped, feeling his limbs melt with relief. He crumpled to the ground beside the Rasta and gripped his arm.

"You know where he is? You have him?" Fear seized hold

again. "Where he is now? What 'bout the men?"

Lion stiffened then sprang up. "Is what you say? Men?" He grabbed Paul by the shoulder. "More dan de one gunman?"

"Another man," Paul choked, "my colour or fairer, but younger. In a car."

"Did hear a car, yes."

He shoved Paul roughly in the direction of Parade.

"De gunman OK. De chile inna one shack a de entrance dere. You go so. Make I cut through ya."

And he was gone into one of the fallen entrances.

Ben saw no details of the road but dim outlines. Nevertheless, he made out a glow blocks away, and he wondered about it idly as people do about fires. Then he realised that it could well be one of the houses near home, set by an oil lamp, perhaps, from the squatters. Then his mind quickened. Or insurance? Evasion of rent? Resentful tenant?

Up to now he had painfully maintained an even, confident pace to be as inconspicuous as possible. Now he moved faster. He clung to the shadows when he could, but found himself glancing involuntarily over his shoulders, feeling that somehow he must be drawing attention to himself. A brown man on the streets at this hour. He shuddered. It seemed hopeless, utterly hopeless that he should get home. And it would not have mattered so much, he thought. It would hardly have mattered but for the receipt. He must get the slip and the diary together and to the police or they might never recover Gerry.

It was strange how much more urgent it became the nearer he drew to home. How the fear grew. How the black shapes under the bougainvillea hedges gathered into crouching figures. How the water hydrant and the uncollected garbage conspired in the darkness, waiting to spring on him. A shot in the back now and the paper was lost again, he thought, and who would know, who would ever know about Gerry and the receipt from Austin Louis. The nearer he drew to the corner the less likely it seemed that he would ever reach it. He did not know that any resemblance to a man of any means had gone from him beyond trace. His hair was matted, his shirt drenched and ripped under the arm, and he stank of sweat, rum and the grave. No one intercepted him as, incredulous at his safety, he neared the corner of his own road where it would all be over.

But when he arrived at the corner of Oxford Close and turned in, the road was alive with writhing shadows and before him the flames danced and beckoned mockingly. The noise was distant still and, somehow, even standing there clear in the middle of the road with the trailer looming to one side and with the stars blotted out and the night fragmented into slivers of red and black, darting, cleaving, splitting, fusing again — even in the midst of it, it was all distant with the remoteness of the impossible. Deep in his pocket his fingers wandered over the plastic flap that housed the receipt and he gasped and hung onto the reality of it. The other thing could not be happening. Life, he began to reason slowly, was not like that. Logically, there among the surreal dance and cackle of the flames, he tried to retrace the steps by which he had wandered into nightmare. He stood there, breaking, straining frantically for the way back into the sane respectable past. But the heat swept out and swelled about him so that when he gasped for breath there was nothing and he stumbled aside, around towards the back of the house to which the fire had not yet spread.

On the porch at the side something moved. The door itself was jammed although the wrought-iron gate was unlocked. The two women had smashed the ornamental glass and broken out the thin ribs of wood between the panes. Sarah pushed something through, "The book, boy," she gasped. "Take the book."

He tried to grasp her arm but she shook him off impatiently.

"Good God! Take the book!"

501

He grabbed Vern's Bible from her blindly and stuffed it into his pants then gripped her arm again. She was frail now, paper thin but pliable enough to slip through the broken door into the yard beside him, but Grace was far too heavy and the heat drove her back towards the kitchen. Outside, Ben and Sarah too stumbled towards the back along the narrow path bordered by blackened rose bushes and blasted pentas. Sarah clutched his arm and hushed him.

"They are around the back, here, somewhere."

"Eh?"

Her fingers dug in, silencing him, and he peered in the direction she indicated. Dimly, in the light over the back door, he made them out. The fire raced behind him. Behind Grace too, then. And there were gunmen at the door.

The tool shed on the other side occurred to him. It was empty though. They had cleared it even before packing the trailer, and then everything that they had taken to the cemetery they had left there. Ben had only his hands. He pushed Sarah against the hedge and she grabbed a broken pipe from the ground and thrust it into his hands.

"Lie still," he breathed, even as she collapsed into the shadows.

Not a second he could spare her for Grace must have reached the door already.

He broke out across the clear space where the car usually parked, lunged away from the hedge towards the other corner of the backyard which was cluttered dark with mango trees. The men swore and swung after him, then one turned.

"You take out de ol' man. Make me keep de door."

As the man blundered among the mango trees Ben spun from behind the thick trunk of a Bombay and fastened onto his back, jamming the end of the pipe onto his spine, and hissed, "Ah not young like you, but I could still pull trigger."

Inside, the front and centre of the house were unbearable, but it was better on the tiles of the narrow room that had been the back porch. Shadows leapt and jumped though, and the smoke spread, thickening. Grace had dropped to the ground, slithered over to the door and centred her eye on the keyhole. Part of him was just distinguishable, and the glint of black metal.

Her eyes flitted, window to window. Bar after bar locked them out, locked her in. Her mind flickered. She forced herself to search it. Old Benton had argued with her when putting in the grillwork, but she had insisted. One set was on hinges, and the key.... At once she was in the kitchen working it loose from the hook to which it had rusted and she struggled with it in the lock but it didn't fit properly. She scrambled away across the porch then nearer to the bedroom and held it up to the light. It was rusty and coated with grease.

She rubbed it desperately in her dress and scratched between the indentations with her fingernails. The kitchen swelled, roared and burst open in a blinding sheet of light, flinging her violently against the wall of the porch. The blow dazed her but not enough to miss the brilliant gush of flame out of the doorway and the almost liquid speed with which it sped up the facing, across the ceiling and along the wooden table on the far side of the porch. She skidded wildly towards the window, coming down hard on the tiles. Now the padlock opened and the rusty hinge yielded to urgent tugging, but the window itself was jammed shut. As she rattled it a voice yelled somewhere underneath.

But it didn't matter anymore. She wasn't frightened anymore. The thunder of the fire entered her heart. Damned if she would burn! She was getting out and she was going to kill them all. She grabbed a chair although one arm was a mass of pain and held it up before her face, its legs pointed out, and hurled herself at the window.

It burst out on the gunman outside the window without warning, a blazing mass of chair and woman that crashed screeching onto him in a rain of broken glass. The gun dropped uselessly as he abandoned it to head her off, but she smashed the chair murderously at his face and he collapsed screaming. A siren wailed in the distance, and Grace pitched the burning chair away to roll over in the wet grass. The man on the ground beside her bawled an obscenity and tried to scramble blindly to his feet, but she grabbed the chair again and swung it once more, with a last effort, at his face.

At the door of the vendor's shack in Parade, Gerry stared at a familiar Porsche cruising towards him and scrambled to his feet in a flood of relief. But it was not Pearl driving, it was Uncle, and he passed unconscious of Gerry, only a few feet away. And what if Lion did not come back? Gerry ran leaping, waving frantically at the driver, but it was useless, and at last he stood still in the middle of the street sobbing bitterly, barely visible in the rear view mirror.

It was difficult to manipulate the car because the barrels from recent barricades were scattered at the side of the street. Gerry stayed near the sidewalk nervously for Lion had gone and now the child wanted only to see someone familiar, only to be picked up and taken to a place he could understand.He could hardly believe his eyes when he saw the Porsche returning. This time the driver distinguished him in the glare of the headlights. The child stood still in the middle of the street with his arms up like a baby begging to be lifted. "Uncle. Uncle!"

Austin Louis never took his eyes off him as he peered determinedly through the glare and pressed the accelerator down to the floor.

When Gerry flung himself out of the way it never occurred to him to run. It never crossed his mind that Uncle had seen him, so he waved frantically from the side of the road, begging to be noticed. The tyres squealed in a last sharp desperate turn and the child's voice grew hysterically shriller.

Paul crashed out into the open, clutching the old Stollmeier rifle and firing wildly towards the car without even raising or aiming it properly, so that one of the bullets found a tyre by accident.

Lion saw the child who had sprung towards the road with his arms spread as if to embrace the car. He plunged at Gerry, clutching, hugging, muttering warm words that quieted the screams.

"Uncle," the child gasped, "tell Uncle I here."

"No, likkle bredda. No. Im see you, you hear. Tu'n way fram Busha, you hear. I an I know 'bout him. Im is abamination — nuh look 'pon him." But Gerry was confused and slipping away and the Rastaman bawled, "I find you Grandaddy fe you." And the child was transfixed for an instant then dived back to him.

A woman's voice shrilled from the emptiness behind the buildings. "Lion! Watch!"

Austin had burst open his car door and centred his magnum accurately on the child even as Lion wrapped his arms and arched his body about him. The shot wasn't very loud and Lion hardly felt it, just hugged the boy tighter and tighter, murmuring as he pressed him to the ground,

"Suffer de likkle children, suffer... suffer...."

But the second bullet ploughed right through Lion and his blood mingled briefly with the child's and trickled away into the dirt of the city.

Around Paul the night exploded into clutching, tearing forms and furious gasps and screams.

"Lion! Im shoot down Lion!"

"De brown shit!"

Austin shrank back towards the Porsche, and the shadows closed on the car, smashing and ripping it. From nowhere, women, men, boys, flung their bodies on it, tugging, slamming it over on its side then upside down with the glass shattered around it. Some continued systematically to wreck it, wrenching off doors and bashing anything they could not detach.

Austin huddled inside but they reached in clawing him out of the leather seat onto the ground and tearing, tearing. Austin's arm clutched above them spasmodically, fingers jerking bloodily at the air. Then a ratchet knife raised, a rum bottle swiped open on the concrete edge of the sidewalk, a pipe swung. Paul buried his face in his hands and tried not to see, not to think of what had become of them, of Gerry, of the Rastaman, of Austin Louis, or of the fury that was unleashed before him. Louis's body, hurled forward, twitched violently and an unrecognisable sound bubbled through the dark stain at his mouth then cut off as a machete hacked down.

"Trow de rass back inna im car."

Paul slid silently down the post of the vendor's shack towards the concrete.

Through the haze a woman bawled, "What 'bout de Reveren'?"

A man ran and put an arm about Paul, supporting him, and the same woman's voice kept shrilling, "De pickney, de pickney. Oh Gawd! Is dead im dead?"

How could it be... allowed? Where was God? Paul's thoughts slipped out of control into the unknown territory of doubt.

"But who pickney it is?" The woman shrieked on and on.

Paul tried to move his feet but he was too old. The horror closed in on him, garrotting his mind. He could not... see anything more tonight.

"De pickney. De pickney, me say."

But Paul knew he was stripped of everything.

A man was bending over him but it was hard to hear. The face above him seemed to expand, shrink, swell again. The man shook him roughly and forced his voice on him.

"Minister! De chile shirt soak up with blood, but is not dead im dead."

Slowly the lines of the face reformed.

"De chile, Minister. De chile living."

Hands held his face and turned it towards the sidewalk. The child was lying with his arms about the Rasta's neck, tugging and whimpering. They detached him and lifted him over to Paul.

Paul and Gerry stared at each other in disbelief. Austin, the gunman, even Lion, faded out of their world. Then Paul touched the child. Stretching a long way to run his fingers over his cheek-bones, along the tilt of his nose, tracing the curl of his lips, the point of his chin. Long afterwards, it seemed, he felt the child's arm, squeezed the flesh of his shoulders. Pressed his arms around his waist. Gerry clutched at him and Paul tried to get hold of him, but the child wriggled all over him, tugging, wrapping his limbs about him and trying to climb him, trying to say, "Grand, Grand," but only gasping great croaking sobs. And when Gerry finally quieted he clung rubbing his face against Paul's shoulder, burying his nose in his neck.

In the distance a weird urgent wail rose and fell and the small crowd around them began to melt again, back into the shadows, pulling in their wake old tyres, boxes, barrels and other refuse of the city and setting it alight.

"Minister," a man said, "none a we cyan't stop, nah."

He pushed a bottle into Paul's hand and closed his fingers over it. "Swallow dis."

"No' stop now," the woman hissed. "Make haste! Come!"

"Lion. Cyan't lef' im ya so."

"Make 'aste, man! Blood 'pon you."

When the squad car came the police were forced to leave their vehicle and approach on foot, for the scrapped Porsche lay mysteriously in a street with barricades at each end, and the lane that crossed the street was blocked too so that every approach blazed. Three figures huddled at the centre of this flame-tipped cross. Blood-soaked and face down on the sidewalk lay a dead Rastafarian. A small child, well-dressed but dishevelled, called him "Lion". The child clung to an older man, who was greying and kindly-looking apart from his antique hunting weapon.

He was shirtless, but a clerical collar hung askew on him. Everything about him reeked of carrion. He seemed too exhausted to speak and the police wandered over to the car.

There in its wreckage they stumbled upon something else that had been a man before some inexplicable fury had broken over it, and one of the younger men edged away and vomited in the dark. The minister handed over his gun thankfully to them and it was obvious from his condition that neither he nor his weapon could be responsible for the mangled remains in the wrecked car. They carried the old man and the child to the patrol car, still clinging to each other.

"I remember you from Sunday School, you know, Rev," murmured one of the younger men. "Feel say I know where you live."

At Oxford Close, police, firemen and an emergency medical crew drifted away eventually, reluctant to leave four battered old people and a small child huddled together on the parched lawn before the blackened shell of a house. One officer insisted on remaining to drive them if only they would get into the car. The police had taken note of their separate nightmares and accepted responsibility for a scorched Bible whose central pages had been ripped out and replaced by an old appointment book. They took also an evil-smelling plastic shield with a single strip of paper, a handwritten receipt. How it all fitted together was clear to no one.

Most incomprehensible of all was the group on the lawn, who sat in the dew, for they could not stand, hugging each other before the ruins and contemplating the lifetime ahead.

"How we'll unpack the trailer, Sugar, now we have no house for the things?"

"Aah, the house doesn't matter, my baby. I didn't want it again anyway, you know."

Paul looked at her scandalised and she stared back stubbornly.

"I'd made up my mind I wasn't leaving it for any damn squatter. I'd a bu'n it down myself first."

"Right, quite correct, Grace child," Sarah nodded.

Ben had retrieved for Sarah a slim stick of wood from the gutted house, and she tapped her approval on the grass by the driveway. The cat separated herself from the bushes and joined them, singed practically nude but otherwise intact. Morgan, still unsteady from whatever drug Ivan had fed him, raised his leg against the tyre of the police car and growled at the patient young policeman at the wheel, then scratched twice dismissively and lurched over to the family as they helped each other up.

Yet they stood together for a minute before getting into the car, and Gerry spread his arms and wove his way in and out among them, swaying with exhaustion but intoxicated with the warmth of their hands on him, breaking away and running back to squeeze and tug at them, rubbing and nuzzling against them, loving them with his body. In the glow of the street light above the trailer the gutted house yawned hollowly before them, but the light itself was busy with insects dipping and reeling in their unending drama.

Around the charred foundations of the house an inner rhythm urged the family together and for an instant Paul recognised the strange, almost immoral, yearning behind the fascination and torment of the moth. It was a familiar sight enough, the light with this alien creature pledging itself to the flame, but he had never understood before the ruthlessness of love. He found himself staring at the moth and seeing it for the first time, gentle and violent. All creativity and destruction was summed up in the control and abandonment of its flight, all freedom and limitation. But its mobility and urgency defied boundaries of space and time, made a mockery of dimensions. It could struggle with the air or ride the wind. It could play upon time, arrest, discard or recapture it, wheel again and again through the phases of experience as through a motif. And when it was gone, beneath the light lay only the ring of dust which marked the immensity of its passion.

Dazedly Ben peered at the trailer. "So we not going after all."

Grace regarded him in astonishment, hugging her injured arm. "You crazy, man?"

Paul spread smeared hands. "Custody...."

"...A house to find...." Grace gasped.

"...And a boy," Ben agreed, his voice low and exultant, "a boy to raise."

"Well we going to stand around idling all night in the dew then?" Sarah snapped at them, struggling to straighten up and emphasising her point with a good swipe of her stick at the fender of the car. "Let's make a start...."

28

The Child

SO THE years were merciful. A season of intricate preparation bore that day when friends who had clung to the island through choice or necessity gathered and celebrated with the family. Then, when the guests had left for their long drive back to Kingston, came the evensong of lingering on the verandah.

Grace darted this way and that, drawing water from the barrel under the eaves for the flowers, carrying in the silver. It was altogether different here from anywhere they had ever lived, yet collectively the family had a sense of belonging on the old grey stone porch. Goldfields. Half of the house still tumbled away in ruin at the side but they had done what they could with the rest, replacing what had been stolen over the years with all they had once packed in the trailer. They had set a few plants too, salvaged from the seared allamanda at Oxford Road. They had caught a few slips from Stella's rose bushes, but mostly they would depend on ferns and anthuriums now, they decided, and perhaps, if they could muster the energy, an orchid or two. Now, in the deep of the evening before them the lights began to twinkle.

They had sat in council together after the fire, Paul and Grace Cohon, Sarah Stollmeier and Ben Goldman, and they had decided that a growing boy must have space. They had not the strength to rebuild, and they wouldn't have known how to raise Gerry in an apartment. They had pondered him, mercurial and fiery, behind bars in Kingston. Suddenly, luminous in its simplicity, the thought kindled. There was nothing to keep them in

Kingston but memories of all they had lost. Strange, they thought, to end up in the country. They had always been Kingston people, and their old people before them, they said. But all they would miss of Kingston, after all, was the city they had known, and it was gone. So now, more than it had ever been, Goldfields was lastingly, hauntingly theirs. For Gerry.

Paul enrolled him in the prep school beside the church; Ben wandered with him on the foam-fringed beach. Quaveringly and then more firmly remembering, they played ring games and plied him with riddles and tales of strange wild creatures that outsmarted and outlived their enemies. And yes, Grace insisted, there was that waterfall of bottomless emerald, not far, not far at all. An old fellow in the area whom Sarah believed to be some distant family of Icelin was garrulous with recollections of it and could guide them to the river. Old man Castries and his daughter helped them around the place and the family paid what they could and let the Castries reap the land. The woman knew about roasting breadfruit in a coalpot behind the kitchen, and she made pepperpot soup with janga fresh from the river for Gerry. There was no proper surface to ride the bicycle they would have liked to give him for his birthday so they arranged that an old horse, patient and dignified, be harnessed to bear him all over Goldfields. Ben kept watch over him, and old man Castries cackled toothlessly, "Yes, Busha, yes!"

No one had been prepared for Gerry's reaction. He hurtled screaming into the house as the memories rose and pitched on him. His mother at Austin's feet. A brown hand on the belt. A brown back bloodied. Once he had felt as if it was his own back, and now it seemed it was his hand too. Madness clutched out at him with gnarled brown fingers.

They tried to hold him but he whirled about the room, always beyond reach, torn by glimpses of the myriad lives that comprised his own. His mother obliterated, Lion ruptured and draining away into a pothole, Uncle... Busha dismembered before him. Then, hard behind them, relief swept gale-force over him and the shame of his own survival and liberty blasted grief and horror away. He swung up onto a railing and perched quivering, his eyes black and turbulent with the maelstrom of the past.

But the Grands were there. Paul lifted his dark, spare face from the book open on his knee, wanting to understand. Ben dropped his tools to take up Gerry, to carry any weight, any distance. Sugar balanced meals, accounts, almost their lives, and her hands were always moving, everywhere raising, opening, smoothing — hands frugal and generous. Goddie Sarah remembered everything. She must have been there, Gerry thought, from the beginning of all things. With relief he reflected that they were wise and good, and that they said he was a whole new boy. It was a new life. Everything was for him.

Now they sat on the porch at Goldfields and the mountains towered over them, the same as always, but nearer. Ben squinted out into the formless twilight, smiling to himself, and reached for Goddie's hand.

"So Mrs Queen write you?"

She nodded, squeezing his fingers with a slight, wavering pressure.

Paul chuckled and reached into the pile of letters and telegrams from their friends all over the world. The McIntyres had written from Canada and a few official ones had arrived in recognition of an extraordinary birthday, Sarah's century. Grace sank onto the doorstep and rubbed her face in Gerry's hair.

"Tired, Gracie?" Sarah gestured shakily. "Too much, too much for one woman. And not robust. You're not robust, Gracie. You do too much."

"Darling," Grace gazed at her then out dreamily into the evening. "To have seen a day like this. Blessed be God."

"Eh?"

Car lights swerved into sight, and before they could retreat into the house the driver was out, nodding to them reassuringly.

"I know you won't recognise me, sir." He extended a firm handclasp to Paul. "I'm Victor Castries."

They crowded around him. So tall, he was. Like a cotton tree among the poincianas.

"Sit down so we can see you," Grace laughed.

"Related to those 'round here?" Sarah asked.

"Yes, same Castries. I worked briefly in Kingston, and just as I was getting to like it the new church was completed and I've been transferred here. It's what I wanted though. I hope you won't mind me as your minister." He extended a five to Gerry and grinned, "What you say, Breds?"

The boy greeted him shyly and wandered back to the table as the adults talked. It was loaded with sandwiches and gifts. The cake, dark and rich with fruit, was leaking wine onto the tablecloth. The tiny flames of its one hundred candles glowed on in Gerry. He reached to it and broke off a piece of icing. His eye caught a basket of fruit, among them a glossy red ball.

"Hey," he breathed, drawing it out and holding it up to the dim light. "I thought they were just pretend."

They stared at him in distress.

"But you were in the States. You must have got apples there."

He did not answer and they let it go.

"He's had a difficult time," Paul muttered to Victor.

"I've heard."

Just what had he heard, Grace wondered quickly.

"I don't know," Goddie quavered fretfully. "I don't know why it had to come to that." She broke off a fat black grape from the plate they had placed within her reach, and she bent stiffly to pop it into his mouth. It was from the Governor General, and of course it was imported, this basket of rare, half-forgotten luxuries. "Good God in heaven. I can never. Never if I live another century. I can never forget how it was. Never forgive... the change."

She breathed shallowly, pressing her hand to her chest.

"It can never be what it was," Ben reflected, almost coldly. "They destroyed it."

Grace knitted her brows.

"Of course, perhaps it shouldn't be quite what it was. There was injustice," she allowed.

Victor glanced at her with interest.

"And what did we get?" Paul was outraged. "And why? Who did we ever hurt? And when everything was taken away from us, who did it help? I want to know where is justice? And there is no answer. There are more hungry children on the island now that ever before."

"Yes, yes. Only...."

"All this holier-than-thou lamentation over the Sufferers. Shams! Rolling in more money than we'll ever see. I've worked all my life," Paul went on. "My grandmother. When I was a baby she dug graves in the night to make a little extra to keep us. When I grew up I worked. Those who don't have, why can't they work? Like I did. Like she did. Let them dig graves."

"My father made coffins after the earthquake," Ben agreed.

"Quite right." Sarah shifted her knees more closely together and smoothed her skirt. "People refuse to work. They should be made to."

"How?" Ben grinned derisively and Sarah turned on him, provoked.

"With the whip, dammit. Excuse me, Pastor. Once I thought with horror what poor people went through. How they were treated. What a history we had, I thought. What a history of brutality. But it's not so simple. Some people work themselves to death so others need not work at all. They should be beaten. Laugh, you fools. Laugh." She broke off chuckling and dismissed it all with a flip of her bony fingers. "Reintroduce the whip, I say."

Sarah paused for breath. "I'm not a wicked woman, son, I mean... Father."

"Victor," he insisted quickly.

"Victor," she said in relief. "But you worked. I remember you working. You never asked for a handout. You worked and did well."

"But it was not enough," he explained gently. "I was lucky. I met with kindness. Now I think of it, the first such kindness was from a very powerful criminal who did not give me a job when I asked for it."

"But how did people get so... so bad?"

"Politics," Paul moaned. "Oh it was a wicked thing, instilling so much hatred into quiet, God-fearing people. Suddenly people like us felt they had to leave. I miss Sam." His voice broke but he stumbled on. "Clem has had a stroke, I'll probably not see him again. We nearly left too, but it would have killed something in us. I know. Why do they hate us? Anyone who works can get anywhere."

"Well, they say people can't find work," Grace faltered.

"Chat nonsense!" Paul exploded. "Coconuts stretching in front of us like the sea and sometimes weeks pass — we can't get one to drink. I can't pay a young man to climb and get a coconut down."

"In the town, they mean, you know."

"OK. And when Victor went off to his studies, and we thank God he did, if you didn't get up every morning at Oxford Close and sweep your driveway who was going to do it?"

"You, my darling," she regarded him sweetly.

"Aah. Well, you see I never had this spine-tingling terror of work."

"What's spine-tingling?"

They stared at Gerry who sat now surrounded with apple pips and scraggly grape stalks, absorbing everything. His electrifying black eyes seemed to fill his face. Paul began to explain the word carefully, but Gerry raced on, "Why does Goddie want to beat people? Who she wants to beat?" He turned to Grace. "And why you made a minister sweep your driveway?" He swivelled back towards Paul. "Who took your things?"

He sat on the ground, arms clasped about his knees, motionless but nonplussing, waiting for answers. Then he raised his shoulders in bafflement.

"And who are They?"

The four stared at him helplessly, and Victor sat still as the mountain itself.

"All kinds of things have happened in this country, son," Paul whispered. "Everyone blames everyone else. Everything is different from what it was when... when I was a boy...." His voice trailed away and he stared at Goddie. "When Goddie was a girl...."

They were silent before the immensity of all she had seen. Of all Gerry had seen in his little life they dared not think. Grace stared out at the hills hunched above Goldfields and they were old, older than them all. Only the hills would see the end of it.

"But things are sweeping back, you know," Grace put in. "And many things are gone that should be gone. Victor, when I was a child there was a girl who wouldn't sit beside me in school because I was coloured. Yesterday we went in town and it's cleaner. Safer. All the madness seems unreal."

"Already people are forgetting what it was like two years ago. It hardly seems real." Paul's voice sank almost to a whisper. "Sometimes I wonder whether I went mad and dreamed it all."

"I feel like that myself sometimes, about the past," Victor stared out into the night wondering where his mother was, here or some other part of the earth, dead or alive. And his mind sobbed for Lion whom he had not found when he was leaving Kingston. (Sufferation, his neighbours lamented. Woulda worse for him if him did live.) "Perhaps it is better to forget?" The pain was audible in Victor's voice.

"But it happened so easily, son," Sarah said softly, "if we forget, it could happen again."

"Will any of them come back?" Gerry's first reference, ever, to his own nightmare hushed them and hung in their silence.

"No, child," Sarah said decisively.

"Not even Lion?"

Victor started, but controlled himself.

"No, child. No."

"He was good," Gerry shouted defiantly.

"Yes," Paul hastened, "he was good."

"The police didn' think so." It must have been boiling in Gerry all along. "They said Lion and Busha were 'one thing'."

Paul intercepted the next, inevitable question smoothly.

"All I know, all that is important, is that Austin Louis was a beast and he's gone. Lion was a kind, brave man who gave you back to us. I'm afraid he's gone too. They certainly were not the same. And, by the way, there's more icing."

As Gerry wandered back to the table they resumed their talk more carefully.

"Tourist coming back," Ben remarked. "Hotel business picking up. But they'll have to begin all over again. The new government — they're just another set of politicians."

"No!" Grace gasped. "Don't say it. It will all come back."

"I won't be here," Sarah snapped. "It will be your trouble, not mine." She paused and looked around at them. "I wouldn't set foot in Kingston again, even if I could still travel. It would be as if we had really taken the trailer and landed in a whole new place. I'm not anxious to live much longer feeling like I've just arrived." Her voice changed to one of sleepy gratification. "But I'm so glad that monster is dead."

Paul remonstrated half-heartedly, but Victor hardly heard him. For there was more, Victor thought, much more than he had heard; his mind rocked from their references to Lion and to Austin, from exposure to their gentle blindness and vulnerability and from the sudden cruel thought of how the years already blurred things he must not forget.

"Is it safe now? Here?" Gerry asked. And Paul could not answer for they had searched for a place beyond guns and rhetoric and he could not believe like Grace that a change of government would rapture them to paradise.

"Goldfields is safe enough. You like it up here, son?"

Gerry stood with them, silent and very still but for the mountain air stirring his curls and his eyes looking out and down over the valley. It was all deep blue now with wisps of mist and Goldfields seemed to be an island in the evening sky and a hole in time. The candles had burnt low and by their parting light Sarah searched his face curiously.

"What does it feel like, child. Tell Goddie."

He didn't turn, and his voice was so quiet she had to lean forward to catch it.

"It's like... riding on God's shoulder."

Paul stared at Gerry's eyes and into his soul. Pain, exultation and fear welled up at the secrets locked in that small head. Adam and Pearl. Austin. Lion. All gone. But Paul knew that they had disappeared by merging into the child's own flesh and their agonies were distributed through him. The unseen dimensions of the boy's life were vast, tangled, massive, unfathomable as the mountains, echoing with dim caverns. A fire blazed in Gerry. He was free, but the relief was guilt-ridden, born of his parents' death. Gerry's mind soared and fluttered along a dark maze of possibilities, sensing somewhere a gleam, an opening. If only they could help him find it. Then he would look out and see, as if from a height, brilliant and dangerous, all that was his for the making. Paul did not mind that he himself would never see it as long as it was there for Gerry — a new, untried shore waiting somewhere in the deeps of time.

And what of the others? Victor bowed his head from memories, time-riven, as the ragged hordes of city children tumbled through his mind. He thought of the boy in the fish-barrel near Lion's shack and knew he must find him. Yet here, even on the porch of the crumbling great house, was another child with only four old people, loving as they were, and a great emptiness yawning beyond. Sarah saw him grab for the seat of the boy's pants as he leaned perilously off the porch and a great weight rolled from her mind.

Grace put her arms around the child and drew him to her painfully, feeling an arthritic joint blaze in warning. The wind stirred the bamboo somewhere below so that the bottomless blue evening moaned around them. The view from the porch blurred, or was it age creeping — she was sure Gerry could see into the valley. And there was so much to say to him; and who were they, with failing limbs and vision and memories, who were they to lead him along the corridors of time, and through the crisscross of past and future? How many of his years would be theirs?

Paul read her thoughts and muttered stubbornly, "My grandmother brought me up."

"She was a younger woman then and ate yam and boiled green banana all her life."

"Eh?"

"Imagine living alone up on that mountain. Old-time people were different, different. Made of old iron...."

Gerry settled down for story time, leaning on her aching shoulder with his cheek so delightful against hers that she never thought to shift him. She was ready to give up fretting over the past and leave the mountains to wait it out and sit in judgement over them. But Gerry's startling black eyes burnt fascinated, fascinating, intent on knowing everything and knowing it at once.

"And were they real, Sugar? All those people you talk about? Were they real or pretend?"

Appendix
Historical Events
referred to in the book

ca. 600-1492   Arawak peoples (Tainos) inhabit Jamaica

1494   Arrival of Columbus

1500-1665   Spanish colonisation
Death of the Tainos
Africans brought to Jamaica as slaves

1665   English invasion; English colonisation begins

1665-1700   White indentured servants: Convicts brought to Jamaica
Increasing numbers of Africans arrive as slaves

1692   Port Royal, buccaneer city, destroyed by earthquake;
survivors rebuild at Hog Craal, now Kingston

1655-1738   Guerrilla war between English and Maroons in mountains
until signing of treaty

1792   Haitian Revolution

1808   Slave trade declared illegal

1834   Slavery abolished in British colonies; Apprenticeships

1838   Emancipation of slaves in British colonies

1840-1860   Indentured labour brought from India and West Africa

1865   Morant Bay Rebellion; Crown Colony rule

1880s   Building of the Panama Canal

521

1890s	Boer War in South Africa
1890s and 1900s	Alexander Bedward preaches in August Town, Jamaica
1907	Kingston destroyed by earthquake and fire
1914-1918	World War I
1930-1950	Impact of Marcus Garvey's teachings Rise of Rastafari
1938	Labour unrest. New political parties
1939-1945	World War II
1940s	Adult suffrage; first local government since 1866
1948-1952	Founding of the University of the West Indies (as the University College, London University), Mona, Jamaica
1950s (early)	Working class migrations to Britain
1950s (mid)-1960s	Economic expansion, real estate boom Accelerated expansion of Kingston
1962	Independence
1968	Rodney Riots; unrest Decline of foreign investment
1972	PNP (People's National Party) victory under new leader, Michael Manley
1970s	Socialism; flight of upper and middle classes to United States and Canada; escalation of political and criminal violence
1980	JLP (Jamaica Labour Party) victory

ABOUT THE AUTHOR

Barbara Lalla (née Ellwood) was born in Jamaica and educated at The Queen's School and the University of the West Indies, Mona. She moved to Trinidad after marrying in 1974 and lives there with her husband and two sons, but returns to Jamaica regularly. She is a Senior Lecturer at the University of the West Indies on the St Augustine Campus, in the Faculty of Humanities and Education, and has produced three books: *Voices in Exile* (coedited with Jean D'Costa), *Language in Exile* (coauthored with Jean D'Costa) and *Defining Jamaican Fiction*. *Arch of Fire* is her first novel.